The Letter and

the Scroll

WHAT ARCHAEOLOGY TELLS US ABOUT THE BIBLE

ROBIN CURRIE AND STEPHEN G. HYSLOP

NATIONAL GEOGRAPHIC

WASHINGTON, D.C.

Contents

Page 1: A fresco of the prophet Jeremiah from the Pinacoteca gallery at the Vatican
Pages 2-3: This sheep-skin scroll of the final chapters of Leviticus was discovered in 1956 but wasn't unrolled until 14 years later.
Page 4: Ezra the scribe copies the sacred texts, from an illustration in the early eighth-century C.E. Codex Amiatinus.
Pages 6-7: In 2007, archaeologist Ehud Netzer located Herod's tomb halfway up a 300-foot-tall, man-made mound, eight miles south of Jerusalem.

SEARCHING FOR THE WORD

No book ever written has been studied more thoroughly or examined at greater length than the Bible. For thousands of years, scholars have probed its chapters and analyzed every verse. Yet those seemingly inexhaustible Scriptures remain open to fresh interpretations as new discoveries are made. Like a river issuing from a distant country not yet fully mapped, the Bible continues to challenge those exploring its sources, or the spiritual and historical currents that converged long ago to produce this phenomenon.

In modern times, the long-standing tradition of literary biblical scholarship, or interpreting Scripture in its original language and context, has been greatly enhanced by the work of archaeologists, who have unearthed biblical manuscripts of ever greater antiquity along with many revealing nonbiblical inscriptions offering fresh insights into the Old and New Testaments and the world that gave rise to them. Written on papyrus or vellum or inscribed in clay or stone, these letters recovered from biblical times and presented here in this book bring us as close to the foundations of Judaism and Christianity as students of the Bible have ever been.

Among the major discoveries that have shed new light on the Bible and its origins are the Dead Sea Scrolls, found in caves near the ruins of Qumran, a community occupied from the mid-second century B.C.E. until the Jewish Revolt (66-70 C.E.), which ended when Roman troops stormed Jerusalem and destroyed its Temple. The inhabitants of Qumran may have been Essenes—a sect whose members strictly observed the Sabbath and other Jewish rites and devoted much of their time to copying and studying Hebrew Scriptures. The first scrolls uncovered near Qumran were found by Bedouin shepherds in 1947 and included a complete version of the Book of Isaiah (see pp. 244-45).

This discovery marked a new millennium in biblical research, for it came nearly a thousand years after the production of the oldest surviving Hebrew Bible, which in turn was written roughly a thousand years after the Isaiah Scroll. The discovery prompted archaeological excavations that uncovered hundreds of additional scrolls—many of them, unfortunately, reduced to shreds that when pieced together yielded only fragmentary texts. Among those scrolls were copies of nearly all the books of the Hebrew Bible and texts revealing the practices and beliefs of worshippers from the Qumran sect or other communities whose writings were stored in the caves during the Jewish Revolt to preserve them from destruction.

"HE WILL BE CALLED GREAT . . . 'SON OF GOD' HE WILL BE CALLED AND 'SON OF THE MOST HIGH' . . . HIS KINGDOM WILL BE AN EVERLASTING KINGDOM."

ARAMAIC APOCALYPSE, DEAD SEA SCROLLS

Archaeologists Gerald Lankester Harding and Father Roland de Vaux sift through debris at the entrance to one of the caves where the Dead Sea Scrolls were found. The scrolls were written in Hebrew, Greek, or Aramaic, a language held in common by Judeans and their neighbors when these documents were produced.

These ancient books, written on papyrus and bound in leather, were found in a jar in a cave near the Egyptian town of Nag Hammadi in 1945. Among the texts were the Gospel of Thomas and other Gnostic scriptures, written in Greek in the second century and translated into Coptic, the language of Egyptian Christians, in the fourth century.

AUTHENTIC OR APOCRYPHAL?

Other recent archaeological discoveries offer insights into the Bible and its world by revealing what was excluded from it, including alternative gospels judged inauthentic or heretical by early Christian authorities. Among these apocryphal Scriptures is the Gospel of Thomas, found in Egypt shortly before the first Dead Sea Scrolls were uncovered. Consisting of sayings attributed to Jesus, the discovery caused great excitement because scholars had long wondered if the gospels of Matthew, Mark, and Luke—called synoptic because they have much in common—drew on an even-earlier account containing the parables of Jesus and other anecdotes. The Gospel of Thomas did contain some sayings found in those synoptic gospels, but it was composed later and represented a mystical tradition called Gnosticism to which leaders of the early Christian church were strongly opposed. Gnostics taught that Jesus was resurrected in spirit, not in the flesh, and pursued secret knowledge and hidden truths at a time when other Christians were trying to speak clearly and plainly to the world and win converts. "What they have published," wrote one bishop in denouncing the Gnostics, "is totally unlike what has been handed down to us by the apostles."

The thorny question of which books to include in the Bible was not quickly or easily resolved. Within Judaism, the five books of law composing the Torah (Genesis, Exodus, Leviticus, Numbers, and Deuteronomy) took precedence early on. Next in importance were prophetic works, including historical accounts with prophetic elements (Joshua, Judges, Samuel, and Kings) and the Books of Isaiah, Jeremiah, Ezekiel, and a dozen other prophets. Other sacred texts were classified as Hagiographa ("holy writings") and were not officially evaluated until around 100 C.E. when rabbis met in council in the Judean town of Jamnia. Some sacred texts composed in recent times like the Wisdom of Solomon were rejected as apocryphal by the council, while others like the

Book of Daniel were accepted and joined beloved Scriptures like the Psalms among the authorized holy writings of the Hebrew Bible.

Whether the Hebrew Bible should be part of the Christian Bible was hotly disputed in the second century C.E. by Marcion, a wealthy and influential son of a bishop, who argued that the God revealed by Jesus was not the same as the God of the Hebrews and that Christians should not hold Jewish Scriptures sacred. Marcion went so far as to reject all gospel passages based on messianic prophecies in the Hebrew Bible. By excommunicating him as a heretic, Christian leaders affirmed the essential link between the Old and New Testaments. Much like the Torah within Judaism, the four gospels became the core of the Christian faith, revealing God's word as conveyed by Jesus to disciples who served like Moses as guardians of that truth.

Next in scriptural importance were the Acts of the Apostles and the letters of Paul, the prophetic apostle who interpreted Christ's message and imparted it to gentiles, or non-Jews, laying the foundation for a church that would spread throughout the Roman Empire and beyond. It took some time for church leaders to determine which other holy writings should be included in the Christian canon (the recognized body of Scriptures). The puzzling and unsettling Book of Revelation met with considerable resistance but was ultimately embraced by authorities in the fourth century C.E. With that, the canon was complete, but the larger project of compiling, translating, and interpreting the Bible had just begun.

DIGGING FOR THE TRUTH

Like biblical archaeologists in later times, scholars who produced the first authoritative Bibles searched for the earliest artifacts of their faith by sifting through old manuscripts to find those closest to the original language and intent of the Scriptures. Such was the task taken on by Jerome, later canonized as a saint, when he began work in the late fourth century on a Latin Bible that would serve Roman Catholics as their standard for more than a thousand years to come. Rejecting as unreliable earlier Latin translations of the gospels, Jerome turned to Greek, the language in which they were written. He could have done all his work in Greek, in which he was fluent, by using a Greek version of the Hebrew Bible called the Septuagint to render the Old Testament

ΤΟΤΟΠΟΤΗΡΙΟΝΗ
ΚΑΙΝΗΔΙΑΘΗΚΗ
ΕΝΤΩΑΙΜΑΤΙΜΟΥ
ΤΟΥΠΕΡΥΜΩΝ·Κ
ΧΥΝΝΟΜΕΝΟΝ
ΠΛΗΝΙΔΟΥΗΧΕΙΡ
ΤΟΥΠΑΡΑΔΙΔΟΝ
ΜΕΜΕΤΕΜΟΥΕΠΙ
ΤΗΣΤΡΑΠΕΖΗΣΟΤΙ
ΟΥΟΓΟΥΑΝΘΡΩΠΟΥ
ΚΑΤΑΤΟΩΡΙΣΜΕ
ΝΟΝΠΟΡΕΥΕΤΑΙ
ΠΛΗΝΟΥΑΙΤΩΝ
ΘΡΩΠΩΕΚΕΙΝ
ΔΙΟΥΠΑΡΑΔΙΔΟΤ
ΚΑΙΑΥΤΟΙΗΡΞΑΝΤ
ΣΥΝΖΗΤΕΙΝΠΡΟ
ΣΑΥΤΟΥΣΤΟΤΙΣΑΡΑ
ΕΙΗΕΞΑΥΤΩΝΕΠ
ΟΤΟΥΤΟΜΕΛΛΩΝ
ΠΡΑΣΣΕΙΝ
ΕΓΕΝΕΤΟΔΕΦΙΛΟΝΙ
ΚΙΑΕΙΣΕΑΥΤΟΥΣ
ΤΟΤΙΣΑΥΤΩΝΔΟ
ΚΕΙΕΙΝΑΙΜΙΖΩΝ
ΟΔΕΕΙΠΕΝΑΥΤΟΙ
ΟΙΒΑΣΙΛΕΙΣΤΩΝ
ΕΘΝΩΝΚΥΡΙΕΥΟΥ
ΣΙΝΑΥΤΩΝΚΑΙΟΙ
ΑΡΧΟΝΤΕΣΤΩΝΕ
ΞΟΥΣΙΑΖΟΥΣΙΝ
ΤΩΝΚΑΙΕΥΕΡΓΕΤ
ΤΑΙΚΑΛΟΥΝΤΑΥ
ΜΕΙΣΔΕΟΥΧΟΥΤ
ΑΛΛΟΜΕΙΖΩΝΕΝΥ
ΜΙΝΓΕΙΝΕΣΘΩ
ΩΣΟΝΕΩΤΕΡΟΣ
ΚΑΙΟΗΓΟΥΜΕΝ·
ΩΣΟΔΙΑΚΟΝΩΝ
ΤΙΣΓΑΡΟΜΕΙΖΩΝ
ΟΑΝΑΚΕΙΜΕΝΟ
ΗΟΔΙΑΚΟΝΩΝΟΥ
ΧΙΟΑΝΑΚΕΙΜΕΝ·
ΕΓΩΔΕΕΝΜΕΣΩ
ΥΜΩΝΕΙΜΙΩΣ·
ΔΙΑΚΟΝΩΝΥΜ·Ι
ΔΕΕΣΤΕΟΙΔΙΑΜΕ
ΜΕΝΗΚΟΤΕΣΜΕ

ΤΕΜΟΥΕΝΤΟΙΣΠΙ
ΡΑΣΜΟΙΣΜΟΥΚΑ
ΓΩΔΙΑΤΙΘΕΜΑΙ
ΥΜΙΝΚΑΘΩΣΔΙ
ΕΘΕΤΟΜΟΙΟΠΑ
ΤΗΡΜΟΥΒΑΣΙΛΕΙ
ΑΝΙΝΑΕΣΘΗΤΑΙ
ΚΑΙΠΙΝΗΤΑΙΕΠΙ
ΤΗΣΤΡΑΠΕΖΗΣΜ
ΕΝΤΗΒΑΣΙΛΕΙΑΜΟΥ
ΚΑΙΚΑΘΗΣΕΣΘΕ
ΠΙΘΡΟΝΩΝΚΡΙΝ
ΤΕΣΤΑΣΔΩΔΕΚΑ
ΦΥΛΑΣΤΟΥΙΗΛ
ΕΙΠΕΝΔΕΟΚΣΣΙ
ΜΩΝΣΙΜΩΝΙΔΟΥΟΣΑΤΑ
ΝΑΣΕΞΗΤΗΣΑΤΟ
ΥΜΑΣΤΟΥΣΙΝΙΑΣ
ΩΣΤΟΝΣΙΤΟΝΕΓΩ
ΔΕΕΔΕΗΘΗΝΠΕρ
ΣΟΥΙΝΑΜΗΕΚΛ
ΠΗΗΠΙΣΤΙΣΣΟΥ
ΚΑΙΣΥΠΟΤΕΕΠΙ
ΣΤΡΑΣΣΤΗΡΙΣΟΝΤ
ΑΔΕΛΦΟΥΣΣΟΥ
ΟΔΕΕΙΠΕΝΑΥΤΩ
ΚΕΜΕΤΑΣΟΥΕΤΙ
ΜΟΣΕΙΜΙΚΑΙΕΙΣ
ΦΥΛΑΚΗΝΚΑΙΕΙΣ
ΘΑΝΑΤΟΝΠΟΡΕΥ
ΕΣΘΑΙ
ΟΔΕΕΙΠΕΝΛΕΓΩ
ΠΕΤΡΕΟΥΦΩΝΗ
ΣΕΙΣΗΜΕΡΟΝΑΛ
ΚΤΩΡΕΩΣΤΡΕΙΣΜ
ΑΠΑΡΝΗΣΗΕΙΔΕ
ΝΑΙ
ΚΑΙΕΙΠΕΝΑΥΤΟΙ
ΟΤΕΑΠΕΣΤΙΛΑΥΜ
ΑΤΕΡΒΑΛΛΑΝΤΙΟΥ
ΚΑΙΠΗΡΑΣΚΑΙΥΠΟ
ΔΗΜΑΤΩΝΜΗΤΙΝΟ
ΥΣΤΕΡΗΣΑΤΕΟΙΔΑ
ΕΙΠΟΝΟΥΔΕΝΟ
ΟΔΕΕΙΠΕΝΑΥΤΟΙ
ΑΛΛΑΝΥΝΟΕΧΩ
ΒΑΛΛΑΝΤΙΟΝΑΡΑ
ΤΩΟΜΟΙΩΣΚΑΙΠΗ

ΡΑΝΚΑΙΟΜΗΕΧΩ
ΠΩΛΗΣΑΤΩΤΟΙ
ΜΑΤΙΟΝΑΥΤΟΥΚΑΙ
ΑΓΟΡΑΣΑΤΩΜΑΧΑΙ
ΡΑΝ
ΛΕΓΩΓΑΡΥΜΙΝΟΤΙ
ΤΟΥΤΟΤΟΓΕΓΡΑΜ
ΝΟΝΔΕΙΤΕΛΕΣΘΗ
ΝΑΙΕΝΕΜΟΙΤΟΚΑΙ
ΜΕΤΑΑΝΟΜΩΝΕ
ΛΟΓΙΣΘΗΚΑΙΓΑΡΤ
ΠΕΡΙΕΜΟΥΤΕΛΟΣΧΙ
ΟΙΔΕΕΙΠΑΝΚΥΟΥ
ΜΑΧΑΙΡΩΔΕΛΥΟ
ΟΔΕΕΙΠΕΝΑΥΤΟΙ
ΙΚΑΝΟΝΕΣΤΙΝ
ΚΑΙΕΞΕΛΘΩΝΕΠΟ
ΡΕΥΘΗΚΑΤΑΤΟΕ
ΕΙΣΤΟΟΡΟΣΤΩΝ
ΕΛΑΙΩΝΗΚΟΛΟΥ
ΘΗΣΑΝΔΕΑΥΤΩ·
ΟΙΜΑΘΗΤΑΙ
ΓΕΝΟΜΕΝΟΣΔΕΕΠΙ
ΤΟΥΤΟΠΟΥΕΙΠΕΝΑΥ
ΤΟΙΣΠΡΟΣΕΥΧΕΣΘΕ
ΜΗΕΙΣΕΛΘΕΙΝΕΙΣ
ΠΙΡΑΣΜΟΝ
ΚΑΙΑΥΤΟΣΑΠΕΣΠΑ
ΣΘΗΑΠΑΥΤΩΝΩΣ
ΛΙΘΟΥΒΟΛΗΝΚΑΙ
ΘΕΙΣΤΑΓΟΝΑΤΑΠΡ
ΗΥΣΑΤΟΛΕΓΩΝ
ΠΑΤΕΡΕΙΒΟΥΛΗΠΑ
ΝΕΓΚΑΙΤΟΥΤΟΤΟ
ΤΟΠΟΤΗΡΙΟΝΤΟΥΓ
ΑΠΕΜΟΥΠΛΗΝΜΗ
ΤΟΘΕΛΗΜΑΜΟΥΑΛ
ΛΑΤΟΣΟΝΓΕΙΝΕ
ΩΦΘΗΔΕΑΥΤΩΝ
ΓΕΛΟΣΑΠΟΥΡΑΝΟΥ
ΕΝΙΣΧΥΩΝΑΥΤΟΝ
ΚΑΙΓΕΝΑΜΕΝΟΣΕ
ΝΑΓΩΝΙΑΕΚΤΕΝΕ
ΣΤΕΡΟΝΠΡΟΣΗΥ
ΧΕΤΟΚΑΙΕΓΕΝΕΤ
ΙΔΡΩΣΑΥΤΟΥΩΣΕΙ
ΘΡΟΜΒΟΙΑΙΜΑΤΟΣ
ΚΑΤΑΒΑΙΝΟΝΤΟ·

ΠΙΤΗΝΓΗΝ
ΚΑΙΑΝΑΣΤΑΣΑΠΟ
ΤΗΣΠΡΟΣΕΥΧΗΣ
ΕΛΘΩΝΠΡΟΣΤΟΥ
ΜΑΘΗΤΑΣΕΥΡΕΝ
ΚΟΙΜΩΜΕΝΟΥ
ΑΥΤΟΥΣΑΠΟΤΗΣ
ΠΗΣΚΑΙΕΙΠΕΝΑΥ
ΤΟΙΣΤΙΚΑΘΕΥΔΕΤ
ΑΝΑΣΤΑΝΤΕΣΠΡ
ΕΥΧΕΣΘΕΙΝΑΜΗ
ΕΙΣΕΛΘΗΤΑΙΕΙΣΠΙ
ΡΑΣΜΟΝ
ΕΤΙΑΥΤΟΥΛΑΛΟΥΝ
ΤΟΣΙΔΟΥΟΧΛΟΣΚ
ΟΛΕΓΟΜΕΝΟΣΙΟ
ΔΑΣΕΙΣΤΩΝΔΩΔ
ΚΑΙΠΡΟΗΡΧΕΤΟΑ
ΤΟΥΣ
ΚΑΙΗΓΓΙΣΕΝΤΩΙ
ΦΙΛΗΣΑΙΑΥΤΟΝΙ
ΔΕΕΙΠΕΝΑΥΤΩ
ΙΟΥΔΑ
ΦΙΛΗΜΑΤΙΤΟΝΥΝ
ΤΟΥΑΝΘΡΩΠΟΥΠΑ
ΡΑΔΙΔΩΣ
ΕΙΔΟΝΤΕΣΔΕΟΙΠ
ΡΙΑΥΤΟΝΤΟΕΣΟΜ
ΝΟΝΕΙΠΑΝΚΕΕΙ
ΠΑΤΑΞΟΜΕΝΕΝ
ΜΑΧΑΙΡΗΚΑΙΕΠΑ
ΤΑΞΕΝΕΙΣΤΙΣΕΞΑ
ΤΩΝΤΟΥΑΡΧΙΕΡΕ
ΩΣΤΟΝΔΟΥΛΟΝ
ΚΑΙΑΦΙΛΕΝΤΟΟΥ
ΑΥΤΟΥΤΟΔΕΞΙΟΝ
ΑΠΟΚΡΙΘΕΙΣΔΕΟΙ
ΕΙΠΕΝΕΑΤΕΕΩΣ
ΤΟΥΤΟΥ
ΚΑΙΑΨΑΜΕΝΟΣΤΟΥ
ΩΤΙΟΥΙΑΣΑΤΟΝ
ΤΟΝ

ΕΙΠΕΝΔΕΙΣΠΡΟΣ
ΤΟΥΣΠΑΡΑΓΕΝΟ
ΜΕΝΟΥΣΕΠΑΥΤΟΝ
ΤΟΝΑΡΧΙΕΡΕΙΣΚΑ
ΣΤΡΑΤΗΓΟΥΣΤΟΥΙ
ΡΟΥΚΑΙΠΡΕΣΒΥΤΕ
ΡΟΥΣΩΣΕΠΙΛΗΣΤ

ΕΞΗΛΘΟΝΤΑΙΜΕΤΑΜ
ΧΗΡΩΝΚΑΙCΥΛ
ΚΑΘΗΜΕΡΑΝΟΝ
ΤΟCΜΟΥΜΕΘΥΜ
ΕΝΤΩΙΕΡΩΟΥΚ
ΞΕΤΙΝΑΤΕΤΑCΧΙ
ΡΑCΕΠΕΜΕΑΛΛΑ
ΤΗΕCΤΙΝΗΩΡΑ
ΗΕΞΟΥCΙΑΤΟΥCΚ
ΤΟΥC
CΥΛΛΑΒΟΝΤΕCΛΕ
ΤΟΝΗΓΑΓΟΝΚΑΙ
CΗΓΑΓΟΝΕΙCΤΗΝ
ΟΙΚΙΑΝΤΟΥΑΡΧΙΕ
ΡΕΩC
ΟΔΕΠΕΤΡΟCΗΚΟΛΟΥ
ΘΙΜΑΚΡΟΘΕΝΠΙ
ΡΙΑΨΑΝΤΩΝΔΕ
ΠΥΡΕΝΜΕCΩΤΗ
ΑΥΛΗCΚΑΙCΥΝΚΑ
ΘΙCΑΝΤΩΝΕΚΑ
ΘΗΤΟΟΠΕΤΡΟCΕ
ΜΕCΩΑΥΤΩΝΙ
ΛΟΥCΑΛΕΧΑΥΤΟΝ
ΠΑΙΔΙCΚΗΤΙCΚΑ
ΘΗΜΕΝΟΝΠΡΟC
ΤΟΦΩCΚΑΙΑΤΕΝΙ
CΑCΑΥΤΩΕΙΠΙ
ΚΑΙΟΥΤΟCCΥΝΑΥ
ΤΩΗΝΟΔΕΗΡΝΗ
CΑΤΟΛΕΓΩΝΟΥΚ
ΛΑΥΤΟΝΠΙΓΥΝΑΙ
ΚΑΙΜΕΤΑΒΡΑΧΥ
ΤΕΡΟCΙΔΩΝΑΥΤ
ΕΦΗΚΑΙCΥΕΞΑΥ
ΤΩΝΕΙΟΔΕΠΕΤ
ΕΦΗΑΝΘΡΩΠΕ
ΚΕΙΜΙΚΑΙΔΙΑCΤΑ
CΗCΩCΕΙΩΡΑCΜΙ
ΑCΑΛΛΟCΤΙCΔΙΙC
ΡΙΖΕΤΟΛΕΓΩΝΕΠ
ΛΗΘΙΑCΚΑΙΟΥΤΟ
ΜΕΤΑΥΤΟΥΚΝΙ
ΓΑΛΙΛΑΙΟCΕCΤΙΝΙ
ΠΕΝΔΕΟΠΕΤΡΟC
ΑΝΘΡΩΠΕΟΥΚΟΙ
ΛΑΙΤΙΛΕΓΕΙCΚΑΙΠΑ
ΡΑΧΡΗΜΑΕΤΙΛΑΛ

ΤΟCΑΥΤΟΥΕΦΩΝΗ
CΕΝΑΛΕΚΤΩΡΚΑΙ
CΤΡΑΦΕΙCΟΚCΕΝΕ
ΒΛΕΨΕΝΤΩΠΕΤ
ΚΑΙΥΠΕΜΝΗCΘΗ
ΟΠΕΤΡΟCΤΟΥΡΗΜΑ
ΤΟCΤΟΥΚΥΩCΕΙ
ΑΥΤΩΟΤΙΠΡΙΝΑΛ
ΚΤΟΡΑΦΩΝΗCΕΗ
ΜΕΡΟΝΑΠΑΡΝΗCΗ
ΜΕΤΡΙCΚΑΙΕΞΕΛΘΩ
ΕΞΩΕΚΛΑΥCΕΝΠΙ
ΚΡΩC
ΚΑΙΟΙΑΝΔΡΕCΟΙCΥΝ
ΕΧΟΝΤΕCΑΥΤΟΝ
ΕΝΕΠΕΖΑΝΑΥΤΩ
ΛΕΡΟΝΤΕCΚΑΙΠΕ
ΡΙΚΑΛΥΨΑΝΤΕCΕ
ΠΗΡΩΤΩΝΑΥΤΟ
ΛΕΓΟΝΤΕCΠΡΟΦ
ΤΕΥCΟΝΤΙCΕCΤΙΝ
ΟΠΑΙCΑCCΕΚΑΙΕ
ΤΕΡΑΓΠΟΛΛΑΒΛΑCΦΗ
ΜΟΥΝΤΕCΕΛΕΓΟΝ
ΕΙCΑΥΤΟΝ
ΚΑΙΩCΗΜΕΡΑΕΓΕΝ
ΤΟCΥΝΗΧΘΗΤΟ
ΠΡΕCΒΥΤΕΡΙΟΝΤΥ
ΛΑΟΥΑΡΧΙΕΡΕΙCΤΕ
ΚΑΙΓΡΑΜΜΑΤΙCΚΑΙ
ΑΠΗΓΑΓΟΝΑΥΤΟΝ
ΕΙCΤΟCΥΝΕΔΡΙΟΝ
ΑΥΤΩΝΛΕΓΟΝΤΕ
ΕΙCΥΕΙΟΧCΕΙΠΟΝ
ΗΜΙΝ
ΕΙΠΕΝΔΕΑΥΤΟΙCΕΑΝΥΜΙΝ
ΕΙΠΩΟΥΜΗΠΙCΤΕ
CΗΤΕΕΑΝΔΕΕΡΩ
ΤΗCΩΟΥΜΗΑΠΟ
ΚΡΙΘΗΤΕ
ΑΠΟΤΟΥΝΥΝΔΕΕ
CΤΑΙΟΥCΤΟΥΑΝΘ
ΠΟΥΚΑΘΗΜΕΝΟC
ΕΚΔΕΞΙΩΝΤΗCΔΥ
ΝΑΜΕΩCΤΟΥΘΥ
ΕΙΠΑΝΔΕΠΑΝΤΕC
CΥΟΥΝΕΙΟΥCΤΟΥΘΥ
ΟΔΕΠΡΟCΑΥΤΟΥC

ΦΗΥΜΕΙCΛΕΓΕΤ
ΟΤΙΕΓΩΕΙΜΙ
ΟΙΔΕΕΙΠΑΝΤΙΕΤΙ
ΧΡΙΑΝΕΧΟΜΕΝΜ
ΤΥΡΙΑCΑΥΤΟΙΓΑΡΗ
ΚΟΥCΑΜΕΝΑΠΟΤ
CΤΟΜΑΤΟCΑΥΤΟΥ
ΚΑΙΑΝΑCΤΑΝΑΠΑ
ΤΟΠΛΗΘΟCΑΥΤΩΝ
ΗΓΑΓΟΝΑΥΤΟΝΕΠΙ
ΤΟΝΠΙΛΑΤΟΝ
ΗΡΞΑΝΤΟΔΕΚΑΤΗΓ
ΡΙΝΑΥΤΟΥΛΕΓΟΝΤ
ΤΟΥΤΟΝΕΥΡΟΜΕΝ
ΔΙΑCΤΡΕΦΟΝΤΑΙΟ
ΕΘΝΟCΗΜΩΝΚ
ΚΩΛΥΟΝΤΑΦΟΡ
ΚΑΙCΑΡΙΔΙΔΟΝΑΙ
ΚΑΙΛΕΓΟΝΤΑΕΑΥΤ
ΧΝΒΑCΙΛΕΑΕΙΝΑΙ
ΟΔΕΠΙΛΑΤΟCΗΡΩ
ΤΗCΕΝΑΥΤΟΝΛΕΓ
CΥΕΙΟΒΑCΙΛΕΥCΤ
ΙΟΥΔΑΙΩΝΟΔΕΑ
ΠΟΚΡΙΘΕΙCΑΥΤΩ
ΛΕΓΕΙCΥΛΕΓΕΙC
ΟΔΕΠΙΛΑΤΟCΕΙΠΙ
ΠΡΟCΤΟΥCΑΡΧΙΕΡ
ΚΑΙΤΟΥCΟΧΛΟΥC
ΟΥΔΕΝΕΥΡΙCΚΩ
ΑΙΤΙΟΝΕΝΤΩΑΝ
ΘΡΩΠΩΤΟΥΤΩ
ΟΙΔΕΕΠΙCΧΥΟΝΛΕ
ΤΕCΟΤΙΑΝΑCΙΗ
ΟΧΛΟΝΚΑΘΟΛΗC διδασκων
ΤΗCΙΟΥΔΑΙΑCΚΑΙ
ΑΡΞΑΜΕΝΟCΑΠΟ
ΤΗCΓΑΛΙΛΑΙΑCΕΩC
ΩΔΕ
ΠΕΙΛΑΤΟCΔΕΑΚΟΥ
CΑCΕΠΗΡΩΤΗCΕΝ
ΕΙΟΑΝΘΡΩΠΟCΓΑ
ΑΙΛΑΙΟCΕCΤΙΝΚΑΙ
ΕΠΙΓΝΟΥCΟΤΙΕΚ
ΤΗCΕΞΟΥCΙΑCΗΡ
ΛΟΥΕCΤΙΝΑΝΕΠΙ
ΨΕΝΑΥΤΟΝΠΡΟΗ
ΡΩΔΗΝΟΝΤΑΚΑΙ

ΑΥΤΟΝΕΝΙΕΡΟCΟ
ΛΥΜΟΙCΕΝΑΥΤΑΙ
ΤΑΙCΗΜΕΡΑΙCΟΠ
ΡΩΔΗCΙΔΩΝΤΟΝ
ΙΝΕΧΑΡΗΛΙΑΝΗΝ
ΓΑΡΕΞΙΚΑΝΩΝΧΡ
ΝΩΝΘΕΛΩΝΙΔΙΝ
ΑΥΤΟΝΔΙΑΤΟΑΚΟΥ
ΕΙΝΠΕΡΙΑΥΤΟΥΚ
ΗΛΠΙΖΕΤΕΙCΗΜΙ
ΟΝΙΔΙΝΥΠΑΥΤ
ΓΕΙΝΟΜΕΝΟΝΟ ΔΕ
ΠΗΡΩΤΑΑΥΤΟΝ
ΕΝΛΟΓΟΙCΙΚΑΝ
ΑΥΤΟCΔΕΟΥΚΑΠ
ΚΡΙΝΑΤΟΑΥΤΩ
ΙCΤΗΚΕΙCΑΝΛΑCΟΙ
ΑΡΧΙΕΡΕΙCΚΑΙΟΙ
ΓΡΑΜΜΑΤΕΙCΕΥ
ΤΟΝΩCΚΑΤΗΓΟΡ
ΤΕCΑΥΤΟΥ
ΕΞΟΥΘΕΝΗCΑC δε αυτο
ΚΑΙΟΗΡΩΔΗCCΥΝ
ΤΟΙCCΤΡΑΤΕΥΜΑΙ
ΑΥΤΟΥΚΑΙΕΜΠ
ΞΑCΠΕΡΙΒΑΛΩΝ
ΑΙCΘΗΤΑΛΑΜΠΡΑ
ΑΝΕΠΕΜΨΕΝΑΥΤΟΝ
ΤΩΠΙΛΑΤΩΕΓΕΝ
ΤΟΔΕΦΙΛΟΙΟΤΕΗ
ΡΩΔΗCΚΑΙΟΠΙΛΑ
ΤΟCΕΝΑΥΤΗΤΗΗΜ
ΡΑΜΕΤΑΛΛΗΛΩΝ
ΠΡΟΥΠΗΡΧΟΝΤ
ΓΑΡΕΝΕΧΘΡΑΟΝ
ΠΡΟCΑΥΤΟΥCΥΝΚΑΛ
ΛΑΤΟCΔΕCΥΝΚΑΛ
CΑΜΕΝΟCΤΟΥCΑΡ
ΧΙΕΡΕΙCΚΑΙΤΟΥCΑΡ
ΧΟΝΤΑCΚΑΙΤΟΝΛΑ
ΟΝΕΙΠΕΝΠΡΟCΑΥ
ΤΟΥCΠΡΟCΗΝΕΓΚ
ΚΑΤΕΜΟΙΤΟΝΑΝΘΡΩ
ΠΟΝΤΟΥΤΟΝΩC
ΑΠΟCΤΡΕΦΟΝΤΑ
ΤΟΝΛΑΟΝΚΑΙΙΔΟΥ
ΕΓΩΕΝΩΠΙΟΝΥ
ΜΩΝΑΝΑΚΡΙΝΑC

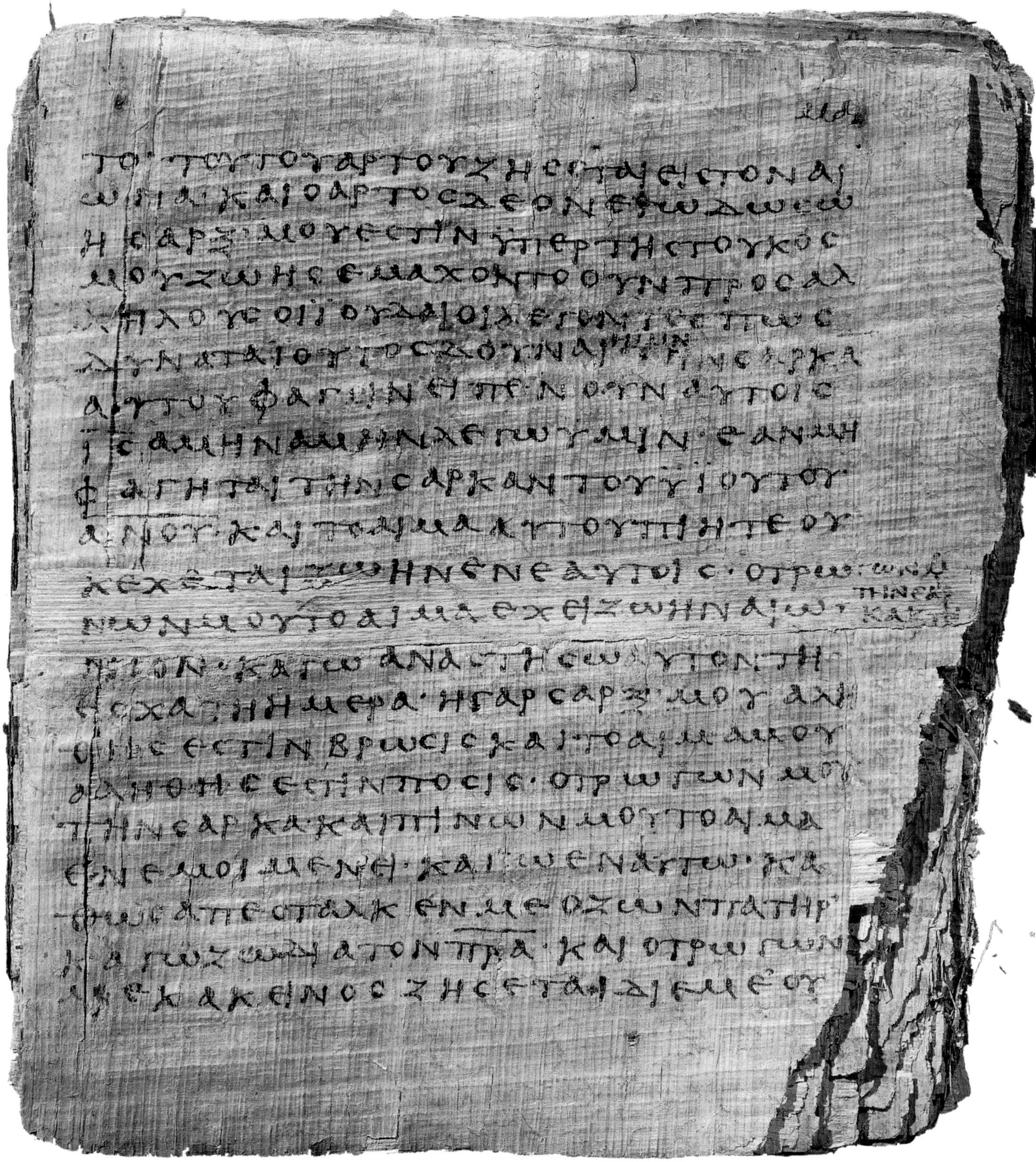

into Latin. But he was convinced that a true translation could be made only from Scriptures in their original language, and proceeded to master Hebrew.

One biblical manuscript that proved particularly helpful to Jerome was the Hexapla, a text in Hebrew and Greek that includes six versions of the Bible in parallel columns. It was produced in the third century by the Christian theologian Origen, who reportedly based his work on Greek and Hebrew scrolls he found in a jar in the Holy Land near Jericho. If so, Origen ranks as one of the first biblical archaeologists. Jerome himself had to do some digging to find Origen's remarkable manuscript, which he uncovered in Caesarea, a Roman town on the Judean coast. Origen's text was lost to posterity, but Jerome's translation, known as the Vulgate because it was the common Bible used by Roman Catholics throughout the Middle Ages, endured as one of the great scholarly achievements of early Christianity.

During the Reformation, Martin Luther and other Protestant leaders translated the Bible into German, French, English, and other modern languages to allow worshippers who had formerly relied on Catholic priests to interpret the text for them to draw lessons directly from Holy Scripture. Like Jerome, Luther went back to the original languages to produce his German Bible, using an authoritative Greek version of the New Testament edited by the Catholic humanist Erasmus and the first printed edition of the Hebrew Bible, set in type at Soncino, Italy, in the late 1400s. The recent introduction of the printing press gave Luther's 1,800-page Bible vast circulation—one printer alone, operating a press in Wittenberg, Germany, published nearly 100,000 copies—and did much to advance Protestantism.

Some Protestant translators were condemned as heretics, including Englishman William Tyndale, who was arrested in Belgium in 1535 and burned at the stake. Tyndale's assistant, Miles Coverdale, found support from King Henry VIII, who broke with the pope in Rome and ordered an English Bible placed in every English church. Catholic leaders soon joined the movement by authorizing their own translations of the Bible in many modern languages.

No English edition of the Bible had broader or longer-lasting appeal than the King James Version, commissioned in 1604 by James I of England, who ordered a translation "as consonant as can be to the original Hebrew and Greek." Although James was a Protestant, he wanted this Bible to unite his kingdom, not divide it, and prohibited interpretive marginal notes, which could accentuate religious differences and cause political unrest. Fifty-four scholars were appointed to perform the task. Divided into six panels, they demonstrated that committees could indeed do great work by basing their efforts on the original Greek and Hebrew but bringing Scripture to life in graceful and stately English. Not until the 20th century did scholars produce an English Bible that improved substantially on the King James Version in terms of accuracy and clarity and took its place in many homes and churches. And even that Revised Standard Version—used for biblical quotations in this book—owed much to its distinguished predecessor and was designed to preserve "those qualities which have given to the King James Version a supreme place in English literature."

Previous pages: Written in Greek on parchment in the fourth century, the Codex Sinaiticus— found at a monastery on Mount Sinai in the 19th century— is one of the oldest surviving Bibles containing both the Old and New Testaments. The Old Testament in this volume was drawn from the Septuagint, an earlier Greek translation of the Hebrew Bible.

Opposite: This second-century manuscript is the earliest existing complete copy of the Gospel of John, composed in Greek in the late first century.

EXPLORING THE BIBLICAL WORLD

The Bible itself is just one of the texts examined by modern scholars studying the origins of Judaism and Christianity and interpreting their Scriptures. Much of what we have learned about the Bible in recent times comes from archaeological excavations conducted throughout the biblical world that brought to light inscriptions written not just by Jews or Christians but by people of various origins and faiths with whom they interacted, including Egyptians, Assyrians, Babylonians, Persians, Greeks, and Romans. The biblical world—which extended from the Near East, or Middle East, westward around the Mediterranean Sea by the early Christian era—was the most literate place on Earth in ancient times and bequeathed to posterity a wealth of texts. It was here that writing began more than 5,000 years ago with the evolution of cuneiform in Mesopotamia and hieroglyphs in Egypt. And it was here that the first concise, phonetic alphabets emerged in various languages more than 3,000 years ago. That crucial simplification of writing systems extended literacy from an elite corps of scribes to much of the region's population and allowed a new faith like Christianity to grow rapidly by circulating its gospels and letters among far-flung communities of believers.

> "AND THE KING WENT UP TO THE HOUSE OF THE LORD . . . AND HE READ IN THEIR HEARING ALL THE WORDS OF THE BOOK OF THE COVENANT."
>
> II KINGS 23:2

Systematic study of the world that gave rise to Judaism and Christianity began around 1800 as archaeologists began excavating ancient monuments and deciphering their inscriptions. The discovery of the Rosetta Stone in Egypt (page 253) and analysis of the Behistun Inscription in Persia, or modern-day Iran, written in three different cuneiform scripts in Old Persian, Elamite, and Babylonian, led to the decipherment of hieroglyphs and cuneiform and opened vast new fields for biblical research. Found on clay tablets in Mesopotamia, for example, were an ancient Sumerian epic containing a story similar to the biblical account of Noah's Flood (see pp. 30-31) and a legend telling how the Assyrian ruler Sargon of Akkad was cast adrift as a baby in a reed basket sealed with pitch, much like the infant Moses (see pp. 86-87). Egyptologists made use of inscriptions, depictions, and other archaeological evidence found in palaces, temples, and tombs to document the migration to the Nile Delta of Asiatic traders and slaves whose ranks may have included Hebrews. One Egyptian monument inscribed around 1200 B.C.E. was found to contain the first known reference to "Israel" and became an archaeological milestone by establishing a date for the presence of Israelites in Canaan (see pp. 96-97).

Excavations within the Holy Land revealed that Israelites engaged in a complex give-and-take with rival groups there, including Philistines, Phoenicians, and pagan Canaanites. Some ancient cities such as Hebron were found to contain layers of destruction that could have been caused by invading Israelites at odds with Canaanites, as related in Joshua and Judges. But other evidence suggested that Israelites had much in common with their Canaanite neighbors. Horned altars like that found at Beersheba (see p. 119), for example, were used by both groups and may originally have been associated with the cults of gods such as Baal and El, worshipped in the form of bulls. Such cults had enduring appeal in the region, causing biblical prophets to denounce Israelites for consorting with pagans and bowing to their idols.

The page opposite from the Aleppo Codex—one of the oldest Hebrew Bibles, produced in the ninth century—contains notations that indicate vowel sounds for Hebrew words, which consist only of consonants and can in some cases be read more than one way. Known as Masoretic Text for rabbinical scholars called Masoretes, this system of notation ensured that the precise meaning of Scripture was clear to the reader and the scribe who copied it.

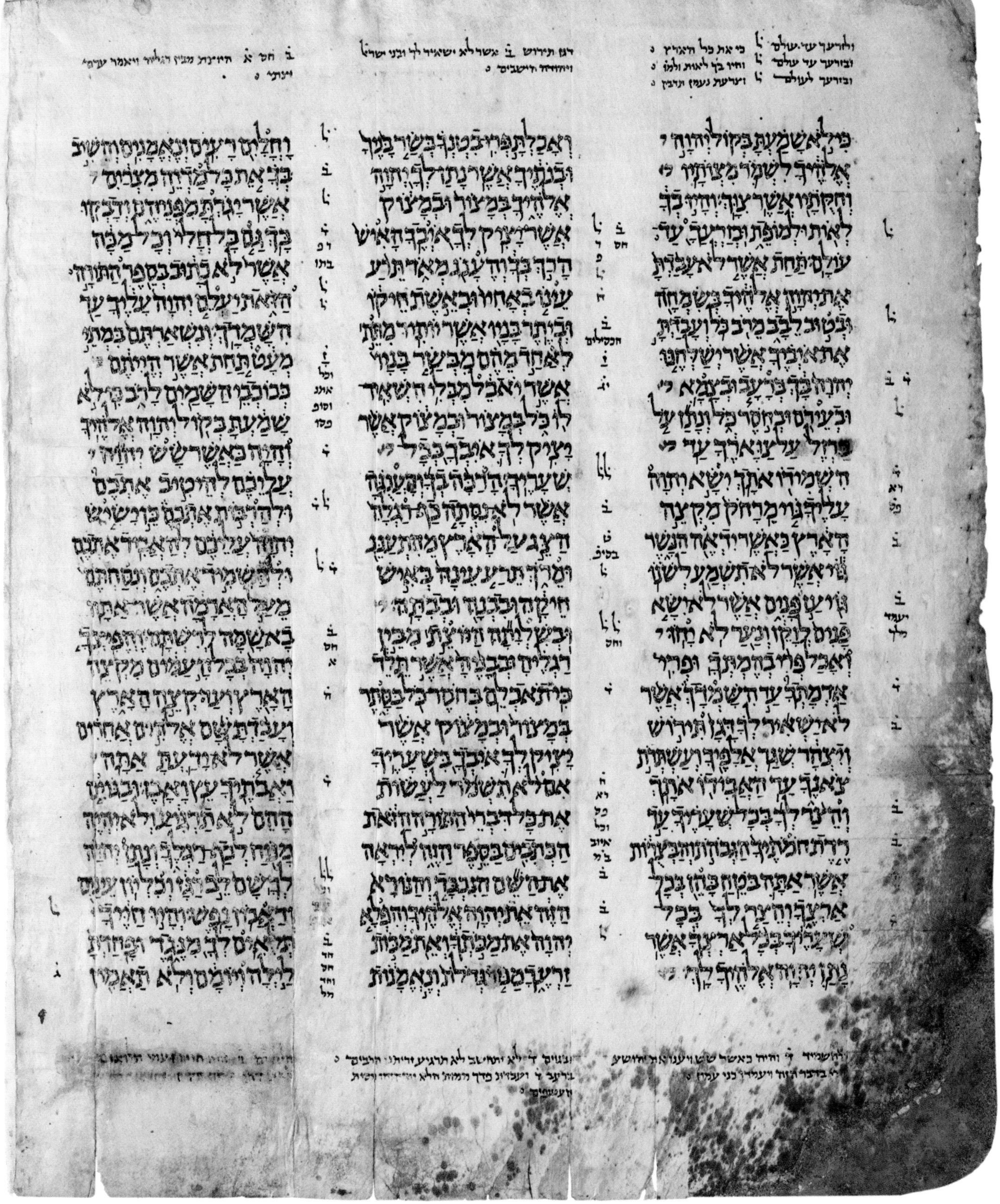

The earliest examples of Hebrew writing found by archaeologists—including the Gezer Calendar (see pp. 160-61) and an inscription discovered recently at Khirbet Qeiyafa—come from around the tenth century B.C.E., or the period when the kingdom of Israel arose. Political consolidation under Kings David and Solomon may have promoted writing by providing royal support for scribes and schools. Although that kingdom soon divided when Israel in the north broke away from Judah in the south, Jewish scribes kept a vivid record of their history, represented in the Books of Kings and Chronicles. Their accounts of tumultuous events such as the siege of Jerusalem by Assyrians around 700 B.C.E. (see pp. 196-97) and the destruction of that city by Babylonians in 586 B.C.E. have been supplemented by the discovery of inscriptions composed by the con-

Found in 2008 by archaeologists excavating at Khirbet Qeiyafa, a fortified city near Bethlehem occupied around the time of King David, this message written on clay is the oldest Hebrew inscription yet discovered, dating to around 1000 B.C.E.

querors. Those reports confirm the essentials of the biblical chronicles but offer a different perspective on the struggles that drove the Jewish people into exile and prompted them to preserve their imperiled traditions and beliefs in their Bible.

Following the Babylonian Exile, Jews were seldom their own masters and had to contend with one imperial power after another—as documented by archaeological finds at many sites, including Jerusalem. Some exiles returned to that holy city after the Persians conquered Babylon and instituted a more tolerant regime in which Jews were able to rebuild their Temple (see pp. 226-27). Not until the second century B.C.E., however, following the conquests of Alexander the Great and a prolonged power struggle between the heirs to his empire, the Ptolemies and Seleucids, did Jews led by Judas Maccabeus regain control of their kingdom, known as Judea, and rededicate their Temple (see pp. 240-41). That brief return to independence only made it harder for them to bear conquest by the Romans, who installed Herod the Great as king of Judea and later took direct control of the province. Opposition to Roman rule and the Roman cult of the divine emperor took two forms—spiritual resistance, as represented by the quest for a heavenly Messiah that gave rise to Christianity (see pp. 254-87); and political resistance, culminating in the Jewish Revolt and the Roman destruction of Jerusalem and its Temple (see pp. 304-05), which renewed the Diaspora that scattered Jews from the very heart of the biblical world to its farthest limits.

Future archaeological discoveries may alter not only our interpretation of the Bible but also the text itself by bringing to light new scrolls containing earlier versions of Scripture that might be recognized by scholars and translators as authoritative. Certainly, new finds will continue to enhance our understanding of the Bible and its world—a universe conceived in words that those who set down Holy Scripture in writing saw as sacred and inspired by a divine author. As John the Evangelist declared in the first verse of his gospel: "In the beginning was the Word, and the Word was with God, and the Word was God."

ABOUT THIS BOOK

This book is divided into eight chapters covering major eras in biblical history as defined by country, kingdom, or faith. The chapters are arranged chronologically, based on when the country achieved prominence or the kingdom or faith arose. The sequence of chapters corresponds roughly to the order of events in the Bible. Readers will find references to Canaan in Chapter 1, dealing with Mesopotamian civilization and the journeys of Abraham and his descendants; and Chapter 2, dealing with Egyptian civilization and biblical accounts of the Exodus. But full treatment of Canaan is reserved for Chapter 3, which examines the settlement of that Promised Land by Israelites and their interactions with rival groups prior to the emergence of the kingdom of Israel around 1000 B.C.E.

Documenting and dating biblical events precisely before that time is difficult because written evidence is limited and the Bible itself had not yet been composed, its stories transmitted only in the oral tradition. The remaining chapters in this book, however, cover well-defined biblical periods for which written records are extensive: the united kingdom of Israel under David and Solomon; the divided kingdom of Israel and Judah; the imperial age when Jews lived in a world dominated by Persians, Greeks or Greek-speaking Macedonians, and Romans; the time of Christ; and the last years of Jerusalem as the spiritual center of Judaism.

Each chapter begins with an introduction providing an overview of the subject and includes a picture essay, displaying works of art emblematic of the various civilizations that made up the biblical world, and one or more maps like the one explained in detail below. The remainder of each chapter consists of articles examining archaeological discoveries related to the Bible or the biblical world. This book is entitled *The Letter and the Scroll* because, with few exceptions, the most significant finds made by biblical archaeologists are inscriptions or manuscripts like the Dead Sea Scrolls.

Most of the articles in the following chapters deal with inscriptions, but many also feature ancient paintings, carvings, or artifacts that support the written evidence or, in some cases, provide the only evidence available on important questions raised by the Bible.

The purpose of this book is not to prove or disprove the Bible but to explore the world that gave rise to its Scriptures and consider them in their historical context—an approach that can enhance one's appreciation for the Bible both as a work of history and as a statement of faith. Reverence for Scripture can withstand careful study, as shown long ago by devout scholars like Martin Luther, who spent many years translating the Bible and likened it to "a mighty tree and every word a little branch." He had no doubt that this wondrous creation existed not simply to be praised and admired but to be examined and explained. "I have shaken every one of these branches," he declared, "because I wanted to know what it was and what it meant."

This map is shown at 36% of the original found on page 172.

chapter 1

SUMER AND AKKAD
Land of Abraham

SUMER AND AKKAD

Between about 3300 and 2600 B.C.E., the foundations of human civilization were being laid in southern Mesopotamia, in a hill-less region between the Euphrates and Tigris Rivers that archaeologists refer to as Sumer. The land between these rivers was a floodplain with rich alluvial soil. Agriculture flourished here, and so did the first cities, bestowing on Sumer the title of "cradle of civilization." It was in this cradle that the biblical patriarch Abraham was nurtured, at the Sumerian city of Ur.

In part, the urbanization of Sumer resulted from the vagaries of its two great, life-giving rivers. While the Nile overflowed its banks in regular cycles, the flooding of the Euphrates and the Tigris was unpredictable, leaving the land alternately well-watered and bone-dry. To avoid this, the Sumerians began to harness the river waters, devising an elaborate system of canals that irrigated agricultural land far inland. The landscape blossomed with vineyards, olive groves, and fields of wheat and barley, a veritable Eden amid the surrounding desert.

> ". . . THEY WENT FORTH TOGETHER
> FROM UR OF THE
> CHALDEANS TO GO INTO
> THE LAND OF CANAAN . . ."
> GENESIS 12:31

THE RISE OF CITY-STATES

The irrigation scheme that was developed around the end of the fourth millennium B.C.E., and the abundant agricultural produce that resulted, was a great spur to human development. Such schemes forced neighboring farmers to cooperate and plan ahead—to dig a network of ditches and dikes to store the floodwaters and channel it to the parched fields. Working together, they also began to live closer together, in communities that eventually grew into city-states. As farmers began to produce surplus crops, many of them were freed up to do other, more specialized jobs. Some became artisans, others herders, others priests serving a pantheon of no fewer than 3,000 gods. Still others became bureaucrats to administer the increasingly complex life of the state on behalf of its ruler or king. These kings built defensive walls around their cities and granaries, wide boulevards and grand temples within. From around 3000 to 2700 B.C.E., the most powerful of these competing Sumerian city-states was Uruk, referred to in the Bible as Erech and, according to some scholars, the origin of the name "Iraq."

Located some 150 miles southeast of the Iraqi capital of Baghdad, Uruk was the largest city-state in Sumer during the late third millennium B.C.E., more than five miles in circumference and home to nearly 50,000 inhabitants. At its heart, on a 40-foot-high mound, loomed the White Temple, perhaps the earliest of the shrines called ziggurats. Made of sun-dried mud bricks covered with an exterior of baked bricks, these distinctive rectangular towers rose, steplike, in successively receding levels that raised the temple's priests, considered to be representatives of the gods, toward the heavens.

Closely related to the forces of nature that could bring prosperity or disaster, the Sumerian pantheon included gods of the sun, moon, water, earth, fertility, and so on. Typically, each city-state also adopted a particular deity as its patron god or goddess. In Uruk, the dominant deities were Inanna, the goddess of fertility, love, and war, and An, the god of heaven and ruler of the constellations. Sumerian craftsmen produced small sculptures of such gods, which rank as history's first instances of statuary. Temples were filled with statues of the gods and of their human worshippers, the latter typically in fringed gowns, hands piously clasped in front. Apparently, the petitioning of the gods could

Previous pages: "The Sacrifice of Isaac" by Michelangelo Merisi da Caravaggio
Opposite: A section of a mural from the royal palace at Mari shows two priests in ceremonial dress leading a bull to sacrifice.

not prevent a great flood dated to around 2900 B.C.E. that seems to have led to a gradual decline in the power of Uruk relative to the other cities of southern Mesopotamia. As an ancient royal genealogy known as the Sumerian King List records, "Erech [Uruk] was defeated, its kingship . . . carried off to Ur."

Located along the banks of the Euphrates River, ancient Ur was by 2750 B.C.E. the most powerful of the rival city-states of Sumer—a center of trade, the commercial links of which reached all the way to Egypt, and a great cultural center boasting magnificent royal tombs and public buildings. Within the space of a couple of centuries, one of Ur's rulers, Mesannepadda (2560-2525 B.C.E.), had exerted his control over all of Sumer.

By now, the cradle of civilization was really beginning to rock. The Sumerians pioneered many great human inventions, including the wheel, the plowshare, monumental architecture, and fine arts. Perhaps their most valuable contribution was the development of writing, first used as a method of recordkeeping by the priests. Because the writing was etched into soft clay that, when baked, is almost impervious to the effects of time, it was also Sumer's greatest gift to later archaeologists and scholars. While entire libraries from the ancient world, filled with papyrus scrolls, have been lost to fire or floods, clay endures; fire only serves to harden it further. The 3,000 years in which cuneiform script was used offers us an invaluable window on the history of Mesopotamia. That history was about to take a dramatic turn when Sargon the Great (2334-2279 B.C.E.), king of Akkad, turned his conquering attentions on the still squabbling city-states of Sumer.

INVASION FROM THE NORTH

The Akkadians were a battle-hardened people from the north and of Semitic origin (the Akkadian language group would later develop into Hebrew and Aramaic). Already they had defeated the kingdom of Mari, upstream on the Euphrates, and the cities of southern Mesopotamia would be no match for them. In short order, Sargon picked off Uruk, Ur, and the others, uniting them all into a single political unit for the first time. In the process, he extended the Akkadian empire even farther, which by 2280 B.C.E. stretched all the way from the Persian Gulf to the Taurus

Marsh Arabs navigate their fishing boats on the waters of the Euphrates near Chebayish, southern Iraq. Life in this part of Mesopotamia has remained largely unchanged for millennia.

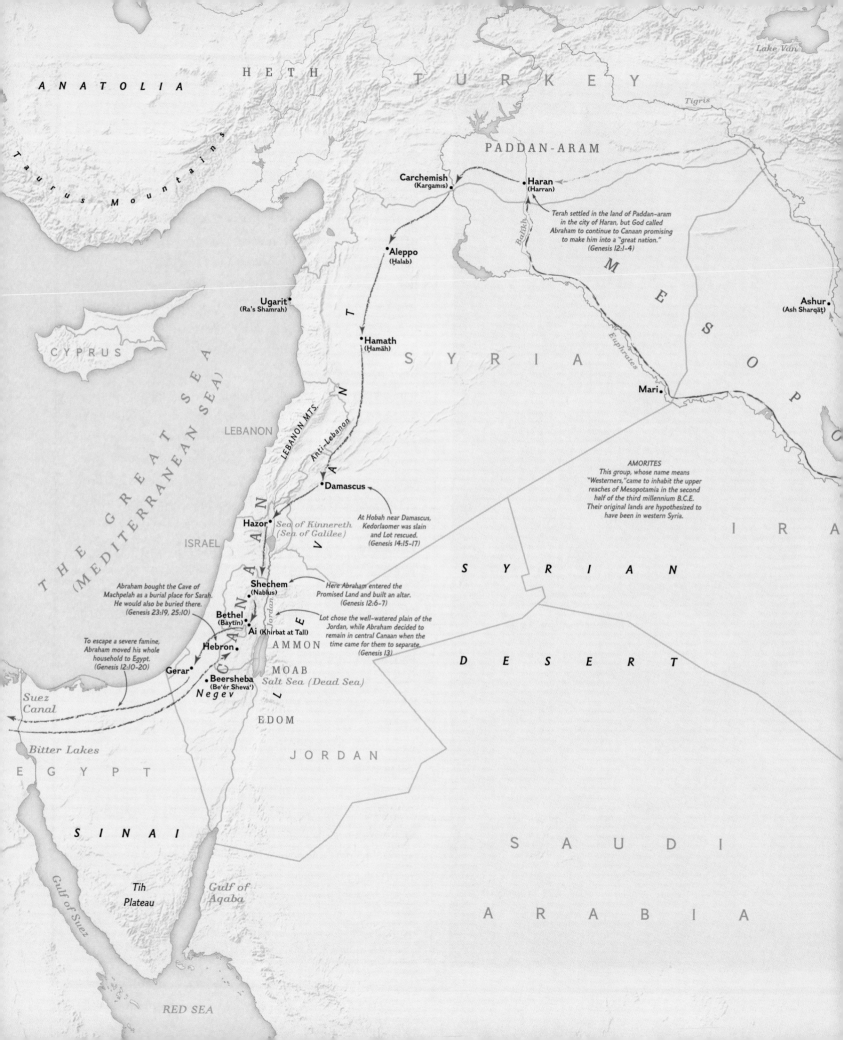

ANATOLIA

HETH

TURKEY

Lake Van

Taurus Mountains

Tigris

PADDAN-ARAM

Carchemish
(Kargamış)

Haran
(Harran)

Balikh

Terah settled in the land of Paddan-aram
in the city of Haran, but God called
Abraham to continue to Canaan promising
to make him into a "great nation."
(Genesis 12:1-4)

Aleppo
(Ḥalab)

MESO

Ugarit
(Ra's Shamrah)

Ashur
(Ash Sharqāt)

CYPRUS

Hamath
(Ḥamāh)

SYRIA

Euphrates

THE GREAT SEA
(MEDITERRANEAN SEA)

LEBANON

LEBANON MTS.

Anti-Lebanon

Mari

MESOP

Damascus

AMORITES
This group, whose name means
"Westerners," came to inhabit the upper
reaches of Mesopotamia in the second
half of the third millennium B.C.E.
Their original lands are hypothesized to
have been in western Syria.

IRA

Hazor

Sea of Kinnereth
(Sea of Galilee)

At Hobah near Damascus,
Kedorlaomer was slain
and Lot rescued.
(Genesis 14:15-17)

ISRAEL

SYRIAN

Abraham bought the Cave of
Machpelah as a burial place for Sarah.
He would also be buried there.
(Genesis 23:19, 25:10)

Shechem
(Nablus)

Here Abraham entered the
Promised Land and built an altar.
(Genesis 12:6-7)

Bethel
(Baytīn)

Ai (Khirbat at Tall)

Lot chose the well-watered plain of the
Jordan, while Abraham decided to
remain in central Canaan when the
time came for them to separate.
(Genesis 13)

DESERT

To escape a severe famine,
Abraham moved his whole
household to Egypt.
(Genesis 12:10-20)

Hebron

AMMON

Gerar

MOAB

Salt Sea (Dead Sea)

Beersheba
(Be'ér Sheva')

Negev

Suez
Canal

EDOM

Bitter Lakes

JORDAN

EGYPT

SINAI

SAUDI

Gulf of Suez

Tih
Plateau

Gulf of
Aqaba

ARABIA

RED SEA

THE JOURNEY OF ABRAHAM

CASPIAN SEA

Lake Urmia

Elburz Mts.

I R A N

Z A G R O S   M O U N T A I N S

Simareh

Babylon

AKKAD

M E S O P O T A M I A

Tigris

SUMERIA

The Elamites invaded lower Mesopotamia, establishing their control of the region including the city of Ur.

ELAM

Erech

Euphrates

Ur

Eridu

Terah, Abraham's father, decided to migrate to the land of Canaan. He took his daughter-in-law Sarah and his grandson Lot along with him. (Genesis 11:31)

C H A L D E A

PERSIAN GULF

K U W A I T

MAP KEY

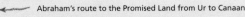

Abraham's route to the Promised Land from Ur to Canaan

Possible alternate route

0   100   200 kilometers

0   100   200 miles

Present-day drainage, coastlines, and country boundaries are represented. Modern names appear in parentheses.

Mountains in what is now Turkey and across to Lebanon in the west. As shown on this map, these were the territories of the Fertile Crescent that the biblical patriarch Abraham would later cross as he moved from his home in Ur in southern Mesopotamia—up the Euphrates Valley to Haran and then west toward the Mediterranean and into the promised land of Canaan.

The Akkadians adopted Sumerian ways, using cuneiform writing to put their own language into written form and taking on the gods of Sumer. After Sargon's death, his heirs strove to hold together his vast realm, one of the world's first great empires. But city-states inside the empire revolted, and nomadic tribes nipped at its borders. Although Akkad's rulers encountered both successes and defeats in countering these threats, by 2218 B.C.E. they had lost control of much of southern Mesopotamia. Eventually, local rulers came back to power. In Ur, King Ur-Nammu presided over a brief but glorious restoration from about 2112 to 2095 B.C.E. Soon other invaders arrived, and confusion continued to reign in southern Mesopotamia.

THE BABYLONIANS

In 1792 B.C.E., however, a man named Hammurabi came to the throne in the city-state of Babylon. The Babylonians were descendants of the Sumerians and Akkadians, though theirs was one of the smaller cities in the region. But under Hammurabi's firm hand, Babylon became the center of a new empire. Hammurabi was more than just a mighty conqueror, though: He was an enlightened ruler, an accomplished builder, and, most significant of all, one of the great lawmakers of the ancient world.

By the reign of Hammurabi—just around the time that Abraham (then called Abram) and his family were about to walk onto the pages of history—Sumer was no longer a political entity. Yet the achievements of Sumerian culture would continue to impact later kingdoms and empires for centuries. Testimony about those achievements, like those of its successors in Mesopotamia, is preserved in the archaeological record, a record that has been painstakingly pieced together by scholars and researchers over the course of the last hundred years or so.

The map shows the migration of Abraham and his clan from the city of Ur in Mesopotamia to Haran in modern-day Turkey and onward to Egypt until they could finally settle in Canaan, the Promsied Land.

"COME, LET US BUILD OURSELVES A CITY,
AND A TOWER WITH ITS TOP IN THE HEAVENS . . .
LEST WE BE SCATTERED ABROAD UPON
THE FACE OF THE WHOLE EARTH."

GENESIS 11:4

THE CITY OF UR

In 1922, a British archaeologist named Sir Leonard Woolley (1880-1960) began excavations at Tell al-Muqayyar, north of Basra in today's Iraq. His site was Ur, a mighty metropolis of the third millennium B.C.E. and home to some 30,000 souls, among them the biblical patriarch Abraham.

Today, the site lies some ten miles from the Euphrates River. But in Abraham's day, the waterway passed much closer, and where there is now bare desert there were once fertile fields. Ur was at that time the preeminent city-state of Sumer, with trade links that extended as far as Egypt, and a cultural center without peer.

During his excavations at Tell al Muqayyar, Woolley uncovered a group of royal tombs containing the remains of 74 people, 68 of them female. The bodies were arranged as if participating in a funerary procession. One tomb had a gold dagger, "its hilt of lapis lazuli decorated with gold studs"; other tombs contained elaborate headdresses, a lovely harp trimmed in gold, and cups and vessels of the finest materials. Woolley theorized that these tombs contained the bodies of King

Abargi and Queen Puabi—and their complete retinue. All the ladies-in-waiting, groomsmen, soldiers, and courtiers were put to death at the time of the funeral so as to continue to serve the royals in the afterlife.

Ur also boasted many magnificent buildings. In the second year of excavations, Woolley's team began to clear away rubble to uncover one of them—the great stepped temple of ancient Sumer, among the greatest finds of the ancient world.

THE ZIGGURATS OF SUMER

Most of the leading cities of southern Mesopotamia built such stepped towers. The Babylonian and Assyrian word for them was *zigguratu,* "temple tower," from which we get the term ziggurat. The one at Ur was constructed by Ur-Nammu, king of Ur from 2112 to 2095 B.C.E. Eighty feet tall, the ziggurat was built on three levels, each accessible via stairways, and topped by a shrine dedicated to

Now partially restored, this great ziggurat once overlooked the ancient city of Ur, where Abraham is said to have been born. The ziggurat's central staircase led up to a shrine dedicated to the moon god Nanna.

the moon god Nanna. The ziggurat was erected inside an elaborate enclosure that included temple facilities, a treasury, and residences for the priestly caste.

The first book of the Bible, Genesis, relates how human beings, at a time "when the whole earth was of one language," purposed to build just such a tower, "with its top in the heavens." Before the construction was completed, however, God intervened, sowing confusion among mankind: At a stroke, people began to "babble" in different languages (in Hebrew, the verb *bala'* means "to confuse"), and hence the tower is called Babel. Scholars believe that the word may also be derived from the Akkadian root of the name Babylon: *bab-ili,* gate of the god.

The ziggurats of Mesopotamia were built of mud brick and mortar made of bitumen. The biblical description echoes this process closely: "And they said to one another, 'Come, let us make bricks, and burn them thoroughly.' And they had brick for stone, and bitumen for mortar. Then they said, 'Come, let us build ourselves a city, and a tower with its top in the heavens'" (Genesis 11:3-4). This, the Bible tells us, occurred in the land of Shinar, a term elsewhere used to denote Babylon. The remains of the ziggurat at Babylon are less impressive than those at Ur. Because the baked bricks used for the Babylon tower have long been removed for use elsewhere, the site today is little more than a water-and-reed-filled hole in the ground.

This fanciful depiction by Flemish painter Abel Grimmer shows the Tower of Babel as a multilevel ziggurat. According to the account in Genesis, chapter 11, the tower was built to reach as high as heaven itself.

"THE FLOOD CONTINUED FORTY DAYS
UPON THE EARTH; AND THE WATERS
INCREASED, AND BORE UP THE ARK,
AND IT ROSE HIGH ABOVE THE EARTH."

GENESIS 7:18

THE GREAT FLOOD

Cuneiform
By the mid-fourth century B.C.E., Sumerian traders were recording their transactions on soft clay tablets (like the one below) marked with small wedge shapes. Eventually, the shapes became a primitive alphabet of pictograms. This form of writing is known as cuneiform, from Latin cuneus, or "wedge."

As Sir Leonard Woolley and his team were excavating at Ur, they came upon a stratum very different from the rest—a uniform layer of clay that had clearly been deposited by water. This clay layer, wrote Woolley, "continued without challenge" through a depth of eight feet, when it ended as suddenly as it had appeared. The archaeologist could find only one possible explanation: It was, he concluded, unmistakable evidence of a great flood—and one "not less than 25 feet deep." News of the discovery generated a buzz of excitement. Finally, it was claimed, here was evidence of the great Flood described in Genesis.

After continued excavations across Mesopotamia, other signs of greater and lesser flooding emerged. Soon it became clear that the ancient "land between the two rivers" was frequently submerged under the waters of the two rivers. The region was one that had repeatedly suffered mild to severe flooding. Literary evidence seems to point to one devastating deluge that may have taken place around 3000-2900 B.C.E., its impact so great that it was enshrined in a number of Mesopotamian myths and tales that have many similarities with the biblical account of the Flood. The most famous of these tales—the world's first great work of literature—is the Epic of Gilgamesh.

Our knowledge of the epic comes from inscribed clay tablets found in the library of Assyria's King Ashurbanipal (ruled 669-627 B.C.E.) at Nineveh and at various other sites in Mesopotamia. Some 3,500 lines long, it recounts the adventures of Gilgamesh, the mighty warrior-king of Uruk. The epic also recalls an original state of innocence for humankind, a temptation, and a fall. And it tells how at one point, because humans made so much noise, the sleep-deprived gods determined to wipe them out in a great deluge that would cover the Earth. However, the god Ea instructs a good man named Utnapishtim to save himself and his family by building a great ark. In language similar to God's instructions to Noah in Genesis, chapter 6, Ea tells Utnapishtim: "Let her beam equal her length, let her deck be roofed like the vault that covers the abyss; then take up in the boat the seed of all living creatures." Utnapishtim obeys. As the floodwaters begin to subside, he releases a dove, a swallow, and then a raven to test whether the Earth had become habitable.

The King List

Compiled around 2100 B.C.E., the Sumerian King List (left) provides an ancient record of Mesopotamian rulers, similar to the Adam-through-Noah genealogy that is found in the fifth chapter of the Book of Genesis. The list describes Eridu as the first city-state on Earth, where Alulim ruled as the first king. And it records how Erech (Uruk) was founded by a mythical ruler named Enmerkar, who was succeeded by Gilgamesh (shown subduing a lion in the eighth-century B.C.E. statue above), builder of the city's great defensive walls.

So devastating was the impact of a great flood that swept the region at the beginning of the third millennium B.C.E. that the king list distinguishes between antediluvian rulers and those who came "after the flood." It records that the decline of Uruk occurred around the time of the deluge, when "its kingship was carried off to Ur."

Fifteen copies of the Sumerian King List have been found, each slightly different, but all a blend of the historical and the mythical. This is particularly so with regard to the unrealistic lengths of the kings' reigns. Some seem reasonable: "Amar-Sin, the son of Shulgi, reigned nine years; Shu-Sin, the brother of Amar-Sin, reigned nine years." But others enter the realms of fantasy, perhaps to enhance the prestige of a particular ruler. The longest reign, for example, is given as 36,000 years. More than a purely dynastic record, however, the list must have had the purpose of helping to legitimize kingship that "came down from heaven."

Similar to the story of Noah, this fragmented Babylonian cuneiform tablet recounts part of the Epic of Atrahasis, in which Atrahasis builds an ark in order to escape a coming flood sent to destroy mankind. The tablet dates from the 17th century B.C.E. and was found in Sippar in southern Iraq.

"When Marduk commissioned me to guide the people aright, to direct the land, I established law and justice in the language of the land, thereby promoting the welfare of the people."

A scene showing Hammurabi standing before the god Marduk adorns a stela inscribed with the law code of the great Babylonian king. The stela is made of black basalt and dates from around 1750 B.C.E.

THE ORIGINS OF LAW

"TEACH THEM THE STATUTES AND THE DECISIONS, AND MAKE THEM KNOW THE WAY IN WHICH THEY MUST WALK AND WHAT THEY MUST DO."

EXODUS 18:20

The magnificent eight-foot-high stela opposite is engraved with the famous Law Code of Hammurabi, and over the millennia it has graced a number of the world's great capitals. Originally, the 18th-century B.C.E. stela may have stood in Babylon's temple of Marduk, the city's patron god, but some 600 years later Elamite invaders carried it off to their capital of Susa, or "Shushan," in the Book of Daniel (8:2), in what is modern-day Iran. There the stela remained for more than 3,000 years until, in 1901, French archaeologists discovered it and shipped it off to Paris, where it now resides in the Louvre Museum.

Through its 282 laws, Hammurabi's code set the highest of goals: "to cause justice to prevail in the land, to destroy the wicked and the evil, that the strong may not oppress the weak." To accomplish this, the code stipulated the punishments associated with each crime. Murderers would pay with their own lives, as would a builder whose negligence resulted in the collapse of a home and the death of its owner. Amputation was the penalty for a physician whose negligence led to a patient's death and for a barber who dared trim the lock of hair that identified a man as a slave.

In its care for the weakest and most vulnerable members of society, the Code of Hammurabi has many similarities with the Law of Moses. The rights of widows and orphans were carefully protected. Men who sexually abused children or committed incest were dealt with most severely of all.

When it was first discovered, the Code of Hammurabi was proclaimed as the oldest known set of laws.

Since that time, however, other law codes have been found that predate Hammurabi's. The oldest of them is the Code of Ur-Nammu, which was written some 300 years before its better-known successor.

The Code of Ur-Nammu takes its name from the founder of the final dynasty of Sumerian kings, the third dynasty of Ur (Abraham's birthplace), whose reign ushered in the last great era of Sumerian literary achievement. Discovered at Ur and at Nippur, near Babylon, the code details some 57 different laws on such subjects as crime, inheritance and other family matters, agricultural and commercial tariffs, and the rights of laborers and slaves. Like Hammurabi's code, it was based on justice by retribution. Because it is older, the Sumerian code might be expected to have an even more punitive character than the "eye-for-an-eye" Code of Hammurabi. But this is not the case, preferring as it does more humane fines rather than mutilation as a punishment for inflicting physical injuries. For example, "If a man knocks out the eye of another man," declares the Code of Ur-Nammu, "he shall weigh out ½ mina of silver," or "if a man cuts off the foot of another man [with his . . .], he shall pay 10 shekels of silver."

Scholars now believe that this enlightened collection of laws may well have been devised by Ur-Nammu's son, Shulgi. Although this set of instructions is the oldest known law code, other written royal decrees had probably been compiled and passed on, ruler to ruler, for centuries before. Yet the Code of Ur-Nammu predates the Ten Commandments that God delivers to Moses in the Book of Exodus by a thousand years.

This cracked and reassembled clay tablet dates from the reign of King Shulgi (2095-2047 B.C.E.) and was the first to contain the entire Code of Ur-Nammu, the world's oldest known law code. The original tablet listed 57 crimes and punishments in its 243 lines of cuneiform script.

This bull's head of gold and lapis lazuli formed part of the sounding box of a lyre. Bulls were symbols of fertility and strength, and the braided beard on this creature may have been a sign of divinity.

THE ROYAL TOMBS OF UR

Ancient grave robbers got to the "Royal Tombs of Ur" ahead of archaeologist Sir Leonard Woolley and plundered what they found. Nonetheless, the excavations Woolley carried out there between 1926 and 1931 revealed some of the greatest treasures of Sumer, dating to about 2600 B.C.E. For in death, as in life, the most lavish trappings were enjoyed by the royalty of Sumerian society.

At Ur, Woolley found 16 royal tombs in all. The underground burial chambers were built of brick and stone, and had been constructed with such architecturally advanced features as the arch, dome, and vault. One of the tombs was the final resting place of a Sumerian king, the one next to it the tomb of a woman thought to be his wife. Also buried in the tombs at Ur were members of the burial party, the musicians, ladies-in-waiting, and soldiers that made up the royal retinue. These attendees were ritually sacrificed at the time of the monarchs' funerals, perhaps drugged into a semiconscious state before being buried alive.

The tombs held some of the finest examples of Sumerian craftsmanship—musical instruments, daggers, ceramic jewelry, gold and silver bowls, and figurines of lapis lazuli. Most of Woolley's finds are today in the possession of the British Museum and the University of Pennsylvania Museum of Archaeology and Anthropology. A selection of these objects are displayed here and on the following pages.

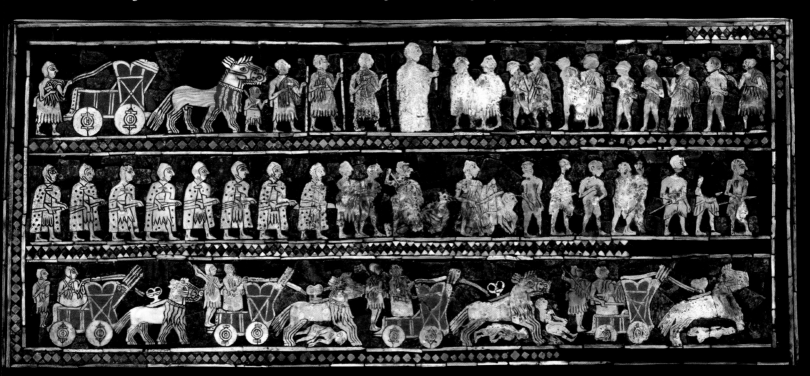

A detail from a mosaic-covered box known as the Royal Standard of Ur shows the king's military forces in action. Two-man Sumerian battle

The sounding box of this reconstructed lyre below is adorned with the head of a bull and its side panels, like the one to the upper right, inlaid with gold and lapis lazuli. Musicians washed their fingers in an act of symbolic purification before playing hymns in honor of the gods.

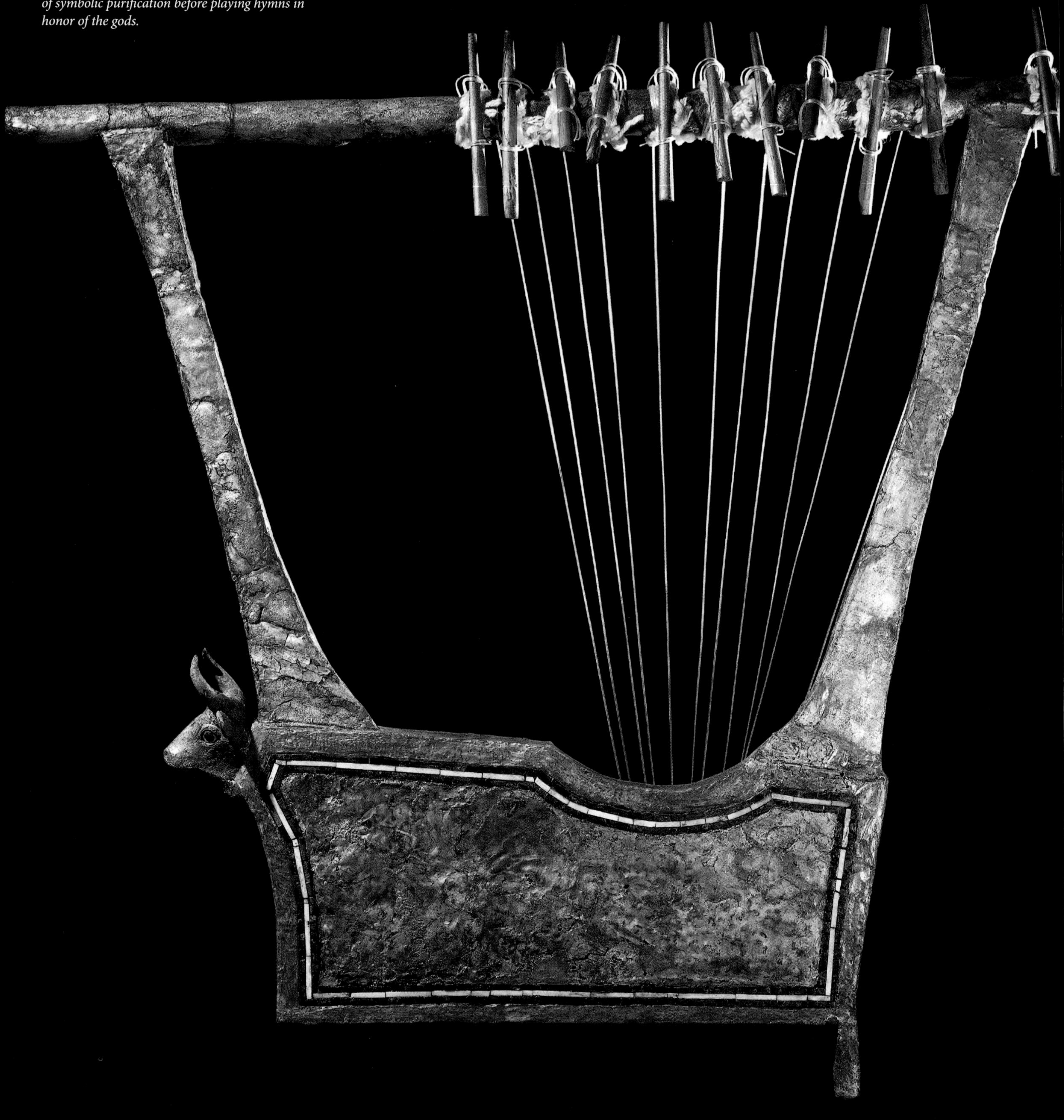

Two goats appear to be nibbling on the leaves of a flowering tree in this shell-and-lapis-inlaid plaque.

This magnificent helmet was made from a sheet of hammered gold that was fashioned to fit the head of a Sumerian king.

THE PALACE AT MARI

> "TERAH TOOK ABRAM HIS SON AND LOT THE SON OF HARAN, HIS GRANDSON, AND SARAI HIS DAUGHTER-IN-LAW, HIS SON ABRAM'S WIFE, AND THEY WENT FORTH TOGETHER FROM UR OF THE CHALDEANS TO GO INTO THE LAND OF CANAAN."
>
> GENESIS 11:31

A seal dating from the time of Mari's temple and palace is adorned with four intertwined figures, a common design during the late second millennium B.C.E. Every important Sumerian had his own distinctive seal that acted as his signature when stamped on soft clay.

When, in early 1933, a Bedouin tribesman found a headless statue on a mound 30 miles from the Syria-Iraq border, French officials in Damascus were immediately interested. They contacted the authorities in Paris, who dispatched a team of archaeologists from the Louvre. Under the direction of André Parrot, they began excavations at the site, known as Tell Hariri. What he found had lain beneath the sands for more than two millennia—the royal palace at Mari. Parrot would spend the next four decades at the site to carry out his "love affair with Mari."

Mari's growth in the early third millennium B.C.E. was a reflection of its location. On the banks of the Euphrates, 250 miles upriver from its rival, Babylon, the city sat astride the region's trade routes. From here, the routes ran northeast to Anatolia, east to Persia, south to the Persian Gulf, and west toward the Mediterranean. Along them traveled caravans laden with olive oil, dried fruits (such as dates), textiles, grain, pottery, and porcelain; cedar wood from Lebanon for the construction of great palaces was transported across to the Euphrates, then floated downriver.

Dedicated to its patron deity Dagan, god of the grain harvest, Mari became a thriving metropolis. Around 2000 B.C.E., the city's population began to swell by the arrival of a nomadic group known as the Amorites, whose homelands are thought to have been in western Syria. Mari enjoyed a golden age as the capital of King Zimri-Lim in the 18th century B.C.E., before it was overrun by King Hammurabi around 1760 B.C.E. Bent on extinguishing all traces of this former rival, Hammurabi ordered Zimri-Lim's 300-room palace burned. Drifting sand gradually covered its remains, hiding them until their discovery by Parrot in the 20th century.

At the Tell Hariri site, the finds came quickly. A month after excavations began, the archaeologists discovered an ancient temple of Ishtar. They declared Mari the most westerly outpost of Sumerian culture and kept on digging. Buried inside the city's ruins, Parrot found a treasure trove of artifacts, including statuettes, earthenware jars, terra-cotta bathtubs, and a functioning plumbing system. He also unearthed colorful murals, fire damaged and in multiple pieces that had to be painstakingly reassembled. But most important was a cache of more than 20,000 cuneiform clay tablets, only a quarter of which have been translated to date. Known as the Mari Archive, it provides detailed information about the economic, cultural, and political affairs of Zimri-Lim's realm, from the minutiae of daily life to the interpretation of omens and the correspondence of kings.

HOMELAND OF THE PATRIARCHS

In Genesis, the Bible recounts how Terah, his son Abraham (then called Abram), and the rest of his family headed north out of Ur, following the Euphrates River across the Fertile Crescent to the city of Haran. Parrot claimed that on their way they passed through Mari, which they would have reached about a month after their departure from Ur. There, they would have encountered the city in its heyday, and saw firsthand the worship of Dagan and other Sumerian gods like Ishtar (Asherah), Baal, El, and Adad.

Just 250 miles from Haran, Mari thus sits within "the homeland of the patriarchs," and its archaeological legacy tells us much about the culture and socioeconomic conditions that Abraham would have experienced. Some of the clay tablets at Mari record many of the practices referred to in the Bible, such as the slaughtering of animals as a mark of covenant, procedures for inheritance and adoption, and the role of judges. Of particular interest are tablets with prophetic messages said to be from one of the gods to King Zimri-Lim.

The Great Temple and palace at Mari in northern Syria, whose remains are shown above, boasted 300 rooms on the ground floor alone. It dates from around 1950 B.C.E., when building began, to around 1760 B.C.E., when it was destroyed by Babylon's King Hammurabi.

THE NUZI TABLETS

Between 1925 and 1933, American archaeologists carried out excavations at the ancient site of Nuzi in northern Iraq. Nuzi was a settlement of a non-Semitic people called the Hurrians. They are believed to have migrated from the Caucasus region to settle in northern Mesopotamia in the middle of the third millennium B.C.E. The influence of the Hurrians came to an end with the invasion of the Assyrians, who destroyed Nuzi around 1400 B.C.E.

Located east of the Tigris River, Nuzi has yielded more than 5,000 cuneiform tablets that date from just before the Assyrian conquest and destruction. Thus Abraham and his family would already have passed through, on their way to Canaan, by the time the Nuzi archive was compiled. But the legal and social customs the tablets describe were doubtless passed down by earlier generations and provide important insights on life during the times of the patriarchs.

The tablets that make up the archive were written in Babylonian, the common language of the region. They address all aspects of the life of this Old Testament people and echo many of the practices referred to in the Book of Genesis. These include marriage arrangements, the significance of the deathbed blessing, and the practices of adoption and inheritance in tradition-honoring Hurrian society.

As documented in the Nuzi tablets, adoption and inheritance were areas of particular concern. For example, the tablets document the importance of passing a family's inheritance on, over the generations, from male heir to male heir—and the two options for a man whose wife could not provide him a son. One was adoption, and the tablets indicate that the prospective candidate might be a relative, a

Known as Nuzi ware, this thin-walled beaker dates from the 15th to 14th centuries B.C.E. and was in widespread use among the Hurrian people of northern Mesopotamia.

nonrelative, or even a slave. In return for undertaking to provide a fitting funeral for his adoptive father, the son would inherit the larger portion of the family estate.

The second option for a sonless patriarch was to father a child with his wife's personal female slave. (One tablet even indicates the region where the best slaves could be obtained for this purpose.) The new mother would no longer be subject to the barren wife's authority but to the husband's only. Her son would have the same rights, as heir, as an adopted son. However, should the original wife eventually bear a son, the latter would become the heir, though the slave wife's son would not be disinherited completely. Should the slave wife forget her place, and behave as an equal with the first wife, she risked being punished by her husband and placed back under the authority of the first wife. Convoluted as all these matters may seem, they were part of everyday life then, and they would all play out in the lives of Abraham and his two wives, Sarah and Hagar, and their sons Ishmael and Isaac (see pp. 52-53).

Another part of the Nuzi archive is made up of the so-called tablets of sistership. These were agreements entered into in which a Hurrian man adopted a Hurrian woman as his sister as well as his wife. This would be done by drawing up two legal documents, one recognizing the marriage and the other conferring sistership. The purpose of such a practice was to enhance the status of the woman involved, for in Hurrian society a wife would enjoy greater legal protection and a more respected position if she could also claim to be a sister. This may explain why Abraham would twice (in Genesis 12:10-20 and later in Genesis 20:1-16) introduce Sarah as his sister.

"*Document of adoption of Tulpunnaya, daughter of Sheltunnaya; and Hurpishenni son of Hashiya adopted [her]. One aweharu of orchard in Temtenash, bordering on the orchard of Hapurshi, son of Puhishenni, to Tulpunnaya he gave in adopting [her]."*

GENESIS 12:13 | GENESIS 16:1-6 | GENESIS 20:1-2

In patriarchal Hurrian society, a woman could be adopted when she bought land as a way to safeguard her rights. Less than four inches tall, the tablet at left documents the adoption of a wealthy businesswoman named Tulpunnaya by a man named Hurpishenni, completed with the seals of the witnesses.

In this clay tablet inscribed in Akkadian script, a resident of Ashur complains to his brother in Kanesh about his family's lack of food, clothes, and fuel. Like many such tablets, it was sent in a clay "envelope" (inset, opposite), this one inscribed with a seal that shows figures approaching a seated king.

"AND ALL THESE JOINED FORCES IN THE
VALLEY OF SIDDIM (THAT IS, THE SALT SEA)."

GENESIS 14:3

LONG-DISTANCE TRAVEL

In ancient times, the Fertile Crescent—the great arc from Sumer to Anatolia and through Canaan to Egypt—described the contours of travel in the Middle East. To reach the Nile Delta from southern Mesopotamia, envoys, traders, and other travelers could not cross the deserts of Arabia. They had to take the more roundabout route following the crescent—up the valleys of the Euphrates and Tigris, west toward the Mediterranean coast, and south past the Phoenician ports of Byblos, Sidon, and Tyre, whose ships traded goods with the rest of the Mediterranean world.

The travels of the Patriarch Abraham are consistent with the geographical, topographical, and climatic realities that the Fertile Crescent represents. In moving with his family across such large distances, he may have followed these well-known routes along the way. Armies likely took the same routes. During the time of Abraham's travels, for example, the combined forces of four kings from northwest Mesopotamia and southeast Anatolia march their armies all the way to Syria and Canaan to conduct a military campaign against a common enemy (Genesis 14).

The first Mesopotamian king to travel long distances throughout the region was Sargon the Great. In the 23rd century B.C.E., this mighty conqueror and his soldiers moved across vast stretches of territory. And he also established trading relationships that linked distant settlements with the empire that he was forging in southern Mesopotamia. Some scholars believe that Sargon was the biblical Nimrod of Genesis, chapter 10. In the genealogy given there, Nimrod is recorded as a descendant of Noah's son Ham who "grew to be a mighty warrior on the earth." According to verses 10-12, "The beginning of his kingdom was Babel, Erech, and Accad, all of them in the land of Shinar. From that land he went into Assyria, and built Nineveh, Rehoboth-Ir, Calah, and Resen between Nineveh and Calah; that is the great city."

Some authorities place the travels of Abraham and his family around the time when Kanesh was growing into an important travel terminus in central Anatolia. In 1925, a Czech scholar named Bedrich Hrozny was excavating at the ancient site (Kültepe in modern Turkey). He unearthed thousands of cuneiform tablets inscribed in Akkadian script. The tablets were written around 1900 B.C.E. by Assyrian merchants who had traveled from their capital, Ashur, 500 miles to the southeast, to settle in Kanesh and establish a *karum,* or trading center. Caravans from Anatolia set out for all points south across the Fertile Crescent.

The clay tablets found at Kanesh include marriage licenses, letters, and other domestic documents. But most of the tablets are records and communications related to trade, such as contracts and invoices. The tablets describe how they used donkeys to transport bolts of fine fabrics and precious tin to Anatolia (a journey of five to six weeks), there selling the wares for measures of silver and gold. It has been estimated that the profits made by the traders on tin was 100 percent and on textiles 200 percent, and not surprisingly some of the traders became fabulously wealthy.

The merchant-colony city of Kanesh, the karum, was burned down and rebuilt, but was eventually abandoned around 1740 B.C.E. The fortunes of this once flourishing city may have been a result of the political strife that all Anatolia was experiencing at that time, which saw the rise of the newest power in the region—the Hittites.

An Anatolian craftsman fashioned this lion-shaped vase from terra-cotta and adorned it with paint. It dates from around 1900 B.C.E.

SOJOURN IN HARAN

Known in Akkadian as Harranu, or "crossroads," Haran was one of the principal Sumerian trading posts in the northern reaches of Mesopotamia. The settlement is mentioned in a number of artifacts down through the ages, including the Babylonian Chronicles, in a letter to the neo-Assyrian king Ashurbanipal, and in the text of at least two ancient treaties. But the earliest reference to Haran is found on a clay prism dating back to the days of King Tiglath-pileser I (ca 1114-1076 B.C.E.). Currently housed in the British Museum, the prism was found at a large ruin along the

The village of Haran in present-day Turkey is famous for its stone-and-brick beehive-shaped houses. In the photograph above, sheepherders tend their flock outside the village.

banks of the Tigris River known as Kalah-Shergat. A celebration of the military campaigns of the great Assyrian ruler, the prism helps document the gradual rise of this new power in the region and describes the construction of palaces and temples during the early part of the king's reign. Among the 811 lines of cuneiform script that cover the prism is a reference to ancient Haran.

TERAH GOES TO HARAN

Haran was well located, sitting astride the trade routes that cut across upper Mesopotamia, between the cities of Carchemish, which lay some 50 miles to the west, and Nineveh, on the headwaters of the Tigris River to the east. It was here that Terah and his family settled after leaving Ur, which, according to some scholars, took place between 2000 and 1800 B.C.E.

To make the 250-mile journey from Mari to Haran, just where the Fertile Crescent begins to arc toward the south, they would have followed the course of the Balikh River, a tributary of the Euphrates. This route would have taken them right into the city. Like Mari and much of the surrounding region, Haran was inhabited by the Amorites, who spoke a local Akkadian dialect. They worshipped a pantheon of Mesopotamian deities, such as the moon god Sin (known as Nanna in Sumerian), whose temple was the most important in the city.

Terah had chosen well. Haran and its district enjoyed a temperate climate and fertile soil. Great stretches of cedars grew here. The family must have settled there for some time, so much so that Abraham, in Genesis, chapter 24, refers to the region as "my country." It was in Haran that Terah died, and Abraham became the patriarch of the family. As such, he was now the one who would decide where the family settled, and Abraham would soon be moving them on. (The Amorite word *huabuaru,* meaning "to immigrate," would help define life for the Hebrews for years to come.)

ABRAHAM MOVES ON

According to the Genesis account, Abraham responded to the voice of God, who told him that the Amorite city was not his home—that Abraham's destiny lay to the south in the land of Canaan. God covenanted to make Abraham a great nation in Canaan. Abraham was 75 years old when he left Haran. But not everyone traveled with him. His brother Nahor decided to remain, and he and his wife, Milcah, raised eight children in Haran. Genesis tells how Abraham's grandson Jacob would later move back to Haran in search of a wife from among his kinsmen. In the end, Jacob would end up with two, the sisters Leah and Rachel, who gave birth to two sons who became tribes of Israel.

"Abraham's Journey from Ur to Canaan" by Hungarian artist Josef Molnar

Abraham's Further Travels

The story of Abraham's journey from Ur of the Chaldees to Canaan is one of the great narratives of the Scriptures. Abraham heeds the call of God and travels with his wife, Sarah, his nephew Lot, other family members, and a large body of retainers, as well as his flocks and possessions, to the Promised Land. (The caravan would have traveled on foot and with donkeys rather than the camels shown above, which did not appear in the Middle East until the tenth century B.C.E.) After following the great arc of the Fertile Crescent, the peripatetic patriarch and his following move southwest from Haran through Syria past Damascus and Aleppo and arrive in the land of Canaan.

The Book of Genesis records how Abraham seems to have found little of promise there. And soon he continues on his journey, trekking the length of Canaan, all the way down to the Negev in the far south. This dry and rocky region was afflicted with a particularly severe drought during that period, and Abraham decides to keep on going. Turning his back on the land he had journeyed so long to reach, he and his clan leave Canaan and set off for the more fertile destination of the well-watered Nile Delta.

In Egypt, Abraham seems to have prospered. But he also has a bizarre run-in with the pharaoh at the time, who cast his eyes on Sarah, and they have to depart in haste. At last the wandering patriarch returns to Canaan, and after a brief dispute over territory with this nephew Lot, who chooses the Jordan Valley, Abraham settles in the Promised Land, a rich man, "heavily laden with cattle, with silver, and gold."

The town of Haran has existed at least since the days of Tiglath-pileser I. The inscription of the Assyrian king on the 22-inch octagonal clay prism at left declares, "Ten large wild buffaloes in the country of Kharran [Haran], and the plains of the river Khabur, I slew."

Alalakh: A Forgotten Kingdom

What he found at Tell Atchana in northern Syria in 1939 inspired Leonard Woolley to write a 1953 book entitled *A Forgotten Kingdom*. And in many ways, before Woolley, Idri-mi's Alalakh had been a forgotten kingdom.

The archaeological record puts the earliest settlement at Alalakh at around 2400 B.C.E., and it is mentioned in the Ebla archives as a dependency of the powerful city-state and one seemingly without a vassal king of its own. Later Bronze Age sources refer to Alalakh as the capital of the Mukish kingdom, with the construction of the first royal palace. During the 18th through 16th centuries B.C.E., Alalakh fell under the sway of a new powerful kingdom centered on Aleppo and became its vassal. However, it also suffered at the hands of conquering Hittites, as did Aleppo itself. King Ilim-ilimma briefly restored Aleppo's independence around 1525 B.C.E., but he was soon overthrown, and his young son Idri-mi fled to Canaan.

While in exile, Idri-mi raised an army and built ships, and eventually landed farther north up the coast. He marched inland and restored himself as king, taking Alalakh as his royal capital and seizing back his father's realm. However, hostilities with the Hittites continued during his 30-year reign, though booty plundered from the enemy to the north enabled him to construct a new palace at Alalakh.

When Idri-mi died, around 1480 B.C.E., his son Adad-nirari ascended the throne and had to cope with another people—the Egyptians. With designs on northern Syria, Pharaoh Thutmose III advanced into the region and made it all the way to the upper Euphrates, in the process receiving tribute from Alalakh in the year 1467 B.C.E. Four years later, the Mitanni were in control, and Idri-mi's other son, Niqmepa, became king and a tribute-paying vassal of the Mitanni. But the Hittite threat remained. It was probably they who around 1430 B.C.E. destroyed a new palace that Niqmepa had built. When the Hittites invaded Syria in 1366 B.C.E., they swept all before them, including Alalakh, whose territories they carved up within their growing empire. The city itself was ruled by Hittite princes, until a final devastating blow—the invasion of the Sea People around 1200 B.C.E.—which destroyed Alalakh completely.

This statue of Idri-mi was unearthed at Tell Atchana, the ancient city of Alalakh, where he was the ruler around 1550 B.C.E.

"I MOVED ON AND WENT TO THE LAND
OF CANAAN. . . . FOR SEVEN YEARS I LIVED
AMONG THE HAPIRU-PEOPLE."

FROM IDRI-MI STATUE

THE LAND OF CANAAN

Some 17 years after the start of his excavations at Ur, British archaeologist Leonard Woolley was working at a site much farther around the curve of the Fertile Crescent, at a mound known as Tell Atchana in northern Syria. This was the site of ancient Alalakh, and there he unearthed a 41-inch-tall statue of a seated figure. The highly stylized statue holds one hand in his lap and the other across his heart, as if pleading earnestly down through the centuries that the tale he has to tell should be believed. For this is the statue of Idri-mi, Alalakh's ruler in the mid-16th century B.C.E., and it did—literally—have a tale to tell. Inscribed on the front of the statue are lines of cuneiform script, some 104 in all, that recount the king's trials and travails, including his time of exile in the land to which, according to the Book of Genesis, God had called Abraham.

The statue's narrative tells how Idri-mi was born in Aleppo, but after "an outrage had occurred," he and his family members had fled for refuge to Emar, a city with trade links to Alalakh. Then, seeking greater security, he himself moved on to "ma-at ki-in-a-nim," the inscription of those words (on the statue's right arm) the earliest known reference to "the land of Canaan." Here and in later cuneiform references from other sites, Canaan is understood to be the strip of land from al Aridah in the north to Gaza in the south and from the Mediterranean coastline to the Bekaa and Jordan Valleys. In the northern part of this region, the king sought protection from the "Hapiru warriors," who "gathered around him."

After living in exile in Canaan for seven years, Idri-mi returned to Alalakh, "my city," and firmly reestablished his rule. The inscriptions on the statue record some of his accomplishments: concluding a treaty with the king of Mitanni, launching a military campaign against the Hittites in the north, and receiving tribute from a number of vassals. His diplomatic agreements with neighboring powers are among the earliest of their kind in all of the Near East. "So I was king over Alalakh," he declared on the surface of the statue. "The kings to my right and to my left came to me."

WHAT LEONARD WOOLLEY MADE OF IT

At Tell Atchana, Woolley discovered a wealth of archaeological remains from Idri-mi's Alalakh, including the ruins of palaces, temples, and fortifications. He also found artifacts, works of art, and more than 500 cuneiform tablets, among them deeds of purchase, deliveries of food, loans, ration lists, legal contracts, and judicial acts. The texts make reference to Alalakh's extensive trade links, not only with Emar (where Idri-mi initially fled) but also with Carchemish, Ugarit, and Cyprus, as well as with distant Babylon. Seizing on the words of the tablets, Woolley waxed lyrical about this region of the eastern Mediterranean, seeing in it links between ancient Mesopotamia and the Aegean:

"It involves continual reference to the great empires of ancient Sumer, of Babylon, and of Egypt, to the Hittite empire centered on Bogazköy in Anatolia and to the less-known powers of Hurri and Mitanni; it bears on the development of that Cretan art which astonishes us in the palace of Minos at Knossos, it is associated with the Bronze Age culture of Cyprus, bears witness to the eastward expansion of the trade of the Greek islands in the proto-historic age, throws an entirely new light on the economic aspects of the Athenian empire and even, at the last, suggests a Syrian contribution to the Italian Renaissance. This is the outcome of seven seasons of excavation."

The Tell Atchana site has yielded many other artifacts over the years, including the pot at left, discovered during a dig in 2004.

"IT WAS A GOOD LAND, NAMED YAA. FIGS WERE IN IT,
AND GRAPES. IT HAD MORE WINE THAN WATER.
PLENTIFUL WAS ITS HONEY, ABUNDANT ITS OLIVES.
EVERY [KIND OF] FRUIT WAS ON ITS TREES."

"THE TALE OF SINUHE"

AN EGYPTIAN VIEW OF CANAAN

The eight lines of script adorning the ostracon, or inscribed potsherd, at right tell the ending of one of the classic poems of ancient Egypt, "The Tale of Sinuhe." The nearly 12-inch-long ostracon is from around 1250 B.C.E., but the tale is considerably older, dating back seven centuries and preserved more fully in a number of papyri and ostraca.

A crude statue (below) dating from the period 2150-2040 B.C.E. is inscribed with an Egyptian execration text. The fact that the figure is without arms may have been an attempt to symbolize the powerlessness of the enemy it represents.

According to the story, Sinuhe, a high official at the Egyptian royal court, is accused of some kind of crime during the turmoil that followed the death of Pharaoh Amenemhet I (ca 1938-1908 B.C.E.). Sinuhe decides to flee and, like Idri-mi, heads to Canaan before traveling on to Syria. There he takes refuge near Byblos, which is ruled by a local leader named Ammi-enshi. It is all a far cry from the royal courts of Egypt, but Ammi-enshi is hospitable to the stranger, and even gives Sinuhe his eldest daughter in marriage. The Egyptian settles there, and raises a family. Eventually, though, homesickness gets the better of him, and he returns to Egypt, where he receives a pardon from the new pharaoh and is restored as a member of the royal court. "And I enjoyed the favors of the royal bounty," the tale concludes, "until the day of death came."

Highly stylized and written as if an autobiography to be placed in a tomb, "The Tale of Sinuhe" is almost certainly a work of fiction. However, it includes descriptions of the lands of Canaan and Syria through which Sinuhe traveled. The fields seem to have been well cultivated, rich in barley, emmer, and olives, and producing plentiful wine and honey. The locals kept flocks, too, and seemed to live a seminomadic existence, not yet dwelling in permanent settlements.

Evidence of firsthand Egyptian knowledge of Canaan also comes in the form of so-called Execration Texts. These are short inscriptions on bowls or figurines, with curses against people the Egyptians considered hostile, that were ritually broken and smashed. Execration Texts are the earliest references to rulers, regions, and cities in Canaan and southern Syria.

One group of texts, from around 1900 B.C.E., mentions a few cities, like Ashkelon, a number of tribes, and the names of several tribal or town leaders. The second group, from around 1800 B.C.E., indicates a growing urbanization in the region. It includes a larger list of cities from throughout the region—from the coast, the central hills, and across the Jordan River—such as Acco, Mishal, Rehob, Jerusalem, Shechem, and Ashtaroth.

"Said he to me . . . 'thou shalt dwell with me, and I will entreat thee kindly.' And he placed me even before his children, and mated me with his eldest daughter. He caused me to choose for myself of his county, of the best that belonged to him . . ."

Written in hieratic script, the cursive version of hieroglyphs used in ancient Egypt, the story of Sinuhe is told as an autobiography, describing Sinuhe's flight from Egypt and his sojourn in Canaan. During the time of Abraham, Egypt had a more direct influence on the land of Canaan than did Mesopotamia.

ABRAHAM ARRIVES IN THE LAND

"AND ABRAM TOOK SARAI HIS WIFE, AND LOT HIS BROTHER'S SON, AND ALL THEIR POSSESSIONS WHICH THEY HAD GATHERED, AND THE PERSONS THAT THEY HAD GOTTEN IN HARAN; AND THEY SET FORTH TO GO TO THE LAND OF CANAAN."

GENESIS 12:5

To get to Canaan, Abraham and his family would likely have followed the main caravan route south from Haran. This would have taken them first to Carchemish then through Aleppo, Ebla, and Damascus. From there, their path would have veered to the west before reaching Hazor and then Shechem. Hazor, located ten miles north of the Sea of Galilee, was a city mentioned in the 17th-century B.C.E. tablets of Mari. Covering 200 acres and home to as many as 20,000 inhabitants, it was a considerable settlement by the mid-19th century B.C.E.

Abraham would have encountered Hazor, but according to the Bible accounts he did not stay there. He was bound for Shechem. Shechem was a prosperous and militarily strategic town, sitting in the pass between Mount Gerizim and Mount Ebal. This was fertile agricultural land, the valley bottom and the hillsides both suitable for cultivation. The settlement, referred to on an Egyptian stela, was likely a center for the worship of Baal, the leading fertility god of Canaan. And here Abraham and his clan are said to have stopped.

Genesis, chapter 12, records that Abraham "built an altar to the Lord" at Shechem, though its exact location is unknown to us today. What is known is the location of the East Gate of the fortified city (opposite), mentioned later in the Book of Judges. In the early 20th century C.E., a team of German archaeologists found the remains during a dig at a low, flat-topped mound called Tell Balata. They unearthed a two-entry gateway with a paved courtyard, measuring about 26 feet by 21 feet, between the two entryways. On either side of the courtyard they found guardrooms linked to the upper floors by stairways.

From here, atop the city gate, the leaders of Shechem would have watched the approach of Abimelech, son of Gideon. Abimelech claimed rule over Shechem, and when the city resisted him he marched there with an army. According to Judges, chapter 9,

"Abimelech and the companies with him rushed forward to a position at the entrance to the city gate. Then two companies rushed upon those in the fields and struck them down. All that day Abimelech pressed his attack against the city until he had captured it and killed its people. Then he destroyed the city and scattered salt over it." In all, the town was destroyed and rebuilt some 22 times over the centuries, and was at one point the first capital of the kingdom of Israel.

SOUTH FROM SHECHEM

Shechem, though, was not to be Abraham's final destination. He continued south, first to Bethel and then to Hebron, building altars to God as he did. He even moved his herds to the edge of the Negev desert, probably during winter when the normally arid grazing lands were sustained by life-giving rains. In so doing, Abraham would have traveled the length of Canaan—the coastal strip bordered by the Mediterranean Sea in the west and the Jordan River in the east, a narrow corridor of fertile valleys and dry highlands that stretched between Mesopotamia and Egypt.

Archaeological remains from ancient Canaan range from ceramics (below) to the ruins of great fortifications such as the East Gate of the city of Shechem (opposite). Shechem is thought to be the first place Abraham and his family stayed after entering the new land.

"AND HE SAID, 'HERE AM I, MY SON.'
HE SAID, 'BEHOLD, THE FIRE AND
THE WOOD; BUT WHERE IS THE
LAMB FOR A BURNT OFFERING?'"

GENESIS 22:7

THE BINDING OF ISAAC

In Genesis, chapter 22, God tells Abraham: "Take your son, your only son, Isaac, whom you love, and go to the region of Moriah. Sacrifice him there as a burnt offering on one of the mountains I will tell you about." The patriarch complies: "Early the next morning Abraham got up and saddled his donkey. He took with him two of his servants and his son Isaac. When he had cut enough wood for the burnt offering, he set out for the place God had told him about." And so begins the story known as the Binding of Isaac.

After three days of travel, father and son arrive at Moriah. Isaac asks where they will find a lamb for the burnt offering, but Abraham insists that God himself will provide the lamb. Then he builds a pyre, binds his son, and lays him on top of it. Only when Abraham raises his knife and prepares to sacrifice his son does an angel intervene. "'Do not lay a hand on the boy,' he said. 'Do not do anything to him. Now I know that you fear God, because you have not withheld from me your son, your only son.'" Then, in what Christians see as a foreshadowing of the sacrifice of Jesus, "the lamb of God," Abraham finds a ram caught in a thicket by its horns and sacrifices it instead of his son.

It is usually assumed that the Isaac who accompanied his father to Moriah was a young boy, which is reflected in many modern depictions of the incident (see, for example, Caravaggio's "The Sacrifice of Isaac" on pp. 20-21). Most traditional sources, however, maintain that Isaac was actually a fully grown man by now. According to the Jewish historian Josephus (ca 37-100 C.E.), Abraham's son was 25 years old at the time of the sacrifice on Mount Moriah. And the writers of the Hebrew Talmud claimed that he was 37 (old enough to resist his father's efforts had he wanted to do so).

WHERE WAS MORIAH?

The Book of Genesis does not provide any further details about the location of Mount Moriah, the Rock of Binding. Just where Moriah was continues to be a matter of speculation and debate. Some authorities believe it was at Shechem, where Abraham built an altar to the Lord shortly after entering the land of Canaan. But Chronicles, chapter 3, places it in the city of Jerusalem, and tradition holds that it is the city's Temple Mount, one of the most contested religious sites in the world. The mount is considered the holiest place in Judaism, where the Temple of Solomon and the later Temple of Herod once stood. Jewish texts regard Mount Moriah as the site of a future, third temple, which will be constructed at the time of the coming of the Jewish Messiah. Islam regards it as the place where the Prophet Muhammad began his ascent to heaven. In the seventh century C.E., Muslims built the Dome of the Rock on the same site, considered the third most holy shrine in Islam.

Like the Hebrews of old, followers of other ancient Middle Eastern faiths performed animal sacrifice. The sculpture at right depicts a Sumerian priest carrying a lamb to slaughter in honor of the gods. The Dome of the Rock (far right) is said to be where Abraham prepared to sacrifice his own son Isaac.

"See the daughter of the Great Lady, your wife, who committed against you a great sin: how long must I continue to guard this villainess? So now, take the daughter of the Great Lady, the villainess, and do with her as you think fit: if you want, kill her, or if you want, throw her in the sea; but do with the daughter of the Great Lady what you want."

The practice of divorce is often referred to in the cuneiform record. Ancient codes, such as the Code of Hammurabi, spell out the terms and conditions of separation. The Ugaritic tablets also make mention of the practice. The clay tablet at right, which dates to around 1250 B.C.E., is a royal decree confirming the divorce of King Ammistomru from Benteshina, the daughter of the king of Amurru.

"THEY SHALL NOT MARRY A HARLOT OR A WOMAN WHO HAS BEEN DEFILED; NEITHER SHALL THEY MARRY A WOMAN DIVORCED FROM HER HUSBAND; FOR THE PRIEST IS HOLY TO HIS GOD."

LEVITICUS 21:7

UGARIT: RAS SHAMRA

I n 1929, French archaeologist Claude Schaeffer began excavations at Ras Shamra, on Syria's Mediterranean coast, that would uncover the huge two-story palace complex of ancient Ugarit. Prior to this, the name of Ugarit was known from various sources but its location was not. It was referred to in correspondence from ancient Mari and in other texts, and known as an ancient cosmopolitan port city.

Like many ancient sites, Ugarit was rediscovered by happenstance. In this case, a local farmer accidentally split open an old tomb while he was plowing a field. In addition to tombs, excavations by Schaeffer uncovered royal residences, administrative quarters, and libraries. And atop the city's acropolis stood two temples, one named the Temple of Baal and the other the Temple of Dagan. Most precious of all, perhaps, he found the first of thousands of clay tablets that were inscribed in several different languages, such as Sumerian and Akkadian, and also in a new Ugaritic script. Dating as far back as the 14th century B.C.E., a time when the city was at its height, the tablets document much of the life of this flourishing city. They also provide a unique window into the cultural practices and religious beliefs of the new land that Abraham called home.

POLYGAMY

For all family patriarchs of the time, the preservation of their lineage was a central consideration. It was especially so for Abraham, whom God promised in the Book of Genesis to make the father of a great nation. So when his wife, Sarah, remained childless, Abraham had two possible options. First, he could have divorced Sarah and taken a new wife, a practice mentioned in the 18th-century B.C.E. Code of Hammurabi and other ancient texts. (According to the code of the great Babylonian lawgiver, the husband merely had to give back "the full amount of her marriage-price and . . . the dowry which she brought from her father's house.") Or second, he could take another wife.

The practice of polygamy is referred to throughout the books of the Old Testament. In Genesis, chapter 4, for example, a descendant of Cain named Lamech takes two

In this painting by Adriaen van der Werff (1659-1722), Sarah presents her slave Hagar to Abraham.

wives, Adah and Zillah. And this is what Abraham does. At Sarah's suggestion, he takes as his wife or concubine (the Hebrew 'ishsha can mean either) an Egyptian slave girl named Hagar, who becomes pregnant.

With the prospect of an heir, Abraham's lineage is now secure. The young slave girl begins to feel more confident. Indeed, according to Genesis 16:4, she "looked with contempt on her mistress," the older, childless Sarah. This sort of situation must have been a common occurrence among Mesopotamian clans. Indeed, Hammurabi made provision for it: "If a female slave has claimed equality with her mistress because she bore children, her mistress may not sell her." However, he goes on, she may put the young woman in her place by marking her "with the slave-mark." In similar manner, while Sarah realizes that she cannot get rid of Hagar, she proceeds to treat her harshly, and Hagar decides to run away. According to Genesis, however, God sends an angel to the young woman who tells her to return. And in due course, Hagar gives birth to a son, Ishmael.

The son of Abraham and Hagar grows up to be a healthy, rugged boy. When Ishmael is 13, the story takes another twist when God promises Abraham a second son, this time from Sarah. Now a hundred years old, Abraham is incredulous. Sarah bursts out laughing when she hears what God has promised. But Sarah does indeed give birth to a boy, and Abraham names him Isaac.

This development echoes the Epic of Aqhat, a tale recorded on one of the tablets found at Ugarit. In it, an elderly and heirless king named Danel prays for his wife to conceive and bear him a son. Baal, the god of storms and fertility, takes up Danel's case, pleading it before El, the supreme god of Canaan. "Let him kiss his wife," El commands, "and she will conceive; in her embracing she will become pregnant." Danel obeys, and his wife gives birth to a son, who is named Aqhat.

ISHMAEL OR ISAAC?

Returning to the account of Abraham, the great Patriarch now has a dilemma. With two sons, the older by an Egyptian slave, the younger by his Hebrew wife, an inevitable question arose: Who would succeed Abraham as leader of the clan? Both women argue that her son is the rightful heir. Again, the Code of Hammurabi weighs in on such a situation.

If, for example, the father "during his lifetime ever said 'My children!' to the issue whom the slave bore him," then this would indicate that the slave's children were to be viewed on par with his other children and would share equally in the inheritance. However, the Babylonian code also declared that the firstborn of the first wife could expect preferential treatment.

Preferential treatment is just what Isaac gets. And Ishmael and his mother are sent away. In Genesis, however, God promises to make Ishmael, too, a great nation, and he in turn becomes the father of many Arab peoples. But God establishes his own covenant with Isaac, and the Old Testament narrative continues to unfold through Sarah's son.

THE CANAANITE PANTHEON

The God of Abraham and Isaac was not the only god in the land of Canaan, of course. As indicated in the Epic of Aqhat and in other Ugaritic tablets, Canaan boasted a whole pantheon of deities. Many of them remain shrouded in mystery, little more than names down through the ages. But we know more about others. The god El mentioned in the epic, for example, was the father of creation—"creator of the created things"—to whom all the other deities were subservient.

Ishtar was another prominent deity, the Babylonian mother goddess. Known as Inanna in Sumer, she was the goddess of sexual love and may also have been the patron goddess of prostitutes. Canaanite worship of such deities involved visits to holy shrines, as well as chants and offerings of animals and crops. In particularly dire circumstances, the Canaanites would sacrifice their firstborn children in an attempt to appease the gods. Seen in this context, the Binding of Isaac may be interpreted as the Hebrew God's rejection of the ancient and barbaric practice of human sacrifice.

The most influential god of the Canaanite pantheon was Baal. A fertility god alternatively referred to as "Lord of the Earth" or "Lord of Rain and Dew," Baal was revered in a semiarid land like Canaan, where life itself depended on sufficient rainfall. He was said to dwell on Mount Zaphon, the tallest mountain in Syria.

The worship of Baal would prove a continual source of temptation for the Hebrews after their arrival in Canaan. Numerous later books of the Bible—Numbers, Deuteronomy, Judges, Samuel, Kings, Chronicles, and the Psalms—warn of the dangers of the cult of Baal and its practice among the descendants of Abraham. They also tell of the Hebrew prophets who spoke out against it. Most famously, I Kings recounts how the prophet Elijah confronts King Ahab and Queen Jezebel for their promotion of Baal worship. The conflict is resolved in chapter 18 when Elijah challenges 450 of the god's prophets to call on Baal to light a sacrifice by fire on Mount Carmel. When they fail to do so, Elijah soaks his sacrifice with water (the very element Baal was said to control) and turns to God in prayer as fire falls from the sky and burns the sacrifice. Retribution on the false prophets comes swiftly. I Kings records, "When all the people saw it, they fell on their faces, and they said, 'The Lord, he is God; the Lord, he is God.' Then Elijah commanded them, 'Seize the prophets of Baal. Don't let anyone get away!' They seized them, and Elijah had them brought down to the Kishon Valley and slaughtered there."

"ABRAHAM TOOK ANOTHER WIFE, WHOSE
NAME WAS KETURAH. SHE BORE HIM
ZIMRAN, JOKSHAN, MEDAN, MIDIAN,
ISHBAK, AND SHUAH."

GENESIS 25:1-2

THE COPPER MINES OF TIMNA

Copper has been mined in the rugged Timna Valley of the southern Negev since the sixth millennium B.C.E. During the 1930s, popular interest in the site rose with the claim that this was the location of King Solomon's Mines (the formidable, mineral-rich rock formations at left are known as Solomon's Pillars). Excavations at Timna have found mine workings and mining tools from various historical periods. Mining at this site, just miles from the Gulf of Aqaba on the Red Sea, reached a peak between the 14th and the 12th centuries B.C.E., first during operation by the ancient Egyptians and then by the Midianites.

The Midianites were famous for their work in copper. Indeed, in the Book of Numbers they are referred to as Kenites, which is related to the word *qain,* or coppersmith in Arabic. A nomadic Arab people from the south and east of Canaan, the Midianites were descendants of Abraham, not through Isaac or through Ishmael, but through another of his sons. For toward the end of his life, the patriarch took another wife, Keturah, who bore him more children, one of whom was Midian. Isaac, though, was his designated heir. And before he died, Abraham secured Isaac's position by giving his other sons gifts and then sending them away to the East, beyond the Jordan River.

Later in Genesis, one of Isaac's grandchildren, Joseph, would fall into the hands of Midianite traders, who bought Joseph from his brothers and carried him off to a life of servitude in Egypt. A young Moses would later spend time in the land of the Midianites, a place of refuge for him after he had killed an Egyptian taskmaster he had caught beating a Hebrew worker. While there, the fugitive Moses was at a well one day when the daughters of Jethro, the high priest of Midian, arrived to water their sheep. When other shepherds tried to drive the women off, Moses intervened and helped the sisters tend to their animals. A grateful Jethro offered him the hand of his daughter Zipporah, who became his wife and the mother of his son Gershom. Moses lived as a shepherd in Midian for some 40 years, taking care of Jethro's herds. He and the Children of Israel would be back this way again, during the Exodus from Egypt, as Moses led them through a desert land with which he would have been more than familiar.

THE ARCHAEOLOGICAL RECORD

Since the early 19th century, archaeologists have found smelting sites and other evidence of mining from many eras of activity at Timna. Excavations carried out between 1959 and 1990 unearthed evidence of the Midianites at Timna, such as metal jewelry and beautifully decorated ceramics. A copper snake with gilded head that was discovered here recalls the copper serpent mentioned in the 21st chapter of the Book of Numbers, during the Children of Israel's trek through the desert toward the land of Canaan: "And the people came to Moses, and said, 'We have sinned, for we have spoken against the Lord and against you; pray to the Lord, that he take away the serpents from us.' So Moses prayed for the people. And the Lord said to Moses, 'Make a fiery serpent, and set it on a pole; and every one who is bitten, when he sees it, shall live.' So Moses made a bronze serpent, and set it on a pole; and if a serpent bit any man, he would look at the bronze serpent and live."

The beautifully decorated pottery below was brought to Timna by Midianites around the 12th century B.C.E. Probably used as votive gifts, they are evidence of a sophisticated Midianite culture.

chapter 2

EGYPT

Pharaoh's Land

EGYPT

Proud, powerful, and enduring, Egypt loomed large in the eyes of the ancient Israelites and figured prominently in their history, legends, and scripture. According to the Bible, Abraham himself went down to Egypt and nearly lost his wife, Sarah, to its grasping ruler, who took her into his harem before "the Lord afflicted Pharaoh and his house with great plagues" and freed Abraham and Sarah to return to Canaan and settle in the promised land (Genesis 12:17). That journey prefigured the migration of Joseph and his brothers to Egypt and the Exodus of their descendants under Moses.

Archaeologists have long sought evidence confirming those stirring biblical accounts. Egyptian inscriptions and depictions indicate that Asiatics from Canaan and surrounding lands in western Asia entered Egypt as traders, captives, or migrants during the second millennium B.C.E., but no proof has surfaced that Hebrews lived there at that time. Some scholars doubt that an entire group of people with distinct customs and beliefs could have entered Egypt, descended into slavery, and escaped en masse without leaving any record of their presence or departure in Egyptian annals. Many consider it likely, however, that some ancestors of those who later founded the kingdom of Israel were among the Asiatics who entered Egypt. They may not have been the huge host described in the Bible, where the followers of Moses are numbered at "about six hundred thousand men on foot, besides women and children" (Exodus 12:37). But the events related in Genesis and Exodus may well be rooted in the historical travails of one or more bands of Hebrews or proto-Israelites who went down to Egypt and had their faith tested and renewed.

> "I AM GOD, THE GOD OF
> YOUR FATHER; DO NOT BE AFRAID
> TO GO DOWN TO EGYPT;
> FOR I WILL THERE MAKE OF
> YOU A GREAT NATION."
>
> GENESIS 46:3

Egyptian history offers clues as to when that might have occurred. Pharaohs of the Old Kingdom, which arose along the Nile around 3000 B.C.E., relied on Egyptians rather than foreigners to administer their realm and build the mighty pyramids that housed their remains. They would not have allowed an outsider like the biblical patriarch Joseph to gain prominence within their state. Nor would Joseph and his brothers have been welcomed by rulers of the Middle Kingdom, which emerged around 2050 B.C.E. following a chaotic interval known as the First Intermediate Period. Pharaohs of the Middle Kingdom restored Egyptian might and sent troops southward into Nubia. But they could not prevent foreigners from entering their country as traders or raiders and lost control of the Nile Delta around 1720 B.C.E. to Asiatics called the Hyksos, whose incursion marked the onset of the Second Intermediate Period. The Hyksos made their capital at Avaris while Thebes to the south remained the seat of a rival Egyptian dynasty. The Bible states that Joseph and his brothers settled in Goshen—the northeastern portion of the Nile Delta—near Avaris, where a Hyksos king might have looked favorably on a gifted foreigner like Joseph and elevated him to a high position.

Rulers from Thebes ousted the Hyksos around 1550 B.C.E. and ushered in the New Kingdom, during which Egypt reached the height of its glory and dominated Canaan. Foreigners entered Egypt as slaves or laborers during this epoch and worked in the fields or helped build royal monuments. New Kingdom inscriptions refer to an influx of nomads, referred to variously as Habiru or Shasu, some of whom may have been Hebrews from Canaan. If so, the biblical account of the sojourn in Egypt was

Previous pages: "Moses Set Adrift on the Waters" by Nicolas Poussin
Opposite: Ramses II ruled Egypt in the 13th century B.C.E., around the time of the Exodus of the Israelites.

inspired not by a single migration during the time of the Hyksos but by the ventures of various nomadic bands over the centuries, some of whom ended up in bondage in Egypt. The tradition that Israelites suffered sorely at the hands of Egypt's rulers, who "set taskmasters over them to afflict them with heavy burdens," is consistent with Egyptian records indicating that Asiatics performed hard labor as slaves or conscripts for pharaohs of the New Kingdom (Exodus 1:11). If, in fact, Israelites built the royal cities referred to in the Bible as Pithom and Ramses, then their flight from Egypt may have occurred during the reign of Ramses II (1279-1213 B.C.E.), who completed construction of a new capital in the Nile Delta, Pi-Ramses, and commissioned another city called Per-Atum, or Pithom, nearby.

OUT OF EGYPT

During the New Kingdom as in earlier times, pharaohs claimed kinship with the gods and took credit for maintaining order and prosperity, achieved through such heavenly blessings as the annual Nile flood that nourished the soil and brought bountiful harvests. Calamities such as drought, famine, epidemics, or infestations like those described in Exodus when Pharaoh refuses to free the Israelites were seen as divine curses and could cause people to lose faith in their ruler if he failed to remove the curse by appeasing the gods. Such was Pharaoh's aim when he told Moses: "Rise up, go forth from among my people, both you and the people of Israel; and go, serve the Lord, as you have said. Take your flocks and your herds, as you have said, and be gone; and bless me also!" (Exodus 12:31-32). When he later went back on his word and sent his army in pursuit of the Israelites, the Bible attests, he again incurred divine wrath and saw his prized troops and chariots swamped when God parted the sea to allow Moses and his followers to pass before flooding the pursuing Egyptians.

Whether viewed as history or legend, the Exodus heralds the emergence of the Israelites as an independent people, no longer subservient to their overbearing Egyptian neighbors. The first reference to Israel in Egyptian records comes from around 1200 B.C.E., when a scribe for Pharaoh Merneptah claimed in writing on a commemorative stela that "Israel is laid waste;

A new day dawns at Mount Sinai (foreground), a 7,500-foot-high mountain near the southern tip of the Sinai Peninsula long identified with the sacred place referred to variously in the Bible as Sinai, Horeb, or the "mountain of God."

his seed is not." This was typical of the boasts pharaohs made after military campaigns—whether those campaigns were successful or not—and indicates that Israelites were established in Canaan by that time and were becoming a matter of some concern to Egypt, which was gradually losing strength.

Spiritually, the biblical accounts of the sojourn in Egypt and the ensuing Exodus reflect the exposure of Hebrews to beliefs and practices that gave them an identity distinct from that of other people in Canaan. According to Genesis, they were not the only descendants of Abraham, who fostered various tribes, including the Midianites, among whom Moses found refuge in the Sinai after killing an Egyptian taskmaster and fleeing the country. Jethro, the priest of Midian, welcomed Moses and became his father-in-law. And it was while tending Jethro's flocks on the mountain called Horeb, or Sinai, that Moses confronted YHWH (the "I AM WHO I AM" of Exodus 3:14, often rendered as the LORD in most English translations) in the burning bush, and became the instrument of his divine will. Scholars have speculated that the worship of YHWH originated among Midianites dwelling around Mount Sinai and that the close ties of Moses to that group made him the conduit by which YHWH became the Lord and savior of the Israelites. It was only by following Moses into the desert and accepting the laws handed down to him at Mount Sinai that Israelites truly became the Chosen People and entered into a unique relationship with God.

Despite their solemn covenant with YHWH, Israelites repeatedly violated his commandments and worshipped graven images like the golden calf. The readiness of the wandering Israelites to bow down to that image while their leader Moses was absent suggests that idolatry was part of their heritage and that their ancestral rituals were not that different from those of rival Canaanites they later denounced as pagans and idol-worshippers. Indeed, some biblical archaeologists have concluded that the Israelites were Canaanites. If so, they distinguished themselves culturally from others there by tracing their roots to the great civilizations of Mesopotamia and Egypt and embracing an exclusive and almighty God whose laws set them apart. Whatever their origins and odysseys, they strengthened their faith and their collective identity by confronting outsiders with powerful traditions like the Egyptians and wrestling with the challenges they posed.

UNCOVERING EGYPT'S PAST

Ancient Egypt left much archaeological evidence in plain view for posterity, thanks to its monumental architecture and dry climate, which helped preserve the remains of temples and tombs. But the significance of that evidence remained largely a matter of speculation until the discovery of the Rosetta Stone in 1799 (see p. 253). Inscribed with the same text in Greek, hieroglyphic, and demotic (a later Egyptian script derived from hieroglyphs), the Rosetta Stone led to the decipherment of hieroglyphs and greatly advanced the scientific study of Egypt's past. By the mid-19th century, museums and collectors were competing ruthlessly for Egyptian antiquities, prompting desecration and destruction as tombs were blasted open and their contents pillaged.

Gradually, order was imposed on the search for ancient treasures through the efforts of Egyptian authorities and foreign organizations such as Great Britain's Egypt Exploration Fund, which supported the work of systematic archaeologists like Flinders Petrie, who in 1896 found the Merneptah Stela containing the first written reference to Israel. In addition to making such groundbreaking discoveries, Petrie introduced scrupulous techniques for excavating sites and preserving and recording all the evidence found there, including such debris as pottery sherds that earlier fortune hunters had ignored but that placed more significant finds made in the same stratum, or soil layer, in their proper historical context. Not all major discoveries in Egypt were made by professional archaeologists like Petrie and Howard Carter, who in 1922 unearthed the mummified remains of Tutankhamun amid what he described as a "strange and wondrous medley of extraordinary and beautiful objects." Other artifacts were found by peasants rummaging among mounds of the accumulated debris of ancient settlements.

Much evidence of ancient Egyptian civilization remains hidden, for only massive stone buildings like the Great Pyramid at Giza withstood collapse. As related in Exodus, where the captive Israelites are described as toiling in "mortar and brick," most Egyptian buildings were made of mud bricks that eventually crumbled, leaving only the foundations, along with such durable items as jewelry, pottery, idols, and inscriptions on stone. As work proceeds at sites such as Avaris, the Hyksos capital in the Nile Delta, important evidence may yet emerge about the foreigners who entered ancient Egypt from Canaan.

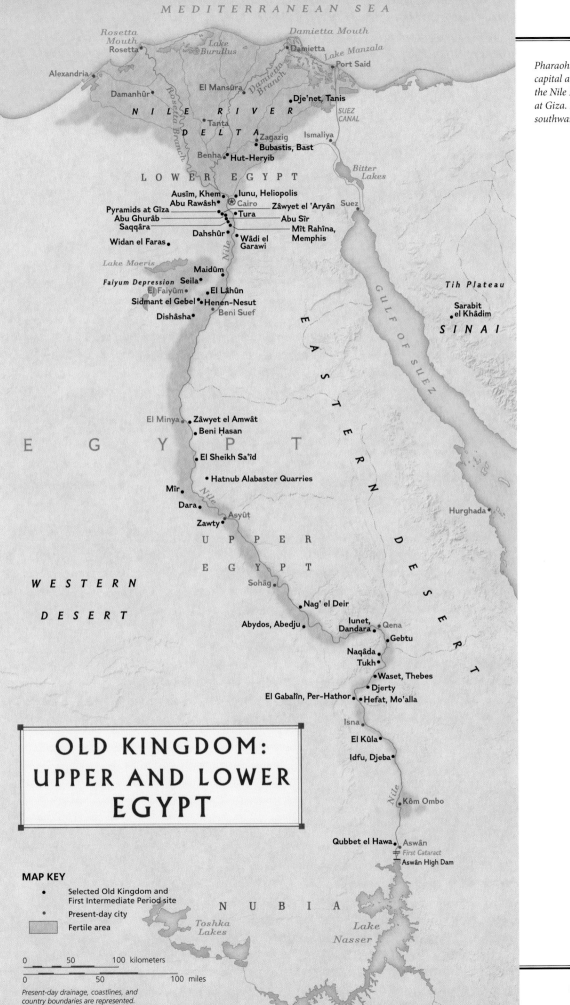

MEDITERRANEAN SEA

Rosetta Mouth
Rosetta •
Damietta Mouth
Alexandria •
Damietta •
Port Said •

Lake Burullus
Lake Manzala

El Mansûra •

Damanhûr •

Dje'net, Tanis •

NILE RIVER
Damietta Branch
SUEZ CANAL

Tanta •

Rosetta Branch

DELTA

Zagazig •
Bubastis, Bast •
Ismaliya •

Benha •
Hut-Heryib •

Bitter Lakes

LOWER EGYPT

Ausîm, Khem •
Abu Rawâsh •
Iunu, Heliopolis •
⊗ Cairo
Suez •

Pyramids at Gîza —
Zâwyet el 'Aryân •

Abu Ghurâb —
• Tura
Abu Sîr •

Saqqâra —
Dahshûr •
Mît Rahîna, Memphis •

Widan el Faras •
Wâdi el Garawi •

Lake Moeris

Maidûm •

Faiyum Depression Seila •
TIH PLATEAU

El Faiyûm •
El Lâhûn •

Sidmant el Gebel •
Henen-Nesut •
Sarabit el Khâdim •

Dishâsha •
Beni Suef
SINAI

GULF OF SUEZ

E G Y P T

El Minya •
Zâwyet el Amwât •

Beni Ḥasan •

E A S T E R N
D E S E R T

El Sheikh Sa'îd •

Hatnub Alabaster Quarries •

Mîr •

Dara •
Hurghada •

Zawty •
Asyûṭ •

U P P E R

W E S T E R N
E G Y P T

Sohâg •

D E S E R T

Nag' el Deir •

Abydos, Abedju •
Iunet, Dandara •
Qena •
Gebtu •

Naqâda •
Tukh •

Waset, Thebes •
Djerty •

El Gabalîn, Per-Hathor •
Hefat, Mo'alla •

Isna •

El Kûla •

Idfu, Djeba •

Nile

Kôm Ombo •

Qubbet el Hawa •
Aswân •
First Cataract
Aswân High Dam

N U B I A

Toshka Lakes

Lake Nasser

MAP KEY

• Selected Old Kingdom and First Intermediate Period site

• Present-day city

▢ Fertile area

0   50   100 kilometers
0   50   100 miles

Present-day drainage, coastlines, and country boundaries are represented.

OLD KINGDOM: UPPER AND LOWER EGYPT

THE LEGACY OF THE HYKSOS

The mysterious Asiatic intruders who swept into the Nile Delta in the 17th century B.C.E. and dominated Egypt for nearly a hundred years were described by their foes as Hyksos, or "rulers of foreign lands," and denounced as bloodthirsty barbarians. "Unexpectedly, from the regions of the East, invaders of obscure race marched in confidence of victory against our land," wrote the Egyptian historian Manetho many centuries later. "By main force they easily overpowered the rulers of the land, they then burned our cities ruthlessly, razed to the ground the temples of the gods, and treated all the natives with a cruel hostility, massacring some and leading into slavery the wives and children of others." In recent times, however, archaeologists have uncovered evidence suggesting that those dreaded Hyksos did much to enhance and advance Egyptian civilization. They were indeed avid warriors who introduced to Egypt horses and chariots and stronger bows. But by mastering those weapons and defeating the Hyksos, Egyptians regained control of their country and reached new heights of glory. In addition to new military technology, the Hyksos bequeathed new forms of artistry to their adopted land.

Archaeological excavations launched in the 1960s by Manfred Bietak of Austria at Tell el Daba, near the eastern margins of the Nile Delta, have revealed what may well be the fabled Hyksos city of Avaris. According to Manetho, Avaris was founded by the first Hyksos ruler in Egypt, King Salitis, who girded the city "with massive walls, planting there a garrison of as many as 240,000 heavy-armed men to guard his frontier.

Here he would come in summertime, partly to serve out rations and pay his troops, partly to train them carefully in maneuvers and so strike terror into foreign tribes." Later Hyksos kings made Avaris their permanent seat and capital. The ruins excavated by Bietak's team at Tell el Daba include a wall more than 25 feet thick, fitting Manetho's description of a great fortress city, and a tomb chamber containing the remains of a high-ranking warrior buried with his weapons, his horse, and a young female servant who may have been sacrificed to honor the man. This form of burial was alien to Egypt, and other evidence found at the site confirms that the inhabitants were of foreign origin, including not only Asiatics but also immigrants from the northern Mediterranean. Fragments of wall paintings discovered here amid the ruins of a palace closely resemble the work of Minoan artists on the island of Crete. Additional Minoan motifs later adorned the tombs of Theban rulers who reunified the country and founded the New Kingdom, reflecting foreign artistic influences that entered the country with the Hyksos.

INVADERS OR IMMIGRANTS?

Whether the Hyksos were in fact invaders, as Manetho declared, or immigrants who infiltrated the Nile Delta and gradually took control there remains unclear. During the Middle Kingdom (ca 2060-1670 B.C.E.), many Asiatics entered Egypt as traders, slaves, or menial laborers. Lower Egypt, or the Nile Delta region, was most affected by the influx of foreigners because it bordered Asia. Controlling that foreign population would have been increasingly difficult for Egyptian rulers as the flow of immigrants increased and they amassed weapons superior to those of their masters. After taking over Lower

These scarabs, excavated in Canaan, were produced by Hyksos artisans who adopted Egyptian designs and techniques after settling in the Nile Delta, where the remains of Hyksos cities have been found below the ruins of later Egyptian monuments like those at Tanis (opposite) and nearby Tell el Daba, the likely site of the Hyksos capital, Avaris.

EXODUS 1:1

Egypt, the Hyksos demonstrated a talent for diplomacy. Rather than warring with the princes of Thebes, who remained in control of Upper Egypt to the south, Hyksos kings exacted tribute from them and took Theban princesses as their wives.

Greatly impressed by Egyptian culture, Hyksos rulers assumed all the attributes of pharaohs, worshipping Egyptian gods and recording their own exploits in hieroglyphs on monuments. Artisans and musicians at Avaris and other Hyksos cities may have come from as far away as Crete or Asia Minor, bringing with them novel designs and instruments, including the lute and the tambourine. But they also adopted Egyptian themes and techniques, turning out scarabs like those shown on p. 69 in vast quantities. Shaped like dung beetles—symbols of regeneration because they seemingly sprang to life spontaneously from decaying matter—scarabs were inscribed with alluring designs and inscriptions and served as seals when pressed into clay or wax, and as amulets, protecting the wearer from harm. Scarabs were often buried with the dead to ensure that their souls would return to life. Shrewd and adaptable, Hyksos artisans placed their own stamps on these Egyptian charms and exported them far and wide.

DECLINE AND FALL

Life in Egypt under Hyksos rule was not as dreadful or calamitous as portrayed by Manetho, but paying tribute to foreign overlords in Lower Egypt was humiliating for the princes of Thebes, and they eventually rebelled. After some preliminary clashes, the war was launched in earnest around 1580 B.C.E. by Prince Kamose, who recorded his fateful decision to defy the Hyksos on a stela erected at Karnak, a ceremonial center devoted to Amun, the patron god of Thebes and its rulers. Conferring with his council of nobles, Kamose announced that he was no longer willing to bow to the Hyksos king at Avaris and meet his demands for tribute. "No man can settle down, when despoiled by the taxes of the Asiatics," he declared. "I will grapple with him, that I may rip open his belly! My wish is to save Egypt and to smite the Asiatics!" Alarmed by the prospect

A ceremonial battle ax, made of bronze overlaid with gold, commemorates the defeat of the Hyksos by Ahmose, the Theban ruler who ushered in the New Kingdom.

of war, councilors urged Kamose to refrain from hostilities as long as the Hyksos king left them in possession of their land and livestock: "Our cattle have not been seized, and have not been tasted. He has the land of the Asiatics, we have Egypt." But Kamose could not bear the thought of sharing with a foreigner a country that had once been united under Egyptian rule. "He who partitions the land with me will never respect me," he concluded. "I will sail north to engage the Asiatics and success will come!"

In his campaign against the Hyksos, Kamose relied mightily on mercenaries from Nubia called Medjay, who sailed with his fleet down the Nile and engaged the enemy at Nefrusis, south of the delta. The Medjay led that fight, but Kamose took personal credit for defeating the Hyksos commander, Teti, and his forces: "When day broke, I was on him as if it were a falcon. When the time of breakfast had come, I attacked him. I broke down his walls, I killed his people, and I made his wife come down to the riverbank. My soldiers were as lions are with their spoil, having serfs, cattle, milk, fat and honey, dividing up their property, their hearts gay." The practice of enslaving defeated people, denounced by Manetho as ruthless and cruel when committed against Egyptians by the Hyksos, was pervasive in the ancient world and a source of great pride to conquerors like Kamose. His victory, however, was far from complete. The Nile Delta remained firmly under Hyksos control, and most of the enemy's assets—including "chariots and horses, ships, timber, gold, lapis lazuli, silver, turquoise, bronze, axes without number, oil, incense, fat and honey"—remained beyond the grasp of Kamose when he died after ruling Thebes for only a few years.

The task of completing the conquest fell to his brother Ahmose, who was a small boy when Kamose died and remained for some time under the guardianship of the Queen Mother, Ahhose. Such regents played an important part in Egyptian history. One of them, Queen Hatshepsut, later delayed the young king under her care from coming to power and ruled as pharaoh in his place. Queen Ahhose made no such attempt to overshadow the heir to the throne, but she evidently played a commanding role until he came of age, for she was hailed in writing as one who cared greatly for Egypt and "looked after her soldiers."

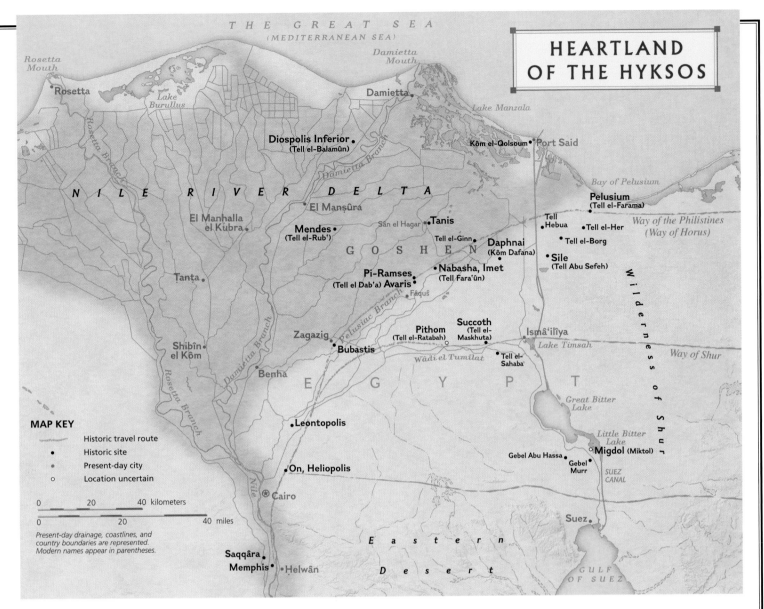

THE GREAT SEA
(MEDITERRANEAN SEA)

Rosetta Mouth
Rosetta
Lake Burullus
Damietta Mouth
Damietta
Lake Manzala

Diospolis Inferior
(Tell el-Balamûn)
Kôm el-Qolsoum • Port Said

NILE RIVER DELTA

Bay of Pelusium

El Manṣûra

Pelusium
(Tell el-Farama)

El Manhalla el Kubra
San el Hagar
Tanis
Mendes
(Tell el-Rub')
Tell el-Ginn
Daphnai
(Kôm Dafana)
Tell Hebua
Tell el-Her
Way of the Philistines
(Way of Horus)
Tell el-Borg

G O S H E N

Tanta

Sile
(Tell Abu Sefeh)

Pi-Ramses
(Tell el Dab'a) Avaris
Nabasha, Imet
(Tell Fara'ûn)
Fâqûs

W i l d e r n e s s   o f   S h u r

Shibîn el Kôm
Zagazig
Bubastis
Pithom
(Tell el-Ratabah)
Succoth
(Tell el-Maskhuta)
Ismâ'ilîya
Lake Timsah
Way of Shur

Benhâ

E G Y P T

Wâdi el Tumilat
Tell el-Sahaba

Great Bitter Lake

MAP KEY

— Historic travel route
• Historic site
• Present-day city
○ Location uncertain

Little Bitter Lake
Migdol (Miktol)
Gebel Abu Hassa
Gebel Murr
SUEZ CANAL

Leontopolis

0   20   40 kilometers
0   20   40 miles

On, Heliopolis

⊕ Cairo

Present-day drainage, coastlines, and country boundaries are represented. Modern names appear in parentheses.

Suez

E a s t e r n

Saqqâra
Memphis • Helwân

D e s e r t

GULF OF SUEZ

After reaching maturity and assuming power, Ahmose led those forces into the Nile Delta and laid siege to Avaris. "Then Avaris was despoiled," declared an Egyptian officer. Those unfortunate inhabitants were left to the mercy of the Egyptians when Hyksos forces abandoned Avaris and fled to Canaan, pursued by Ahmose, who claimed another victory over his foes before returning in triumph to Thebes to rule a reunited Egypt. A ceremonial bronze ax proclaiming his victory (opposite) may have been presented as a gift to Queen Ahhose.

In victory and defeat, the Hyksos helped set the stage for the emergence of the prosperous New Kingdom, inaugurated by Ahmose. Perhaps their greatest legacy was to eliminate any possibility that Egypt would remain isolated from the turmoil and creative ferment in Canaan and Mesopotamia, where the art of warfare and other technologies were fast advancing as innovative groups like the Hittites swept down from the north, introducing

horses and chariots and later iron. Pharaohs of the New Kingdom sought to avoid any repetition of the humiliating Hyksos incursion by subjugating Canaan and vying with the Hittites for control of Syria. In the process, they drew Egypt deeper into a vibrant cultural web that extended for nearly a thousand miles from the Nile to the Euphrates and Tigris Rivers. At the center of that web lay what would later be called the Holy Land, where Judaism emerged and inspired Christianity and Islam. Some scholars believe that the biblical sojourn of the Israelites in Egypt, as described in Genesis and Exodus, has its roots in a Hebrew migration that occurred during the Hyksos era. Others emphasize later contacts between the Israelites and their Egyptian neighbors. In any case, the Hyksos incursion linked Egypt inextricably to Canaan and helped make that emerging Holy Land a spiritual hub where religious currents from Egypt, Arabia, and Asia Minor intermingled and spawned new faiths.

Shown here are archaeological sites in the Nile River Delta associated with the Hyksos—who came in from the east and established their capital at Avaris—and with later Egyptian kings such as Ramses II, who completed the city of Pi-Ramses near Avaris.

Thutmose III, portrayed here wearing the false beard that linked pharaohs with Osiris, lord of the underworld, expanded the Egyptian empire in the 15th century B.C.E. with his far-reaching campaigns.

LORDS OF THE
NEW KINGDOM

The concept of divine kingship had ancient roots in Egypt, but it reached full bloom artistically during the New King- dom when pharaohs were idolized in magnificent sculp- tures like that of Thutmose III (opposite). After his death in 1425 B.C.E., that conqueror was likened in a funerary text inscribed on the wall of his tomb chamber to the sun god, Re, who dies in the west at night and descends into the underworld, only to be resur- rected in the east at dawn in a blaze of glory. Hailed as descen- dants of the gods, Egyptian kings were considered immortal and associated not only with the eternal brilliance of the sun but also with the dark mysteries of death as personified by Osiris, lord of the underworld, whose crook and flail (see p. 74) and long beard were awe-inspiring symbols of royal authority in a land where the ordeals of this life were regarded as a mere prelude to the trial the soul faced after death. Only if the soul passed that trial and was judged worthy by Osiris could it cross safely into the world beyond. "I shall sail rightly in my bark," read one funerary text. "I am lord of eternity in the crossing of the sky."

No Egyptian was more certain of achieving such everlasting glory than the king. When Moses asked Pharaoh to set Israelites free, as described in Exodus, he did so as a servant of the almighty confronting a man who was almighty, or claimed to be. "Who is the Lord, that I should heed his voice and let Israel go?" Pharaoh replied haughtily, with the emphasis on "I." As lord and master of Egypt when its power was at its zenith, he would not be humbled by anything less than a miracle of biblical proportions.

Seti I, who ruled Egypt in the early 13th century B.C.E., began construction of the royal city Pi-Ramses, completed by his successor, Ramses II. Some believe that Seti was the biblical pharaoh who set taskmasters over the Israelites and forced them to build the cities referred to in Exodus as Pithom and Ramses before he died, while Moses was taking refuge in the land of Midian.

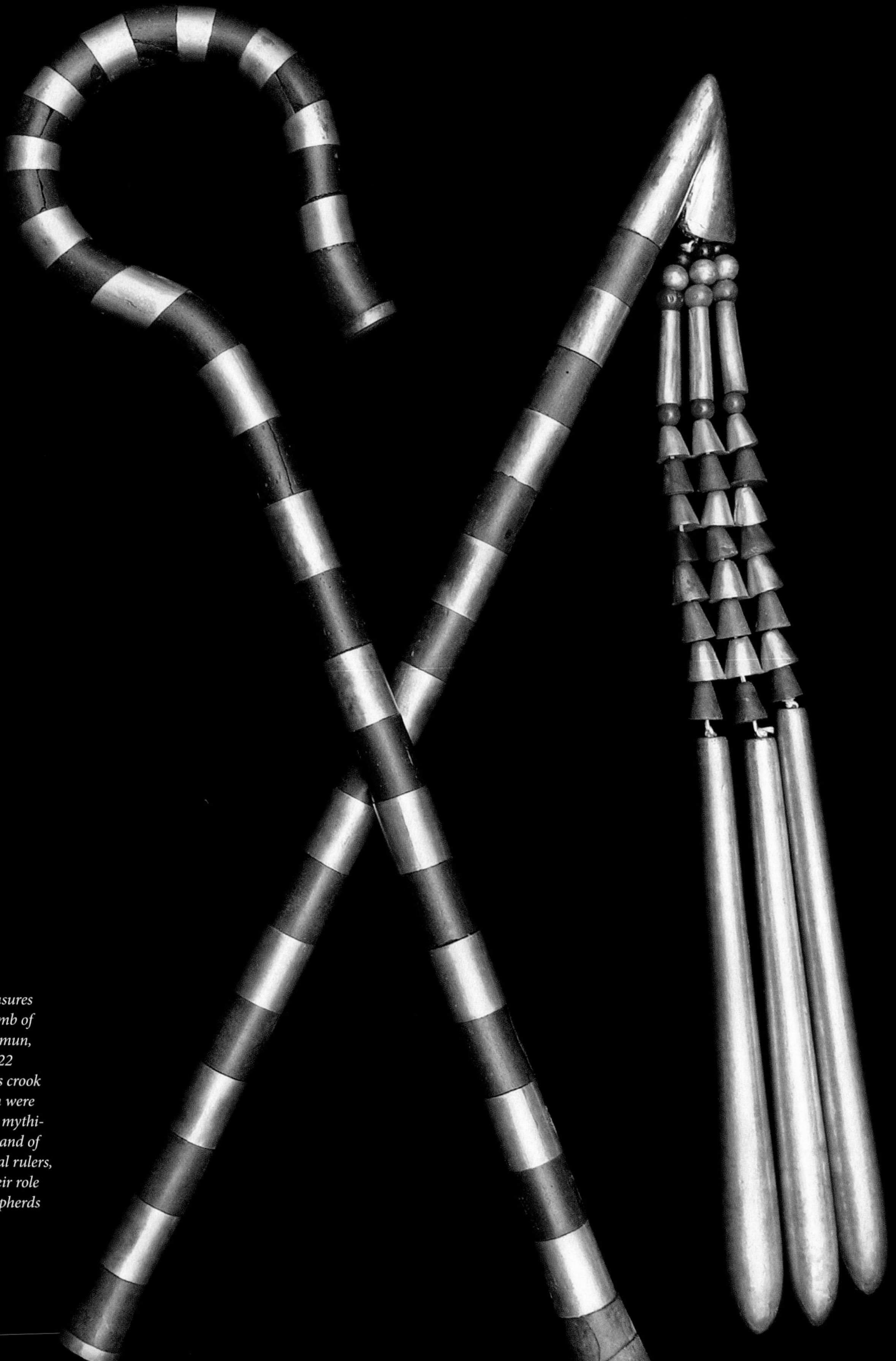

Among the treasures found in the tomb of King Tutankhamun, who died in 1322 B.C.E., were this crook and flail, which were emblems of the mythical King Osiris and of Egypt's historical rulers, symbolizing their role as watchful shepherds of the people.

Also found in Tutankhamun's tomb were the dagger and sheath below and necklace at bottom, representing the soaring falcon god, Horus, another deity closely associated with Egyptian kings.

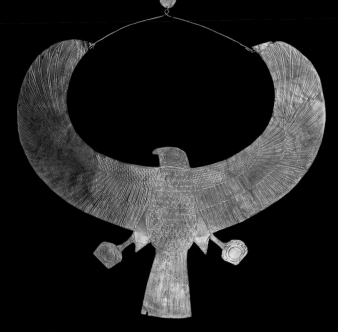

King Akhenaten, who took power in 1353 B.C.E., rejected other Egyptian cults and devoted himself exclusively to Aten, a solar deity within whom earlier gods of kingship such as Re and Horus were subsumed.

"THE HABIRU SACK THE TERRITORIES OF THE KING . . . ,
IF THERE ARE NO ARCHERS, THE TERRITORIES OF
THE KING, MY LORD, WILL BE LOST!"

KING ABDU-HEBA OF JERUSALEM

ROYAL CORRESPONDENCE

Much of what we know about Egypt, when it dominated Canaan and other foreign lands, comes from tablets discovered at Tell el Amarna, site of a royal city founded by King Akhenaten around 1350 B.C.E. Rejecting the cult of Amun, worshipped by his predecessors at Thebes, Akhenaten established his capital here to honor the god Aten, who was worshipped by the king to the exclusion of all other Egyptian deities. The city crumbled when Akhenaten's rebelled and returned to Thebes and their traditional forms of worship. From the rubble emerged the Amarna tablets, nearly 400 of which have been recovered. Written in Akkadian, the international language of the Near East at that time, they contain messages to Egypt's king from the lords of foreign lands and shed light on the political situation in Canaan before Israelites became firmly established there.

The Amarna letter shown here was sent to Akhenaten by King Abdu-Heba (perhaps the Adoni-zedek mentioned in Joshua 10:1-5) of Jerusalem, one of several rival city-states in Canaan whose rulers recognized Egypt's king as their overlord. King Abdu-Heba described himself as falling "at the feet of the king, my Lord, seven times and seven times." Denying charges that he was disloyal to Egypt, he blamed rivals in Canaan for making false accusations. It was they, he claimed, who were stirring up roving bands of troublemakers called Habiru and turning them against faithful servants like him. He implored Akhenaten to send him archers so that he could restore order: "The Habiru sack the territories of the king. If there are archers [here] this year, all the territories of the king will remain [intact]; but if there are no archers, the territories of the king, my Lord, will be lost!" Scholars once thought "Habiru" might be synonymous with "Hebrew," but the inscriptions make clear that the term has a broader meaning, referring to vagrants of various origins who haunted Canaan, Egypt, and other lands.

The rising sun at Tell el Amarna reveals the foundations of a temple built by King Akhenaten to honor the solar deity Aten.

Hieroglyphic inscriptions lend deeper meaning to Egyptian murals like this one in the tomb of Pharaoh Horemhab (1350-1315 B.C.E.).

Sacred Writing

The Greeks referred to Egyptian writings as hieroglyphs, or "sacred inscriptions," because they often adorned temples and tombs. In fact, hieroglyphs were used to inscribe accounts of battles, medical prescriptions, and love letters. But the beauty of hieroglyphs lent them a spiritual charm much like that of the illuminated manuscripts produced by medieval monks to glorify the word of God. Egyptian scribes had to practice for years to master their complex writing system, which contained nearly 700 characters. Most were pictographs, representing objects or concepts, but some were phonetic characters resembling pictographs but representing sounds. Egyptian scribes also evolved a cursive script that allowed them to write more quickly than when inscribing traditional, angular hieroglyphs like those above, showing the king as the falcon god, Horus, wearing the crown of Upper and Lower Egypt. These formal hieroglyphs remained in use on monuments and in religious texts inscribed on papyrus. Among the most inspiring of those writings was the Great Hymn to the Aten, carved on the tomb of King Ay, who commissioned the monument before he succeeded Akhenaten and rejected his monotheistic cult devoted to Aten. The hymn, containing language echoed in Psalm 104, may have been written by Akhenaten and reflects his devotion to his shining Lord in heaven: "Your dawning is beautiful in the horizon of the sky, / O living Aten, Beginning of life! / When You rise in the Eastern horizon, / You fill every land with Your beauty."

TRADERS AND IMMIGRANTS

> "LOOKING UP THEY SAW A CARAVAN OF ISHMAELITES,
> COMING FROM GILEAD, WITH THEIR CAMELS BEARING
> GUM, BALM, AND MYRRH, ON THEIR WAY
> TO CARRY IT DOWN TO EGYPT."
>
> GENESIS 37:25

Ancient Egyptian artists left archaeologists vivid pictorial evidence placing in historical context biblical accounts that Semitic people such as Ishmaelites, or Arabs, entered Egypt in trade caravans. In Genesis, for example, Joseph is betrayed by his brothers and carried as a slave to Egypt by Ishmaelites, leading a caravan of camels. Camels were not domesticated in the Near East until around 1000 B.C.E., long after the events described in Genesis are thought to have taken place but before those stories were set down in writing by chroniclers who filled out the narrative with details from their own era. As revealed by the Egyptian tomb painting shown below—from the crypt of an Egyptian provincial governor of the Middle Kingdom named Khnumhotep, buried at Beni Hasan in the 19th century B.C.E.—camels were preceded as beasts of burden in Near Eastern trade caravans by donkeys, or asses. Accompanied by women and children, the traders in this painting are distinguished as Semitic, or Asiatic, by their full beards, light complexion, and colorful garb, in contrast to the plain white tunics of the two darker-skinned, clean-shaven Egyptians at the front of the procession. One prominent 20th-century biblical archaeologist, William F. Albright, concluded

This scene from the tomb of Khnumhotep shows Asiatic traders with exotic goods and animals being escorted into his presence.

that the clothing of these traders was probably similar to that worn by the biblical patriarchs. "We can scarcely go wrong if we picture Jacob and his family clad in much the same way," Albright wrote.

According to an inscription accompanying this scene, the Asiatics came to Egypt to trade in galena, or eye shadow, but they brought other valuable goods with them, including a bellows (shown in detail at upper right, opposite), used to smelt ore. Metalworking technology entered Egypt from western Asia, and Egyptian smelters found the bellows a great improvement over their earlier technique of blowing through pipes to raise the fire to a higher temperature. The arrival of such a caravan was an exciting and memorable occasion, recorded as one of the most significant events in the career of Khnumhotep.

EGYPT'S POROUS BORDERS

The trading expedition portrayed here came at a time when Egypt was increasingly exposed to foreigners and foreign influences. Pharaohs of the Old Kingdom had attempted to control foreign trade—and keep foreigners at bay—by sending expeditions abroad to bring back spices and other prized goods. It proved impossible to seal off Egypt's borders, however, and inroads by bands of

Asiatics like these traders during the Middle Kingdom were followed by the incursion of the Hyksos, who overran the Nile Delta. The Hyksos came from Asia and would have welcomed well-stocked Asiatic traders like the Ishmaelites described in the biblical account of Joseph. Some of those traders dealt in slaves, and some of those slaves could have earned their freedom and risen to high positions in the land of Goshen, along the eastern fringe of the Nile Delta, as Joseph does in Genesis. After he achieves prominence, his brothers visit him, bringing gifts similar to the goods Ishmaelites offered. "Take some of the choice fruits of the land in your bags," their father, Jacob, tells them, "and carry down to the man a present, a little balm and a little honey, gum, myrrh, pistachio nuts, and almonds" (Genesis 43:11). In return, Joseph sends them back to Canaan to fetch Jacob and prepare to settle in Goshen, equipping them not with camels but with "ten asses loaded with the good things of Egypt, and ten she-asses loaded with grain, bread, and provision for his father on the journey" (Genesis 45:23). Thus the old animosity between Joseph and his brothers is resolved partly through an exchange of goods reflecting the ongoing commerce between Egypt and lands to its east and north.

Egypt's greatest natural asset was its grain or bread, made possible by the annual flood of the Nile—fed by monsoon rains in central Africa—which brought the country ample harvests even when little or no rain fell in the Near East and people in Canaan suffered famine. Such was the case when Jacob first sent his sons to Egypt. "Behold, I have heard that there is grain in Egypt," he tells them; "go down and buy grain for us there, that we may live, and not die" (Genesis 42:2). As their story suggests, the bountiful land along the Nile was a powerful lure for people from Canaan and environs. Some arrived as traders in caravans, others as slaves offered in trade, and still others as refugees, who settled in Goshen and earned their daily bread laboring for Egyptians.

A trader carrying a lyre—an instrument introduced to Egypt from western Asia—accompanies a donkey with a bellows and a spear strapped to its back.

GENESIS 37:25 | GENESIS 42:2 | GENESIS 43:11 | GENESIS 45:23

In a relief from the tomb of Ankhmahor, a high-ranking Egyptian buried at Saqqara around 2300 B.C.E., an attendant holds a boy's arms as he undergoes circumcision while another youngster receives a soothing ointment to ease the procedure.

"THEN PHARAOH SENT AND CALLED JOSEPH, AND THEY BROUGHT HIM HASTILY OUT OF THE DUNGEON; AND WHEN HE HAD SHAVED HIMSELF AND CHANGED HIS CLOTHES, HE CAME IN BEFORE PHARAOH."

GENESIS 41:14

HYGIENE AND RITUAL

According to Scripture, Joseph was so "handsome and good-looking" that the wife of his Egyptian master Potiphar found him irresistible (Genesis 39:6). A handsome man by Egyptian standards was neat, clean, and well-shaven, and a trusted domestic servant of foreign origin like Joseph would have conformed to those standards by trimming his hair and shaving with a razor like the one shown below. His smooth good looks spelled trouble for him when he refused to "sin against God" by yielding to Potiphar's seductive wife. Enraged, she accused him of assaulting her, and he ended up in prison. Released from the dungeon two years later to interpret Pharaoh's dreams, he was bearded, bedraggled, and in no condition to appear before royalty. Not until Joseph "had shaved himself and changed his clothes" did he enter the king's presence.

The meticulous grooming habits of ancient Egyptians were partly a matter of hygiene. Trimming one's hair or shaving one's head—as Egyptian women did before putting on wigs—helped people avoid lice. But such customs also helped distinguish respectable Egyptians from those they considered barbarians, including slaves or menial laborers of Asiatic origin, who were portrayed with rough beards and long, tangled hair. Some men of distinction were shown in Egyptian art with neatly trimmed goatees, and pharaohs with a long, slender beard associated with Osiris, god of death and rebirth. But most Egyptian men remained clean-shaven—a habit that sometimes had ritual significance. Egyptian priests removed all their body hair, including their eyebrows. For them as for monks of various faiths going bald was a form of self-purification and self-mortification that made them humbler and more devout.

Another custom that may have been hygienic but also had great ritual importance was circumcision, practiced by Egyptians, Hebrews, and other people of the ancient Near East. As shown opposite, in a relief from the tomb of an Old Kingdom nobleman, Egyptian boys were circumcised in groups when they reached puberty.

Ointments were applied to make the procedure less painful, but like all rites of passage this was an ordeal that tested the youngster's fortitude. In the inscription, the assistant grasping the boy at far left is told: "Hold him firmly. He might swoon." Symbolically, the removal of the foreskin marked the boy's transition to manhood and may have served as an offering to the gods, who might then reward the youngster for his sacrifice by making him potent.

Unlike Egyptians, Hebrews circumcised males in infancy, as decreed by God when he appeared to Abraham after the birth of his son Ishmael: "This is my covenant, which you shall keep, between me and you and your descendants after you: Every male among you shall be circumcised. . . . He that is eight days old among you shall be circumcised. . . . So shall my covenant be in your flesh an everlasting covenant" (Genesis 17:10-13). This rite may have been inspired by the custom of sealing a contract with drops of one's own blood. The covenant between God and the descendants of Abraham was a solemn contract that had to be renewed each time parents were blessed with a son. This was not an offering like the rite of the Egyptians; it was an obligation owed to God in exchange for the gift of life he granted and would continue to grant to his people as long as they honored the covenant.

Who Was Ishmael?

The son of Abraham and Hagar—an Egyptian servant of Abraham's wife, Sarah, who gave Hagar to Abraham to provide him with an heir—Ishmael was later overshadowed by Isaac, born to Abraham and Sarah in their old age. Cast out of the household with his mother, Ishmael was nonetheless favored by God, who promised to make of him "a great nation" (Genesis 21:18). As the biblical forefather of Bedouins, or Arabs, he was hailed by Muslims as their patriarch and Abraham's rightful heir. The circumcision of Ishmael was cited as sanctifying that practice in Islamic culture.

GENESIS 17:10-13 | GENESIS 21:18 | GENESIS 39:6 | GENESIS 41:14

The blade of this bronze razor, crafted in Egypt around 1400 B.C.E., could be honed to a keen edge for shaving the face or trimming hair, a service performed by barbers who visited people at home or set up shops outdoors.

"SO IN THE MORNING HIS SPIRIT WAS TROUBLED; AND HE
SENT AND CALLED FOR ALL THE MAGICIANS IN EGYPT AND ALL
ITS WISE MEN; AND PHARAOH TOLD THEM HIS DREAM, BUT
THERE WAS NONE WHO COULD INTERPRET IT TO PHARAOH."

GENESIS 41:8

DREAM INTERPRETATION

The prophetic power that Egyptians and other people of the ancient Near East attributed to dreams is reflected in the biblical story of Joseph, who rose to prominence by interpreting a dream that none of Pharaoh's wise men could fathom. Joseph had special powers of interpretation in this case because the dream came from God and he alone was able to read God's will. But the technique Joseph used was much like that employed by Egyptian soothsayers who composed guides to dream

Joseph interprets the dream of Pharaoh, seated on his throne, in this work by the 19th-century French artist Jean Adrien Guignet.

interpretation such as the text shown here, to help people distinguish good omens from bad in their dreams and recognize what they foretold. As Joseph declared, when Pharaoh dreamed that "there came up out of the Nile seven cows sleek and fat," that was a good omen, betokening seven years of plenty. But when he dreamed that seven cows "gaunt and thin" emerged from the Nile and "ate up the seven sleek and fat cows," that foretold seven years of famine, during which all the bounty stored up during the years of plenty would be consumed. An Egyptian tradition of seven lean years, caused by inadequate monsoon rains at the source of the Nile, was documented

on the so-called Famine Stela (see p. 89), which told of a time when the river failed to overflow its banks and replenish the fields "for a space of seven years." It was Joseph's task as the king's vizier, or chief administrator, to ensure that enough grain was set aside in the plentiful years to sustain Egypt through the lean years.

Soothsayers advising Pharaoh were portrayed in the Bible as deluded worshippers of false gods, unable to decipher symbolic messages whose meaning was clear to followers of the one true God. But this text—which belonged to a scribe at Deir el Medina, a village occupied by artisans who labored on the majestic tombs of New Kingdom pharaohs—suggests that dream interpretation in Egypt was a complex task, which involved seeking meaning in ambiguous messages that could be viewed either as good or bad omens. Dreaming of plunging into a river, for example, might be seen as foretelling danger or disaster. But entering the river was interpreted as a good omen, signifying that the dreamer would be cleansed of evil. To dream of birds being snared was not a sign that the dreamer would gain wealth or wisdom, as some might hope, but meant that his property would be seized. Unlike the God of Joseph, who spoke clearly and unambiguously to his people, the gods of the Egyptians communicated in ways that were often cryptic and hard to decipher. Even the god-kings who ruled Egypt sought advice from wise men and soothsayers as to what lay in store for them.

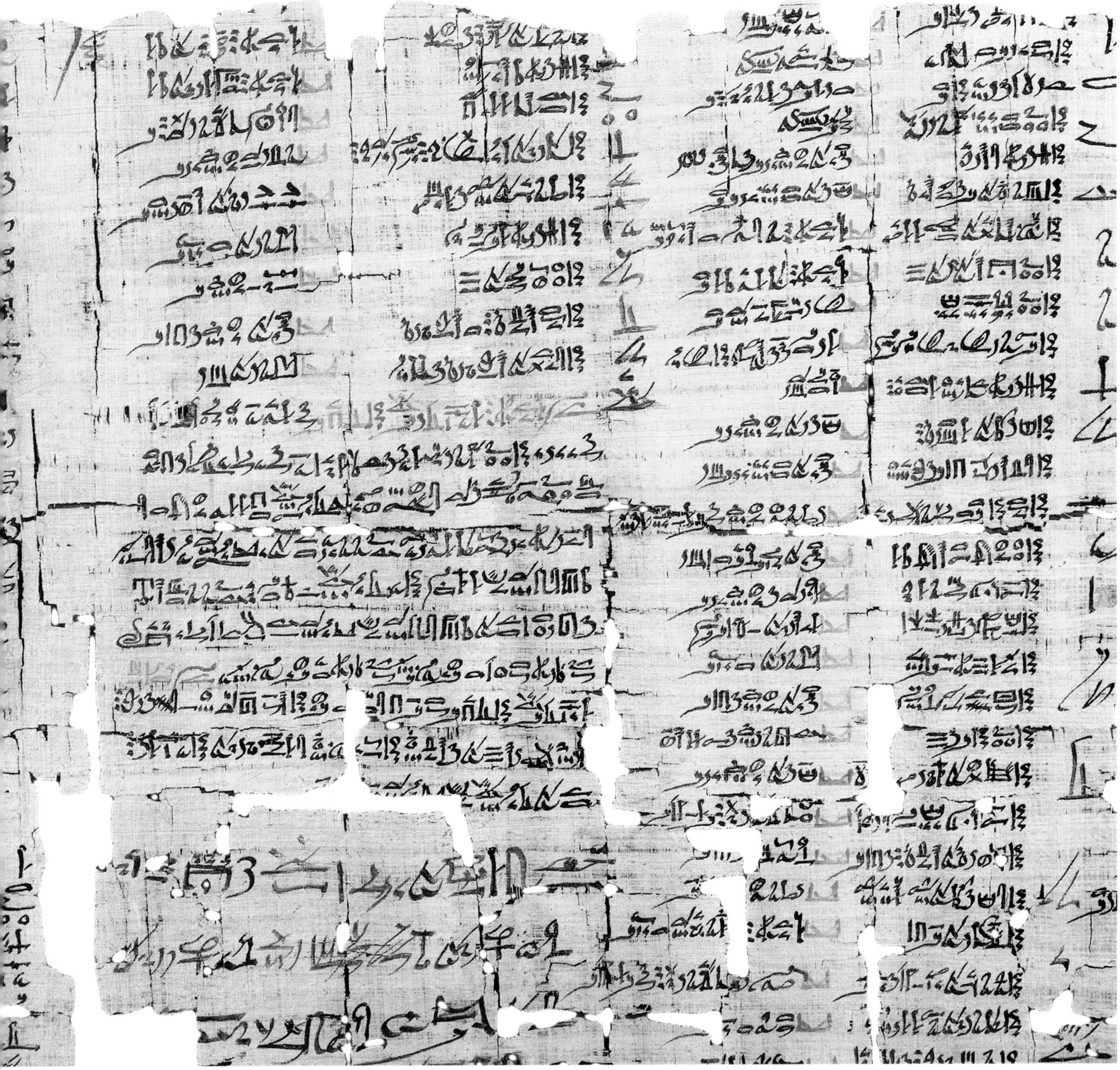

This dream guide, defining various motifs as good or bad omens, was written around the time that Ramses II ruled Egypt, as revealed by a poem inscribed on the back of the papyrus describing the Battle of Kadesh, waged by Ramses II against the Hittites in 1275 B.C.E. The lore compiled here, however, probably went back many centuries, for Egyptians had long been obsessed with dreams and the task of interpreting them.

"Seeing a large cat . . . good: it means a large harvest will come to him. Seeing the moon as it shines . . . good: forgiveness to him by his god. Seeing his face in a mirror . . . bad: it means another wife."

"AND THE EGYPTIANS WERE IN DREAD OF THE PEOPLE OF ISRAEL. SO THEY MADE THE PEOPLE OF ISRAEL SERVE WITH RIGOR, AND MADE THEIR LIVES BITTER WITH HARD SERVICE, IN MORTAR AND BRICK, AND IN ALL KINDS OF WORK IN THE FIELD."

EXODUS 1:12-14

SLAVERY

Archaeological evidence confirms that pharaohs of the New Kingdom used forced labor of the sort described in Exodus to build palaces and other monuments. Unlike the workers who erected the soaring pyramids of the Old Kingdom, these laborers were not free Egyptians, conscripted seasonally to serve their ruler. Most were of foreign origin and were seized as slaves by Egyptian troops or sold into slavery. Others, like the Israelites in the biblical account, may have entered Egypt of their own accord in times of unrest like the Second Intermediate Period, when the Hyksos took control of the Nile Delta, and lived freely there until they were rounded up by rulers of the New Kingdom and placed under taskmasters who treated them much like the slaves Egyptians seized abroad.

A vivid depiction of slaves at work (opposite) adorns the tomb of Rekhmire, who served as vizier to King Thutmose III in the 15th century B.C.E. An inscription identifies the laborers portrayed there as prisoners of war seized in the "south lands" (Nubia) and "north lands" (Canaan and Syria). The dark-skinned southerners and light-skinned northerners are shown toiling together at a brickyard, mixing water with clay to shape it in molds, from which the sun-dried bricks are then removed and carried off. According to the inscription, these slaves were well fed but kept under strict control by their overseer, who reminded them forcefully: "The rod is in my hand; be not idle." Straw served as a binding agent in the brickmaking process, as indicated in Exodus, where Pharaoh adds to the burdens of Israelites by insisting they gather straw themselves: "Go now, and work; for no straw shall be given you, yet you shall deliver the same number of bricks" (Exodus 5:18).

Egyptian sources confirm that brickmakers had to meet daily production quotas. Some laborers were granted holidays to honor their gods, but in Exodus that privilege is denied to the Israelites by Pharaoh, who, in refusing to recognize their God and release them from bondage, subjects Egypt to devastating plagues. Although the king who made that fatal miscalculation is not named in the Bible, the story seems to be set during the reign of Ramses II, who completed work on a new capital in Goshen called Pi-Ramses—recently located by archaeologists near the ruins of the Hyksos capital, Avaris. Ramses also commissioned a cult center in the same region called Per-Atum, devoted to the god Atum. The Bible states that enslaved Israelites built for Pharaoh the cities Pithom (Per-Atum) and Ramses (Pi-Ramses) before being delivered from captivity, thus relating the Exodus to the reign of mighty Ramses II and underscoring the central theme of this sacred story—that no power on Earth could defy the Lord of Israel.

Two depictions of slaves held in Egypt indicate that captives of Asian and Nubian origin served side by side there. Traditionally, Egyptians were disdainful of all foreigners, regardless of their complexion.

Nubians in Egypt

In forging an empire that extended from Nubia in the south to Canaan and Syria in the north, Egyptians increased their dependence on foreign labor and their exposure to foreign influences. Egyptian forces began to expand into Nubia during the Old Kingdom, when they advanced beyond the First Cataract of the Nile, marking Egypt's southern border, to the Second Cataract and established an outpost at Buhen. Pharaohs of the Middle Kingdom delved deeper into Nubia and tightened their grip on its people and natural resources, including gold. Over the centuries, many Nubians entered Egypt as slaves like the dark-skinned captive at left, portrayed here on the sole of a sandal beside a light-skinned Asiatic prisoner. Other Nubians served under Egyptian commanders as soldiers like the hard-fighting Medjay who helped the princes of Thebes oust the Hyksos and were rewarded with booty and grants of land. Nubians who remained in their homeland assimilated the culture of their Egyptian colonizers, burying their dead rulers in pyramids and forging a kingdom called Kush that grew stronger as Egyptian power waned. Ultimately, Nubians supplanted their former masters. In the eighth century B.C.E., they gained control of Thebes—which had long relied on Nubian mercenaries—and went on to extend their authority over the whole of Egypt. Founding their own dynasty at Thebes, Nubian pharaohs ruled there until the seventh century B.C.E.

Inscribed on this clay tablet is the birth legend of Sargon of Akkad, bearing a haunting resemblance to the story of the infant Moses.

"MY MOTHER, THE HIGH PRIESTESS CONCEIVED ME,
SHE BORE ME IN SECRET. SHE PLACED ME IN A REED BASKET,
SHE SEALED MY HATCH WITH PITCH.
SHE LEFT ME TO THE RIVER. . . ."

BIRTH LEGEND OF SARGON OF AKKAD

THE STORY OF MOSES

In the 19th century, archaeologists excavating at Nineveh, the ancient Assyrian capital near the Tigris River, discovered fragments of a clay tablet that when pieced together shed new light on the story of the infant Moses, left floating in the Nile in a reed basket. Inscribed in Akkadian, the tablet describes the legendary birth of Sargon of Akkad, who forged a great empire around 2300 B.C.E. that reached from the Persian Gulf to the Mediterranean. According to this tale, related by Sargon, he was the son of a high priestess who engaged in an illicit union with an unidentified man and hid her guilt by bearing the child in seclusion, placing him in a reed basket sealed with pitch, and casting him adrift in the river. Sargon was rescued by a common man named Aqqi, who found the infant in the basket as he was drawing water from the river and raised him as his adopted son. Later, as young Sargon was working in his father's orchard, the goddess Ishtar was drawn to him and loved him, setting him on the path to immortality. The story of his birth and deliverance may have been composed during his lifetime, but it was not recorded in Nineveh until long afterward, perhaps by scribes of the Assyrian ruler Sargon II (721-705 B.C.E.), who proudly bore the name of that great Akkadian conqueror of old. The resemblance between the story of Moses and the Sargon legend and similar Near Eastern tales of heroes rescued after being exposed as infants suggests that such myths may have influenced the biblical account as it was told and retold over the centuries before being set down in writing. But the differences between the Moses story and the Sargon legend are as striking as the similarities and show that the Israelites, in framing their account of the hero who led them to freedom, were expressing values and beliefs unlike those of the Akkadians or Assyrians. Sargon's mother sets him adrift to hide her shame and never sees him again. Moses' mother, however, is proud of the "goodly child" she bears and leaves him amid the bulrushes in a basket daubed with pitch only because she fears he will be seized and drowned after Pharaoh orders every boy born to the Hebrews cast into the Nile (Exodus 1:22; 2:3). She later becomes his nurse after he is adopted by Pharaoh's daughter, thus preserving his Hebrew identity, which might have been lost without her enduring presence and care. Sargon ascends with divine help from obscurity to majesty, but Moses falls from a high position as a member of Pharaoh's household when his sympathy for his fellow Israelites leads him to slay their Egyptian taskmaster and flee to the desert as an outlaw. Unlike Sargon, who consorts with gods and becomes lord and master of a vast empire, Moses acts as God's servant and renounces wealth and worldly power in order to redeem his people.

This imposing bronze head from Mesopotamia may represent Sargon of Akkad, shown with a long beard, which symbolized wisdom and authority in many Near Eastern cultures and became conventional in depictions of biblical patriarchs like Moses, portrayed at left by Rembrandt bearing tablets inscribed with God's commandments.

"FOR IF YOU REFUSE TO LET MY PEOPLE GO, BEHOLD,
TOMORROW I WILL BRING LOCUSTS INTO YOUR COUNTRY,
AND THEY SHALL COVER THE FACE OF THE LAND."

EXODUS 10:4-5

THE PLAGUES

Swarming locusts arriving from Egypt cloud the sky over fields in southern Israel in November 2004. In ancient times, such plagues and other natural disasters like the one recorded on the Famine Stela (opposite) were viewed by Egyptians and Hebrews alike as acts of God.

The afflictions visited on Egypt in Exodus when Pharaoh refuses to free the Hebrews accurately reflect not only the natural history of the Nile region—where plagues of locusts and other pests are well documented—but also the beliefs and legends of the ancient Egyptians, who viewed such calamities as divine punishments. In one Egyptian myth, the sun god, Re, swears vengeance on humans, who have turned against him. "I myself will be master over them as king," he declares, "and I will destroy them." He sends the goddess Hathor to carry out that destruction, and she spills blood in rivers. Taking pity on humanity, Re mixes beer with the blood and Hathor laps it up and becomes drunk, avoiding further carnage. Visions of blood-swollen rivers, as described in

Exodus and in Egyptian lore, may have been inspired by a natural phenomenon in the Nile Valley, where excesses of algae or bacteria sometimes turned the water red, killing fish and sickening those who drank from the river. In ancient times, this was seen as a supernatural disaster—a curse on the land by an angry god.

The kings of Egypt, who claimed kinship with the gods and served as intermediaries between them and the populace as a whole, were responsible for seeking an end to such afflictions and restoring order through prayers, offerings, and the building of temples. The royal rituals conducted to end one terrible misfortune, a seven-year famine caused by the failure of the Nile to overflow its banks and replenish the soil, are spelled out on a granite boulder erected on Sehen, an island in the Nile near the First Cataract. Although inscribed around the third century B.C.E., when Egypt was ruled by the Ptolemaic dynasty of Macedonian origin, this Famine Stela (opposite) harks back more than 2,000 years to the reign of King Djoser, an early pyramid builder of the Old Kingdom. As the famine worsened and order collapsed, Djoser turned to Imhotep, a great architect and wise man, who advised him to erect a temple on the island of Elephantine, a religious center near Sehen, and dedicate the shrine to Khnum, the god who controlled the flow of the Nile and enriched the fields with silt. One of the oldest and greatest of Egyptian deities, Khnum was overshadowed during the Old Kingdom by Re. Imhotep may have concluded that Khnum was holding back his gifts because he felt slighted.

According to the inscription, Djoser dedicated the temple by first making offerings to goddesses at Elephantine and then went into a trance, during which Khnum appeared to him and blessed him: "I am Khnum, your creator. My arms are around you, to steady your body, to safeguard your limbs. . . . I will make the Nile swell for you . . . so the plants will flourish, bending under their fruit." Unlike the hard-hearted king in Exodus, who breaks his promise to heed God and release the Israelites, Djoser increased his temple offerings to Khnum so that he would no longer withhold his blessings.

"THEN THE LORD SAID TO MOSES, 'STRETCH OUT YOUR HAND OVER THE SEA, THAT THE WATER MAY COME BACK UPON THE EGYPTIANS, UPON THEIR CHARIOTS, AND UPON THEIR HORSEMEN.'"

EXODUS 14:26

CHARIOTS OF WAR

No miracle attributed to God by the Israelites was greater than the parting of the sea for Moses and his followers and the closing of those waters over the army pursuing them in chariots—preeminent symbols of power in Egypt and rival kingdoms. Rulers of the New Kingdom, which emerged when Egyptians mastered the horse-drawn chariots introduced by the Hyksos, were portrayed hunting from chariots and riding them into battle. Among the mightiest of those hard-driving warrior-kings was Ramses II, during whose long reign in the 13th century B.C.E. the Exodus may have occurred. Soon after taking power, Ramses II led an army to Syria to challenge the rival Hittites, led by King Muwatallis. That campaign culminated around 1275 B.C.E. in the Battle of Kadesh, where each side deployed hundreds of chariots. The battle ranks as one of the best documented conflicts of ancient times, thanks to accounts by Egyptian chroniclers and the discovery in Turkey of Hittite tablets with the peace treaty that ended hostilities (right).

According to those accounts, the Egyptian army—consisting of four divisions, each 5,000 men strong, named for the Egyptian gods Amun, Re, Ptah, and Seth—became strung out as it crossed the Orontes River and approached the city of Kadesh, a Hittite stronghold. Ramses was up front with the division of Amun, from whom he claimed descent, when opposing charioteers slammed into the Re division to his rear and routed it. As shown opposite in a wall carving at Abu Simbel, Ramses' temple in Nubia, he reportedly saved his army from collapse by vanquishing thousands of enemies from his chariot single-handedly: "Then his majesty drove at a gallop and charged the forces of the Hittites, being alone by himself." This was, of course, royal propaganda, designed to portray Ramses as superhuman. He could not have entered battle alone because Egyptian war chariots required two men—one to handle the reins and the other to fight as an archer or to hurl javelins. Ramses may have led charioteers in a successful counterattack, but the timely arrival of Egyptian reinforcements and lack of discipline among the Hittites

helped him to avoid defeat. The battle was no great triumph for Ramses, who returned to Egypt without having won any concessions from his foe. The inconclusive contest showed that the two sides were evenly matched and led to a treaty between Ramses and Muwatallis's successor in which they pledged eternal friendship. That pact was later reinforced when Ramses wed the Hittite king's daughter, who joined his large harem of wives.

Only a miracle could have allowed Moses and his followers to prevail against the armed might of a ruler like Ramses. After parting the sea and allowing the Israelites to cross, God "discomfited the host of the Egyptians, clogging their chariot wheels so that they drove heavily." Bogged down in the exposed seabed, the charioteers are doomed when Moses stretches out his hand and the waters return, covering "the chariots and the horsemen and all the host of Pharaoh" (Exodus 14:24-28). To skeptics, this story might appear as improbable as the tale of Ramses II vanquishing the Hittites single-handedly. But while that legend was designed to invest the king with godlike powers, the biblical account attributed no such superhuman strength to Moses, who was simply the vehicle chosen by God to work his divine will.

In the Treaty of Kadesh, inscribed on these fragments in Akkadian, Ramses II entered into a mutual-defense pact with the Hittites. A relief, opposite, at Abu Simbel shows Ramses II in his war chariot.

THE ARK OF THE COVENANT

"THEY SHALL MAKE AN ARK OF
ACACIA WOOD. . . . AND YOU SHALL
PUT INTO THE ARK THE TESTIMONY
WHICH I SHALL GIVE YOU."

EXODUS 25:10-16

Built to hold the sacred stone tablets inscribed with God's commandments, the Ark of the Covenant symbolized both the unique spiritual identity of the Israelites and the traditions they held in common with other cultures of the Near East. Their covenant with YHWH set them apart from other people, but the ark itself and the tabernacle in which it was housed were similar in function and design to shrines of the ancient Egyptians, Mesopotamians, and Arabians.

According to the Bible, God instructed Moses to place four rings of gold at the base of the ark through which poles were inserted to carry the gilded wooden chest, which measured two and a half cubits (about four feet) long and one and a half cubits wide and high. A gilded wooden shrine of similar dimensions, equipped with carrying poles, was discovered by archaeologist Howard Carter in the tomb of King Tutankhamun. Perched atop the shrine was a jackal representing Anubis, the god of mummification, guarding the king's internal organs, which were preserved in jars. A similar shrine served as the throne of the Egyptian god Amun during the religious festival of Opet, when it was placed on a ceremonial bark and ferried across the Nile from Karnak to Thebes. Priests then lifted the bark on poles atop their shoulders and carried it to a temple dedicated to Amun.

THE SHRINE

The Ark of the Covenant served a similar purpose, for on its top was a *kapporet,* or "mercy seat," envisioned as God's throne or footstool. Guarding the mercy seat were two cherubim—winged creatures found at the entrances to temples and palaces in Mesopotamia and similar in function to Egyptian guardian spirits such as Anubis and the Sphinx. Shielded by their wings, God makes his presence felt. "There I will meet with you," he promises Moses, "and from above the mercy seat, from between the two cherubim that are upon the ark of the testimony, I will speak with you of all that I will give you in commandment for the people of Israel" (Exodus 25:22). Much as the Israelites placed the laws of their covenant with God under his throne or footstool, worshippers of other Near Eastern deities deposited treaties or agreements between parties in boxes at such shrines to make those covenants sacred and inviolable.

The tabernacle built to hold the ark, as described in Exodus, was an elaborate structure containing three sections: an outer courtyard for sacrificial offerings, a holy place with an altar lit by lamp stands called menorahs, and an inner sanctum, or Holy of Holies, where the ark was kept. Biblical scholars believe this description refers to the Temple of Solomon in Jerusalem—where the ark was enshrined after Israelites achieved power in Canaan—and doubt that Moses and his followers could have maintained and transported such an ornate tabernacle as they wandered in the desert. Artists in later eras pictured the tabernacle and the lost ark itself as resembling places of worship in their own

A relief from the synagogue at Capernaum portrays the Ark of the Covenant as a miniature temple adorned with Greek columns and mounted on wheels.

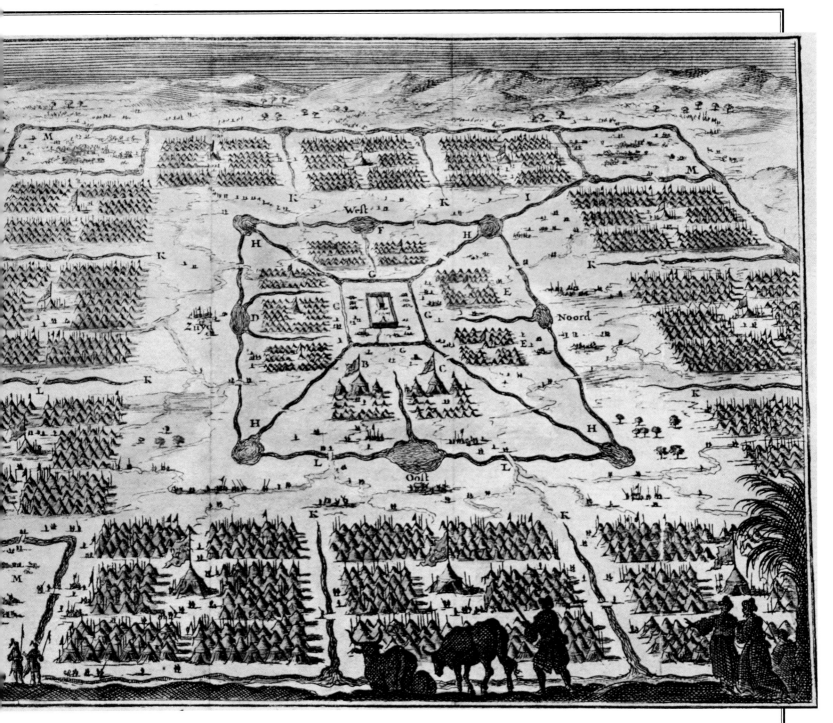

time, like the classical shrine on wheels shown opposite, portrayed at a synagogue built at Capernaum along the Sea of Galilee in the early Christian era. But the original tabernacle may have been more like the tents used by Bedouin chieftains of Arabia or the throne rooms set up in camp for Egyptian kings when they advanced with their troops.

Like the Egyptians, the Israelites believed that their God, if properly honored, would accompany them into battle and bring them victory. As portrayed above in an 18th-century Dutch etching, showing the 12 tribes of Israel camped in military style with the tabernacle in their midst, the Ark of the Covenant was central to the campaigns that brought Israelites to power in Canaan. Yet the shrine remained sacrosanct, and only priests could approach it. As Joshua told his followers when they were about to cross over the Jordan River into Canaan: "When you see the ark of the covenant of the Lord your God being carried by the Levitical priests, then you shall set out from your place and follow it. . . . Yet there shall be a space between you and it, a distance of about two thousand cubits; do not come near it" (Joshua 3:3-4).

This depiction of the 12 tribes of Israel camped around their sacred tabernacle, at center, evokes militant biblical passages such as I Samuel 4:5: "When the ark of the covenant of the Lord came into the camp, all Israel gave a mighty shout, so that the earth resounded."

WORSHIPPING THE GOLDEN CALF

"AND HE RECEIVED THE GOLD AT THEIR HAND, AND FASHIONED IT WITH A GRAVING TOOL, AND MADE A MOLTEN CALF; AND THEY SAID, 'THESE ARE YOUR GODS, O ISRAEL, WHO BROUGHT YOU UP OUT OF THE LAND OF EGYPT!'"

EXODUS 32:4

The Levites
An Israelite tribe who traced their ancestry to Levi, son of Jacob, the Levites served as priests. Moses and his brother Aaron were Levites. After destroying the golden calf, Moses has the Levites punish those who worshipped that idol. "Today you have ordained yourselves for the service of the Lord," he says, "each one at the cost of his son and of his brother" (Exodus 32:29). As a priestly caste, they receive no allotment of their own in the Promised Land.

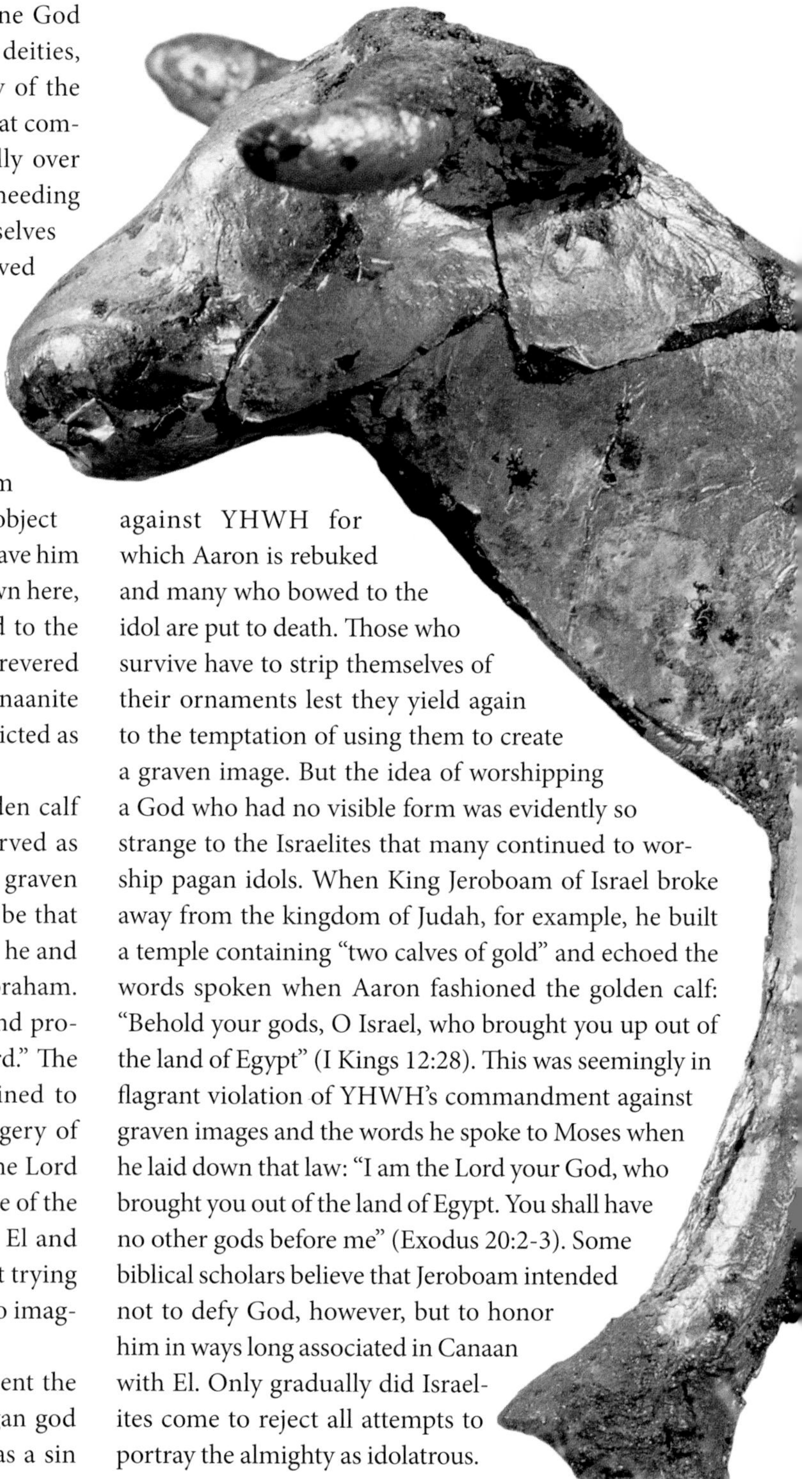

The gold-plated figurine at right, which was found at Byblos, may represent the Canaanite god Baal, one of many Near Eastern deities portrayed as a bull or cow, including the Canaanite goddess Baalat and the Egyptian goddess Hathor.

Monotheism, or worshipping one God to the exclusion of all other deities, was the great spiritual legacy of the Israelites. But they came to that commitment slowly and painfully over the centuries, often worshipping idols before heeding the warnings of prophets and devoting themselves strictly to YHWH. No sooner had Moses received the Ten Commandments on Mount Sinai—the first of which required the Israelites to have no other gods and shun graven images—than they broke that law. Losing faith when Moses remained in seclusion on Mount Sinai, they turned to his brother Aaron and asked him to "make us gods, who shall go before us." The object Aaron fashioned from the golden earrings they gave him was a "molten calf," resembling the figurine shown here, found at a temple in Byblos, Lebanon, devoted to the goddess Baalat. Portrayed as a cow, Baalat was revered as the mistress or mother of Baal, a mighty Canaanite god associated with storms and fertility and depicted as a horned bull like this gold-plated idol.

One question raised by the story of the golden calf is why a God-fearing man like Aaron, who served as spokesman for Moses, would have fashioned a graven image in defiance of YHWH. The answer may be that Aaron intended the calf as an image of the Lord he and his people had worshipped since the time of Abraham. After making the idol, he built an altar for it and proclaimed: "Tomorrow shall be a feast to the Lord." The Israelites had roots in Canaan and were destined to return there. They used the language and imagery of Canaan to refer to God. In the Hebrew Bible, the Lord is often referred to as "El," which was also the title of the supreme god in the Canaanite pantheon. Both El and Baal were portrayed as bulls. If Aaron was in fact trying to picture the Lord, it was only natural for him to imagine the almighty in that shape.

Whether the golden calf was meant to represent the Lord of Abraham and his descendants or a pagan god such as Baal, worshipping this graven image was a sin against YHWH for which Aaron is rebuked and many who bowed to the idol are put to death. Those who survive have to strip themselves of their ornaments lest they yield again to the temptation of using them to create a graven image. But the idea of worshipping a God who had no visible form was evidently so strange to the Israelites that many continued to worship pagan idols. When King Jeroboam of Israel broke away from the kingdom of Judah, for example, he built a temple containing "two calves of gold" and echoed the words spoken when Aaron fashioned the golden calf: "Behold your gods, O Israel, who brought you up out of the land of Egypt" (I Kings 12:28). This was seemingly in flagrant violation of YHWH's commandment against graven images and the words he spoke to Moses when he laid down that law: "I am the Lord your God, who brought you out of the land of Egypt. You shall have no other gods before me" (Exodus 20:2-3). Some biblical scholars believe that Jeroboam intended not to defy God, however, but to honor him in ways long associated in Canaan with El. Only gradually did Israelites come to reject all attempts to portray the almighty as idolatrous.

A painting by Italian artist Andrea Celesti portrays the destruction of the golden calf, as ordered by Moses.

This ten-foot-high granite slab, inscribed with lavish tributes to Merneptah's victories, was recycled for that purpose and commemorates the exploits of an earlier king, Amenhotep III, on its opposite side. The crucial reference to Israel is outlined in white here.

Israel is laid waste,
his seed is not.

"THE GREAT LORD OF EGYPT IS POWERFUL;
VICTORY BELONGS TO HIM. . . . FOOLISH AND
WITLESS IS HE WHO TAKES HIM ON!"

MERNEPTAH STELA

MERNEPTAH'S BOAST

Few finds caused greater excitement among biblical archaeologists—or raised more questions—than the discovery by Flinders Petrie of the Merneptah Stela, inscribed with verses hailing the conquests of King Merneptah, who succeeded Ramses II in 1213 B.C.E. "This stela will be better known in the world than anything else I have found," declared Petrie, who recognized that much would be made of a single sensational line here: "Israel is laid waste, his seed is not." This was the first known reference outside the Bible to the people of Israel and demonstrated that they had achieved a distinct identity—and notoriety—in Egypt by the time this stela was installed at Thebes in the mortuary temple of Merneptah, who died around 1203 B.C.E.

Written in hieroglyphs, the inscription on the stela deals largely with a triumphant campaign Merneptah mounted against hostile Libyans and allied Sea People, fearsome raiders who swept down from the northern Mediterranean in ships around this time. "The great Lord of Egypt is powerful; victory belongs to him," the royal scribe boasts here. "Who can fight, knowing his unhindered stride? Foolish and witless is he who takes him on!" This was typical of the tributes paid in writing to the kings of Egypt and other powerful countries in the region who sent their forces into battle and were heaped with praises, even when their campaigns ended inconclusively. Historians have determined from supporting evidence that Merneptah's troops did indeed defeat the Libyans and Sea People, but questions linger about another campaign described on this stela that caused defeated princes in Canaan and surrounding lands to cry "Mercy!" (Merneptah's scribe used the Canaanite word *Shalam!* here, akin to the Hebrew Shalom, or Peace!) Canaan had long been under Egypt's control, but the country was unstable and Merneptah's forces evidently put down a rebellion there. Israel is mentioned as among those crushed, a defeat so thorough that their "seed is not" (an obvious exaggeration since the Israelites endured and grew stronger in years to come).

Petrie's team was able to decipher the term "Israel" because Egyptian hieroglyphs contain not only pictographs, representing objects or concepts, but also phonemes—phonetic characters derived from pictographs. (A crude example in English of using pictographs phonetically would be combining pictures of a cat and a log to represent the word "catalog.") The word "Israel," written in hieroglyphs from right to left, appears in the outlined portion of the inscription shown opposite. The first phoneme in that word, at far right, resembles two upright feathers, side by side, and represents the sound "y" as in "slowly." To its left are two phonemes, one atop the other, representing the combined sounds "s" and "r." The remaining phonemes complete the term "Ysrael," or "Israel," followed at far left by pictographs of a seated man and woman, which function as a determinative, indicating that the term refers not to a nation or state but to a people.

In other words, the people of Israel were established in Canaan when this stela was inscribed but had not yet achieved nationhood there. If, in fact, the people who founded Israel came out of Egypt and settled in Canaan after wandering in the desert, then that process must have been completed by the time Merneptah died.

Merneptah, portrayed at left in stone as an idealized young king, took the throne name "Soul of Re, Beloved of the Gods" when he was crowned pharaoh in his late 50s and had that title inscribed by the sculptor here in an oval cartouche on his right shoulder.

chapter 3

CANAAN

The Promised Land

CANAAN

No event described in the Bible has provoked greater interest or livelier debate among archaeologists recently than the conquest of Canaan by Israelites as portrayed in the Books of Joshua and Judges. Those sources do not entirely agree in their accounts of the conquest, depicted as a more sweeping and devastating campaign in Joshua than in Judges, which deals with the formative experiences of Israelite tribes in Canaan when they were governed by leaders called judges. The difference between those two biblical versions of the conquest story is minor, however, compared to the gap between their shared view of how Israelites became established in Canaan and recent theories based on archaeological findings. Although excavations have shown that Jericho and several other Canaanite cites reportedly destroyed by Joshua and his followers were in fact reduced to rubble in ancient times, only a few such layers of destruction have been dated to around 1200 B.C.E., when an Israelite presence in Canaan was first recorded in Egypt, on the Merneptah Stela (see pp. 96-97). That proposed date for the conquest was favored by many scholars. They based their conclusion on descriptions from the Bible suggesting that the Exodus occurred in the 13th century B.C.E., around the time that Ramses II ruled Egypt, and on the Merneptah inscription, which indicates that the Israelites were an emerging group in Canaan around 1200 B.C.E., not a dominant political force there, arguing against an earlier date for a wholesale conquest as told in the Bible.

> "SO JOSHUA TOOK THE WHOLE LAND, ACCORDING TO ALL THAT THE LORD HAD SPOKEN TO MOSES; AND JOSHUA GAVE IT FOR AN INHERITANCE TO ISRAEL ACCORDING TO THEIR TRIBAL ALLOTMENTS."
>
> JOSHUA 11:23

No widespread pattern of destruction has been found in Canaan that can be attributed with any confidence to the Israelites. What archaeologists have detected instead is a seemingly peaceful process of settlement beginning around 1200 B.C.E. in the central highlands of Canaan, away from cities listed as targets of Joshua and his forces. To scholars studying the material evidence left behind by those settlers, they look less like invaders than refugees, seeking sanctuary from the turmoil and deprivation that haunted the region around this time—the tumultuous dawn of the Iron Age, when the Egyptian empire declined, the Hittite empire collapsed, and fearsome intruders called Sea Peoples swept down from the northern Mediterranean.

LINGERING QUESTIONS

Despite recent findings challenging biblical accounts of the conquest, the issue of how Israelites occupied Canaan is by no means resolved. Further evidence from the field may support or call into question the theory of peaceful settlement. For now, archaeologists who hold that view must contend with serious objections raised by those who maintain that biblical accounts of Joshua's triumphant campaign, like those of the Exodus and the wanderings of Moses and his followers in the wilderness, must have some foundation in the history and traditions of the Israelites or they would never have been accepted as authoritative. Archaeological findings have confirmed significant details in Joshua and Judges, including frequent references to the five cities of the Philistines, a branch of the Sea Peoples who invaded coastal Canaan in the 12th century B.C.E. Did the authors of the Bible add those verifiable

Previous pages: "Abraham's Journey to Canaan" by Jacopo Bassano
Opposite: This haunting three-horned goddess was found amid the relics of an Edomite shrine at Horvat Qitmit in the Negev desert.

details to a largely fictional account to lend it authenticity, as historical novelists do today? And if they did—if Joshua was an invention and his conquest a myth—why was the story presented as history in the Bible rather than as a poetic fable like the Book of Job?

One possible explanation of the current gap between Scripture and archaeological findings is that Joshua was a real figure whose feats grew substantially in legend during the 600 or more years that elapsed between the time he may have lived, around 1200 B.C.E., and when his story was set down in writing as we have it today. Perhaps Moses and Joshua were leaders not of all Israelites but of one determined band of exiles who fled bondage in Egypt, found strength in the wilderness through their defining encounter with YHWH at Mount Sinai, and battled their way into Canaan, their Promised Land, where the survivors imparted their faith and fighting spirit to Hebrews among whom they settled, preparing the way for the emergence of a kingdom. If so, they could have come to represent Israel as a whole in Jewish lore much as George Washington and others who fought the British—rebels who constituted a small minority of the American colonial population—have come to represent their emerging nation in American lore. Over the centuries, perhaps, the ordeals and accomplishments of Moses, Joshua, and their followers became those of all 12 tribes of Israel, acting in unison, and Joshua's victories expanded to embrace cities that were destroyed long before he entered Canaan or were seized by expansive Israelites long after he died.

This conquest story assumed profound significance for Israelites as the kingdom established by Saul and David around 1000 B.C.E. divided and later collapsed under assault by Assyrians and Babylonians (sometimes called Neo-Babylonians or Chaldeans to distinguish them from those who forged the first Babylonian empire a millennium earlier). The Books of Joshua and Judges were drawn from ancient Israelite lore but were probably not completed in their present form until after the Babylonian conquest of Jerusalem in 587 B.C.E. and the resulting exile. For those exiles, the conquest story served as a

The famed cedars of Lebanon were prized by Israelites in neighboring Canaan, who obtained them from Phoenicians and used the timber to build Solomon's Temple in Jerusalem.

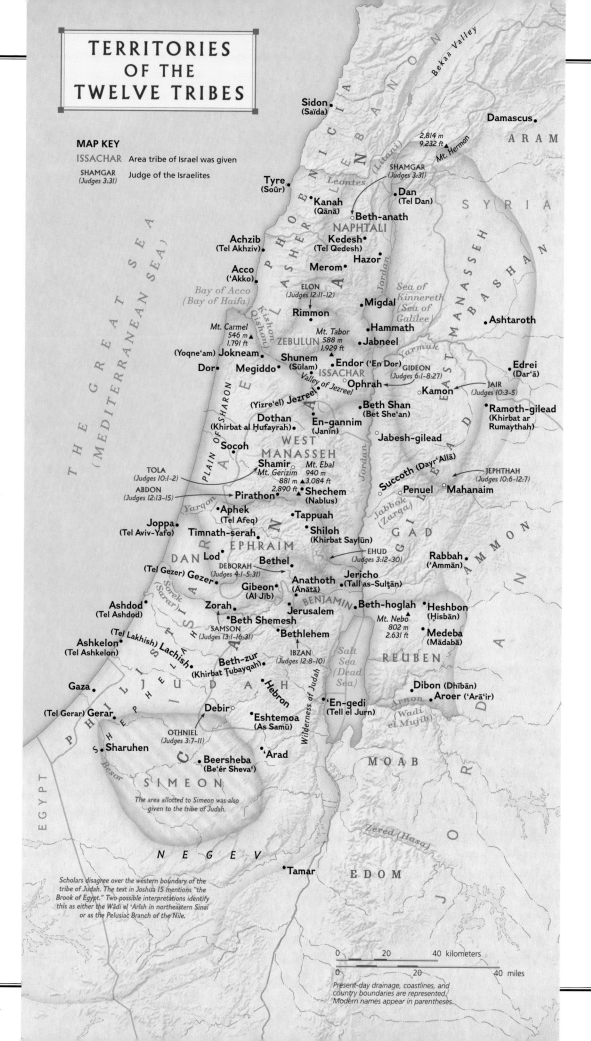

TERRITORIES OF THE TWELVE TRIBES

This map shows the territories allotted to the 12 tribes of Israel in Canaan, according to the Bible, and the locations of groups with whom those Israelites came in contact, including the Philistines, Phoenicians, Aramaeans, Moabites, and Edomites.

MAP KEY

ISSACHAR — Area tribe of Israel was given

SHAMGAR (Judges 3:31) — Judge of the Israelites

Sidon (Saïda)

Damascus

ARAM

2,814 m 9,232 ft Mt. Hermon

SHAMGAR (Judges 3:31)

SYRIA

Tyre (Soûr)

Kanah (Qānā)

Dan (Tel Dan)

Beth-anath

NAPHTALI

Achzib (Tel Akhziv)

Kedesh (Tel Qedesh)

Hazor

BASHAN

Acco ('Akko)

Merom

Bay of Acco (Bay of Haifa)

ELON (Judges 12:11-12)

Rimmon

Migdal

Sea of Kinnereth (Sea of Galilee)

Ashtaroth

Mt. Carmel 546 m 1,791 ft

Mt. Tabor 588 m 1,929 ft

Hammath

ZEBULUN

Jabneel

(Yoqne'am) Jokneam

Shunem (Sūlam)

Endor ('En Dor)

GIDEON (Judges 6:1-8:27)

Edrei (Dar'ā)

Dor

Megiddo

ISSACHAR

Ophrah

Kamon

JAIR (Judges 10:3-5)

(Yizre'el) Jezreel

Valley of Jezreel

Beth Shan (Bet She'an)

Ramoth-gilead (Khirbat ar Rumaythah)

Dothan (Khirbat al Ḥufayrah)

En-gannim (Janīn)

Jabesh-gilead

Socoh

WEST MANASSEH

EAST MANASSEH

TOLA (Judges 10:1-2)

Shamir

Mt. Ebal 940 m 3,084 ft

Succoth (Dayr 'Allā)

JEPHTHAH (Judges 10:6-12:7)

ABDON (Judges 12:13-15)

Mt. Gerizim 881 m 2,890 ft

Shechem (Nablus)

Penuel

Mahanaim

Pirathon

Aphek (Tel Afeq)

Tappuah

GILEAD

Joppa (Tel Aviv-Yafo)

Timnath-serah

Shiloh (Khirbat Saylūn)

GAD

DAN

Lod

Bethel

EHUD (Judges 3:12-30)

Rabbah ('Ammān)

AMMON

(Tel Gezer) Gezer

DEBORAH (Judges 4:1-5:31)

Anathoth (Anātā)

Jericho (Tall as-Sulṭān)

Ashdod (Tel Ashdod)

Gibeon (Al Jīb)

Zorah

BENJAMIN

Beth-hoglah

Heshbon (Ḥisbān)

Jerusalem

Mt. Nebo 802 m 2,631 ft

Beth Shemesh

SAMSON (Judges 13:1-16:31)

Bethlehem

Medeba (Mādabā)

Ashkelon (Tel Ashkelon)

(Tel Lakhish) Lachish

IBZAN (Judges 12:8-10)

REUBEN

Beth-zur (Khirbat Ṭubayqah)

Salt Sea (Dead Sea)

Gaza

Hebron

Dibon (Dhībān)

Aroer ('Arā'ir)

(Tel Gerar) Gerar

Debir

En-gedi (Tell el Jurn)

JUDAH

Eshtemoa (As Samū)

Arnon (Wadi el Mujīb)

OTHNIEL (Judges 3:7-11)

Sharuhen

'Arad

MOAB

Beersheba (Be'ér Sheva')

SIMEON

The area allotted to Simeon was also given to the tribe of Judah.

Zered (Hasa)

NEGEV

Tamar

EDOM

Scholars disagree over the western boundary of the tribe of Judah. The text in Joshua 15 mentions "the Brook of Egypt." Two possible interpretations identify this as either the Wâdi el 'Arîsh in northeastern Sinai or as the Pelusiac Branch of the Nile.

EGYPT

THE GREAT SEA (MEDITERRANEAN SEA)

PHOENICIA

PHILISTIA

0   20   40 kilometers

0   20   40 miles

Present-day drainage, coastlines, and country boundaries are represented. Modern names appear in parentheses.

poignant reminder of what they lost when they were no longer united as a people and wholly dedicated to a sacred cause like Joshua's followers. At a time when defeat and exile signaled the impotence of one's gods, the biblical narrative made clear that the fault lay not with YHWH—who remained almighty and superior to any power on Earth—but with his faithless followers, who broke his laws and met with disaster. That outcome was prefigured by God's warning to Joshua when one of his men disobeyed a solemn order to set aside all treasure taken from Jericho as an offering to the Lord: "Israel has sinned; they have transgressed my covenant which I have commanded them. . . . Therefore the people of Israel cannot stand before their enemies" (Joshua 7:11-12). When the culprit confessed and was punished, God again blessed Joshua and his forces with great victories, a redemption that hold out the promise of deliverance for exiles in Babylon if they repented and trusted anew in God.

A Cultural Crossroads

Most biblical archaeologists working today in Canaan—or the modern nation of Israel and adjacent Palestinian territories—are not seeking either to prove or to disprove the Bible. Their goal rather is to uncover and interpret the complex archaeological record of the various societies that occupied Canaan and interacted there in biblical times. As a cultural crossroads where people from Mesopotamia, Egypt, Arabia, Asia Minor, the Aegean Islands, and the larger Mediterranean world met and exchanged goods, techniques, ideas, and beliefs, Canaan cannot be fully understood or explained by scholars focusing on one culture or faith. A single archaeological site there such as Tel Dor, located on the Mediterranean coast south of modern-day Haifa, may contain material contributions made by a dozen or more societies over thousands of years. They included the original Canaanites; Egyptians who became their overlords during the New Kingdom; Philistines and other Sea Peoples who invaded as Egyptian power waned; Phoenicians from the coast of Lebanon who ventured here as traders or colonists; Israelites who clashed with Canaanites and Philistines and reached an accommodation with Phoenicians; and in later times Assyrians, Babylonians, Persians, Macedonians, Greeks, and Romans.

Archaeologists investigating sites where many cultures converged sometimes find it difficult to distinguish the relics of one group from another. What set the early Israelites apart materially from others in Canaan? Their pottery was basic, and much of it could have been produced by other people of limited means, living outside the larger towns or cities where skilled potters turned out more decorative ware. One distinctive pot found in many highland settlements in Canaan of the early Iron Age was a tall jar called a *pithos* with a rim collar. Another distinguishing feature of those settlements was a four-room pillared house with a central courtyard that could serve as a stable for livestock at night. But such traits offer archaeologists few clues as to the rituals and beliefs of the occupants and whether they were in fact Israelites or pagan Canaanites. More intriguing and significant is the absence of the remains of pigs in those settlements, for Israelites were the only group in the region at that time known to have dietary laws against eating pork. Later settlements in Canaan offer further evidence of Hebrew cultic practices, which were not always observed to the exclusion of pagan rituals, as evidenced by the discovery of images of fertility goddesses and other idols within Israelite communities. Evidently, prophets like Jeremiah were not exaggerating when they accused YHWH's Chosen People of having "burned incense to other gods, and worshiped the works of their own hands" (Jeremiah 1:16).

From the remarkable mingling of cultures in Canaan came achievements that cannot be attributed to any one group who left their mark on what became the Holy Land. The first phonetic alphabets—which launched a cultural revolution in the Mediterranean world by extending the power of the written word from the few to the many—evolved in and around Canaan. The far-ranging Phoenicians played a major role in disseminating that gift, but others contributed to the process, including Egyptians, Hebrews, and Aramaeans, whose language became the lingua franca of this diverse region and was mastered by Jews along with Hebrew as their kingdom crumbled and they were thrown together with people of other faiths and tongues. The Book of Daniel was written in Aramaic and offered disheartened exiles the inspiring vision of the coming of a new Canaan or Promised Land, ruled by God: "His kingdom shall never be destroyed, and his dominion shall be to the end" (Daniel 6:26).

This Canaanite board game, with squares etched in limestone and two sets of pieces shaped like pyramids and thimbles, resembles board games found in Egyptian tombs.

"THEY SAID TO THEM AT SHILOH IN
THE LAND OF CANAAN, 'THE LORD
COMMANDED THROUGH MOSES THAT WE
BE GIVEN CITIES TO DWELL IN, ALONG WITH
THEIR PASTURE LANDS FOR OUR CATTLE.' "

JOSHUA 21:2

LUXURY IN CANAAN

Touted in the Bible as a land of milk and honey, Canaan was also a place of wealth and refinement, whose cities posed temptations for Israelites, warned by their leaders not to be led astray by luxuries and treasures and end up worshipping mammon. Before attacking Jericho, Joshua commands his followers to claim no spoils for themselves. "All silver and gold, and vessels of bronze and iron, are sacred to the Lord," he declares; "they shall go into the treasury of the Lord" (Joshua 6:19).

Archaeological evidence indicates that the earliest Israelite settlements in Canaan were small villages in the highlands whose occupants had few possessions other than clothing, tools, and simple clay pots. Most cities that were not destroyed during the conflicts that convulsed the region remained for a time in the hands of pagan Canaanites or the Philistines, who occupied the coast. Israelites, however, regarded all of Canaan as their inheritance, including not just its bountiful fields but also its bustling cities where artisans produced splendid goods like those shown here. In taking possession of Jerusalem and other centers of population and production, Israelites became lovers of luxury and artistry and fashioned their own alluring objects, much to the dismay of prophets like Isaiah, who lamented, "Their land is filled with silver and gold, and there is no end to their treasures" (Isaiah 2:7-8).

Some villagers in Canaan produced pottery for their own use, but fine ware like this was made by skilled artisans who congregated in cities.

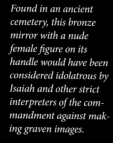

Images of animals like the flying-hawk amulet below and the cosmetics box at bottom, shaped like a waterfowl, also had pagan associations in Canaan, where many people revered animal spirits.

Found in an ancient cemetery, this bronze mirror with a nude female figure on its handle would have been considered idolatrous by Isaiah and other strict interpreters of the commandment against making graven images.

Ornamental lotus seeds on this necklace were symbols of regeneration because they could be preserved indefinitely before being planted and yielding new life.

"I HAVE COME DOWN TO DELIVER THEM OUT OF
THE HAND OF EGYPTIANS, AND TO BRING THEM UP
OUT OF THAT LAND TO A GOOD AND BROAD LAND,
A LAND FLOWING WITH MILK AND HONEY."

EXODUS 3:8

THE LAND OF MILK AND HONEY

God's promise to Moses on Mount Sinai to deliver the Israelites from captivity in Egypt and bring them into a land of "milk and honey" is one of more than a dozen passages in the Bible using those evocative words to refer to Canaan. In one passage, the words are turned against Moses by opponents who have lost faith in him after wandering for years in the desert and who complain that by leading them away from Goshen in the bountiful Nile Delta, he exiled them from the real Promised Land: "Is it a small thing that you have brought us up out of a land flowing with milk and honey, to kill us in the wilderness, that you must also make yourself a prince over us?" (Numbers 16:13). Moses replies that "the Lord has sent me to do all these works, and that it has not been of my own accord." YHWH then upholds Moses in spectacular fashion by opening the earth and swallowing up his opponents. Shortly before his death, Moses invests his God-given authority in Joshua, one of 12 men from each of the 12 tribes of Israel who were sent to spy on the land of Canaan and returned with a cluster of grapes, signaling that the Lord's promise to Moses would soon be fulfilled: "We came to the land to which you sent us; it flows with milk and honey, and this is the fruit" (Numbers 13:27).

As shown by those grapes, milk and honey were not the only natural blessings awaiting the Israelites in Canaan, where the fruitful corridor along the Jordan River (opposite) formed part of the Fertile Crescent, extending from the Nile Valley to Mesopotamia. Wheat was cultivated in Canaan, for example, and made into bread. Few of the region's assets meant more to its inhabitants, however, than milk and honey. Milk from goats and cows provided more sustenance than meat because the animals furnishing it remained alive and offered nourishment in that form for years. Honey—which in Hebrew meant the product of bees as well as nectar or paste made from figs, dates, and other fruits—was prized in all forms because it was sweet, satisfying, and virtually imperishable.

Archaeologists long looked in vain for evidence that Israelites tended bees in Canaan and concluded that most of the "honey" they consumed came from fruit. Then in 2007 a team from the Hebrew University of Jerusalem excavated the first ancient apiary found anywhere in the Near East at Tel Rehov, located west of the Jordan River below the Sea of Galilee. Found there were more than 30 cylindrical clay hives like those shown below. Bees entered and exited through a small hole in one end of the clay cylinder; a lid at the opposite end could be removed

by beekeepers to extract the honeycomb. Dating from around the tenth century B.C.E., this site included an altar adorned with images of fertility goddesses—evidence confirming frequent biblical charges that many Israelites were not exclusively devoted to YHWH and made offerings to other gods or idols, who were credited with making people fertile and their land fruitful. "You defile yourselves with all your idols to this day," railed the Prophet Ezekiel in the sixth century B.C.E. He likened wayward Israelites of his time to the faithless followers of Moses, who despite being promised "a land flowing with milk and honey, the most glorious of all lands," broke God's commandments and yearned "after their idols" (Ezekiel 20:15-31).

The clay beehives above, found recently at Tel Rehov in Israel, provided the first evidence that ancient Israelites kept bees in the fabled land of milk and honey. Other forms of honey were derived from fruit that grew in Canaan's fertile river valleys (opposite) or at desert oases.

"AND THE TERRITORY OF THE CANAANITES
EXTENDED FROM SIDON, IN THE DIRECTION
OF GERAR, AS FAR AS GAZA."

GENESIS 10:19

GAZA:
WHERE CANAAN AND EGYPT MET

In ancient as in modern times, Gaza lay on a frontier where people of different origins and faiths interacted, sometimes peacefully and sometimes violently. As defined in Genesis, the land of Canaan extended along the Mediterranean coast from Sidon in the north, in modern-day Lebanon, to Gaza in the south, bordering Egypt. Gaza served as a gateway for traders and troops passing to and from Egypt. As such, it was of great strategic importance to Egypt's rulers, who eventually gained control over that city. Flinders Petrie, a pioneering figure in ancient Near Eastern archaeology, thought he had found ancient Gaza when he began excavations in 1930 at Tell el-Ajjul, a mound located about seven miles from the modern city of Gaza. As it turned out, the site he uncovered was a separate settlement within what is now the Gaza Strip, one that rivaled nearby Gaza in importance in ancient times.

Petrie's most spectacular finds at Tell el-Ajjul came from the early second millennium B.C.E.—the period when the Hyksos moved down through Canaan and infiltrated Egypt, taking control of the Nile Delta. In one burial chamber, he found the remains of a Hyksos nobleman, interred with his horses and chariot. The lords of this city amassed considerable wealth, including gold from Nubia, which went into the crafting of the treasures shown here, including a stunning golden plaque bearing the seductive features of a Canaanite goddess (opposite). Her "curiously impassive expression," Petrie wrote, signified "the impartial rule of reproductive Nature."

Tell el-Ajjul declined in population and importance during Egypt's New Kingdom, whose rulers, having ousted the Hyksos, asserted control over Canaan and made their administrative center in nearby Gaza, which expanded as a result. Local rulers in Gaza were subject to

A necklace crafted of pearl and gold was among the glittering relics of the Hyksos era unearthed by Flinders Petrie's team at Tell el-Ajjul, near Gaza.

Egypt's pharaohs and paid them lavish tribute in writing, as revealed in one of the Amarna Letters, sent to Egypt's king by a Canaanite prince called Yabitri, who served as governor of both Gaza and Joppa, a coastal city to the north. "Behold, I am thy servant, true to my lord, my king," Yabitri declared. "I look on one side, and I look on the other side, and there is no light; but I look on my lord my king, and there is light. . . . Let my lord my king ask his agent if I do not guard the gate of Gaza and the gate of Joppa. . . . The yoke of my lord is on my neck, and I bear it."

Around 1200 B.C.E., Egypt lost hold of Canaan, creating an opening there for other factions. Among those vying with Canaanites for control were the Israelites—who considered this their Promised Land—and the Philistines, who conquered Gaza and other cities near the coast. According to the Bible, the Israelite folk hero Samson clashed repeatedly with those Philistines, who on one occasion laid a trap for him in Gaza, surrounding him in the night while he was visiting a harlot. But Samson got the better of them, Scripture attests, "and took hold of the doors of the gate of the city, and the two posts, and pulled them up, bar and all, and put them on his shoulders and carried them to the top of the hill that is before Hebron" (Judges 16:3). Aside from that fabled exploit, Israelites never had a very firm grip on Gaza. Although it was described in the Hebrew Bible as part of the territory allotted by Joshua to the tribe of Judah along with two other Philistine cities, Ashkelon and Ekron, a later version of the Old Testament, the Greek Septuagint, said that Judah did not take those cities, and biblical scholars agree with that conclusion. Over the ages, Gaza fell to one great power after another, including the Assyrians, Macedonians, Romans, Arabs, Turks, and British. By the time Petrie conducted his excavations at Tell el-Ajjul in the 1930s, Gaza was once again disputed territory as Palestinians vied with incoming Jewish settlers. Rising tensions and old age took their toll on the venerable archaeologist. "I begin to find that camp life is becoming too much for me," he remarked, "but I do love the freedom of it."

Flinders Petrie

With his majestic white beard, William Matthew Flinders Petrie—who began excavating at Tell el-Ajjul at the age of 77—looked like a biblical patriarch. He was, in fact, one of the founding fathers of modern archaeology, a prodigy who formulated the vital technique of using pottery sherds to define and date the successive levels, or strata, at an excavation site. His career began in 1880 when he surveyed the Great Pyramid at Giza, seeking to confirm a theory that its dimensions had mystical significance. When his findings disproved that thesis he readily discarded it, leaving it to "the flat earth believers and other such people to whom a theory is dearer than a fact." By the 20th century, other archaeologists had improved substantially on his methods, but he remained an inspirational figure to young men and women drawn to the field, who eagerly worked under him despite the dangers associated with his campsites, where he was notorious for dining on canned meat that often went bad. "Why hasn't he died of ptomaine poisoning?" wrote T. E. Lawrence, who joined Petrie on a dig before winning fame during the First World War as Lawrence of Arabia. He and others ate from "week-opened tins after scraping off the green crust inside" while Petrie instructed them in professional matters and personal hygiene. "He is a man of ideas and systems," Lawrence observed, "from the right way to dig a temple to the only way to clean one's teeth."

Petrie identified this alluring plaque as a representation of Asherah, a Canaanite mother goddess associated with fertility and reproduction who was worshipped by some unorthodox Israelites as YHWH's consort or feminine counterpart.

Petrie examines pottery found at one of the many sites he excavated in Palestine and Egypt.

BALAAM'S CURSES AND BLESSINGS

The Amorites
A wide-ranging people who spoke a Semitic language like the Hebrews, Amorites lived at one time in Mesopotamia, Syria, Canaan, and the Transjordan (east of the Jordan River and the Dead Sea). When King Sihon of the Amorites barred the Israelites from crossing his territory, the Bible states, they "slew him with the edge of the sword, and took possession of his land" (Numbers 21:24).

One of the more mysterious figures in the Bible is a seer and sorcerer named Balaam, portrayed alternately as a friend and foe to the wandering Israelites advancing toward Canaan. In the main account of his deeds, Balaam is described as a pagan wizard from Mesopotamia who nonetheless heeds the command of God and refuses to curse his followers as urged by Balak, King of Moab. Balak's aim is to avoid the fate suffered by the ruler of the neighboring Amorites, who loses his life and his kingdom to the Israelites after refusing passage to them. Fearing that they will now overrun Moab—a sparsely settled land along the eastern rim of the Dead Sea and the lower Jordan River—Balak sends messengers to Balaam to appeal for help: "Come now, curse this people for me, since they are too mighty for me" (Numbers 22:6). Balaam is then visited by the angel of the Lord and realizes that no spell he casts can prevent the Israelites from achieving what almighty God has ordained for them. Instead of cursing them, Balaam blesses them and foretells the downfall of Balak: "a scepter shall rise out of Israel; it shall crush the forehead of Moab" (Numbers 24:17).

This favorable view of Balaam is contradicted elsewhere in Scripture, where he is charged with counseling the "daughters of Moab" to seduce Israelites, who then bow to pagan idols, inviting God's wrath, "and so the plague came among the congregation of the Lord" (Numbers 25:1; 31:16). Balaam reportedly dies at the hand of Israelites after joining their foes. These contradictory passages so puzzled biblical interpreters that some imagined there were two Balaams—a good wizard and his evil twin.

The angel of the Lord confronts Balaam in a painting by Italian artist Luca Giordano.

Light was shed on this mystery in March 1967, when a team led by Dutch archaeologist Henk Franken excavating at Tell Deir Alla, east of the Jordan River, uncovered fragments of a wall on which a text had been written in Aramaic in the eighth century B.C.E. Although the text was fragmentary, its import was clear and startling. It told of Balaam, "the man who was a seer of the gods," and how gods came to him in the night and warned him of a looming apocalypse, when the sun would cease to shine and darkness would descend on the world. Balaam may have used his powers to avert that catastrophe, but the conclusion of the story was lost. Linguists determined that its language was archaic and that it was probably composed several centuries before it was copied here. That meant that Balaam was a fabled soothsayer of great antiquity, known to Hebrews and pagans alike for his potent curses and blessings before the Bible was set down in writing. Two traditions evidently emerged: In one Balaam was seen as evil like the Egyptian wizards described in Genesis—but more dangerous than them because his powers were greater. The other tradition regarded all seers as powerless before God, who transformed the dreaded Balaam into his dutiful servant.

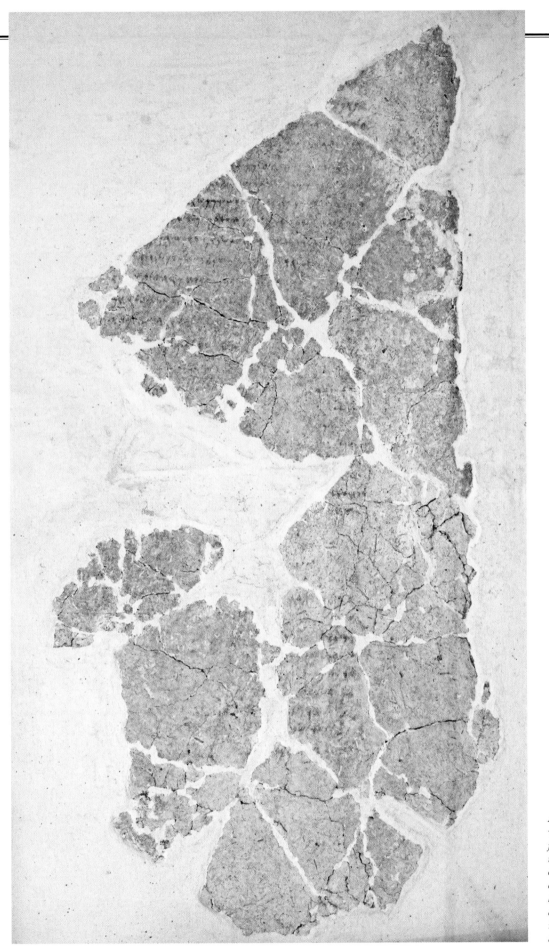

"Balaam, [son of Be]or,
the man who was a seer
of the gods. Lo! Gods
came to him in the night
[and spoke to] him . . .
'Sew shut the skies with
your thick cloud. There let
there be darkness.'"

*Archaeologists exca-
vating in the Trans-
jordan found this
nonbiblical account
of Balaam written
on a wall that may
have been part of
a school, shattered
in an earthquake
around 750* B.C.E.

THE DESTRUCTION OF JERICHO

"AND WHEN THEY MAKE A LONG BLAST WITH THE RAM'S HORN, AS SOON AS YOU HEAR THE SOUND OF THE TRUMPET, THEN ALL THE PEOPLE SHALL SHOUT WITH A GREAT SHOUT; AND THE WALL OF THE CITY WILL FALL DOWN FLAT."

JOSHUA 6:5

For more than a century, archaeologists have sought evidence confirming the stirring biblical account that invading Israelites led by Joshua brought down the walls of Jericho, located just west of the Jordan River near where it enters the Dead Sea. Systematic excavations in the 1950s, conducted by British archaeologist Kathleen Kenyon, revealed that the foundations of ancient Jericho—unearthed at Tell as Sultan, near the modern town of Jericho—were laid more than 10,000 years ago, making it one of the world's oldest settlements. The first city there, fortified with a massive stone tower (opposite) and walls six feet thick, collapsed around 6000 B.C.E., perhaps as a result of an earthquake. Subsequently, Jericho suffered many further shocks or assaults and was rebuilt at least 17 times. Kenyon dated the destruction of City IV, the last substantial ancient settlement here, to around 1550 B.C.E. That was far too early to fit any chronology proposed for the Exodus of Israelites from Egypt and their entry into Canaan. Invaders who arrived in later times would have found nothing at Jericho resembling the mighty stronghold described in the Bible, a city "great and fortified up to heaven" (Deuteronomy 9:1). If Kenyon was correct, then the story of Israelites bringing down the walls of Jericho with a great shout when they heard their priests blowing trumpets—shofars made from rams' horns—was a myth, inspired by ancient ruins associated in folklore with Joshua and his followers, who may have taken some other towns or cities in Canaan.

Not all scholars accepted Kenyon's interpretation of the archaeological evidence. Some have dated the destruction of City IV to around 1400 B.C.E. That would allow for the possibility that Jericho was attacked by Israelites who left Egypt in the 15th century B.C.E., during the early stages of Egypt's New Kingdom. But a conquest around 1400 is not supported by the Merneptah Stela

(see pp. 96-97), which implies that Israelites were present in Canaan around 1200 B.C.E. but had yet to establish a state or kingdom there. Furthermore, it conflicts with the biblical assertion that before Israelites fled Egypt they built the cities Pithom and Ramses, which could only have occurred around the time of Ramses II, in the 13th century B.C.E.

Another problem facing those seeking to verify the biblical story of Jericho scientifically is explaining how

the city fell to the Israelites. One proposed scenario is that the attack mounted by Joshua was preceded by a severe earthquake, which dammed up the Jordan, allowing the Israelites to cross over on dry ground, and so weakened the city's foundations that their thunderous shout was enough to bring down its walls. Like other efforts to rationalize wondrous events, however, that explanation ignores the core message of the Bible, which attributes the parting of the Jordan and the destruction of Jericho not to any natural cause but to God's miraculous power. As Joshua assures the Israelites who have crossed with him into Canaan: "For the Lord your God dried up the waters of the Jordan for you until you passed over . . . so that all the peoples of the earth may know that the hand of the Lord is mighty" (Joshua 4:23-24).

Excavations at Jericho uncovered the sturdy foundations of what may be the oldest continuously occupied city in the world and impressive artifacts. But no evidence has surfaced to confirm the biblical story of Jericho's destruction, which inspired the medieval depiction above.

"AND THEY AROSE AND WENT TOGETHER TO BEERSHEBA; AND ABRAHAM DWELT AT BEERSHEBA."

GENESIS 22:19

BEERSHEBA: WHERE ABRAHAM DWELLED

Among the sacred places reclaimed by Israelites in the biblical account of their conquest of Canaan was Beersheba, an oasis in the Negev fed by wells that sustained settlements here for thousands of years. Abraham himself dug a well there, it was said, and affirmed his right of occupancy by making a covenant with King Abimelech, who acknowledged Abraham's claim to the well (*beer* in Hebrew) by taking an oath *(shevua)*: "Therefore that place was called Beersheba, because there both of them swore an oath" (Genesis 21:31).

Like ancient Jericho, the biblical Beersheba was excavated at a mound located near the modern town bearing the same name (Beer Sheva). Archaeologists found evidence that people were living in this area as early as the fourth millennium B.C.E. But the oldest remaining structures unearthed at the mound date from around 1100 B.C.E., when Israelites were vying for control of Canaan. By the tenth century B.C.E., Beersheba was girded by a thick wall of mud bricks, set on a stone foundation. Guarding the southern frontier of the emerging kingdom of Israel, this outpost was well equipped to withstand a siege, with a well more than 60 feet deep.

Among the revealing discoveries here was a horned altar (right), found in fragments. This kind of altar, with a horn-shaped stone at each of its four corners, was used for sacrificial offerings both by those devoted to YHWH and by Canaanites who worshipped other gods. One theory is that those cornerstones originally symbolized the horns of Canaanite gods such as El and Baal, represented as bulls. Worshippers of YHWH preserved the basic shape of the ancient Canaanite altar, which lost its pagan associations for them. In Exodus, God commands Moses to build such an altar of acacia wood: "And you shall make horns for it on its four corners; its horns shall be of one piece with it, and you shall overlay it with bronze" (Exodus 27:1-2). People accused of crimes could obtain sanctuary, or immunity, by grasping the horns of the altar.

Authorities may have had the altar at Beersheba dismantled because it violated a commandment that no altar be built "of hewn stones; for if you wield your tool upon it you profane it" (Exodus 20:25). Not only were these stones hewn with a tool, but one of them was incised with the figure of a snake, defying the commandment that worshippers make no likeness "of anything that is in heaven above, or that is in the earth beneath" (Exodus 20:4). Perhaps the snake was meant to represent a serpent idol said to be the work of Moses, who was instructed to fashion that graven image by God after he sent snakes to punish wayward Israelites. Called Nehushtan, the bronze image became the focus of a cult that alarmed the devout King Hezekiah, who reigned around 700 B.C.E. Fearing that its worshippers were reverting to idolatry, he "broke in pieces the bronze serpent that Moses had made," and tore down altars like the one at Beersheba, insisting that sacrifices be made only by the high priest at the temple in Jerusalem (II Kings 18:4).

Excavations at Tel Beer Sheva (opposite) revealed the horned altar below, reconstructed from the disassembled stones. According to Genesis, Abraham's son Isaac built an altar here at Beersheba to honor the Lord.

"THEN JOSHUA WENT UP WITH ALL ISRAEL FROM EGLON
TO HEBRON; AND THEY ASSAULTED IT, AND TOOK IT,
AND SMOTE IT WITH THE EDGE OF THE SWORD."

JOSHUA 10:36-37

HEBRON:
RESTING PLACE OF THE PATRIARCHS

If Joshua indeed conquered Hebron and crushed the Canaanites who held that well-fortified city, as written, then he and his fellow Israelites were laying claim to hallowed ground. For this was the legendary burial place of the biblical patriarchs Abraham, Isaac, and Jacob, laid to rest here in the Cave of Machpelah along with their wives Sarah, Rebecca, and Leah. In the late first century B.C.E., King Herod the Great began work on a massive wall enclosing that sacred cave (opposite), which has long drawn Jewish, Christian, and Muslim pilgrims to Hebron. In recent times, archaeologists have delved deeper into the history of this holy city by excavating at a nearby mound, where ancient Hebron once stood. Their findings have shed some light on the question of whether the conquest of Canaan could have occurred as described in the Bible.

The walls of ancient Hebron date back to the third millennium B.C.E. and were built on a prodigious scale. The original city, surrounded by a stone rampart more than 20 feet thick, was destroyed around 2300 B.C.E. in a catastrophe of unknown origin. Several centuries later an imposing new city arose, with walls made of massive uncut boulders. Wrestling those ponderous stones into place was a herculean task and helped foster the legend that Hebron was inhabited by giants, referred to as the children of Anak. As related in the Bible, spies sent by Moses to reconnoiter Canaan before the Israelites entered that land returned with an alarming tale, reporting that the cities were "fortified and very large" and that the men were of "great stature," particularly the sons of Anak, who stood so tall that the Israelites were "like grasshoppers" in comparison to them (Numbers 13:28-33). All but two of the spies advised against invading Canaan—Joshua and a stalwart named Caleb from the tribe of Judah. Fittingly, it was to Caleb and his clan that Joshua later assigned Hebron after its conquest.

Excavations at Hebron indicate that the city suffered significant damage around 1200 B.C.E., a date that fits the proposed chronology for the conquest of Canaan by Israelites following their Exodus from Egypt during the reign of Ramses II. The archaeological evidence does not indicate who or what caused that damage, however, and it does not support the assertion in the Book of Joshua that Hebron was "utterly destroyed" along with "every person in it" (Joshua 10:37). If invading Israelites took the city at this time, they most likely did so as described in the Book of Judges, which portrays the campaign as less devastating. When Hebron was granted to Caleb, "he drove out from it the three sons of Anak" (Judges 1:20), suggesting that the occupants were routed rather than annihilated. By whatever means, the Canaanite stronghold of Hebron fell to Israelites and became their first capital before they captured Jerusalem under King David.

Jars like this one at left found at Hebron were marked with a seal designating them as "property of the king," indicating that the city served as a royal administrative center around the time of King Hezekiah, long before Herod the Great built a wall enshrining the Cave of Machpela (opposite).

"SO JOSEPH WENT AFTER HIS BROTHERS AND FOUND THEM AT
DOTHAN. . . . AND REUBEN SAID TO THEM, 'SHED NO BLOOD;
CAST HIM INTO THIS PIT HERE IN THE WILDERNESS.'"

GENESIS 37:17-22

DANGER AT DOTHAN

Manasseh and Ephraim
The tribes of Manasseh and Ephraim bore the names of Joseph's two sons. Ephraim was younger than Manasseh, but when their grandfather Jacob lay dying, he could no longer see and gave Ephraim priority by blessing him with his right hand while placing his left hand on Manasseh. Joseph asked Jacob to reverse the blessing but he refused, foreseeing that the "younger brother shall be greater" (Genesis 48:19). In fact, the tribe of Ephraim produced such prominent biblical figures as Joshua, Deborah, and Samuel.

As chronicled in the Book of Joshua, the Israelite conquest of Canaan proceeded from south to north, retracing ancient paths trod by the patriarchs celebrated in Genesis. When Joseph was a young man, for example, he left Hebron, where his father, Jacob, and forefathers Isaac and Abraham had sojourned, and went north to join his brothers, who found pasture for their flocks in the fertile Dothan Valley (opposite). That was a land of plenty compared to the drier country to the south, but it was also a dangerous place, for the valley served as a corridor for traders, troops, and other wayfarers who were not always to be trusted. It was here, according to Scripture, that Joseph's envious brothers cast him into a pit before selling him to Ishmaelites who dealt in slaves, among other commodities, and carried him in bondage to Egypt. Local tradition identifies that pit with a deep well at Dothan.

FOR THE TRIBE OF MANASSEH

The ancient town of Dothan—whose foundations were uncovered along with a profusion of pottery during excavations that began in the 1950s—lay between the cities of Shechem to the south and Beth Shean to the northeast, within the area allotted to the Israelite tribe of Manasseh, as described in Joshua. The tribe did not have complete possession, however, for "Canaanites persisted in dwelling in that land" (Joshua 17:12). Low-lying cities such as Beth Shean, near the Jordan River, remained Canaanite enclaves for some time while Israelites occupied the highlands, a pattern confirmed recently by archaeologists. This settlement pattern is reflected in the words of Joshua, who tells the tribes of Manasseh, Ephraim, and Joseph: "the hill country shall be yours, for though it is a forest, you shall clear it and possess it to its farthest borders" (Joshua 17:18). He promises the hill dwellers that they will "drive out the Canaanites, though they have chariots of iron and are strong." That was a slow process, however, and rival Canaanites were just one of the forces with whom Israelites would have to contend here in centuries to come.

A 14th-century C.E. fresco in the Collegiata church of San Gimignano, Italy (above, right), depicts the story of Joseph being thrown into the well at Dothan by his brothers.

That Dothan remained a dangerous place is suggested by the story of the Prophet Elisha, who lived there and played an inspirational role in a struggle that unfolded around the ninth century B.C.E. between the kingdoms of Israel and Aram, located in southern Syria and inhabited by people referred to in some versions of the Bible as Aramaeans and in other versions as Syrians. Hailed in Scripture as a miracle worker with extrasensory perception, who can hear the hostile plans made by the Aramaean king in his distant camp, Elisha is targeted by that ruler, who sends "horses and chariots and a great army" to surround Dothan at night (II Kings 6:14). Calling on the Lord to strike the Aramaeans blind, Elisha eludes capture and diverts his enemies to the city of Samaria, where they regain their sight only to be seized by the king of Israel and his forces. Like Joseph, who survives his ordeal at Dothan and later forgives his brothers and hosts them in Egypt, Elisha implores his king not to punish the captives: "You shall not slay them. . . . Set bread and water before them, that they may eat and drink and then go to their master" (II Kings 6:22).

An Egyptian sculptor portrayed this Philistine captive with his hands bound and a collar around his neck after those invading Sea Peoples were repelled near the mouth of the Nile River.

"AND THE PEOPLE OF ISRAEL AGAIN DID WHAT WAS EVIL IN THE SIGHT OF THE LORD; AND THE LORD GAVE THEM INTO THE HAND OF THE PHILISTINES FOR FORTY YEARS."

JUDGES 13:1

CONTENDING WITH THE PHILISTINES

During the 12th century B.C.E., a powerful new force entered the contest for Canaan, posing a formidable challenge to the disunited tribes of Israelites there, who had not yet formed a kingdom to secure their claim to the Promised Land. Known as the Philistines, those invaders were one branch of the marauding Sea Peoples who swept down from the north. Described in Scripture as coming "from the coastland of Caphtor" (Jeremiah 47:4), meaning most likely Crete or Cyprus, the Philistines may indeed have migrated from that vicinity, for as shown here their exquisitely painted pottery reflected Mycenaean artistic traditions that spread from mainland Greece to islands around the Aegean Sea. After being repulsed by the Egyptians, who captured some Philistines and portrayed them in stone (opposite), they occupied the coast of Canaan and seized five cities there: Ekron, Ashkelon, Ashdod, Gath, and Gaza. Better organized than the Israelites, they formed a confederacy called Philistia and had such a profound impact on Canaan that it was known to posterity as the land of the Philistines, or Palestine.

Among the Israelites defeated or displaced by the invading Philistines were the Danites, or people belonging to the tribe of Dan, who were especially vulnerable because their settlements lay near the coast. Significantly, Samson—hailed for standing up to the Philistines when they appeared unstoppable—is identified in Judges as a Danite, born to a woman who is barren but gives birth through divine intervention. Although the Lord has recently punished Israelites for their sins by delivering them "into the hands of the Philistines," he brings Samson into the world to give them hope of redemption. Before the boy is born, his mother is instructed by the angel of the Lord never to shave his head, for he is destined to become a Nazirite, or one who dedicates himself to the Lord by taking vows that include leaving his hair uncropped. Not until the end of his days, however, when he brings down a pagan temple on the heads of his Philistine captors at the cost of his own life, does Samson truly emerge as a holy man, sacrificing all for the Lord and his people. Before then, he is subject to worldly temptations, including the attractions of Philistine women, against whom his parents warn him: "Is there not a woman among the daughters of your kinsmen, or among all our people, that you must go to take a wife from the uncircumcised Philistines?" (Judges 14:3). The danger of consorting with uncircumcised heathens who know nothing of YHWH and his laws becomes all too clear when Samson's scheming Philistine wife Delilah shaves his head, leaving him weak until his hair begins to grow back in captivity and he destroys his foes.

The story of Samson and Delilah reflects an era when Israelites were hard-pressed to contend with the expansive Philistines, who were stronger not only politically but also technologically, thanks to their mastery of ironworking, which gave them tools and weapons that were sturdier than those made of bronze. That the Philistines helped introduce the Iron Age in Canaan is suggested by archaeological evidence and by a biblical passage describing conditions during the reign of King Saul, around 1000 B.C.E., which states that there was "no smith to be found throughout all the land of Israel . . . but every one of the Israelites went down to the Philistines to sharpen his plowshare" (I Samuel 13:19-20). Israelites did not lag too far behind the rival Philistines, however, in mastering ironworking. One of the benefits they reaped as their kingdom coalesced under David and Solomon was improved trade with regions such as Asia Minor, a major source of iron ore. Well equipped with iron weapons to challenge the Philistines and other foes, they had no need to combat them in the primitive manner of their folk hero Samson, who, it was said, once slew a thousand men with the jawbone of an ass.

Philistines preserved their ancestral traditions by continuing to craft Mycenaean-style pots like this one after they occupied Canaan.

EKRON: WHERE PHILISTINE CULTURE ENDURED

"THERE ARE FIVE RULERS OF THE PHILISTINES, THOSE OF GAZA, ASHDOD, ASHKELON, GATH, AND EKRON."

JOSHUA 13:3

In 1996, archaeologists excavating Tel Miqne, a mound some 20 miles west of Jerusalem, found written confirmation that it was the Philistine city of Ekron—an inscription identifying Ikausu, "ruler of Ekron," as the builder of a temple erected there around 700 B.C.E. The name Ikausu was of Aegean origin, and the deity to whom he dedicated the temple was addressed as "his lady," a form of address used for goddesses in ancient Greece. As noted by Seymour Gitin, co-director of this project with Trude Dothan, the inscription proved that the people of Ekron "retained their ethnic identity as Philistines" long after they left the Aegean islands and invaded Canaan. Philistine culture did not decline after Ekron and the other four cities named in the Bible came under assault by Israelites or Egyptians in the tenth century B.C.E. Ekron revived in the eighth century B.C.E. under Assyrian control and became a major producer of olive oil, extracted in presses using stone weights. Ikausu paid tribute to his Assyrian overlords but honored Philistine traditions until Babylonians destroyed Ekron in 603 B.C.E., a disaster seen in the Bible as ordained by God: "I will turn my hand against Ekron; and the remnant of the Philistines shall perish" (Amos 1:8).

The press below, used to extract olive oil at Ekron, was much like those employed by Israelites and Judeans in Canaan, from whom Philistines probably acquired the technology.

*"The temple which he built, 'kysh [Achish, Ikausu] son of Padi,
Ysd son of Ada, son of Ya'ir, ruler of Ekron,
For Ptgyh his lady. May she bless him, and
protect him, and prolong his days, and bless
his land."*

Discovered at Ekron, this inscription was the first found at a biblical site to identify the place by name. Lacking such written proof, archaeologists have been unable to identify some sites positively even after decades of work.

ASHKELON BY THE SEA

Like Gaza and Ekron, Ashkelon was a Canaanite city that was conquered by the Philistines in the 12th century B.C.E. and became a thorn in the side of the emerging kingdom of Israel. Devout Israelites made little distinction between the cults of the Philistines and those of the Canaanites they displaced, who worshipped idols like the sacred calf shown below, discovered at Ashkelon alongside a ceramic cowshed that housed the image. Both groups were denounced in the Bible as heathens who had to be defeated if God's promise to the Israelites was to be fulfilled. No Philistine stronghold was more formidable than Ashkelon, which profited from maritime trade as well as traffic on a coastal road running northward from Egypt along the Mediterranean. Protected by a wall nearly 50 feet high and 80 feet wide, this was Philistia's chief seaport and may have been its largest city.

Ashkelon is mentioned several times in the Bible, notably in the impassioned lament of David following the death of King Saul and his son Jonathan, defeated by Philistines in battle on Mount Gilboa: "How are the mighty fallen! Tell it not in Gath, publish it not in the streets of Ashkelon; lest the daughters of the Philistines rejoice, lest the daughters of the uncircumcised exult" (II Samuel 1:19-20). As king of Israel, David would avenge that defeat and scourge the Philistines, but that reversal of fortune would not bring an end to mighty Ashkelon. As late as the seventh century B.C.E. the prophets Jeremiah and Zephaniah were denouncing it as a godforsaken place and forecasting its utter desolation, a fate seemingly fulfilled when conquering Babylonians razed Ashkelon shortly before they destroyed Ekron.

Unlike Ekron, however, which never regained its stature as a major city after that devastating blow, Ashkelon rose from the ashes to become one of Palestine's leading ports and trading centers during the Roman conquest. It was the birthplace of Herod the Great and remained a prosperous and privileged place, immune to the tumult that ravaged other cities in the region, until the Middle Ages, when it became caught up in the holy war between Christian crusaders and the Muslim leader Saladin, who reluctantly ordered it leveled. "I would rather be bereaved of all my children than destroy a single stone of it," he remarked by one account. "But if God foreordained anything, it is bound to be carried out."

Ashkelon's favorable location along land and maritime trade routes (opposite) made it wealthy in ancient times—and a treasure trove for modern archaeologists, who found pots shipped here from Cyprus and Greece and so many cult objects of Egyptian design that Lawrence Stager of Harvard University, director of excavations at Ashkelon, concluded that it was "home to a permanent Egyptian enclave with its own sanctuary."

Sacred Cows

Found at Ashkelon, the idol shown here beside its ceramic shed was not exactly a golden calf. Measuring barely four inches high, it was made of bronze and plated with silver. But the sacred nature of this figurine is indicated by the fact that it was found amid the remains of a Canaanite temple, built in the 16th century B.C.E. Idols like this one, representing cows or bulls, were associated with various Canaanite gods and goddesses, including the supreme deity El (Lord). They may have been regarded as images of those gods or as props or pedestals for them. That some Israelites clung to the Canaanite custom of revering such idols is indicated by archaeological findings—including a bull figurine found in Samaria and dated to the early days of Israelite occupation there—and by biblical passages, including the story of the golden calf fashioned by Aaron at Mount Sinai. In the eighth century B.C.E., the

Prophet Hosea denounced Israelites who were crafting "molten images, idols skillfully made of their silver," which they kissed and offered sacrifices (Hosea 13:2). So esteemed were cows in Canaan that even devout Jews who knew that bowing to a golden calf was sacrilege atoned for their sins by sacrificing a live calf to the Lord at a horned altar, as Aaron did to show repentance: "So Aaron drew near to the altar, and killed the calf of the sin offering . . . . and he dipped his finger in the blood and put it on the horns of the altar" (Leviticus 9:8-9).

"YOUR BORDERS ARE IN THE HEART OF THE
SEAS; YOUR BUILDERS MADE PERFECT YOUR
BEAUTY. . . . THEY TOOK A CEDAR FROM
LEBANON TO MAKE A MAST FOR YOU."

EZEKIEL 27:4-5

THE PHOENICIANS

U nlike the Philistines, the Phoenicians dwelling along the coast of Lebanon sought to avoid hostilities with Israelites and their rulers in Canaan. Great seafarers, who used the prized cedars of Lebanon to build ships like the galley pictured at right and exported timber and other resources to distant lands, Phoenicians expanded their power and influence through trade and colonization rather than through conquest. They largely escaped devastation by the Sea Peoples and emerged as one of the most prosperous and accomplished societies in the Mediterranean world. Their city-states, including the bustling ports of Tyre, Sidon, and Byblos, were independent, and each had its own ruler. According to Scripture, King Hiram of Tyre made a diplomatic gesture to David shortly after he became king of Israel by sending him "cedar trees, also carpenters and masons who built David a house" (II Samuel 5:11). Relations between the two rulers may have been strained when King David's forces later advanced up the Mediterranean coast and conquered the Phoenician port of Dor, south of Tyre, as confirmed by recent excavations at that site, a mound called Tel Dor near modern-day Haifa. But King Hiram continued to seek an accommodation with the expansive Israelites by reaching out to David's son and successor, Solomon, who asked Hiram to send cedars of Lebanon for the great temple he built in Jerusalem: "And there was peace between Hiram and Solomon; and the two of them made a treaty" (I Kings 5:12).

Despite that alliance, Ezekiel and other prophets later denounced the Phoenicians for abandoning Jerusalem to its fate when the city was attacked by Babylonians and for carrying captive Jews into bondage aboard their ships. Their chief failing, in Ezekiel's judgment, was the sin of pride: "Your heart has become proud in your wealth." Because Phoenicians considered themselves as wise as gods, he added, YHWH would send troops against them from "the most terrible of the nations; and they shall draw their swords against the beauty of your wisdom and defile your splendor" (Ezekiel 28:5-7). The Phoenicians indeed underwent fierce trials. Tyre was besieged by Babylonian forces and later shattered by Alexander the Great. By then, however, Phoenician colonies were thriving, including mighty Carthage, which vied with Rome for mastery of the Mediterranean. The Phoenicians' greatest legacy, however, was the phonetic alphabet.

Avid merchants and seafarers, Phoenicians spanned the Mediterranean in their galleys and spread their phonetic alphabet.

The Alphabet

T he Phoenician arrowhead at left—made in the 11th century B.C.E. and inscribed with the name of its owner, "Ada, son of Bala"—testifies to an invention that did more to break down barriers than any weapon devised in ancient times: the phonetic alphabet. Earlier scripts such as cuneiform and hieroglyphs were derived from pictographs (representing objects or concepts pictorially) and consisted of hundreds of characters, which meant that only priests or scribes were able to read or write. Although the Egyptians incorporated into their writing system some phonetic symbols, based on sounds in the spoken language, the first fully phonetic alphabets developed only in lands to the northeast, including the Sinai Peninsula, Canaan, Aram (in southern Syria), and coastal Lebanon, home of the Phoenicians. Consisting of only two dozen or so characters, those alphabets could be mastered without formal schooling and made it possible for larger segments of the population to read and write. Hebrew was akin to Phoenician, and the Hebrew alphabet may have evolved from the Phoenician alphabet. This script was later adopted in modified form by the Greeks and helped promote literacy and the wisdom of classical civilization.

This expressive terra-cotta mask suggests that Phoenicians were forerunners of the Greeks both artistically and linguistically.

NEW LINGUA FRANCA

"PRAY, SPEAK TO YOUR SERVANTS IN THE ARAMAIC LANGUAGE, FOR WE UNDERSTAND IT; DO NOT SPEAK TO US IN THE LANGUAGE OF JUDAH WITHIN THE HEARING OF THE PEOPLE WHO ARE ON THE WALL."

II KINGS 18:26

Who Were the Judeans? Originally, the Judeans were one of 12 Israelite tribes. They became closely identified with the kingdom of Israel under King David. That kingdom later divided: The northern kingdom of Israel came to an end when conquered by the Assyrians, but the southern kingdom of Judah persisted until shattered by Babylonians. The kingdom revived under the Maccabees, a priestly family whose Judean kingdom, embracing Jerusalem, became synonymous with Judaism.

No neighboring group with whom Israelites interacted as they laid claim to Canaan, not even the Phoenicians, had a greater impact on their language and culture in the long run than the Aramaeans. Described in Genesis as a kindred people to the Hebrews descended from Abraham's brother Nahor, they ranged widely across the ancient Near East. Some Aramaean tribes settled in Mesopotamia, where they warred with the Assyrians, who ultimately defeated them but adopted the Aramaic language. Others occupied southern Syria and made Damascus their capital. Those people, referred to in the Bible as Aramaeans or Syrians, clashed repeatedly with the Israelites. King David, it was written, "put garrisons in Aram of Damascus; and the Syrians became servants to David and brought tribute" (II Samuel 8:6). Those Aramaeans later regained independence, however, and remained a powerful force in the region until Assyrians conquered

Portrayed on a stela found near Damascus, this Aramaean ruler who lived around 800 B.C.E. holds a spear and a tulip, perhaps symbolizing his readiness to fight foes and make peace with others.

Damascus in the eighth century B.C.E. and went on to threaten the Judeans in Jerusalem. Officials there had mastered Aramaic for diplomatic purposes and used it to communicate with Assyrians sent to demand their surrender. Fearing that the surrender talks would demoralize common Judeans, who knew only Hebrew, those officials asked the Assyrian emissaries to speak Aramaic and not use "the language of Judah" within the hearing of the people of Jerusalem, who were waiting anxiously atop the wall.

In time, Judeans found themselves at the mercy of one imperial power after another, including the Babylonians and the Persians, who made Aramaic the official language of their vast empire and allowed people exiled from Judah by the Babylonians to return there.

According to the Book of Ezra, a dispute arose between those repatriated exiles and inhabitants who opposed their efforts to rebuild the temple in Jerusalem and wrote a letter in Aramaic to King Artaxerxes

"Greetings to Micalah from Jedaniah. Now, lo I sent [word] to you yesterday in the name of Hodaviah son of Zechariah saying 'Come this day' but you did not come. Into the hand my daughters send [word] to me."

45035

The message in Aramaic on the ostracon at left was written by an Aramaean or Judean soldier of the Persian army about 475 B.C.E., garrisoned in Aswan and Elephantine in Egypt, where the soldiers lived with their families.

of Persia, claiming that those Jews were rebellious by nature and if allowed to have their way would not pay him "tribute, custom, or toll" (Ezra 4:13). That letter caused the king to order work on the temple suspended, demonstrating the power of the written word and the importance of the Aramaic language in the sprawling, multilingual Persian domain. The empire later fell to Alexander the Great and his generals and ultimately passed to the Romans.

The lesson was not lost on Jews, many of whom learned Aramaic and came to favor it over their ancestral language, Hebrew. Indeed, parts of the Hebrew Bible were written in Aramaic. Among those fluent in both languages was Jesus of Nazareth, who according to Scripture cried out in Aramaic before he died on the cross: " '*Elo-i, Elo-i, la'ma sabach-tha'ni?*' which means, 'My God, my God, why hast thou forsaken me?' " (Mark 15:34; Matthew 27:46).

chapter 4

THE UNITED MONARCHY
Kingdom of David and Solomon

THE UNITED MONARCHY

The Israelites prospered in Canaan. They cultivated great olive groves, vineyards, and orchards, and raised flocks of sheep, goats, and cattle. The people were growing in numbers, too. But so were the hostile nations who hemmed them in on all sides. Only by uniting against their enemies, they realized, would Israel be able to survive.

In the west, one of those enemies, the Philistines, seemed ever ready to strike. Around the year 1050 B.C.E., they came storming out of Aphek, killing some 4,000 Israelite warriors. According to the Book of I Samuel, they went on to destroy the shrine at Shiloh and carry off the Ark of the Covenant to Ashdod. There, they triumphantly paraded the ark through the streets and put it on display in the Temple of Dagon. Only when the statue of Dagon crashed to the ground, and a plague ravaged Ashdod, did the Philistines return the ark to the Israelites.

To the east, another threat emerged. From the heights above the Jordan River Valley, Nahash, fearsome king of the Ammonites, descended on Jabesh-gilead, laying siege to the city and threatening to gouge out the right eye of every one of the Israelite inhabitants. In response to the city's cry for help, a young warrior named Saul mobilized troops from all across Israel and marched on Jabesh. Encircling the besiegers, Saul led a surprise dawn attack and slaughtered or scattered the Ammonites by midday. In the aftermath, the Prophet Samuel anointed Saul to rule over all Israel.

Israel's new ruler soon had to move across Canaan to confront the Philistines. After early successes, the Israelites got bogged down, however, and the war began to drag on. Saul's

> "HAS NOT THE LORD ANOINTED YOU TO BE PRINCE OVER HIS PEOPLE ISRAEL? AND YOU SHALL REIGN OVER THE PEOPLE OF THE LORD AND YOU WILL SAVE THEM FROM THE HAND OF THEIR ENEMIES ROUND ABOUT."
>
> I SAMUEL 10:1

mood darkened. Eventually, the Philistines went on the offensive, gathering for battle in a valley west of Bethlehem. There they unveiled a new champion, a giant named Goliath, who strode forward to challenge any Israelite to single combat. Only one man would take him on—a boy, in fact, a young shepherd who had recently become Saul's armor-bearer: David, son of Jesse.

In the account in I Samuel, David boldly confronts the Philistine champion, who stands fully clad in armor, wielding an immense bronze javelin. Carrying only a slingshot, the shepherd boy approaches—and hurls a stone that hits the giant in the forehead and kills him. Then David takes Goliath's own sword and cuts off his head, and the Philistines flee.

A grateful King Saul puts David in charge of his army and heaps praise on the young warrior. For a time, all is well. But as David's popularity rises among the people, Saul sinks into jealousy and his thoughts turn murderous. To save himself, David flees to the land of the Philistines, Saul's men in pursuit. Meanwhile, the Philistines launch another invasion of Israel, sweeping the army of Saul before them. The king himself is badly wounded in the battle and in despair, according to one account, falls upon his own sword (I Chronicles 10:3-6).

With the Israelites in full retreat across the Jordan River, all of Israel—leaderless, beaten, and divided—lies open to the Philistines. Once again, David steps forward. Dismissing the claims of Saul's remaining male offspring, Ishbaal, he rallies "all the tribes of Israel" at Hebron, where they pledge their loyalty to him. "We are your bone and flesh," they declare (II Samuel 5:1). The shepherd boy becomes the shepherd of Israel, king of a united kingdom.

Previous pages: "David Playing the Harp for King Saul" by (Sir Jacob) Jehuda Epstein
Opposite: A drinking cup shaped like a goat's head

Before moving against the Philistines, David moves to make sure that all the tribes of Israel are truly behind him. If they are a united people, they will need a real capital—a seat of government for Israel and a center for the tribes' common worship of the God of Abraham, Isaac, and Jacob. To be acceptable to all, it would have to be centrally located and in neutral territory. For his new capital, David selects the stronghold of the Jebusites—Jerusalem.

Strategically positioned, Jerusalem sat at the crossroads between Jericho in the east and the Mediterranean in the west, and along the main roads connecting north and south, astride the traditional boundary between Judah and the northern tribes. But it was also perched securely on a high ridge, and when David marched his troops there they had to fight their way in. Word of his conquest soon reached the Philistines. Immediately, they dispatched an army to dislodge the Israelites. But David and his men lay waiting for them and crushed the Philistines, driving them back toward the coast.

With the enemy routed, the Israelites set about building their capital, henceforth known as the City of David. The Ark of the Covenant is brought there, and David sends for architects, builders, and precious cedar wood from Lebanon to construct his palace. Meanwhile, Israel's army confronts the threats to the nation's other borders—defeating Aram-Damascus (Syria) in the north, Ammon and Moab (Transjordan) in the east, and Edom (the Negev) in the south. By the early tenth century B.C.E., the nation's frontiers were secure.

Things on the domestic and family front, however, were less secure. To consolidate his power, David had taken a bride from each of the 12 tribes of Israel and also from neighboring lands. Perhaps not surprisingly, the House of David was wracked by jealousies and intrigue, and the great achievements in his public life are mirrored by tragedies and turmoil in his private life, including the death of several of his sons. In his waning years, David's heirs jockey for supremacy, each attracting the support of various factions. His oldest surviving male offspring, Adonijah, seemed to favor restoring power to each of the tribes, thus

Wildflowers bloom along the shores of the Sea of Galilee, deep in the Jordan Great Rift Valley. At 685 feet below sea level, the Sea of Galilee is the lowest freshwater lake on Earth.

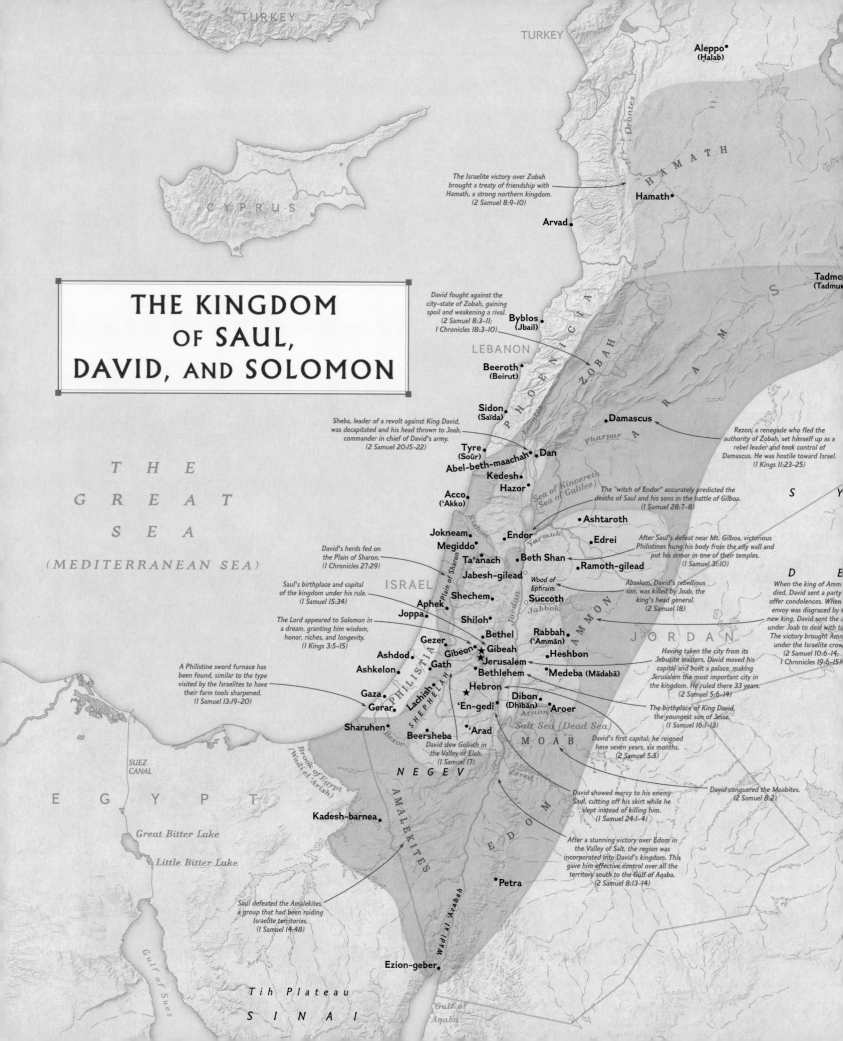

THE KINGDOM OF SAUL, DAVID, AND SOLOMON

TURKEY

TURKEY

Aleppo• (Halab)

CYPRUS

The Israelite victory over Zobah brought a treaty of friendship with Hamath, a strong northern kingdom. (2 Samuel 8:9-10)

Hamath•

Arvad•

Tadmo (Tadmu

David fought against the city-state of Zobah, gaining spoil and weakening a rival. (2 Samuel 8:3-11; 1 Chronicles 18:3-10)

Byblos• (Jbail)

LEBANON

Beeroth• (Beirut)

Damascus•

Rezon, a renegade who fled the authority of Zobah, set himself up as a rebel leader and took control of Damascus. He was hostile toward Israel. (1 Kings 11:23-25)

Sidon• (Saïda)

Sheba, leader of a revolt against King David, was decapitated and his head thrown to Joab, commander in chief of David's army. (2 Samuel 20:15-22)

Tyre• (Soûr)

Abel-beth-maachah• Dan•

Kedesh•

Hazor•

Acco• ('Akko)

The "witch of Endor" accurately predicted the deaths of Saul and his sons in the battle of Gilboa. (1 Samuel 28:7-8)

S Y

THE GREAT SEA

(MEDITERRANEAN SEA)

Ashtaroth•

Jokneam•

Megiddo•

Endor•

Edrei•

David's herds fed on the Plain of Sharon. (1 Chronicles 27:29)

Ta'anach•

Beth Shan•

Ramoth-gilead•

After Saul's defeat near Mt. Gilboa, victorious Philistines hung his body from the city wall and put his armor in one of their temples. (1 Samuel 31:10)

D E

Saul's birthplace and capital of the kingdom under his rule. (1 Samuel 15:34)

ISRAEL

Jabesh-gilead○

Wood of Ephraim

Absalom, David's rebellious son, was killed by Joab, the king's head general. (2 Samuel 18)

When the king of Amm died, David sent a party offer condolences. When envoy was disgraced by new king, David sent the under Joab to deal with t The victory brought Amm under the Israelite crow (2 Samuel 10:6-14; 1 Chronicles 19:6-15

Aphek•

Shechem•

The Lord appeared to Solomon in a dream, granting him wisdom, honor, riches, and longevity. (1 Kings 3:5-15)

Joppa•

Shiloh•

Succoth•

Bethel•

Rabbah• ('Ammān)

JORDAN

Gezer•

Gibeon• ★Gibeah

A Philistine sword furnace has been found, similar to the type visited by the Israelites to have their farm tools sharpened. (1 Samuel 13:19-20)

Ashdod•

Gath•

Heshbon•

★Jerusalem

Ashkelon•

Bethlehem•

Medeba (Mādabā)•

Having taken the city from its Jebusite masters, David moved his capital and built a palace, making Jerusalem the most important city in the kingdom. He ruled there 33 years. (2 Samuel 5:6-14)

Gaza•

Hebron★

Dibon• (Dhibān)

Gerar•

'En-gedi•

Aroer•

The birthplace of King David, the youngest son of Jesse. (1 Samuel 16:1-13)

Sharuhen•

Beersheba•

'Arad•

Salt Sea (Dead Sea)

MOAB

David's first capital; he reigned here seven years, six months. (2 Samuel 5:5)

David slew Goliath in the Valley of Elah. (1 Samuel 17)

NEGEV

David conquered the Moabites. (2 Samuel 8:2)

David showed mercy to his enemy Saul, cutting off his skirt while he slept instead of killing him. (1 Samuel 24:1-4)

SUEZ CANAL

EGYPT

Kadesh-barnea•

Great Bitter Lake

Little Bitter Lake

AMALEKITES

EDOM

After a stunning victory over Edom in the Valley of Salt, the region was incorporated into David's kingdom. This gave him effective control over all the territory south to the Gulf of Aqaba. (2 Samuel 8:13-14)

Petra•

Saul defeated the Amalekites, a group that had been raiding Israelite territories. (1 Samuel 14:48)

Gulf of Suez

Ezion-geber•

Tih Plateau

SINAI

Gulf of Aqaba

PHOENICIA ZOBAH A R A M

Sea of Kinnereth (Sea of Galilee)

Kishon

Leontes

Orontes

Pharpar

Yarmuk

Jordan

Jabbok

AMMON

PHILISTIA

SHEPHELAH

Plain of Sharon

Besor

Brook of Egypt (Wadi el-'Arish)

Zered

Arnon

Wadi al-'Arabah

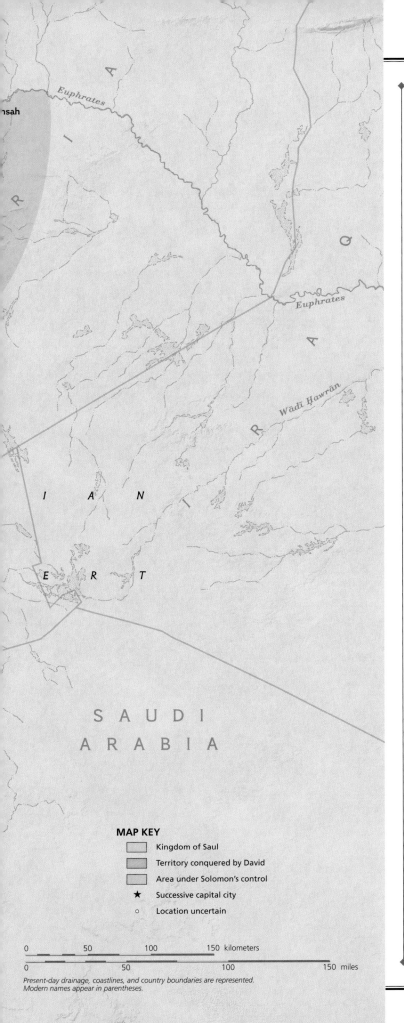

effectively fissuring David's young kingdom. Before his death in about 960 B.C.E., David anoints as his successor Solomon, the son of his beloved wife Bathsheba.

Educated and urbane, Solomon was very different from his passionate and impetuous father. But he, too, believed strongly in a united and centralized monarchy, and soon after ascending the throne moved decisively to tighten his grip on power. He eliminated the enduring threat of Adonijah, putting him and his chief backers to the sword and banishing his remaining supporters.

To keep his kingdom, the new king would need much wisdom, a trait for which Solomon—like King Hammurabi in Abraham's days—is most associated. In addition to being credited with writing the Book of Proverbs, Solomon is said to have composed some 3,000 other wise and philosophical sayings. And like the great Babylonian ruler, Solomon was also an accomplished builder.

According to biblical accounts, Solomon did not launch military campaigns to expand the kingdom given to him by his father. He preferred to secure what he held through marriage alliances with princesses from neighboring and vassal powers and through trade with neighbors rather than warfare. Instead of increasing the size of the kingdom, he chose to adorn it with grand building projects, financed by the extraordinary wealth generated through trade. The most elaborate was a permanent sanctuary for the Ark of the Covenant. Known as Solomon's Temple, or the First Temple, it was the crowning glory of Jerusalem.

In Solomon's waning years, the seeds of decline were already evident. The northern tribes were increasingly restless, resentful of what they saw as the privileges enjoyed by the southern tribe of Judah—and, perhaps, by the king's Asiatic-style harem, where the worship of foreign deities had always continued. For according to I Kings 11:4, "As Solomon grew old, his wives turned his heart after other gods, and his heart was not fully devoted to the Lord his God, as the heart of David his father had been." With the death of Solomon around 930 B.C.E., the tribal fault lines would deepen and the kingdom split apart. Israel's golden age would be no more.

The map (left) shows key events in the lives of Saul, David, and Solomon and the extent of the kingdom of Israel during their reigns.

MAP KEY

Kingdom of Saul
Territory conquered by David
Area under Solomon's control
★ Successive capital city
○ Location uncertain

0   50   100   150 kilometers
0   50   100   150 miles

*Present-day drainage, coastlines, and country boundaries are represented.
Modern names appear in parentheses.*

"BUT THE PEOPLE REFUSED TO LISTEN TO THE VOICE
OF SAMUEL; AND THEY SAID, 'NO! BUT WE WILL HAVE
A KING OVER US, THAT WE ALSO MAY BE LIKE ALL
THE NATIONS, AND THAT OUR KING MAY GOVERN US
AND GO OUT BEFORE US AND FIGHT OUR BATTLES.'"

I SAMUEL 8:19-20

THE MONARCHY

Before the Prophet Samuel anointed Saul as king, the Israelites were little more than a loose confederation of tribes, ruled over by judges and coming together only at times of dire threat to face a common enemy. In the Philistines, Israel faced a deadly enemy and a threat of existential proportions.

The Israelites had always resisted monarchy. A king, they believed, would pose a challenge to the authority of God, especially the kind of supposedly divine king that ruled in Egypt and in other neighboring nations. God alone would rule over Israel, through his servants the judges. These were prophets and priests, like Samuel, and also military and political leaders. Samson was a judge, as were Deborah and Gideon. Their role, under the direction of God, was to redeem Israel at times of crisis, and thus they were referred to as "saviors" (*moshia* in Hebrew).

By the beginning of the first millennium B.C.E., however, when the Israelites faced annihilation at the hands of the Philistines, they desperately sought a savior of more royal proportions. With Samuel's anointing of Saul, the office of the judge in Israel ended and the era of monarchy began. The artifacts on this and the following pages are a sampling of objects from royal Israel.

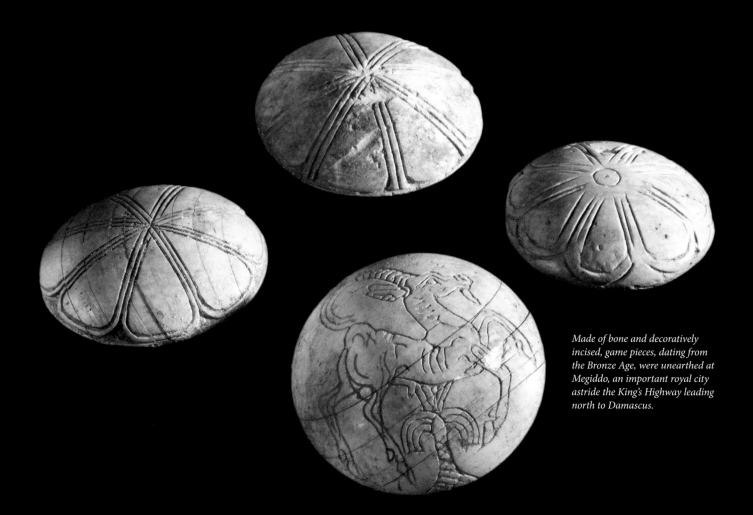

Made of bone and decoratively incised, game pieces, dating from the Bronze Age, were unearthed at Megiddo, an important royal city astride the King's Highway leading north to Damascus.

This bronze tripod and vessels from Megiddo date to around 900 B.C.E., close to the time of King Solomon, when the city was prosperous. They were probably used for ceremonial purposes.

This bluestone vessel, decorated with gold leaf, dates to the Late Bronze Age, and was found in Megiddo.

The incense stand above, in the form of a shrine and decorated with female figures sitting at the window, dates to 1200-1000 B.C.E.

Seven inches tall and amply proportioned, these clay figures from Lachish likely represent a Canaanite fertility goddess from the seventh century B.C.E.

The ivory carving (below) was found at Megiddo. It shows an Israelite king—or perhaps an Egyptian pharaoh—seated on a sphinx-adorned throne.

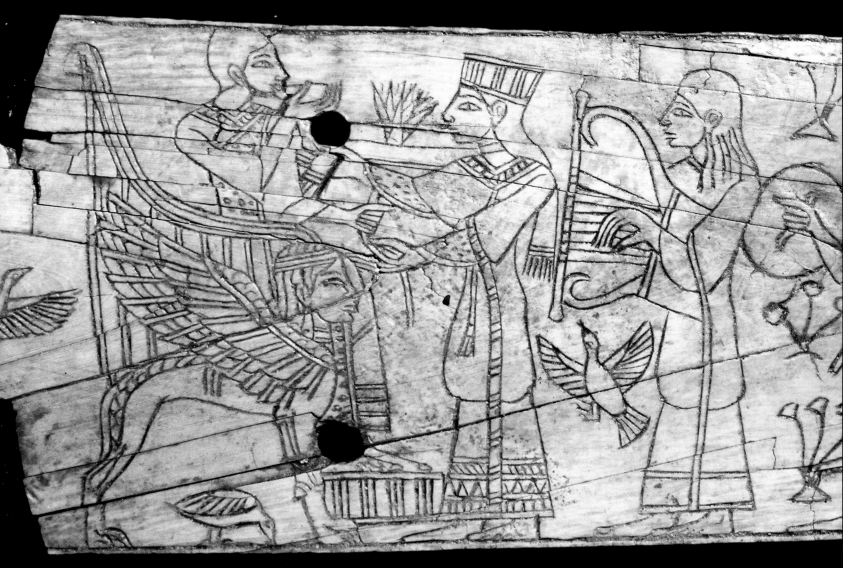

SAMUEL'S TOMB

At various times in history, key events have taken place at the hill of Nebi Samwil. It was from here, on the morning of June 7, 1099, that the Christian knights of the First Crusade to the Holy Land saw the city of Jerusalem for the first time, at the end of three long years of bloody fighting. There they built a mighty fortress to protect Jerusalem from Muslim raids from the north. Since that time, Jerusalem-bound pilgrims have begun their final approach to the city from here, walking the last three miles after spending the night at a hostel on what the crusaders called Mount Joy. Today a mosque stands on the site of a church that once took shelter within the crusader fortress. A cave beneath the mosque is the traditional burial place of the Prophet Samuel, making it a place revered by Jews, Christians, and Muslims alike.

One other momentous event is linked with Nebi Samwil and with the life of Samuel. For it was here, in his capacity as the reigning judge over Israel, Samuel is said to have proclaimed Saul as Israel's first king. Up until this point, the Israelites had never had a royal ruler. But now the people were demanding a king like the neighboring peoples, someone who would protect them from their enemies. Samuel resisted, believing that God would be their protection. Relenting only when instructed to do so by God, Samuel anointed the young Saul with oil and declared him king of the Israelites. At this, the judgeship—rule over Israel by a religious leader—came to an end and the monarchy began.

Israeli excavations at Nebi Samwil began in the early 1990s and have uncovered artifacts from throughout its long history. Most spectacular are the remains of the crusader fortress and the building complex that lay outside its walls. A cave beneath the mosque is said to hold the tomb of Samuel, whose bones had been taken from the Holy Land to the city of Chalcedon in Asia Minor during Byzantine times.

> "THEN SAMUEL TOOK A VIAL OF OIL AND POURED IT ON HIS HEAD, AND KISSED HIM AND SAID, 'HAS NOT THE LORD ANOINTED YOU TO BE PRINCE OVER HIS PEOPLE ISRAEL?'"
>
> I SAMUEL 10:1

A mosque sits amid the archaeological ruins at Nebi Samwil (right), said to be the site where the prophet Samuel crowned Saul as the first king of Israel. The hill, which provides a view of Jerusalem just eight miles to the southeast, is also the traditional burial place of the prophet.

"And Joab, the son of Zeruiah, and the servants of David, went out and met them at the pool of Gibeon."

II Samuel 2:13

THE POOL OF GIBEON

Another hill just to the north of Jerusalem and spiked with ancient ruins is El Jib, said to be the site of ancient Gibeon. It was at Gibeon, during Joshua's conquest of Canaan, that the Hebrews routed the forces of King Adonizedek of Jerusalem. Chapter 10 of the Book of Joshua tells how the enemy troops retreated before Joshua's men, plunging down into the valley of Aijalon. As darkness began to fall, Joshua feared that the fleeing soldiers would escape. So he prayed for the sun to stand still over Gibeon, and when it did, the Hebrews proceeded to finish off Adonizedek's soldiers.

Digging Begins

An American team began digging here in the late 1950s, financed by the University of Pennsylvania Museum and the Church Divinity School of the Pacific, and unearthed fortifications, dwellings, and caves. But they also found the rim of a pool fully 36 feet in diameter. Calling in the help of a hundred locals, they began to dig down, working two shifts a day to haul out dirt and debris. Soon they had uncovered an elaborate water cistern (opposite) sunk 82 feet into the ground. A spiral staircase with 79 steps leads all the way down to the bottom of the well.

The ancient water system must have required a monumental, multiyear mobilization of labor. Scholars speculate that it may be the pool mentioned in the Book of II Samuel. In chapter 2, David's warriors, led by his commander Joab, defeated Saul's men at the pool: "And they caught every one his fellow by the head, and thrust his sword in his fellow's side, so they fell down together."

Later, David's son Solomon visits Gibeon soon after becoming king. The Book of I Kings records how the new ruler takes decisive action to secure his throne, moving against his most dangerous rival, David's oldest son, Adonijah. Maneuvered out of the succession, Adonijah nevertheless still seems to harbor kingly ambitions and wins the support of powerful figures at the royal court, among them his father's military commander, Joab. Solomon responds ruthlessly, and has both Adonijah and Joab put to the sword.

The enmity between Saul and David has often been portrayed as here by 16-century C.E. artist Francesco Salviati in "Saul Throwing His Spear at David."

After the purge against his rival, Solomon visits a shrine near the pool of Gibeon, where he sacrifices and prays for God's guidance. In I Kings, chapter 3, God asks him what he desires above all else. After reflection, Solomon asks not for wealth or power or long life, but for wisdom. "Give thy servant therefore an understanding mind to govern thy people, that I may discern between good and evil."

The location of the pool of Gibeon was lost for centuries. After Babylonian King Nebuchadnezzar's destructive raids against the settlement, the pool must have been contaminated and closed permanently.

Below the ruins of Mareshah (right), once stood the city of Edom. Underneath the ruins, excavations have revealed subterranean workshops and caves to house oil presses such as the one above, which has an altar carved into the wall.

MARESHAH'S OIL PRODUCTION

Mentioned some hundred times in the Bible, the Edomites traced their ancestry back to Esau, the son who lost his birthright to his brother Jacob. In Genesis, chapter 27, Esau plans to kill his deceiving brother, who escapes only by fleeing to his mother's relatives. Years later Jacob returns with his two wives and family, though he fears that his brother is still plotting to take his life. Thus he first sends Esau gifts of a large number of sheep, goats, cows, asses, and camels. What follows is one of the great reconciliations in Scripture:

"Jacob looked up and there was Esau, coming with his four hundred men; so he divided the children among Leah, Rachel, and the two maidservants. He put the maidservants and their children in front, Leah and her children next, and Rachel and Joseph in the rear. He himself went on ahead and bowed down to the ground seven times as he approached his brother. But Esau ran to meet Jacob and embraced him; he threw his arms around his neck and kissed him. And they wept" (Genesis 33:1-4).

The reconciliation between Isaac's two sons was complete. But the same cannot be said of their descendants. In the biblical account, Edom became the implacable enemy of the Israelites, a threat that often had to be dealt with by King David and his successors.

UNDERGROUND TREASURE TROVE

Archaeologists have been working at the Edomite settlement of Mareshah for more than a hundred years. Early excavations revealed the city's walls and dwellings, which had been destroyed and rebuilt several times throughout the centuries. But in 1980, a team with the Israel Antiquities Authority came upon a find that was unrivaled in the ancient world and contained the best preserved artifacts of ancient Judaea. Underneath the ruins of the city's commercial district, they discovered an elaborate complex of caves that the once nomadic Edomites had started to dig out of the soft limestone some 2,800 years ago.

The caves provided a place where hundreds of Mareshah's townsfolk could work in comfort, sheltered from the heat of the Middle Eastern sun. In them they stored goods and stabled horses. And in dozens of multistoried dovecotes they raised flocks of pigeons, as many as a hundred thousand. The birds were an important source of food and their droppings a valuable fertilizer.

Most impressive of all, the inhabitants of Mareshah operated a number of great stone presses for producing olive oil. In as many as 20 different sites, the city's underground olive oil production was a thriving undertaking, supplying enough olive oil to meet Mareshah's demands—and more. Each season, some 190 tons of olive oil were surplus to requirements and could be traded to other towns.

Throughout the Scriptures, Edom is an enemy of the Hebrews, a threat that had to be dealt with by kings David and Solomon. Edom was finally conquered in 113 B.C.E. by the Maccabean John Hyrcanus, and Mareshah was destroyed for the last time. But while structures above ground suffered at the hands of these latest invaders, the caves of Mareshah were sealed for posterity. Safely concealed underground, they escaped the privations of raiders and the ravages of nature, yielding up an amazingly well-preserved site that tells us much about what life must have been like in biblical Edom.

The Edomites
A Semitic-speaking tribal group from the Negev and the Arabah Valley, south of Judah, the Edomites were the descendants of Esau, the firstborn son of Isaac and Rebecca. Despite the biblical ban on marrying people from different cultures, he took Canaanite wives, causing his parents much grief. Esau's sobriquet, "the red" ("Edom" in Hebrew), was transferred to his descendants, who became known as the Edomites.

GENESIS 25:25 | GENESIS 33:1-4 | GENESIS 36:1 | GENESIS 36:43

Despite being descendants of Isaac, the Edomites did not worship the God of Israel. The winged creature (above, left), found in a shrine, may have represented one of their deities.

"AND THERE CAME OUT FROM THE CAMP OF THE PHILISTINES A CHAMPION NAMED GOLIATH, OF GATH."

I SAMUEL 17:4

THE STORY OF GOLIATH

Tell es-Safi is a mound in southern Israel, halfway between Jerusalem and Ashkelon, that has been identified as the site of the Philistine city of Gath. Excavations there have unearthed artifacts from various periods during Philistine history. They include remains dating back some 2,800 years to the reign of King Aram and evidence of Gath's destruction at the hands of Hazael, which is described in the Book of II Kings. But one particular find, a tiny sherd of pottery unearthed in 2005, electrified the scholarly world with two names that it bore—"Alwt" and "Wlt," which are strikingly close to that of the most famous Philistine of them all, Goliath of Gath.

The Philistines have a long history in this part of the eastern Mediterranean. They arrived in the southern part of Canaan around 1200 B.C.E., eventually giving to the entire region the name the Romans would know it by: Palestine. The Philistines were fearsome warriors, career soldiers who thundered across the coastal plain in great war chariots and extended their realm at the expense of their comparatively weak neighbors. Along this coastal strip, they established a string of confederated city-states, the famous Philistine Pentapolis—Ashdod, Ashkelon, Ekron, Gaza, and Gath—that reached their peak during the 10th and 11th centuries B.C.E. The Philistines' domination of the region came to an end only when they were conquered by the Assyrian Empire in 723 B.C.E.

Relations with the neighboring Israelites must have been cordial at times. When fleeing from King Saul, David finds refuge in Gath. And earlier in the Old Testament, one of Israel's judges, Samson, marries a Philistine woman. But Samson is better known as the scourge of his warlike neighbors, he who "shall begin to deliver Israel from the hand of the Philistines" (Judges 13:5). The Hebrew strongman kills a thousand of them with the jawbone of a donkey, carries off the city gates of Gaza, and destroys the temple of the Philistine god Dagon, perishing himself in the act. After the rule of the judges in Israel, conflict continues with the Philistines during the reigns of Saul, David, and Solomon, the most celebrated of the encounters being with the great Philistine champion Goliath:

He stood and shouted to the ranks of Israel, "Why have you come out to draw up for battle? Am I not a Philistine, and are you not servants of Saul? Choose a man for yourselves, and let him come down to me. If he is able to fight with me and kill me, then we will be your servants; but if I prevail against him and kill him, then you shall be our servants and serve us." And the Philistine said, "I defy the ranks of Israel this day; give me a man, that we may fight together." When Saul and all Israel heard these words of the Philistine, they were dismayed and greatly afraid. (I Samuel 17:8-11)

A SMALL SHERD WITH A BIG NAME

The pottery sherd is little more than two inches long. Unearthed some six and a half feet underground, it dates from the tenth or early ninth century B.C.E., making it the earliest Philistine inscription found so far. Inscribed with Proto-Canaanite letters, it contains also two non-Semitic, Indo-European names. And the Philistines are believed to have migrated from the Aegean region to the Levant. There they adopted local ways, blending them with their own, as exemplified by the Semitic script and Indo-European name of this now famous sherd.

The sherd dates to about a hundred years prior to the time of the biblical Goliath, but this is the first evidence of a name like Goliath outside the Scriptures.

Warriors slinging stones (opposite) adorn a relief from the palace of Assyria's King Sennacherib in Nineveh that dates to around 700 B.C.E. Sling-throwers were common to all armies in the ancient world, including the Israelite army, and generally led the attack. Slingshots were among the deadliest weapons, with an effective range of about one hundred yards.

HOUSE OF DAVID

I n July 1993, archaeologists from the Hebrew Union College-Jewish Union Institute were excavating at the site of the old city of Dan in northern Israel. There they made one of the most significant finds in recent biblical archaeology.

Working at a large square that lay just outside the city's gates, the surveyor from the team came upon a stone fragment that had been used in the construction of the square's east wall. It measured 12.6 inches by 8.6 inches and dated from the ninth century B.C.E. An inscription in Aramaic was clearly legible on the basalt stone, each word of which was separated by a single dot, as was the case with two other, smaller fragments that were later found and which are part of what is now known as the Tel Dan Stela. Among the few words on the stela is the phrase *"bytdwd."* This, most scholars agree, means that the stela contains the only known reference outside the Old Testament to a dynasty whose name had become synonymous with the Israelite kingdom: the House of David.

> "THEN KING DAVID WENT IN AND SAT BEFORE THE LORD, AND SAID, 'WHO AM I, O LORD GOD, AND WHAT IS MY HOUSE, THAT THOU HAST BROUGHT ME THUS FAR?' "
>
> II SAMUEL 7:18

Likely erected in the city of Dan by Hazael, king of neighboring Aram-Damascus (in present-day Syria), the stela appears to commemorate the ruler's victory over Jehoram, king of Israel, and Ahaziah, king of the House of David. But, according to archaeologist Eric Cline this interpretation contradicts the account in II Kings 9, which states that Jehu, not Hazael, killed the two kings. Cline suggests that perhaps the two accounts should be combined, with Jehu acting as the "hatchet man" for Hazael. Scholars have further supposed that Jehoash, the Israelite king who later recovered Dan from the Arameans, may have smashed the stela in the triumph of his victory—thus forming the fragments that were recycled into the building at the city's entrance.

The Tel Dan Stela confirms other events described in the Old Testament, in both books of Kings and II Chronicles. The verses in II Chronicles 22 specifically refer to the war between the expanding kingdom of Aram-Damascus and the kings of Israel. And II Kings 8 describes an encounter between Hazael and the Prophet Elisha, who was visiting Damascus just before Hazael became king. Beginning in verse 12 it states:

And Hazael said, "Why does my lord weep?" He answered, "Because I know the evil that you will do to the people of Israel; you will set on fire their fortresses, and you will slay their young men with the sword, and dash in pieces their little ones, and rip up their women with child." And Hazael said, "What is your servant, who is but a dog, that he should do this great thing?" Elisha answered, "The Lord has shown me that you are to be king over Syria." Then he departed from Elisha, and came to his master. . . . But on the morrow he took the coverlet and dipped it in water and spread it over his face, till he died. And Hazael became king in his stead.

Tel Dan Stela
Despite containing only 14 lines of script, the Tel Dan Stela has become one of the most important recent discoveries in biblical archaeology. It is the oldest non-biblical text to refer to the kingdom of Israel and the only one to the House of David.

The outer walls of the ancient city of Dan (above) stand today in the northernmost region of Israel.

"[I] killed [Ahaz]iahu son of [Jehoram, kin]g of the House of David. And I set [their towns into ruins and turned] their land into [desolation]"

The City of Dan

Tucked into the northeast corner of present-day Israel, at the foot of Mount Hermon, Tel Dan, or "mound of Dan," has become one of its country's most significant archaeological sites. Excavations, which began in 1966 and have continued to the present, have unearthed barely a third of the ancient city, but the discoveries have shed important light on Old Testament narratives. The Tel Dan Stela, the most famous of these finds, contains the oldest nonbiblical, Semitic-language reference to Israel as well as the only ancient, nonbiblical reference to the House of David. Other finds include an elevated stone platform, which may have been the high place (or *bamah*) erected by Jeroboam to serve as the base for the golden calf (I Kings 12:31).

Situated on the trade route from Galilee to Damascus, Dan was one of ancient Israel's most important points of commerce. During the Canaanite period, in the 18th century B.C.E., the city was known as Laish or Leshem and was fortified with large man-made ramparts that today are some of the best preserved examples of defense systems in the ancient world.

In Genesis 14 it is recorded that Abraham came to the Canaanite city after defeating the kings of the north. Laish became Dan when it was conquered by the tribe of Dan in the 12th century B.C.E.; the settlement is described in Judges 18. The city was newly constructed with places of worship, courtyards, and an elaborate entrance gate complex—discovered accidentally by the Tel Dan archaeological team during a site cleanup in 1992.

"AT THE KING'S COMMAND, THEY
QUARRIED OUT GREAT, COSTLY STONES
IN ORDER TO LAY THE FOUNDATION OF
THE HOUSE WITH DRESSED STONES."

I KINGS 5:17

JERUSALEM

The Dome of the Rock (opposite), built over the rubble of Solomon's and Herod's Temple, rises above the old City of David. The Hulda Gate (below) was once one of the main entrances to Herod's Temple.

The Jebusite city that David selected to be the capital of his new kingdom was one of the oldest settlements in the world. Finds of scattered pottery suggest that Jerusalem was inhabited as early as the third millennium B.C.E. And the city is mentioned in Egyptian execretion texts from the 19th and 18th centuries B.C.E., when Jerusalem's rulers paid tribute to the pharaohs. The Book of Genesis records an encounter between Abraham and Melchizedek, king of Shalem, or Jerusalem. And later, when the Children of Israel return to Canaan under the leadership of Joshua, Jerusalem is one of the cities they occupy, but they leave its citizens undisturbed—until, that is, when David sets his sights on the strategically placed city as the location for his new capital.

As recounted in I Samuel 6, one of David's first acts as Jerusalem's new ruler was to bring there the Ark of the Covenant, to which all the tribes of Israel gave allegiance. But David did little to expand the size of Jerusalem, which was probably no more than 15 acres in all. He commissioned Phoenician builders to construct his royal palace, importing cedars and other materials from Lebanon, and renamed the capital the "City of David." Toward the end of his reign, he chose a site in the southeast to build the Temple, which tradition holds was the same Mount Moriah where Abraham had prepared to sacrifice his son Isaac. But despite David's intentions, the Prophet Samuel instructed him that he, a man of war, would not be permitted to build the Temple, a place of peace. That task would fall to his son Solomon.

Solomon was the city's great builder, doubling the size of the Jebusite city and constructing a huge royal complex. For his Temple, he called on Phoenician craftsmen and materials, and within seven years a magnificent edifice arose, completely covered in gold. Deep inside the Temple lay the inner sanctum that housed the ark and could be entered only by the high priest.

The Temple was at the heart of Hebrew religious worship. There the faithful would present offerings and, on Yom Kippur, seek to atone for their sins. With its construction right next to the royal palace, political power and religious life were now centralized in the capital and under the sole control of the Israelite king.

Nothing of Solomon's complex survives today, having been destroyed by Babylon's King Nebuchadnezzar II in 586 B.C.E. A smaller temple replaced the grand structure after the Babylonian Exile. It was extensively renovated by Herod the Great in the first century B.C.E. Later, the Romans raised a temple to Jupiter on the Mount, and later still Muslims built a mosque, the Dome of the Rock, opposite. Today, Jews gather to pray at an exposed wall, the Western Wall, the only remnant associated with the Temple of Herod.

"THE BOUNDARY SHALL RUN FROM TAMAR TO THE WATERS OF MERIBATH-KADESH, THENCE ALONG THE BROOK OF EGYPT TO THE GREAT SEA."

EZEKIEL 48:28

SOLOMON'S FORTRESS

Archaeologists have long shown an interest in the ruins at Hatzeva, a low hill in the Arava Valley some 22 miles south of the Dead Sea where several Israelite fortresses appear to have been built and rebuilt over the centuries. Excavations carried out at the site between 1987 and 1995 have identified it as the biblical Tamar, a small fortification on the border with Edom first constructed during the tenth century B.C.E. during the time of King Solomon.

Hatzeva, in fact, was part of a network of strongholds designed to protect Israel's southern border. It also stood to safeguard the trade routes leading to the Gulf of Aqaba and beyond, and along this way passed spices, perfumes, and other valuable goods from Arabia. Hatzeva eventually burgeoned into a new fortress with walls some ten feet thick, inside which the earlier stronghold became an inner fortress; there, archaeologists have found remnants of wheat and barley in one of the stores where provisions were kept in case of siege.

By the mid-eighth century B.C.E., Hatzeva was about a hundred yards long and a hundred yards wide, the size of many towns of the period. But it appears to have been damaged at that time by an earthquake that rocked the region, which is referred to in the first chapter of the Book of Amos. The ever hostile Edomites were expanding their influence and may well have been the perpetrators of the fortress's destruction, which soon followed.

Evidence of settlement by these traditional Hebrew enemies comes from a cache of ritual objects discovered at an open-air Edomite temple, including anthropomorphic incense stands like those opposite, used for cultic practices. Such idols may have led to the religious reforms that took place under King Josiah in the seventh century B.C.E. The Book of II Kings records, "The king ordered Hilkiah the high priest, the priests next in rank . . . to remove from the temple of the Lord all the articles made for Baal and Asherah and all the starry hosts. He burned them outside Jerusalem in the fields of the Kidron Valley and took the ashes to Bethel."

The ruins at Hatzeva testify to the importance of this site to the rulers of Israel over the centuries. A succession of fortresses stood here to guard the southern borders and protect trade with distant Arabia.

Painted in reddish hues, these three human-formed incense stands were found in an Edomite temple at Hatzeva that dates to the seventh century B.C.E. The limbs and facial features were molded separately and then attached to the vessels.

II KINGS 23:4 | EZEKIEL 48:28 | AMOS 1:1

"Two months of ingathering, two months of sowing, two months of late sowing, one month of chopping flax, one month of barley harvest, one month of harvest and completion, two months of grape cutting, one month of summer fruits."

The Gezer Calendar is a limestone plaque with a Paleo-Hebrew inscription that provides details about the agricultural calendar and tells us much about the rigors of a farmer's life in biblical times.

"THEN HORAM KING OF GEZER CAME UP TO HELP LACHISH; AND JOSHUA SMOTE HIM AND HIS PEOPLE, UNTIL HE LEFT NONE REMAINING."

JOSHUA 10:33

THE GIFT OF GEZER

According to the Old Testament, when Joshua entered Canaan with the Children of Israel, the king of Gezer joined forces with other rulers to resist him—and paid for it with his life. However, the Israelites were unable to conquer Gezer itself, and the city remained under Canaanite control until Siamun (ca 978-960 B.C.E.), Pharaoh of Egypt, captured it in a daring raid that is described in the Book of I Kings. Upon Solomon's marriage to one of his daughters, Pharaoh granted the city as a wedding present to the Israelite king, who promptly fortified his newly gained city.

As a result of excavations made in 1870, the site of Gezer has been identified as Tell Jezer, a 33-acre mound five miles south of Ramleh. Its strategic location explains its importance, guarding as it does one of the most important crossroads in Canaan—where the Via Maris (Way of the Sea) crosses the road leading to the valley of Aijalon. It also explains why Solomon decided to strengthen it. Excavations at Gezer have revealed one of the city's fortified gateways that dates to the time of the Israelite king and matches others perhaps built by Solomon elsewhere. Constructed with six guard chambers and four separate gates, the huge gateway was built of large fieldstones covered in ashlar masonry.

Another important find, made early in the 20th century, was the so-called Gezer Calendar (opposite), which is dated to the late tenth century B.C.E. Just 4.37 inches high and 2.83 inches wide, the soft limestone tablet is regarded as the work of a schoolboy, a certain "Abiya," practicing his writing—and is one of the earliest known examples of the written Hebrew language. Of more monumental proportions is the famous "High Place" (below), which consists of a row of ten monoliths, some more than ten feet high, erected in a north-south line inside Gezer's inner wall. The stelae were part of a Canaanite sanctuary on the site between 1400 and 1200 B.C.E.

A series of standing stones now covers the high ground at Tell Jezer, site of ancient Gezer. They were probably part of Canaanite cultic practices.

"HAZOR SHALL BECOME A HAUNT OF JACKALS,
AN EVERLASTING WASTE."

JEREMIAH 49:33

HAZOR, SOLOMON'S CITY

Another of the Canaanite strongholds rebuilt by Solomon to protect the borders of his kingdom was Hazor in northern Galilee. Hazor had a long history; it was an established and prominent city-state and trading center by the mid-19th century B.C.E. and the largest city in the southern Levant. In diplomatic dispatches on tablets recovered from the capital of Pharaoh Akhenaten, King Ashtaroth of the Transjordan complains to the Egyptian king that the ruler of Hazor "took from me three cities."

Hebrew leaders well before the time of Solomon had had dealings with the city. Abraham and his family would have encountered it on first entering Canaan. When Joshua led his Israelite army back into the Promised Land, Hazor was one of the fortified cities that stood in the way. According to the Book of Joshua, Hazor was considered "the head of all those kingdoms" and its ruler, Jabin, rallied those northern kingdoms into a defensive coalition against the Israelites. Joshua defeats the coalition, captures Hazor, and burns it to the ground, the only city torched during the conquest of the Promised Land.

Excavations carried out at the site in 1955 by Yigael Yadin, the pioneer of Israeli archaeology, uncovered a large building that he identified as the king's palace. In the building, he found traces of soot and concluded that Hazor had, indeed, been razed around 1230 B.C.E. Work at the site, in the 1990s, uncovered the results of a fire so intense that it cracked the palace's basalt-lined walls and left a layer of ash in places up to three feet deep. The palace also held the remains of Canaanite cult figurines, dating to the time of settlement by the idol-shunning Israelites, that had been

A pottery mask (right), probably used for ceremonial purposes, was found at the Canaanite stronghold of Hazor, whose ruins are shown opposite. The mask is dated to the 15th century B.C.E., well before Joshua's army is said to have burned Hazor to the ground.

purposefully destroyed. Hazor, declared Yadin, "is not just any ancient city, but one which is biblical in all its aspects. For many of us, the names of Joshua, Sisera, Deborah, Solomon, Ahab, and Jezebel—to mention but a few—are associated with chapter and verse; here they are connected with strata, buildings, and artifacts."

THE ISRAELITE CITY

The Israelites did not immediately establish their own permanent settlement at Hazor, and for 200 years only a small outpost existed there. But according to the Book of I Kings, this was one of the Canaanite strongholds that King Solomon tasked his architects with rebuilding from the ashes, and during his reign it grew into a royal city ten times the size of his capital, Jerusalem.

Rich in artifacts, Hazor is now the largest biblical-era archaeological site in Israel, spreading across some 200 acres. Recent excavations have dated its six-chambered gate, casemate wall, and other constructions to the mid-tenth or ninth century B.C.E. At the western edge rose a fortress that likely also served as the residence of the governor, who would have been tasked to rule over the northern part of the kingdom.

Israelite Hazor would reach its height of prosperity in the ninth century B.C.E., during the reign of King Ahab. By then it boasted a population twice the size of Solomon's city, substantial public buildings, and an impressive water system that would have guaranteed continued water supply even in times of siege. But the city fell into decline and, as recorded in II Kings, was finally destroyed in 732 B.C.E. by the Assyrian king Tiglath-pileser III (II Kings 15:29-30). Most of the city's inhabitants were deported to Assyria, and Hazor never recovered.

ARMAGEDDON

Megiddo was a key fortress in northern Israel that guarded the caravan routes between the King's Highway from Damascus and the coastal trade route to Egypt. Settled as early as the seventh millennium B.C.E., the site has been built over, time and time again, with no fewer than 30 cities occupying the site over the centuries. Its location, at the western approach to the 18-mile-long plain of Jezreel, placed it in the most fertile region of ancient Canaan. It also put it in a prime battlefield site.

When King Thutmose III (ca 1479-1435 B.C.E.) launched a campaign to reassert his influence in Canaan and Syria, he led his army right up to the gates of Megiddo and routed the troublesome Canaanites, who had rebelled as soon as he became king. "Thou hast smitten the Sand-dwellers as living captives!" trumpets the inscription carved in the Temple of Amun at Karnak around 1460 B.C.E. "Thou hast made captive the heads of the Asiatics." There, too, Saul clashed with the Philistines. And as Armageddon, it is the place where the kings of the Earth will congregate to witness the penultimate battle between the forces of good and evil at the end of time, as chronicled in the Book of Revelation.

THE ARCHAEOLOGICAL RECORD

Working at Megiddo, Israeli archaeologist Yigael Yadin discovered a casemate portal of an almost identical design to those at Hazor and Gezer. All of the monumental gates feature a long and narrow passageway flanked by three large chambers on either side that could house guards, weapons, or other goods. As archaeologist Amihai Mazar wrote, the "ashlar masonry, stone molding, and specificity" of these gates all point to a new,

royal style. The gates may have been built by Solomon's architects or a later monarch.

Yadin's other claim, that the area adjacent to the palace precinct of Megiddo is likewise from the time of Solomon, has been a source of greater controversy. It appears to be a vast exercise yard bordered by rows of rectangular shelters or stalls. Each one of these stalls is furnished with hollow stone blocks that may be feeding troughs.

The Old Testament tells us that Solomon had "forty thousand stalls of horses . . . and twelve thousand horsemen," enough to outfit a division of 4,000 chariots (I Kings 4:26). Seeing the troughs, the excavators readily identified the Megiddo stalls as stables.

It is not hard to see why they did so. Viewed from the center of this marshaling yard, this does indeed appear to be the famed "Solomon's stables" that at one time would have been filled with snorting war horses hitched to swift chariots. However, new research has shown that the complex was probably built by a later monarch, King Ahab (874-853 B.C.E.) of the Omride dynasty of the kingdom of Judah, who reigned a century after Solomon. The stalls may indeed have been used as stables. Or they may have served as storage facilities, similar to another such, also from the time of Ahab, that has been found at Hazor.

Before Ahab, during the golden age of David and Solomon, Israel had been able to blunt Egyptian designs on the region. But five years after Solomon's death, Pharaoh Shoshenq I saw and seized his opportunity. As his hieroglyphs on the Temple of Amun in Karnak proclaim, Shoshenq invaded Canaan and made it as far north as the stronghold of Megiddo, which he captured. Almost 3,000 years later, archaeologists at Megiddo found fragments of a victory stela dedicated to Shoshenq's triumph.

Doom-laden Word
Few words are as evocative—or as chilling—as "Armageddon," the place where the penultimate battle between good and evil is said to take place. The word is a combination of the Hebrew *Har*, meaning "hill" or "mountain," and *Megiddo*, the name of the ancient fortress city in the plain of Jezreel. The location that has been fought over so many times in the past will, according to the Book of Revelation, be the site of the final battle.

The inscription on a seal (above), found at Megiddo in 1904, reads "servant of Jeroboam," one of the kings of Israel. The roaring lion on the eighth-century B.C.E. seal is likely a reference to the Lion of Judah.

chapter 5

ISRAEL AND JUDAH
The Divided Kingdom

ISRAEL AND JUDAH

The separation of the northern kingdom of Israel from the southern kingdom of Judah following the death of Solomon greatly reduced the power and influence of the House of David, or the royal descendants of King David in Jerusalem. Ten tribes seceded to form the northern kingdom, leaving only Judah—which had absorbed the tribe of Benjamin—under the House of David. Turning his back on Jerusalem, King Jeroboam of Israel made his own capital in the north at Tirzah and established cult centers at Dan and Bethel, where he placed calves of gold, according to Scripture, and proclaimed to his people: "You have gone up to Jerusalem long enough. Behold your gods, O Israel, who brought you up out of the land of Egypt" (I Kings 12:28). Like Aaron when he fashioned the golden calf in the wilderness, Jeroboam may have been trying to honor YHWH using the familiar imagery of enduring Canaanite cults such as those devoted to El and Baal. To the biblical chroniclers, however, this was a great sin against God and one that Jeroboam's successors perpetuated, dooming their kingdom to destruction: "The Lord will smite Israel, as a reed is shaken in the water, and root up Israel out of this good land which he gave to their fathers, and scatter them beyond the Euphrates" (I Kings 14:15).

Like other accounts in the books of Kings and Chronicles dealing with the divided kingdom, this passage was written after Israel was overwhelmed by Assyrian forces in the late eighth century B.C.E. That conquest was seen as God's judgment on Israel, not for rebelling against the House of David—a rift for which Solomon and his son Rehoboam were blamed in the Bible—but for rebelling against the Lord. The destruction of

> "SO ISRAEL DEPARTED TO THEIR TENTS. . . . THERE WAS NONE THAT FOLLOWED THE HOUSE OF DAVID BUT THE TRIBE OF JUDAH ONLY."
>
> I KINGS 12:16-20

Israel by Assyrians in the late eighth century B.C.E. and the subsequent conquest of Judah by Babylonians, or Chaldeans, in the early sixth century B.C.E. cast a tragic light on preceding events and led biblical chroniclers to hold leaders of both realms morally responsible for the disasters that later befell their people.

Archaeological findings, including proclamations inscribed on stone by Assyrians and others with whom Israelites and Judeans clashed, confirm many details in those biblical accounts but offer different perspectives on rulers and their deeds. King Omri, for example, who ruled Israel around 880 B.C.E., a half century or so after it broke away from Judah, is described in the Bible as an army commander who took power by force by defeating a usurper named Zimri and went on to build a new capital at Samaria, near the Mediterranean coast, where he "did what was evil in the sight of the Lord" by practicing paganism and idolatry (I Kings 16:26). That brief and unflattering portrait of Omri is countered by archaeological evidence indicating that he was a dynamic and expansive ruler in the manner of King Solomon. Like Solomon, he challenged some rivals on his borders, including the Moabites, and made peace with others, notably the Phoenicians, whose talents as traders, builders, and artists helped enrich his realm and beautify his new capital. He sealed that alliance by having his son and heir, Ahab, marry the Phoenician princess Jezebel, and they in turn had their daughter Athaliah wed King Jehoram of Judah, thus renewing ties between Israel and the smaller kingdom to its south.

Biblical chroniclers saw no reason to extol Omri as they did Solomon. They were, after all, Judeans who composed their accounts after Israel was destroyed by Assyrians in what they

Previous pages: "King Hezekiah Displays His Treasure" by Vicente Lopez y Portana
Opposite: Assyrians, like these officials portrayed in a fresco from the eighth century B.C.E., defeated Israel with their formidable weaponry and vastly superior numbers.

viewed as God's retribution on that wayward kingdom. That did not make them indifferent to the fate of the defeated Israelites or blind to their own sins. Even Solomon, hailed for his strength and wisdom and for building a magnificent temple to the Lord, was condemned in one biblical passage for being led astray in old age by foreign wives, who "turned away his heart after other gods" (I Kings 11:4). Later Judean rulers were denounced for straying farther in the direction of paganism and bringing down on Judah much the same punishment God inflicted on Israel when the southern kingdom, too, was assailed by Assyrians and ultimately conquered by Babylonians. Yet the priests and prophets who composed the biblical accounts of this era never lost faith in the House of David or in the sacred nature of Jerusalem, Judah's capital. The promise of Zion—the heavenly city of Jerusalem founded by David as a beacon for a united Israel—would one day be redeemed and renewed, they believed, but the breakaway kingdom of Israel was lost forever through the unforgivable crimes of Jeroboam, Omri, Ahab, and other rulers whose idolatry poisoned their own realm and infected Judah when it reconciled with the northern kingdom. That harsh portrait of Israel's rulers was colored by knowledge of the terrible fate their kingdom suffered. But the historical evidence as a whole suggests that they were indeed tolerant of paganism and lacked the exclusive commitment to YHWH demonstrated by some later Judean rulers, notably Kings Hezekiah and Josiah, whose reforms helped make monotheism intrinsic to Judaism.

A PROPHETIC ERA

Prophecy can be found throughout the Bible, but the great prophetic era when holy men testified courageously against the high and mighty, denouncing them for impiety and injustice, began after Israel rebelled against Jerusalem. Seeking to appeal to devotees of other cults within their borders and beyond, the northern kingdom's rulers defied the biblical injunction that Israelites must make no covenant with heathens "or with their gods" (Exodus 23:32). That set the Prophet Elijah, who preached in the mid-ninth century B.C.E., against King Ahab and his pagan wife Jezebel, accused of persecuting YHWH's

A shepherd tends his flock on a hillside near Jerusalem, pursuing a way of life that changed little over the centuries as the royal City of David and Solomon became the capital of Judah and later fell under the sway of one conqueror after another.

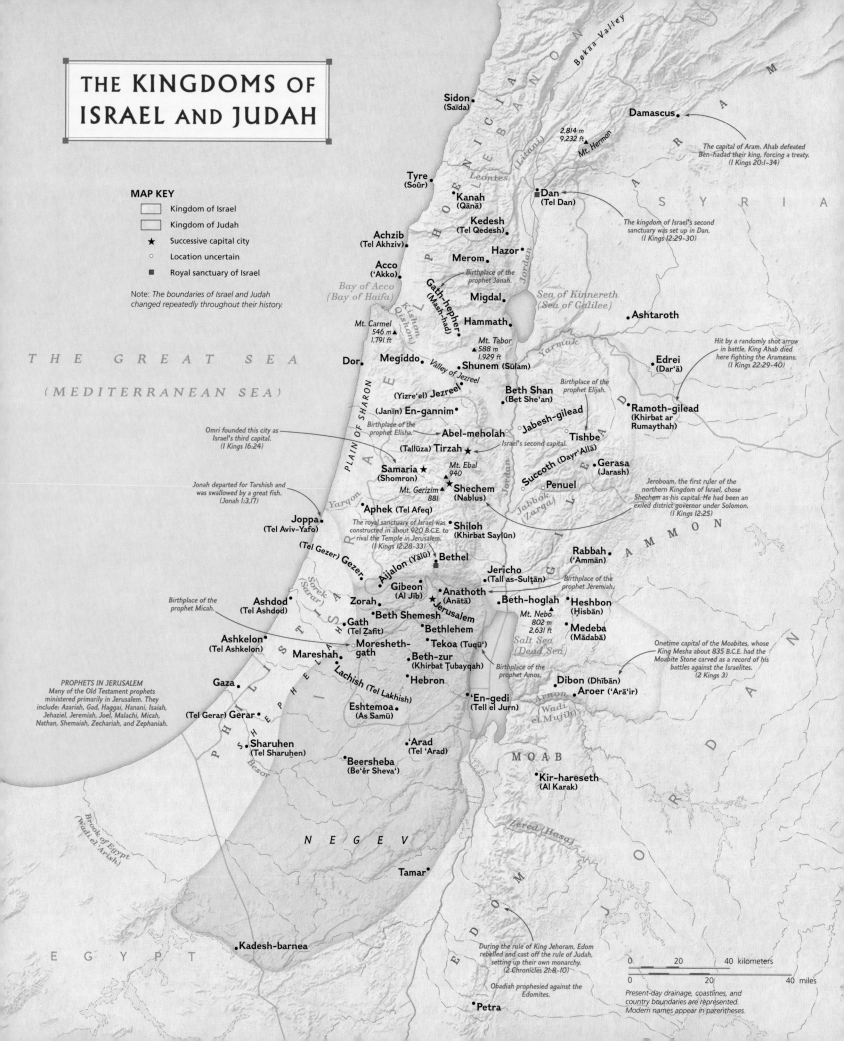

THE KINGDOMS OF ISRAEL AND JUDAH

MAP KEY

| | Kingdom of Israel |
| | Kingdom of Judah |
★ | Successive capital city
○ | Location uncertain
■ | Royal sanctuary of Israel

Note: *The boundaries of Israel and Judah changed repeatedly throughout their history.*

The capital of Aram. Ahab defeated Ben-hadad their king, forcing a treaty. (1 Kings 20:1–34)

The kingdom of Israel's second sanctuary was set up in Dan. (1 Kings 12:29–30)

Birthplace of the prophet Jonah.

Birthplace of the prophet Elijah.

Hit by a randomly shot arrow in battle, King Ahab died here fighting the Arameans. (1 Kings 22:29–40)

Birthplace of the prophet Elisha.

Omri founded this city as Israel's third capital. (1 Kings 16:24)

Israel's second capital.

Jonah departed for Tarshish and was swallowed by a great fish. (Jonah 1:3,17)

Jeroboam, the first ruler of the northern Kingdom of Israel, chose Shechem as his capital. He had been an exiled district governor under Solomon. (1 Kings 12:25)

The royal sanctuary of Israel was constructed in about 920 B.C.E. to rival the Temple in Jerusalem. (1 Kings 12:28–33)

Birthplace of the prophet Micah.

Birthplace of the prophet Jeremiah.

Onetime capital of the Moabites, whose King Mesha about 835 B.C.E. had the Moabite Stone carved as a record of his battles against the Israelites. (2 Kings 3)

Birthplace of the prophet Amos.

PROPHETS IN JERUSALEM
Many of the Old Testament prophets ministered primarily in Jerusalem. They include: Azariah, Gad, Haggai, Hanani, Isaiah, Jehaziel, Jeremiah, Joel, Malachi, Micah, Nathan, Shemaiah, Zechariah, and Zephaniah.

During the rule of King Jehoram, Edom rebelled and cast off the rule of Judah, setting up their own monarchy. (2 Chronicles 21:8–10)

Obadiah prophesied against the Edomites.

Present-day drainage, coastlines, and country boundaries are represented. Modern names appear in parentheses.

Sidon (Saïda)
Damascus
2,814 m / 9,232 ft ▲ Mt. Hermon
Tyre (Soûr)
Kanah (Qānā)
Dan (Tel Dan)
Kedesh (Tel Qedesh)
Achzib (Tel Akhziv)
Hazor
Merom
Acco ('Akko)
Gath-hepher (Mash'had)
Migdal
Hammath
Ashtaroth
Dor
Mt. Carmel 546 m ▲ 1,791 ft
Megiddo
Mt. Tabor ▲ 588 m 1,929 ft
Shunem (Sūlam)
Edrei (Dar'ā)
(Yizre'el) Jezreel
Beth Shan (Bet She'an)
Ramoth-gilead (Khirbat ar Rumaythah)
(Janīn) En-gannim
Jabesh-gilead
Abel-meholah
Tishbe
(Tallūza) Tirzah ★
Succoth (Dayr 'Allā)
Gerasa (Jarash)
Samaria (Shomron) ★
Mt. Ebal 940
Penuel
Mt. Gerizim 881
Shechem (Nablus)
Aphek (Tel Afeq)
Shiloh (Khirbat Saylūn)
Joppa (Tel Aviv-Yafo)
Rabbah ('Ammān)
(Tel Gezer) Gezer
Bethel
Jericho (Tall as-Sultān)
Aijalon (Yālū)
Gibeon (Al Jīb)
Anathoth (Anātā)
Beth-hoglah
Heshbon (Hisbān)
Ashdod (Tel Ashdod)
Zorah
Jerusalem ★
Mt. Nebo 802 m 2,631 ft
Medeba (Mādabā)
Beth Shemesh
Gath (Tel Zafit)
Bethlehem
Ashkelon (Tel Ashkelon)
Moresheth-gath
Tekoa (Tuqū')
Dibon (Dhībān)
Mareshah
Beth-zur (Khirbat Tubayqah)
Aroer ('Arā'ir)
Gaza
Lachish (Tel Lakhish)
Hebron
'En-gedi (Tell el Jurn)
(Tel Gerar) Gerar
Eshtemoa (As Samū)
Sharuhen (Tel Sharuhen)
'Arad (Tel 'Arad)
Beersheba (Be'ér Sheva')
Kir-hareseth (Al Karak)
Tamar
Kadesh-barnea
Petra

THE GREAT SEA (MEDITERRANEAN SEA)
Bay of Acco (Bay of Haifa)
Sea of Kinnereth (Sea of Galilee)
Salt Sea (Dead Sea)
Bekaa Valley
Leontes
Litani
Jordan
Yarmuk
Kishon
Valley of Jezreel
Plain of Sharon
Yarqon
Sorek (Sarar)
Besor
Zered (Hasa)
Arnon (Wadi el Mujib)
Brook of Egypt (Wadi el Arish)
NEGEV
MOAB
EGYPT
EDOM
AMMON
GILEAD
SYRIA
ARAM
PHOENICIA
LEBANON
PHILISTIA
SHEPHELAH
SHARON

0 — 20 — 40 kilometers
0 — 20 — 40 miles

true believers. Jezebel also brought false charges against Naboth, a farmer whose vineyard Ahab coveted, resulting in Naboth's death. For that sin against man and repeated sins against God, Elijah condemned the king and queen and foretold that dogs would lick their blood. His grim prophecy was fulfilled when Ahab was killed in battle and Jezebel was later thrown to her death from a palace window at the command of Jehu, a usurper who destroyed what remained of Ahab's legacy at the urging of Elijah's disciple, Elisha.

They and other biblical prophets were credited with the ability to foresee the future, but these visionaries were not mere soothsayers or fortune-tellers. Often, the doom they prophesied involved far-reaching historical events that were already under way. Assyrians had conquered Israel and posed an imminent threat to Judah, for example, when the Prophet Isaiah, preaching just before 700 B.C.E., described the fate awaiting Judeans: "Your country lies desolate, your cities are burned with fire; in your very presence aliens devour your land" (Isaiah 1:7). Later chapters of the Book of Isaiah prophesying the downfall of Babylon, an event that occurred more than a century after he died, were composed by another witness in the spirit of Isaiah and added to the book in his name.

What distinguished the great biblical prophets was not their ability to peer into the future but their capacity to tell right from wrong and speak hard truths to those in power and their complacent subjects. Like Elijah, who denounced his king and queen not just for paganism but for dispossessing and destroying Naboth, the Prophet Amos saw idolatry and greed as twin evils, rooted in the delight people took in wealth and worldly possessions, which they loved more than God or their neighbor, leading them to oppress the poor and "crush the needy" (Amos 4:1). As confirmed by the findings of archaeologists and historians, tolerating pagan cults in fact helped rulers such as King Omri and the aristocratic elite of Israel promote trade with foreigners and amass wealth, increasing the gap between the rich and the poor, whose cause Amos and other prophets embraced. Their eloquent testimony heightened the emphasis on charity and shared sacrifice within Judaism and later imbued Christianity with a similar spirit.

GENESIS OF THE BIBLE

The tumultuous era that began with the breakup of Solomon's kingdom and concluded with the Assyrian conquest of Israel and the Babylonian conquest of Judah was a defining time for Judaism not only because of the teachings of the prophets. This was also the period when priests and scribes began setting down in writing their sacred laws and oral traditions and laying the foundations for the Hebrew Bible. The earliest Hebrew inscriptions discovered thus far by archaeologists date from around the tenth century B.C.E. Some scholars have proposed that Israelite scribes could have begun recording their history and beliefs in writing as early as the reign of King David and that of Solomon, who succeeded David around 960 B.C.E. But the oldest known biblical inscription—found in a tomb near Jerusalem and beginning with the memorable words "The Lord bless you and keep you" (Numbers 6:24)—was recorded not long before the Babylonian conquest of Jerusalem in 586 B.C.E. The Bible itself states that the first book of Scripture came to light during the reign of King Josiah of Judah (640-609 B.C.E.) when a priest named Hilkiah "found the book of the law" in the Temple and had it conveyed to Josiah, who pledged to obey its commandments and keep the covenant with God as "written in this book" (II Kings 23:3).

That sacred text was probably an early version of the Book of Deuteronomy, in which God's laws and purposes are elaborated by Moses. Frequent warnings in Deuteronomy that foreign enemies would one day assail wayward Israelites in their Promised Land and force them into exile suggest that the book was composed sometime after the Assyrians conquered Israel and besieged Judah and did not reach its final form until after the Babylonian Exile. The priest Hilkiah who "found" or brought forth the version presented to Josiah may also have been its keeper or compiler. If so, his achievement marked the first step in a long process by which sacred writings from relatively recent times (dating back perhaps to the ninth or tenth century B.C.E.) and oral traditions of greater antiquity were assembled and edited to produce the Bible as we know it today. From this tragic era of division, defeat, and exile came holy Scriptures that defined and sustained Judaism and preserved its lessons down through the ages.

Opposite: As shown here, much of the territory encompassed by Judah after its rupture with Israel was desert. The northern kingdom was more populous and productive, and its conquest by Assyria left Judah in a precarious position.

"BEHOLD, I AM ABOUT TO TEAR THE KINGDOM
FROM THE HAND OF SOLOMON, AND WILL
GIVE YOU TEN TRIBES."

I KINGS 11:31

ISRAEL:
THE NORTHERN KINGDOM

Two reasons are given in the Bible for the collapse of the united kingdom ruled by David and Solomon, which shattered around 930 B.C.E. when Israel in the north broke away from Judah in the south. One explanation is that Solomon, in taking wives from foreign lands, was seduced into worshipping their gods, so angering the Lord that he split the kingdom after Solomon died and left his son Rehoboam with the smaller portion, Judah, including people of that tribe and the subordinate tribe of Benjamin. The other ten tribes of Israel went to Jeroboam, an official under Solomon who rebelled after the Lord spoke to him through a prophet and promised him all of the kingdom except Judah and its capital, Jerusalem, which God reserved for the descendants of King David because he "kept my commandments and my statutes" (I Kings 11:34).

The other reason offered for the division of the kingdom is that the ten northern tribes resented having to perform "hard service" for Solomon, whose building projects, including the Temple in Jerusalem, were strenuous and costly. "Your father made our yoke heavy," their leaders complained to Rehoboam when he succeeded Solomon, but he dismissed them with harsh words: "My father chastised you with whips, but I will chastise you with scorpions" (I Kings 12:10-11; II Chronicles 10:14). Rallying around the rebellious Jeroboam, the ten tribes then formed their own kingdom and left Judah to Rehoboam, a paltry successor to his imposing father.

Excavations that began at Samaria in the early 20th century revealed that the hilltop city (opposite), founded by King Omri as the capital of Israel, was a place of considerable wealth and refinement, where palace scribes kept receipts on pottery fragments called ostraca, such as the tax receipt at right.

Whether charged to the sins of the father or to the foolish arrogance of his son, the breakup of the united kingdom was viewed in the Bible as a calamity that might have been avoided if David's successors had governed according to his precepts: "When one rules justly over men, ruling in the fear of God, he dawns on them like the morning light" (II Samuel 23:3-4). Viewed in retrospect by biblical chroniclers writing long after the breakup of Solomon's realm, this was the first act in a national tragedy that continued with the transgressions of later rulers, including King Jeroboam and his successors in the north, and culminated with the destruction of Israel by the Assyrians and the ensuing conquest of Judah by the Babylonians.

Jeroboam's great sin was to place golden calves in temples he raised at Bethel and Dan in the north to rival Solomon's Temple in Jerusalem. Recent excavations at Tel Dan, site of the biblical city of Dan, uncovered a raised stone platform that could have been one of the suspect "high places" where Jeroboam installed a golden calf or allowed other illicit practices. To the chroniclers, this was blatant idolatry and paganism, crimes for which Jeroboam's breakaway kingdom would pay dearly in generations to come. Any hope that God might relent and pardon Israel, they concluded, was lost when Jeroboam's successors followed in his path and fell under the evil spell of Phoenicians and other heathens.

Archaeologists have confirmed that rulers of the northern kingdom were receptive to pagan idols and foreign influences, as shown by excavations at Samaria, founded as Israel's capital by King Omri in the early ninth century B.C.E. Set on a hilltop offering a distant view of the Mediterranean Sea to the west, this site was chosen by Omri

Archaeologists shed light on biblical accounts of the notorious King Ahab and his "ivory house" (I Kings 22) when they found at Samaria carved ivory adornments reflecting the influence of foreign cults, including motifs from Egyptian mythology (above), a winged sphinx drawn from Egyptian and Mesopotamian lore (opposite), and the ring at right bearing the seal of "Ahab of Israel."

because it could not easily be attacked and guarded trade routes linking his kingdom to wealthy Phoenician cities along the coast, including Byblos, Sidon, and mighty Tyre. (Phoenicians are referred to in the Bible as Sidonians, for Sidon, but Tyre was preeminent at this time.) Although King Hiram of Tyre had earlier been allied with Solomon and contributed to the building of his temple in Jerusalem, Hiram's successors were closer geographically and politically to Israel and its new capital of Samaria than to Judah. Friendship with Tyre brought Omri the services of Phoenician artisans who helped make Samaria an opulent new Jerusalem, where royalty reportedly slept on beds of ivory and scribes writing in Hebrew kept track of goods received and distributed. Israel grew stronger and wealthier than Judah and overshadowed that southern kingdom. This northern renaissance, however, was viewed with alarm by biblical prophets, who denounced the kings of Israel for coveting wealth and worshipping false idols and warned them of a terrible reckoning to come.

AHAB AND JEZEBEL

The alliance between Samaria and Tyre was formalized when Omri's son and successor, Ahab, wed Jezebel,

daughter of the king of Tyre, referred to in the Bible as "Ethbaal king of the Sidonians" (I Kings 16:31). As his name suggests, he was a devotee of Baal, a god worshipped in various guises by Phoenicians as well as Canaanites. (The Bible does not distinguish between those incarnations, referring to them collectively as Baals.) Ahab is condemned in Scripture for honoring the beliefs of his wife and her father by erecting a temple to Baal in Samaria. Archaeologists have found no trace of that temple, but there is little reason to doubt that Jezebel adhered to the cult in which she was raised. It was customary in the Near East for rulers who brought foreign wives or workers into their realm to allow them to worship their native gods, and Ahab would have been insulting his allies had he not permitted his Phoenician queen or the Phoenician artisans who helped build Samaria to do the same. Such tolerance for paganism was not uncommon among Israelites or Judeans in Ahab's time, but some holy men took strong exception to it, notably the Prophet Elijah (meaning "YHWH is my Lord"), who hailed from Gilead, east of the Jordan River. As portrayed in the Book of I Kings, he counters the aggressive paganism of Jezebel—who has prophets of the Lord executed—by pitting his sacred powers against those of 450 prophets of Baal on Mount Carmel, where he first puts them to shame by performing a miracle beyond their capacity and then puts them to death.

Archaeology sheds no light on whether the notorious Jezebel in fact engaged in a lethal vendetta with Elijah and others who honored YHWH as the one true God. Excavations at Samaria have confirmed, however, that its privileged occupants lived in high style amid luxuries unknown to the poor, as testified by the Prophet Amos, who preached in the mid-eighth century B.C.E. when the northern kingdom of Israel reached the peak of its wealth and influence under King Jeroboam II. As a native of Judah, which was now allied with Israel and beholden to it as the weaker partner in their pact, Amos risked alienating both Israelites and Judeans when he spoke out against the elite in Samaria and their hedonistic ways: "Woe to those who lie upon beds of ivory, and stretch themselves upon their couches . . . who drink wine in bowls, and anoint themselves with the finest oils, but are not grieved over the ruin of Joseph!" (Amos 6:4-6). By likening the aristocrats of Samaria to Joseph's brothers, who sold him into slavery, Amos accused those lovers of luxury—a vice often equated with idolatry in the Bible—of ignoring the plight of the needy and profiting at their expense. God would punish Israel, he prophesied, because their lords and masters continued not only to worship false idols but also to "trample the head of the poor into the dust of the earth, and turn aside the way of the afflicted" (Amos 2:7).

IVORY IDOLS

Among the treasures unearthed at Samaria were splendid ivory carvings lending substance to Amos's depiction of palace life there. Some of those carvings may have adorned wooden furniture in the palace, fostering the impression that lords and ladies here lay on beds of ivory. Luxury and idolatry indeed went hand in hand in Samaria, as shown by the mythic figures depicted in ivory there, including a winged sphinx and other sacred images of foreign origin. The artists may well have been Phoenicians, who found a ready market for their alluring idols in Samaria, where those in power tolerated paganism or practiced it. Indeed, many of the personal names inscribed at Samaria on seals or ostraca—pottery sherds on which scribes recorded shipments of goods—contained the name "Baal" or some variation of it, as in the case of Jezebel and her father, Ethbaal. Some of the people who bore these names may have been Phoenicians residing around Samaria. Others may have been Israelites who honored Baal as one guise of the almighty they worshipped in various forms. In any case, prophets like Elijah had reason to regard Samaria as a place where people had "forsaken the commandments of the Lord and followed the Baals" (I Kings 18:18).

The willingness of the elite in Samaria to tolerate or worship pagan gods was a reflection of the wealth they gained through trade with Phoenicia and other foreign lands. Then as now, foreign trade was both an economic and a cultural exchange that exposed those who engaged in it to new values and beliefs. Far from viewing this as a blessing, Amos saw it as a curse that led the wealthy and powerful astray and caused them to

abandon customs and traditions that once bound Israel together as one people under God and obligated the rich to the poor, as stated in Scripture: "You shall not harden your heart or shut your hand against your poor brother, but you shall open your hand to him, and lend him sufficient for his need, whatever it may be" (Deuteronomy 15:7-8).

Instead, the wealthy were giving the poor the back of their hand, Amos lamented, and were so attached to foreign treasures and heathen idols that they were now hopelessly estranged from YHWH and would be treated by him as he treated any pagan nation that grew proud and arrogant. Speaking for God, Amos told of

the grim fate that awaited Israel as Assyrians menaced their kingdom in the late eighth century B.C.E. and targeted their capital: "Woe to those who are at ease in Zion, and to those who feel secure on the mountain of Samaria. . . . I abhor the pride of Jacob, and hate his strongholds; and I will deliver up the city and all that is in it" (Amos 6:1-8).

"I am Mesha, son of Chemosh, the king of Moab. . . . Omri was the king of Israel, and he oppressed Moab for many days."

The Mesha Stela (also known as the Moabite Stone), containing a victory proclamation by King Mesha of Moab over Israelites and their God YHWH, was eventually obtained in fragments from Bedouins in the 19th century and reconstructed.

"AND THERE CAME GREAT WRATH UPON ISRAEL; AND THEY WITHDREW FROM HIM AND RETURNED TO THEIR OWN LAND."

II KINGS 3:27

KING OMRI'S WAR

Omri's accomplishments as king of Israel earned little notice from biblical chroniclers, who dismissed him as an idolator. He made a powerful impression on foreigners, however, including the Assyrians, who later referred to Israel's royalty as "the house of Omri." Proof that Omri was a formidable figure abroad was provided by the Mesha Stela (opposite), found in 1868 at Dhiban (below), located east of the Dead Sea in what was once the kingdom of Moab. Inscribed around 850 B.C.E., a few decades after Omri died, the stela bears a proclamation from King Mesha of Moab, described in the Bible as a ruler who paid steep tribute to Israel before rebelling. Those tribute payments may have been imposed by Omri, who in Mesha's words "afflicted Moab many days." Like Israelites, Moabites attributed their misfortunes to their supreme deity, called Chemosh, who subjected them to defeat because he was "angry with Moab." Mesha then regained the god's favor by honoring him at a shrine and went on to repulse Omri's son, presumably Ahab, when he too tried to afflict Moab. Like the Merneptah Stela (see pp. 96-97) and other ancient victory proclamations, this one claimed that the enemy had been annihilated. "Israel perished everlastingly," Mesha boasted. Among the trophies he seized were sacred "vessels of YHWH"—the first written reference to the God of Israel to appear outside the Bible—which were then offered to Chemosh.

Mesha's proclamation differs substantially from the biblical account, which states that the war began after Ahab died and ended when Mesha, facing imminent defeat, sacrificed his eldest son to Chemosh. Then "there came great wrath upon Israel; and they withdrew from him and returned to their own land" (II Kings 3:27). Clearly, Israel was not extinguished, as Mesha claimed, but that retreat allowed him to declare victory on behalf of his god. Taken together, these two versions of history demonstrate that King Omri faced stiff challenges on his borders, not only from Moabites but also from Aramaeans and Assyrians. The tolerance for pagan cults was meant to bolster Israel against such threats by strengthening its alliance with the Phoenicians and by appealing to its people, who feared that if they abandoned idols long honored in Canaan, Israel would feel their wrath.

The Mesha Stela was found at Dhiban, Jordan, once known as the biblical Dibon, the Moabite capital. According to the Bible, Israelites clashed in this region with Moabites before entering Canaan and remained at odds with them in later times.

II KINGS 3:27

"THUS SAYS THE LORD, THE GOD OF DAVID YOUR
FATHER. . . . I WILL DELIVER YOU AND THIS CITY
OUT OF THE HAND OF THE KING OF ASSYRIA."

II KINGS 20:5-6

JUDAH:
THE SOUTHERN KINGDOM

When Israel broke away from Judah, it left that tiny kingdom and its capital, Jerusalem, exposed to danger on all sides. King Rehoboam of Judah, whose threats and insults drove the northern tribes to secede, could not stop Egyptians from exploiting that rift and plundering Jerusalem, where they seized "the treasures of the house of the Lord and the treasures of the king's house" (II Chronicles 12:9). Rehoboam's successors fought with Israelites, Philistines, and Moabites, among other foes, before recognizing that Judah's only hope lay in forming alliances with stronger powers or yielding and paying tribute to them. King Jehoram of Judah reconciled with Israel by wedding Athaliah, the daughter of King Ahab of Israel and Queen Jezebel of Phoenicia—a marriage pact denounced in the

Water flowing through a tunnel constructed during the reign of King Hezekiah poured out here at the Pool of Siloam, enabling Jerusalem to withstand a siege mounted by King Sennacherib of Assyria. These waters were credited with healing properties and in one gospel account were used by Jesus to restore sight to a blind man (John 9:1-12).

Bible for exposing Judah to the malicious pagan influence of Jezebel's daughter.

How could Judah bargain with heathen powers without breaking its covenant with God and selling its soul? That was the problem devout Judeans faced as their rulers came to terms with Israel, where pagan cults were tolerated, and with more distant kingdoms that knew nothing of YHWH. To pay tribute to a ruler in those days was to pay homage to his gods, a point driven home in the late eighth century B.C.E. as Assyrian forces descended on

"Then the water flowed from the spring to the pool, a distance of one thousand and two hundred cubits."

Judah. King Ahaz of Judah defied Israel and other countries allied against Assyria and bowed to the Assyrians, offering them treasure from his own house and the Lord's house, the Temple, which was once again despoiled. Ahaz then had a replica of an Assyrian altar installed in Jerusalem and cast on it "the blood of his peace offerings" (II Kings 16:13). In so doing, he was not simply submitting to the Assyrians but sacrificing to them and their gods.

Ahaz's son and successor, King Hezekiah, was so unlike his father that he was seen as the spiritual heir of an earlier ruler, the devout King David: "And he did what was right in the eyes of the Lord, according to all that David his father had done" (II Kings 18:3). Through rigorous reforms, Hezekiah sought to cleanse Judah of paganism and make the Temple in Jerusalem the focus of a cult devoted strictly to YHWH in keeping with his commandments. He then joined a rebellion against Assyria and prepared for a siege by engineering a tunnel that funneled water from a spring outside Jerusalem to the Pool of Siloam (opposite), within the fortified city. That feat,

This Hebrew inscription found carved into the roof of Hezekiah's Tunnel describes how it was excavated: Two teams of men wielding pickaxes advanced from either end and met in the middle.

described in an inscription on the tunnel wall, helped spare Jerusalem from destruction by the Assyrians, who regained control but left Judah under its own kings and priests—a reprieve that allowed for the continued development here of Judaism as professed by Hezekiah and others who shared his exclusive commitment to YHWH.

PROPHET OF REDEMPTION

Among those who counseled Hezekiah was the Prophet Isaiah, who believed that Zion, or Jerusalem, was the city of God, where heaven and earth met, and that from the House of David, who claimed Jerusalem for the Lord, would come a redeemer called Immanuel ("God with us"). Some biblical scholars have suggested that Isaiah saw Hezekiah as that Messiah, who would restore Jerusalem to grace and glory by ruling in the righteous manner of his forefather David, son of Jesse: "There shall come forth a shoot from the stump of Jesse, and a branch shall grow out of his roots. And the Spirit of the Lord shall rest upon him" (Isaiah 11:1-2). Others have interpreted such passages as referring to a future savior, a Messiah so close to the Lord in spirit that he would be seen as the son of God: "For to us a child is born, to us a son is given; and the government will be upon his shoulder, and his name will be called 'Wonderful Counselor, Mighty God, Everlasting Father'" (Isaiah 9:6).

Isaiah's stirring prophecies would long be subject to varying interpretations by Jews, Christians, and people of other faiths. But there is little doubt that Hezekiah, if not the savior hoped for by Isaiah, was a ruler who shared the prophet's vision of redeeming the House of David, which had fallen into disrepute under Ahaz and other recent kings, and making Jerusalem once again, as in David's time, "the stronghold of Zion" (II Samuel 5:7). Hezekiah ordered the Temple in Jerusalem purified so that sacrifices could properly be offered to the Lord there and nowhere else. All "high places" in Judah where offerings had been made to idols or other commandments had been violated were torn down.

Hezekiah instituted those reforms before he rebelled against Assyria. They were not meant as protests against his Assyrian overlords, who did not impose their cults on foreigners under their authority. But he may well have feared that if he failed to cleanse Judah of paganism, God would punish the kingdom as he did neighboring Israel, which had recently been shattered by Assyria. Hezekiah's reforms were also part of a wider effort to assert his authority and bind Judeans to Jerusalem spiritually and politically. Archaeologists excavating ancient Hebron and other Judean sites have found large numbers of storage jars from this period marked with a seal identifying them as the king's property, suggesting that Hezekiah set up regional administrative centers where supplies were distributed to his officials or troops. Such efforts to organize and centralize the kingdom made it stronger but did not prevent Assyrians from wreaking havoc here in the conflict that ensued.

The rebellion against Assyria in which Hezekiah took part began after the death in 705 B.C.E. of Sargon II, one of the greatest Assyrian rulers. He reportedly died in battle, which may have been a sign of Assyria's waning power. According to Scripture, however, Hezekiah remained wary of its might and was so distraught when Assyrian envoys demanded the surrender of Jerusalem that he "rent his clothes, and covered himself with sackcloth." Only after Isaiah prophesied that the Lord would spare Jerusalem from destruction "for the sake of my servant David" did Hezekiah stand firm (II Kings 19:1-34). He bolstered the city walls and closed off Gihon Spring to divert water to the Pool of Siloam. He thus denied the oncoming Assyrians access to the spring and "brought water into the city" to sustain the populace during the siege (II Kings 20:20).

An Assyrian account boasted that King Sennacherib had Hezekiah penned in Jerusalem "like a bird in a cage." In the end, Hezekiah managed to save his city only by yielding to Sennacherib and paying him tribute. By staving off destruction for Jerusalem and exile for its people, however, Hezekiah preserved the city as a haven for Judaism until the Babylonian conquest a century later—a crucial interval during which King Josiah renewed Hezekiah's reforms and priests began compiling the laws, wisdom, and prophecies enshrined in the Bible.

II SAMUEL 5:7 | II KINGS 19:1-34 | II KINGS 20:20 | ISAIAH 9:6 | ISAIAH 11:1-2

Who Was the Messiah?

The term "messiah," meaning "anointed one," was used in the Hebrew Bible to refer to an ideal king, anointed by God as his earthly representative. King David came closest to that ideal, as attested by the Prophet Nathan in II Samuel 7:5-14. Isaiah described the Messiah as a messenger from God, bringing "good tidings to the afflicted" (61:1). Disciples of Jesus believed he was that messenger, summoning them into the kingdom of God his father, but some Jews continued to hope for a Messiah who would restore their kingdom on earth.

Among the relics of King Hezekiah's reign uncovered by archaeologists are objects carrying this royal seal—identifying the property as belonging to "Hezekiah (son of) Ahaz King of Judah"—and foundations of the massive city wall (opposite) that he strengthened and expanded to shield Jerusalem before the Assyrians attacked.

This marriage contract was written in 427 B.C.E. at Elephantine, where Jewish colonists recorded such covenants in Aramaic on papyrus and stored the documents in clay containers.

"THEN ALL THE PEOPLE, BOTH SMALL AND
GREAT, AND THE CAPTAINS OF THE FORCES
AROSE, AND WENT TO EGYPT; FOR THEY
WERE AFRAID OF THE CHALDEANS."

II KINGS 25:26

A JEWISH COLONY IN EGYPT

The journey of Joseph and his brothers to Egypt was not the last such migration by Hebrews chronicled in writing. Revealing documents found at Elephantine, an island in the Nile near the First Cataract—the ancient border between Egypt and Nubia—tell of a Jewish military colony established there by exiles from Judah. Just when this colony was founded remains uncertain. It may have originated in the seventh century B.C.E. when King Manasseh of Judah sent troops to Egypt to affirm an alliance with the ruler of that country against their common foe, the Assyrians. Or it may have taken shape a century later when rebels in Judah killed the governor imposed on them by the Chaldeans, or Babylonians, and fled to Egypt to avoid retaliation, as related in the Bible: "Then all the people, both small and great, and the captains of the forces arose, and went to Egypt." Once established at Elephantine, the Jewish exiles and their descendants helped guard Egypt's southern border for generations to come, serving faithfully under the Persians, who conquered Egypt in 525 B.C.E.

The documents found at Elephantine were written on papyrus in Aramaic, the common language of the Persian Empire. As revealed in those manuscripts, this Jewish community was unorthodox in that its members honored YHWH at a temple here—ignoring the biblical precept that there was only one rightful temple, in Jerusalem—and recognized the gods of foreigners in Elephantine with whom they intermarried. They may have brought a tolerance for pagan cults with them from Judah. King Manasseh, for example, spurned the reforms of his predecessor King Hezekiah and was denounced for building altars to various gods and worshipping "all the host of heaven" (II Kings 21:3). These colonists also granted women a right restricted to men in biblical law by allowing either marriage partner to initiate divorce.

Among the documents found at Elephantine are marriage contracts like the one shown opposite, in which "Ananiah son of Azariah, a servitor of YHWH the God who is in Elephantine," took as his wife Tamet, the handmaiden of an Aramaean named Meshullam. As a servant, Tamet brought no dowry to this union other than a few personal possessions. The contract specified that if she and Ananiah divorced, which either party could do by public declaration, "all that she brought in her hand, she shall take out." In another marriage contract, a man named Yedoniah, "a Jew of Elephantine," granted as a dowry to his daughter Mibtahiah and her husband land on which to live. "Build and equip that site," he told his son-in-law, "and dwell thereon with your

II KINGS 21:3 | II KINGS 25:26

Ancient Elephantine, shown here in ruins, contained both a Jewish temple and shrines to Egyptian deities, worshipped at this site long before colonists arrived from Judah.

wife." That marriage did not last, for a later document told of Mibtahiah's divorce from her second husband, an Egyptian, who declared in writing: "Let us make a division of the silver, grain, raiment, bronze, iron, and all goods and possessions." Mibtahiah agreed to this settlement by swearing an oath to the Egyptian goddess Sati. She then entered into a third marriage to an Aramaean named Ashor, who offered her father a bride price of five shekels. All property she brought into the marriage she could if they divorced "take out, shred and thread, and go whither she will, without suit or process."

"HAS ANY OF THE GODS OF THE NATIONS
EVER DELIVERED HIS LAND OUT OF THE
HAND OF THE KING OF ASSYRIA?"

II KINGS 18:33

THE ASSYRIANS

Great warriors and strategists, the Assyrians had much in common with the Romans who later took Jerusalem and forced Jews to render tribute to Caesar. Like the Romans, the Assyrians were merciless to foes who refused to yield to them, shattering the walls of cities and slaughtering or deporting the inhabitants. But like the Romans they too were builders as well as destroyers, whose rulers erected splendid monuments and promoted artistry and learning. In the same way that Romans later absorbed Greek culture, Assyrians drew on the cultural legacy of the Babylonians, who preceded them as masters of Mesopotamia, and preserved that legacy at cities like Nineveh, where archaeologists uncovered tens of thousands of clay tablets inscribed with legal, scientific, and literary texts such as the Epic of Gilgamesh.

Nothing the Assyrians created or produced, however, so impressed the world as their capacity for conquest and destruction. Their principal deity, Ashur, was an overpowering force to whom they prayed for victories. The Assyrian people were named for him, as was the city where Assyria was founded—Ashur, on the upper Tigris River—and some of its rulers, including Ashurnasirpal II (opposite), who set the kingdom on the path to greatness in the ninth century B.C.E. Assyrian rulers amassed huge armies, equipped them with iron weapons and fearsome siege engines, and forged an empire reaching all the way to Egypt. So dreaded were their armies that some rulers submitted without a fight when Assyrians demanded surrender, as King Sennacherib's envoys did upon reaching Jerusalem: "Do not let Hezekiah deceive you, for he will not be able to deliver you out of my hand" (II Kings 18:29).

Among the emblems that signaled strength and majesty among Assyrians were a long, braided beard—as shown in this sculpture of King Ashurnasirpal II (opposite) found at Nimrud, his capital—and crowns of gold like the one at left, discovered in a tomb at that same site.

Scale armor like that shown at top shielded Assyrian warriors as they advanced across the Near East and collected booty or tribute, including the silver-studded bowl above, made in Syria and found in the palace of Ashurnasirpal II.

Shown here in a relief from the ninth century B.C.E., Assyrian bowmen fire from a platform at an enemy stronghold (right) while a wheeled siege engine in the foreground batters the wall with its iron-tipped ram.

King Jehu of Israel bows meekly before King Shalmaneser III of Assyria on the Black Obelisk, documenting tribute paid by Jehu to the Assyrian ruler.

"'SO JEHU SLEW ALL THAT REMAINED OF THE HOUSE
OF AHAB IN JEZREEL, ALL HIS GREAT MEN, AND HIS
FAMILIAR FRIENDS, AND HIS PRIESTS,
UNTIL HE LEFT HIM NONE REMAINING."

II KINGS 10:11

BOWING TO ASSYRIA

For ages, all that was known about King Jehu of Israel was what was written of him in the books of Kings and Chronicles. An army commander urged by the Prophet Elisha to rid the land of paganism, he conducted a bloody purge in which he did away with Jezebel and her son by Ahab, King Joram of Israel, as well as her grandson, King Ahaziah of Judah, and other princes or prophets related to Jezebel or devoted to the cult of Baal she promoted. No mention was made in the Bible of any dealings between Jehu and the Assyrians, and it was assumed that they had not yet imposed on Israel when Jehu reigned (841-814 B.C.E.).

In 1846, however, Austen Henry Layard, a British diplomat, collector of antiquities, and pioneering archaeologist, opened a new chapter in biblical history when he extracted from the rubble of an Assyrian palace at Nimrud a black marble obelisk about seven feet high on which scenes were sculpted in relief above an inscription. As Layard recalled, "the figures were as sharp and well defined as if they had been carved but a few days before." Portrayed atop the Black Obelisk was King Shalmaneser III of Assyria (858-824 B.C.E.), receiving tribute from a submissive foreign ruler, as shown opposite. According to the inscription, this supplicant was none other than Jehu of Israel, the dreaded figure who had spilled the blood of kings in his own land but was now kowtowing to Shalmaneser.

Further light was shed on relations between Assyrians and Israelites during this period by the discovery in 1861 of a stela recounting a battle waged by Shalmaneser in 853 B.C.E., when Jehu's predecessor, Ahab, was king of Israel. As revealed by that inscription, Ahab joined with the Aramaean ruler Hadadezer of Damascus and other kings in the region in opposing Shalmaneser's forces at Qarqar in Syria. The Israelites alone committed 10,000 troops and 2,000 chariots to that battle, which is not mentioned in the Bible. Shalmaneser claimed victory, but the fact that he returned home afterward suggests that he was in fact stymied by the Israelites and their cohorts. What became of that powerful alliance and reduced defiant Israel to bowing to Assyria?

Apparently, the bloodbath that brought Jehu to power isolated and weakened his kingdom. In doing away with the Phoenician Jezebel and her followers, he surely offended Tyre and other Phoenician city-states that Israel had been profitably allied with under Ahab. And the fatal blow he struck against King Ahaziah of Judah must have strained relations with that kingdom as well. Jehu may have been encouraged to carry out this purge not just by the Prophet Elisha but also by King Hazael of Damascus—if, as suspected by scholars, Hazael was the foreign ruler who authorized the Tel Dan inscription found in 1993 and claimed credit there for killing King Joram of Israel and King Ahaziah of Judah. That claim would not contradict the biblical account that Jehu eliminated those kings if he was doing the bidding of Hazael, who then turned against him. As stated in the Bible, after Jehu completed his purge, he was challenged by Hazael, who "began to cut off parts

Israelite porters bear tribute to be laid before King Shalmaneser III in another scene carved on the Black Obelisk.

of Israel" (II Kings 10:32). The biblical chronicler saw this as God's judgment on the impious Jehu, whose motives for destroying Jezebel and her kin were probably more political than spiritual. Having alienated Phoenicia and Judah and been outmaneuvered by Hazael, he evidently had little choice but to pay tribute to Shalmaneser and seek protection from the Assyrians, who posed a greater threat to Israel in the long run than any other opponent.

"THEN THE KING OF ASSYRIA INVADED ALL
THE LAND AND CAME TO SAMARIA, AND
FOR THREE YEARS HE BESIEGED IT."

II KINGS 17:5

CONQUEST OF SAMARIA

F ollowing the death of King Shalmaneser III in 824 B.C.E., Assyria remained at peace with Israel for some time, accepting tribute from its kings, who ruled from Samaria, and serving their immediate interests by attacking their archrivals, the Aramaeans, and reducing the power of Damascus. The long reign of King Jeroboam II of Israel (786-746 B.C.E.) was stable and prosperous, but it proved to be a lull before the storm. Soon after he died, the Assyrians embarked on a new phase of imperial expansion that continued relentlessly through the reigns of Kings Tiglath-pileser III (745-727 B.C.E.), Shalmaneser V (727-722 B.C.E.), Sargon II (721-705 B.C.E.), and Sennacherib (705-681 B.C.E.).

Not content simply to conquer territory and exact tribute, those kings deported people who defied them. Exiling them left them dependent on their Assyrian masters. A defiant ruler could sometimes spare his people the ordeal of defeat and deportation if he submitted to the Assyrian king, but any renewed sign of rebellion on his part might result in his kingdom being essentially wiped off the map. Such was the fate of Israel.

Facing a renewed Assyrian threat, Israel's first response was to seek an alliance with its neighbors. This new pact joined Israelites with Phoenicians and Aramaeans, but Damascus had lost strength and the allies were further weakened when King Ahaz of Judah opposed them and pledged fealty to the Assyrians. When Assyrian forces overwhelmed the allies and invaded Israel, its ruler King Hoshea (732-724 B.C.E.) followed the lead of Ahaz and submitted to Tiglath-pileser III and his successor, Shalmaneser V, who spared the northern kingdom further devastation. As related in the Bible, "Hoshea became his vassal, and paid him tribute. But the king of Assyria found treachery in Hoshea." Foolishly hoping for aid from Egypt—which was ill equipped to resist Assyrian might—Hoshea defied Shalmaneser and withheld tribute. But there would be no reprieve for him: "The king of Assyria shut him up, and bound him in prison. Then the king of Assyria invaded all the land and came to Samaria, and for three years he besieged it" (II Kings 17:3-5).

Who Fathered Sargon II?

The parentage of King Sargon II of Assyria—portrayed at right—remains something of a mystery. Historians suspect that he was a younger son of King Tiglath-pileser III who overthrew his older brother Shalmaneser V and may have caused his death. If so, he cloaked his treachery by inventing a new identity, linking himself to the ancient conqueror Sargon of Akkad, another ruler of mysterious origins, who was reportedly cast adrift as a baby in a reed basket like the infant Moses (see p. 87).

The conquest was completed by Sargon II after he supplanted Shalmaneser V in 721 B.C.E. For the people of Samaria, penned up in that hilltop city as the Assyrians cut off their food supply and slowly broke down their defenses, it must have been a terrible ordeal. But for Sargon, it was just one of many victories recorded on the tablet shown opposite and warranted only a few sentences, free of the bombast that often characterized such proclamations. "I besieged and conquered Samaria, led away as booty 27,290 inhabitants of it," he declared. "The town I rebuilt better than it was before and settled therein people from countries which I myself had conquered." As confirmed in the Bible, "the king of Assyria captured Samaria, and he carried the Israelites away to Assyria" (II Kings 17:6). Not all the people of Israel were exiled, but their kingdom was divided into several Assyrian provinces and would never be reconstituted. In the words of the Prophet Hosea: "Israel is swallowed up; already they are among the nations as a useless vessel" (Hosea 8:8).

"I besieged and conquered Samaria, led away as booty 27,290 inhabitants of it. . . . The town I rebuilt better than it was before and settled therein people from countries which I myself had conquered."

Scribes serving under Sargon II recorded his conquest of Samaria and other exploits in cuneiform on this hexagonal clay tablet, known as a prism.

"HEZEKIAH KING OF JUDAH SENT TO THE KING OF ASSYRIA
AT LACHISH, SAYING, 'I HAVE DONE WRONG; WITHDRAW
FROM ME; WHATEVER YOU IMPOSE ON ME I WILL BEAR.' "

II KINGS 18:13-14

SIEGE OF LACHISH

The most spectacular discovery made by Austen Henry Layard as he unearthed the monuments of ancient Assyria in the mid-1800s was the palace of King Sennacherib at Nineveh, whose walls were adorned with stunning reliefs offering a panoramic view of the king's achievements, including the conquest of Lachish, shown here. The struggle that doomed Lachish, the second most important city in Judah after Jerusalem, began when Sennacherib succeeded his father, Sargon II, in 704 B.C.E. and faced a rebellion that spread from Babylon to Judah and beyond, including Philistine and Phoenician cities along the Mediterranean coast.

In joining that revolt, King Hezekiah of Judah broke with the compliant policy of his father, King Ahaz, hoping that his own efforts to strengthen Judah would allow it to withstand retaliation by the Assyrians. Only in Jerusalem, however, were his defensive preparations sufficient to avert disaster when Sennacherib's forces swept down

The conquest of Lachish unfolds in sequence from left to right on these panels from the walls of Sennacherib's palace at Nineveh.

the coast, subdued the Phoenicians and Philistines, and invaded Judah. By Sennacherib's reckoning, he took 46 Judean cities and deported some 200,000 inhabitants. None of the strongholds he targeted posed a greater challenge to his army than Lachish, a well-defended city with inner and outer walls. Its capture stood as the crowning achievement of his campaign, as shown by the lavish attention devoted to the siege on his palace walls.

Like a medieval tapestry, these depictions portray side by side a sequence of events that occurred at Lachish over an extended period. At the far left, Assyrian archers and troops wielding slings target the city's defenders. To the right of the archers, infantrymen carrying shields and spears prepare to join in the climactic assault on Lachish, led by armored battering rams, which have ascended ramps laid down by Assyrian engineers and are pounding the city walls. Judean troops toss firebrands down on those siege engines, hoping to set them aflame, but Lachish is doomed. At center, victorious Assyrians carry plunder from the fallen city and herd captives toward

the camp of Sennacherib, who sits on his throne at far right as an official surrenders to him and other Judeans kneel or raise their hands in submission to the conqueror, identified in an accompanying inscription as "Sennacherib, king of the world, king of Assyria."

The fall of Lachish, which was destroyed by the Assyrians, came as a terrible blow to King Hezekiah in Jerusalem, who did what he could to prevent his capital from suffering the same fate. According to the Bible, he sent a message to Sennacherib at Lachish: "I have done wrong; withdraw from me; whatever you impose on me I will bear." Ultimately, Hezekiah submitted to the Assyrian ruler, who allowed him to remain king of Judea as his vassal. Lachish was rebuilt, only to be destroyed again during the Babylonian conquest.

Discovered by archaeologists amid the debris of that later conflagration were reports written on pieces of pottery, sent to the Judean commander at Lachish before the Babylonians attacked. In vocabulary and phrasing, those reports were similar to the early books of the Bible and often invoked the name of God. "May YHWH cause my lord to hear tidings of peace!" officers wrote to the commander. Here as elsewhere in the Near East, subordinates used submissive language when addressing their superior. "Who is thy servant but a dog, that my lord should remember his servant?" they wrote, using terms much like those spoken in the Bible to the Prophet Elisha by Hazael of Damascus before he seized power there: "What is your servant, who is but a dog, that he should do this great thing?" (II Kings 8:13).

The message written on this ostracon (left) to the Judean commander at Lachish reads in part: "We are watching for the beacon from Lachish following the signals you, sir, gave."

"Then upon Hezekiah, there fell the fear of the power of my arms, and he sent out to me the chiefs and the elders of Jerusalem with 30 talents of gold and 800 talents of silver."

The Taylor Prism—
one of several such
tablets on which King
Sennacherib recorded
his campaigns—offers
a different interpreta-
tion of the struggle for
Jerusalem than pre-
sented in the Bible.

THE FATE OF JERUSALEM

Sennacherib recorded his war against the rebellious Judeans not only in pictures carved on his palace walls but also in words inscribed on tablets like the one opposite, known as the Taylor Prism for the British official who acquired it in 1830. Found at Nineveh, it posed a difficult question for biblical scholars: Did the siege of Jerusalem that concluded Sennacherib's campaign allow him to return home in triumph as claimed here, or was it in fact a victory for the Judeans defending that city as stated in the Bible?

Sennacherib never declared that he took Jerusalem, but he insisted that he had Hezekiah at his mercy: "He himself, I locked up within Jerusalem, his royal city, like a bird in a cage. I surrounded him with earthworks, and made it unthinkable for him to exit by the city gate." In the end, Hezekiah reportedly agreed to resume yearly tribute payments to Sennacherib and meet additional demands imposed by his "lordship." After returning to Nineveh, Sennacherib boasted, he received from Hezekiah 30 talents of gold, 800 talents of silver, and other treasures, trappings, and implements of war.

A comparison of Sennacherib's claims with biblical accounts of the siege reveals some similarities between them and suggests that the struggle for Jerusalem ended in such a way as to allow both sides to claim success. For example, the Bible states that after receiving a conciliatory message from Hezekiah promising to bear "whatever you impose on me," Sennacherib demanded "three hundred talents of silver and thirty talents of gold" (II Kings 18:14). This figure is close enough to what Sennacherib claimed he received to leave little doubt that such a payment was in fact part of a settlement intended to resolve the conflict.

That payment was probably not made before Assyrians demanded the surrender of Jerusalem and laid siege to it, as implied in the Bible. Sennacherib stated that he received the tribute after he returned home, and that

arrangement would have been more in Hezekiah's interest than paying off his foe beforehand in the hope that he would withdraw. In all likelihood, it was not until both sides grew weary of the struggle that terms were agreed upon and the siege of Jerusalem was lifted. Sennacherib's forces may have been exhausted by the long campaign or depleted by disease, as suggested by biblical references to devastation inflicted on the Assyrian camp by the "angel of the Lord" (II Kings 19:35; II Chronicles 32:21). In any case, he chose to settle with his opponent and head home. The result may not have been the crushing victory

An Assyrian cavalryman fires his bow deftly from horseback on a relief from Sennacherib's palace.

he hoped for, but he could still take credit for stamping out the rebellion and reclaiming Judah as a vassal state. People in Jerusalem had reason to feel vindicated as well. Although Hezekiah had to pay tribute to Sennacherib with silver and gold from the Temple and his own treasury, Jerusalem was spared the fate suffered by Lachish and other cities. It was indeed a day of deliverance—not so much for Hezekiah, who remained subject to Sennacherib, but for the City of David and the faith nurtured there, which survived this ordeal and grew stronger.

"LET THE OUTCASTS OF MOAB SOJOURN
AMONG YOU; BE A REFUGE TO THEM
FROM THE DESTROYER."

ISAIAH 16:4

THE OUTCASTS OF MOAB

Reckoning with mighty Assyria was a challenge not just for Israel and Judah but for many of the small kingdoms or city-states along their borders. At one time or another, most of them paid tribute to Assyrian kings. When rebellions broke out, their rulers had to decide whether to remain vassals of the Assyrians—which meant continuing to make payments to them in silver, gold, or other treasure—or join the uprising, which could be much costlier if the Assyrians regained control

This desolate but hauntingly beautiful terrain east of the Dead Sea belonged to the Moabites in ancient times and inspired in them visions of a heavenly power who watched over them, not unlike the God of their rivals the Israelites and Judeans.

and exacted punishment. The clay tablet shown opposite records tribute paid to Assyria around the time that King Sennacherib succeeded Sargon II. Judah had not yet rebelled against Sennacherib, because it is listed here as one of the kingdoms still paying tribute along with Ammon, Edom, and Moab. Rulers of those three small countries along Judah's eastern border may have considered rebelling but decided they had little chance of prevailing against the dreaded Assyrian army and remained loyal to Sennacherib.

That decision set Moab at odds with Jerusalem and was one of many slights or offenses for which the Moabites were denounced by biblical prophets. The relationship

between them and the Israelites or Judeans was close and conflicted. Described in Genesis as products of the incestuous union between Abraham's nephew Lot and Lot's elder daughter, Moabites were regarded by Israelites as disreputable distant cousins much like the neighboring Ammonites, said to be descendants of Lot and his younger daughter. Both groups are portrayed in the Bible as hindering the progress of Israelites into the Promised Land and are prohibited from entering "the assembly of the Lord" (Deuteronomy 23:3). Yet Moabites in particular had much in common with the Israelites. Their language was close to Hebrew, and their god Chemosh, while not the only deity they recognized, resembled YHWH in that he punished them severely when they were unfaithful to him. Despite the enmity between the two groups, one passage in the Bible holds that Moabites were not harassed because the Lord gave their domain "to the sons of Lot for a possession" (Deuteronomy 2:9). A Moabite woman was among the ancestors of King David, and a Moabite chieftain named Ithmah was one of the "mighty men" of his army (I Chronicles 11:26-46).

Reverence for King David and kindred feeling for the Moabites may have led the Prophet Isaiah to temper his condemnation of them with compassion. He recognized that the tribute they paid to Sennacherib would not long spare them from conquest. "They have sent lambs to the ruler of the land," he declared, recalling the tribute that Moabites once paid to hostile Israel—reckoned at 100,000 lambs and the wool of 100,000 rams annually—and the offerings they later made in other forms to Assyria. That could not buy them lasting protection. As further convulsions swept the troubled Assyrian Empire, Moabites were caught in the upheaval and would ultimately lose their kingdom. Envisioning their plight, Isaiah urged Judeans to offer their afflicted neighbors sanctuary. "Let the outcasts of Moab sojourn among you," he counseled; "be a refuge to them from the destroyer. When the oppressor is no more . . . then a throne will be established in steadfast love, and on it will sit in faithfulness in the tent of David one who judges and seeks justice and is swift to do righteousness" (Isaiah 16:1-8).

"Tribute from Ammon—
two manus of gold;
Moab—one manu
of gold; Judah—ten
manus of silver;
Edom and Byblos . . ."

*Tallied here in cune-
iform are tribute
payments to Assyria
from the rulers
of Judah, Moab,
Ammon, Edom,
and the Phoenician
city-state of Byblos.
A manu of silver or
gold weighed about
500 grams.*

EARLIEST KNOWN BIBLICAL INSCRIPTION

In 1979 a team led by Israeli archaeologist Gabriel Barkay excavating a burial cave on a ridge called Ketef Hinnom near Jerusalem's Old City found two silver amulets, rolled up like scrolls, amid a stash of precious items that belonged to the deceased or were left there as gifts for them. It took years for technicians at the Israel Museum to devise a method of unrolling the ancient silver scrolls, which had grown brittle over time, without destroying them. Finally, in 1982, Barkay was able to examine the text inscribed on the amulets. "When I saw the unrolled silver strip and placed it under the magnifying glass," he wrote, "I could see that the surface was covered with delicately made characters, scratched with a sharp instrument onto the very thin and fragile sheet of silver." One word above all commanded his attention: "YHWH." As Barkay noted, the Lord's name occurs thousands of time in the Hebrew Bible, yet this was its "first appearance on an archaeological find from the city of Jerusalem—the city where the Lord's Temple was built."

That alone made the discovery noteworthy, but the full text when deciphered proved even more significant. Inscribed on both scrolls was this memorable passage: "May YHWH bless and keep you; may YHWH cause his face to shine upon you and grant you peace." This was an abbreviated version of the blessing that God instructed Moses to confer on the people of Israel, as related in the sixth chapter of the Book of Numbers. The scrolls were dated to around 600 B.C.E., before the Babylonian conquest of Jerusalem, making this the earliest known biblical inscription. That did not mean this text was taken from Numbers, which may not have been compiled by then, but it did suggest that such sacred passages were well established in writing by this time and that the Bible had its origins in the days before the Babylonian Exile.

Silver amulets (opposite), tightly rolled and containing a biblical blessing, were found in Jerusalem on Ketef Hinnom, a ridge overlooking the Hinnom Valley (right).

> "THE LORD BLESS YOU AND KEEP YOU:
> THE LORD CAUSE HIS FACE TO SHINE UPON
> YOU AND BE GRACIOUS TO YOU: THE LORD
> LIFT UP HIS COUNTENANCE UPON YOU,
> AND GIVE YOU PEACE."
>
> NUMBERS 6:24-26

The date assigned to the amulets was greeted skeptically by scholars who believed that even the first books of the Bible—the Torah comprising Genesis, Exodus, Leviticus, Numbers, and Deuteronomy—were composed in the centuries following the Exile. Further analysis by researchers at the University of Southern California, however, confirmed that the silver scrolls were inscribed shortly before the Babylonian conquest and "preserve the earliest known citations of texts also found in the Hebrew Bible." That conclusion was consistent with the view that compilation of the Bible began no later than the reign of King Josiah of Judah (640-609 B.C.E.). Scholars holding that view believe that the "the book of the law" presented to Josiah (II Kings 22:10-20; II Chronicles 34:14-31) was an early version of Deuteronomy and that during his reign priests and scribes began compiling other parts of the Torah and the Books of Joshua, Judges, Samuel, and Kings, all of which underwent revision after the Babylonian Exile before reaching their present form. If so, the blessing found on the amulets could have been drawn not just from Hebrew oral traditions but from Scripture.

The silver amulets worn by the deceased also testify to the ancient Jewish custom of keeping sacred writings close to one's heart and home. That tradition endures in the practice of placing in a case called a mezuzah, located at the doorpost of a house—or in a pouch called a phylactery, strapped around the left arm and forehead—scriptures of central importance to Judaism, notably the Shema (Hebrew for "hear"), found in Deuteronomy: "Hear, O Israel: The Lord our God is one Lord; and you shall love the Lord your God with all your heart, and with all your soul, and with all your might. And these words which I command you this day shall be upon your heart. . . . And you shall write them on the doorposts of your house and on your gates" (Deuteronomy 6:4-9). As shown by the amulets, the idea that such sacred writings are dear to God and confer the Lord's blessing on those who hold them close was established in Jerusalem before the Babylonian Exile and may help explain the care and devotion given to preserving and expounding holy Scripture in the trying times that followed.

"May YHWH bless and keep you; may YHWH cause his face to shine upon you and grant you peace."

"NOW THE CANAANITE, THE KING OF ARAD
WHO LIVED IN NEGEV IN THE LAND OF CANAAN,
HEARD OF THE COMING OF THE SONS OF ISRAEL."

NUMBERS 33:40

TEL ARAD:
ONE GOD, ONE TEMPLE

By the late seventh century B.C.E., as a result of the reforms of Kings Hezekiah and Josiah of Judah, the Temple in Jerusalem was widely recognized as the one and only house of the Lord. At no other shrine were offerings to be made to God, for he had chosen Jerusalem as the place "to put his name and make his habitation" (Deuteronomy 12:5). Archaeological evidence of those reforms was found at Tel Arad, site of an ancient settlement located east of Beersheba at the edge of the Negev desert. Arad is first mentioned in the Bible as the seat of a Canaanite king defeated by the Israelites. By 1000 B.C.E., they had built a fortress here. Within its walls was a broad-room temple of Canaanite design, with a sacrificial altar in its outer courtyard. In the late eighth century B.C.E., when Hezekiah ruled Judah, that altar was abandoned. The fortress was destroyed by Sennacherib's army and rebuilt in the late seventh century B.C.E., but the temple remained in ruins in keeping with the reforms of Josiah.

That efforts to centralize worship at the Temple in Jerusalem were indeed taking effect was confirmed by the discovery at Tel Arad in 1967 of an ostracon inscribed with a message written around 600 B.C.E. to an official named Eliashib, who may have been the commander at Arad. "To my lord Eliashib," the letter began. "May YHWH seek your welfare." The writer went on to inform Eliashib that a man about whom he had inquired was staying in the "house of YHWH." There was no need for the writer to state which house he was referring to, for the Temple in Jerusalem was the only place officially dedicated to YHWH and the only sanctuary recognized by authorities as a place of asylum, which may be why the man in question was staying there. This was the earliest mention of the Temple yet discovered. Along with evidence of the abandonment of the shrine at Arad, the letter demonstrated that the idea of one God, honored at one Temple, was gradually taking hold.

Temple or Synagogue?
The destruction of Solomon's Temple by Babylonians in 586 B.C.E. left Jews without a central sanctuary at which to honor God. Instead synagogues arose wherever Jews lived in substantial numbers and gathered to worship through prayers and readings of the Torah. No sacrificial offerings were made to the Lord at synagogues.

Amid the remains of the hilltop fortress excavated here at Tel Arad—a site within the ancient kingdom of Judah—archaeologists found striking evidence of the emergence of the Temple in Jerusalem as the only recognized house of God.

"To my lord Elyashib, may YHWH seek your welfare . . . as to the matter which you commanded me—it is well; he is in the House of YHWH."

This message written on an ostracon found at Tel Arad refers to the Temple as the "house of YHWH."

"Belonging to Berechiah, son of Neriah, the scribe."

This seal stamped on clay is the bulla of Jeremiah's scribe, Baruch. His name appears here as Berechiah, with the suffix "iah" representing the Hebrew letters "YHW," signaling his devotion to YHWH.

"THEN JEREMIAH CALLED BARUCH THE SON OF NERIAH, AND BARUCH WROTE UPON A SCROLL AT THE DICTATION OF JEREMIAH ALL THE WORDS OF THE LORD WHICH HE HAD SPOKEN TO HIM."

JEREMIAH 36:4

JEREMIAH'S SCRIBE

The Hebrew Bible offers few insights into how its books were composed. One notable exception is the book of Jeremiah, where that prophet dictates revelations he received from God to a scribe named Baruch, the son of Neriah, whose seal was impressed in clay as shown here, which was once attached to his scrolls. The prophecies set down by Baruch warned that Judah was being led astray by King Jehoiakim (609-598 B.C.E.), whose father, King Josiah, had lost his life opposing Egyptian forces allied with the Assyrians. Jeremiah supported Josiah's religious reforms and was appalled when Jehoiakim tolerated pagan cults. Jeremiah also opposed the king's alliance with Phoenicians and other foreigners against the Babylonians, who had recently defeated the Assyrians and Egyptians and were now the dominant power in the region. Having lost God's favor, Jehoiakim had no chance of withstanding the might of the Babylonians, the prophet warned, and would bring Judah to ruin.

That was the essential message Jeremiah dictated to Baruch and had him convey to "all the men of Judah," including the king, who learned of the prophecies when his counselor Jehudi obtained Baruch's scroll and read it to him, as related in Scripture: "The king was sitting in the winter house. . . . As Jehudi read three or four columns, the king would cut them off with a penknife and throw them into the fire in the brazier, until the entire scroll was consumed. . . ." This was an offense against God, for the words written by Baruch came from the Lord. In burning the words, Jehoiakim was sealing his fate, as revealed by YHWH: "And I will punish him and his offspring and his servants for their iniquity; I will bring upon them, and upon the inhabitants of Jerusalem, and upon the men of Judah, all the evil that I have pronounced against them, but they would not hear" (Jeremiah 36:22-31).

This remarkable chapter says much about how the Book of Jeremiah and other parts of the Bible were composed. Although most of the surviving writings in biblical history are inscribed on clay or stone, Baruch wrote in ink on papyrus scrolls, which were perishable and endured only in extraordinary circumstances, as in the case of the Dead Sea Scrolls (see pp. 244-245). Conceivably, Baruch's bulla was once affixed to scrolls containing the very words and deeds of Jeremiah. His original scrolls did not survive, but they were copied and revised by priestly editors who produced two versions of the book of Jeremiah, a shorter edition in Greek and a longer edition in Hebrew.

In an etching by French artist Gustave Doré, the Prophet Jeremiah dictates his visions to Baruch. A figure revered in posterity by Jewish scholars, Baruch may well have produced the original version of the Book of Jeremiah.

Many parts of the Hebrew Bible were composed in similar fashion, beginning with the testimony of an inspired prophet or leader, whose words were recorded in his lifetime by a scribe like Baruch or recaptured in later times by a biblical chronicler who drew on earlier written accounts and Hebrew oral traditions. For true believers, however, the real author of such sacred texts was not the scribe or the prophet but God himself, speaking through the prophet.

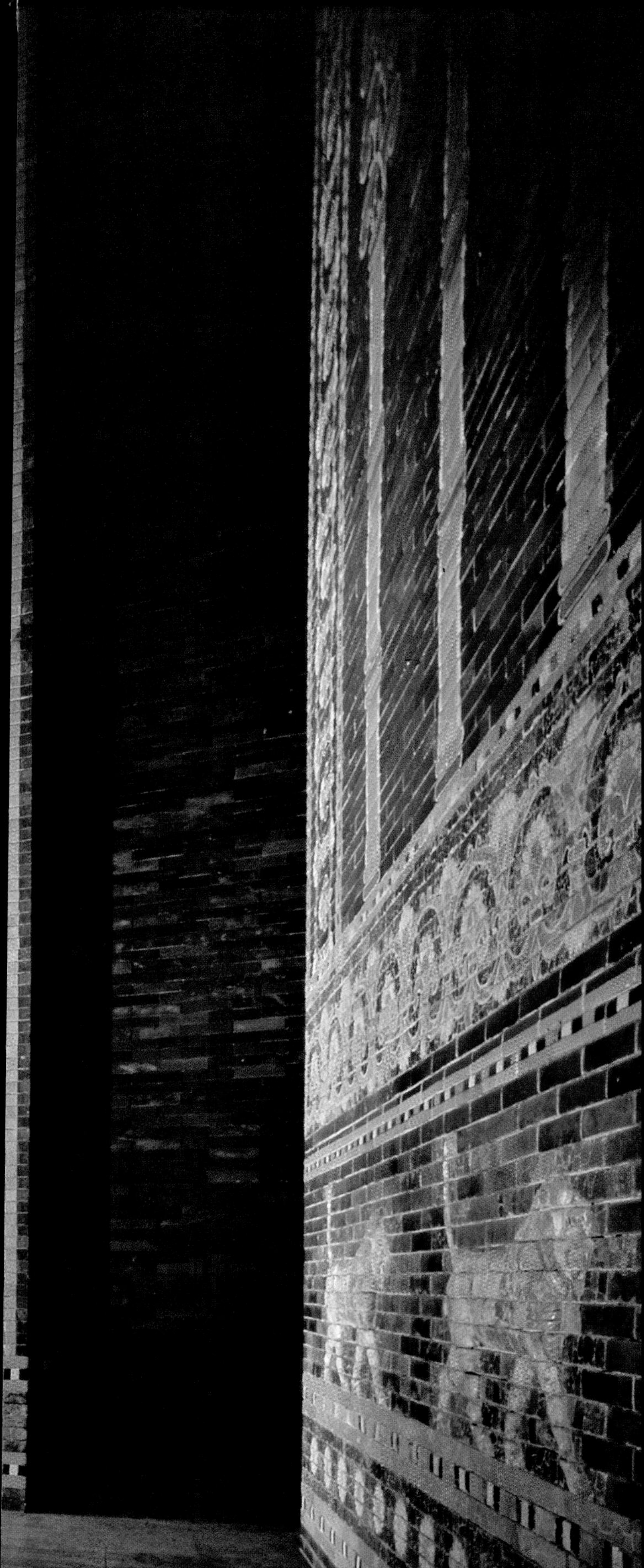

"I PLACED WILD BULLS AND FEROCIOUS DRAGONS IN THE GATEWAYS AND THUS ADORNED THEM WITH LUXURIOUS SPLENDOR SO THAT PEOPLE MIGHT GAZE ON THEM IN WONDER."

NEBUCHADNEZZAR II

THE BABYLONIANS

The Babylonian conquest and exile of Judeans in the early sixth century B.C.E., as portrayed in the Bible, made Babylon synonymous with oppression. "By the waters of Babylon, there we sat down and wept," lamented one psalmist. "O daughter of Babylon, you devastator! Happy shall he be who requites you with what you have done to us!" (Psalm 137:1-8). Yet some exiles settled in Babylon. "Build houses and live in them, plant gardens and eat their produce," Jeremiah advised them; "seek the welfare of the city . . . and pray to the Lord on its behalf, for in its welfare you will find your welfare" (Jeremiah 29:5-7).

Like the Assyrians—whom they overthrew to establish a Neo-Babylonian empire that recalled the time when King Hammurabi dominated Mesopotamia—Babylonians were ruthless in suppressing rebellions. The reckless decision of Judean kings to defy their Babylonian overlords led to the destruction of Jerusalem in 586 B.C.E. But those who survived and were exiled to Mesopotamia were not entirely at a loss, for they were returning to the land of Abraham, born according to Genesis in Ur of the Chaldeans (a term for the Neo-Babylonians, applied here to their ancient predecessors). Babylon was the heart of Mesopotamian civilization, the city that inspired the legend of the Tower of Babel and that under King Nebuchadnezzar II (604-562 B.C.E.) was indeed a place of towering monuments teeming with people speaking sundry languages. For the exiles, entering its gates must have been both dreadful and awe-inspiring.

The crowning emblem of Babylonian might was the Gate of Ishtar, shown here. Built by Nebuchadnezzar around 575 B.C.E. to honor the mother goddess Ishtar, it was "made of bricks with blue stone on which wonderful bulls and dragons were depicted," proclaimed the inscription. But the days of Babylonian glory were numbered and the deliverance that prophets envisioned would not be long in coming.

The spectacular Ishtar Gate, built in Babylon during the reign of King Nebuchadnezzar II, was excavated by a team led by German archaeologist Robert Johann Koldewey in the early 1900s and later reconstructed at the Berlin Museum of the Ancient Near East.

*Babylonians wearing peaked caps lead a
zebu in this relief depicting tribute offered to
Emperor Darius I of Persia in Persepolis. The
Persians conquered the Babylonians in the late
sixth century B.C.E. and absorbed their empire.*

This is one of many inscriptions bearing the words of Nebuchadnezzar II, who thanked deities such as Ishtar and Marduk, the "Lord of the Gods," for success by dedicating temples and monuments to them. Babylonian culture strongly influenced the Assyrians, whose ruler Ashurnasirpal II built a temple devoted to Ishtar adorned with the sculpted lion below. Lions were common in Mesopotamia and symbolized the might of its rulers in Scripture: "Israel is a hunted sheep driven away by lions. First the king of Assyria devoured him, and now at last Nebuchadnezzar king of Babylon has gnawed his bones" (Jeremiah 50:17).

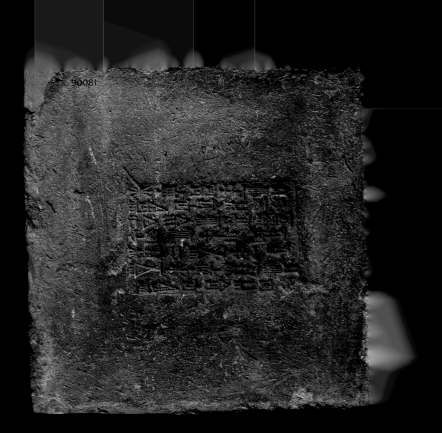

". . . t[o] Ia-'-u-kin, king . . ."

"10 (sila of oil) to . . . Ia-'-kin, king of Ia[. . .]"

"2½ sila to [...so]ns of the king of Ia-a-hu-du" (Judah)

10 (sila) to Ia-ku-u-ki-nu, the son of the king of Ia-ku-du
2½ sila for the 5 sons of the king of Ia-ku-du"

This ration tablet, which confirms the story of King Jehoiachin's captivity in Babylon, was one of many discovered, bearing the names of Judeans, Phoenicians, Egyptians, and others.

JEHOIACHIN'S RATION TABLETS

"EVIL-MERODACH KING OF BABYLON . . . GRACIOUSLY FREED JEHOIACHIN KING OF JUDAH FROM PRISON . . . A REGULAR ALLOWANCE WAS GIVEN HIM BY THE KING, EVERY DAY A PORTION, AS LONG AS HE LIVED."

II KINGS 25:27-30

The conquest and exile of Judeans by Babylonians did not occur all at once. The ordeal began in 598 B.C.E., 12 years before the destruction of Jerusalem, when King Jehoiakim, who launched Judah's rebellion against Babylon, died and was succeeded by his son, King Jehoiachin. Just 18 at the time, Jehoiachin reigned only a few months before Babylonian forces sent to crush the uprising encircled Jerusalem. According to Scripture, King Nebuchadnezzar II arrived soon after that siege began and accepted the surrender of Jehoiachin along with "his mother, and his servants, and his princes, and his palace officials." He was replaced on the throne by his uncle, King Zedekiah, who ruled Judah as Nebuchadnezzar's vassal. The Babylonian king then carried away Jehoaichin and his household along with "ten thousand captives . . . none remained, except the poorest people of the land" (II Kings 24:12-14).

Perhaps because he did not initiate the rebellion, Jehoiachin fared well in captivity. According to the Bible, he remained a prisoner until Nebuchadnezzar died in 562 B.C.E. and was succeeded by King Amel-Marduk (Evil-merodach), who then freed him and gave him a "regular allowance." That Jehoiachin in fact received generous rations while in exile in Babylon was confirmed by the tablet shown here, discovered by Robert Koldewey's team in a vault where official records were kept, near the Ishtar Gate. The ration tablet specified that "Johoiachin king of Judah" was to receive the equivalent of 32 pints of sesame oil and that his sons and other men of Judah were to receive lesser amounts. The tablet was inscribed during the reign of Nebuchadnezzar II, indicating that Jehoiachin was treated well even before he was freed by Amel-Marduk. A ration of that size suggests that he was a privileged prisoner, living with his retinue under house arrest.

Babylonians imposed escalating reprisals on those who defied them. For a first offense, a rebellious ruler who yielded might be allowed to remain if he offered tribute, or kept in lenient confinement like Jehoiachin. If the offender or his successor rebelled again, the punishment was terrible, as shown when King Zedekiah defied Babylon and Nebuchadnezzar's forces captured him: "They slew the sons of Zedekiah before his eyes, and put out the eyes of Zedekiah, and bound him in fetters, and took him to Babylon." With him went those Judeans who survived the destruction of Jerusalem: "So Judah was taken into exile out of its land" (II Kings 25:7-21).

The prophet Jeremiah, shown lamenting the destruction of Jerusalem in this painting by Rembrandt, believed that resistance to Babylonian might was futile and that the only safe course for Judeans was to seek God and trust in him to deliver them from evil in due time.

chapter 6

PERSIA, GREECE, AND ROME
Imperial Overlords

PERSIA, GREECE, AND ROME

One empire, the Babylonian, had carried the Hebrews into captivity. Another empire, the Persian, would provide them their means of freedom. The Persians had been on the rise since around the year 553 B.C.E., when their king, Cyrus II (559-529 B.C.E.), led a revolt that overthrew the neighboring Medes. With Cyrus's victory he had control over the vast imperial realm of the Medes, which stretched from the Persian Gulf to the Black Sea. His appetite thus whetted, the king set about further earning the name, Cyrus the Great, that history would remember him by. He cast his eyes on the other great empire in the region at the time, the Babylonian, and started drawing up his plans.

Although no one knew it then, the once mighty empire of lower Mesopotamia had already entered the reign of its last ruler. King Nabonidus (ca 556-539 B.C.E.) was little inclined to the exercise of power, and he had appointed as co-regent his son, Bel-shar-usur (ca 553-540 B.C.E.), who may well be the Belshazzar referred to in the prophecies of Daniel.

The Book of Daniel tells how Belshazzar decides to throw a grand feast, with the meal served to his guests on nothing less than the sanctified vessels that the Babylonians had pillaged from Solomon's Temple in Jerusalem. As he and his dinner guests begin to eat, however, a hand appears and begins writing a message on the wall of the ornate banquet hall: "Mene mene tekel parsin." Terrified, Belshazzar calls for an interpreter, but none can be found to translate the unknown words for the king. Finally, the Hebrew prophet Daniel is summoned. He explains the meaning of the message to Belshazzar: *Mene* meant that

> "THEN ROSE UP THE HEADS OF THE FATHERS' HOUSES OF JUDAH AND BENJAMIN, AND THE PRIESTS AND THE LEVITES, EVERY ONE WHOSE SPIRIT GOD HAD STIRRED TO GO UP TO REBUILD THE HOUSE OF THE LORD WHICH IS IN JERUSALEM."
>
> EZRA 1:5

God had numbered the days of his kingdom and brought it to an end. *Tekel* meant that he had been weighed in the balance and found wanting. And *peres* meant that his kingdom was divided and given to the Medes and the Persians. Belshazzar, the story continues, was dead within hours, slain by an assassin.

Soon, Cyrus and his armies were indeed marching, pouring across the Babylonian frontier and moving on the ancient capital. According to the Verse Account of Nabonidus, a Babylonian tablet recovered in 1924, the citizens of Babylon threw open wide the city gates in advance of the arrival of the Persian invaders. Cyrus himself, says the Book of Ezra, credits his spectacular success to a very specific source—the God of the Hebrews. "The Lord, the God of heaven, has given me all the kingdoms of the earth," he declares. Now it remained to be seen what the king would do with them.

A WORLD EMPIRE

As conqueror turned ruler, Cyrus revealed to the world another aspect of his greatness. Unusual for a king of the time, he showed respect and tolerance for the beliefs and practices of the various "kingdoms of the earth" that were now under his dominion. Cyrus not only gave the Hebrew exiles permission to leave Babylon and return to their homeland, he went further. According to the first verses of the Book of Ezra, he stated: "Whoever is among you of all his people, may his God be with him, and let him go up to Jerusalem, which is in Judah, and rebuild the house of the Lord, the God of Israel—he is the God who is in Jerusalem."

What's more, Cyrus gathered together all the Temple articles that Nebuchadnezzar had plundered and brought back to

Babylon, and gave them to the returning exiles. So laden, the Jews set off for home, doubtless following the same arc of the Fertile Crescent that their great patriarch Abraham had traveled on his historic journey from southern Mesopotamia to the land of Canaan.

As soon as the exiles returned to Jerusalem, they laid the cornerstone for construction of the Temple. But progress on the rebuilding was slow, despite the financial support provided by Cyrus's successor, Darius I (522-486 B.C.E.). Twenty years later, the Temple still remained unfinished, provoking the Prophet Haggai to demand of the people, "Is it a time for you yourselves to dwell in your paneled houses, while this house lies in ruins?" (Haggai 1:4).

Finally, by 515 B.C.E., the new temple was completed. It was less ornate than Solomon's Temple had been, and did not contain the Ark of the Covenant. But a temple for the Jews now once more stood in Jerusalem and would do so until the year 70 C.E. In the meantime, though, the region would come under the rule of two other outside powers and dominant cultures, this time emerging from the West. The first of these were the Greeks, their arrival in the region beginning with Alexander the Great's assault on the Persian Empire in 333 B.C.E. A year later he had occupied Judah, an early conquest in a campaign that would take him all the way across the Hindu Kush to the banks of the Indus and borders of India. Within a decade Alexander was dead. But in that short time, Greek customs and practice spread across much of the Near East. Alexander's generals divided the empire after his death, with Ptolemy taking charge of Judah (which became known as Judea during that time) and making it an Egyptian province ruled from the great city of Alexandria. Later, though, the descendants of another of Alexander's generals, Seleucus, pushed the Ptolemies out and seized control of Judea from their base in Syria and Mesopotamia.

The Hellenization of Judea

Whether ruled by Ptolemies or Seleucids, for Judea the process of Hellenization continued in all realms of life. It was reflected in the choice of everyday language—Greek instead of Hebrew or Aramaic—and in the naming of children. It could also be

A herd of sheep crosses the Euphrates—one of the "waters of Babylon" of Psalm 137, where the Jewish exiles wept in memory of Zion.

found in the adoption of Greek educational institutions, the study of Greek literature and philosophy, and the construction of theaters and stadiums. Many Jews, including those of the Diaspora, actively immersed themselves in Greek ideas, as can be seen in the works of the Jewish philosopher Philo of Alexandria in Egypt. Under the rule of the Seleucid King Antiochus IV Epiphanes, however, the process of Hellenization went too far. The king imposed punitive taxes on the people of Judea and stationed his troops in the country. Under penalty of death, he banned the Jews from practicing their religion and proceeded to plunder their temple, as Nebuchadnezzar had done before him, rededicating it to the worship of the Greek god Zeus.

THE REVOLT

Religious Jews were appalled at the king's actions. Under the leadership of a priest named Mattathias from the family of the Hasmoneans, they revolted. After Mattathias's death, his son Judas Maccabeus ("the Hammer") took charge of the rebels, who were known as the Maccabees, and they kept on fighting. In the year 164 B.C.E., Judas Maccabeus managed to recapture the Temple in Jerusalem, which he rededicated to God. But Judas was not yet done. He and his brothers, Jonathan and Simon, continued the struggle until they had driven the Seleucids out of Judea entirely and won complete independence.

For the first time since the Babylonian conquest, the Jewish people were in control of their land. Under the rule of the Hasmonean dynasty that followed, the state grew in power and size. But toward the middle of the first century B.C.E., internal squabbles began to weaken the ruling family and gave a foothold in the region to the next rising world power: Rome.

The Romans were on the move across much of Europe and the Near East. In 63 B.C.E. their general Pompey marched into Judea and made it a vassal of Rome. Within a quarter century, the Roman senate had set up Herod the Great as its king, and he ruled the territory with an iron hand until his death in the year 4 B.C.E. Herod's monumental building projects included the renovation of Jerusalem's Temple, but he left behind him an impoverished, rebellious kingdom. For Judea and its people, a time of unprecedented turmoil lay ahead.

The empire of Cyrus the Great stretched from his homeland in Persia across Mesopotamia and Canaan all the way to Asia Minor and the very borders of Europe.

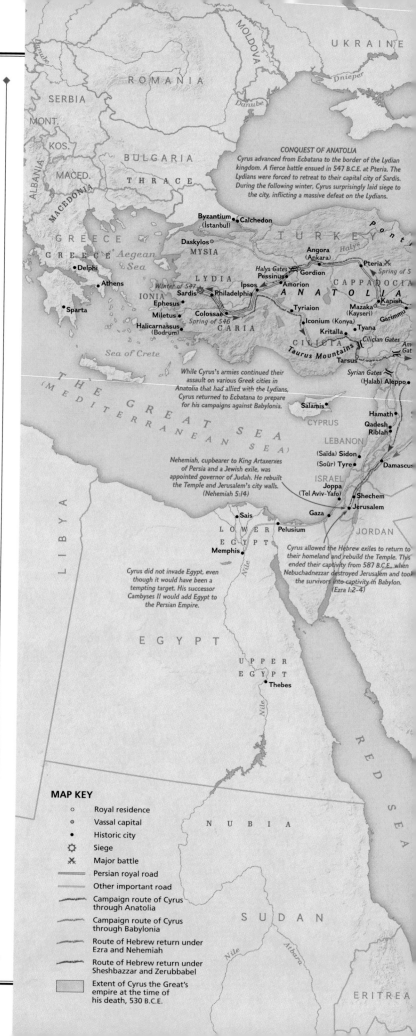

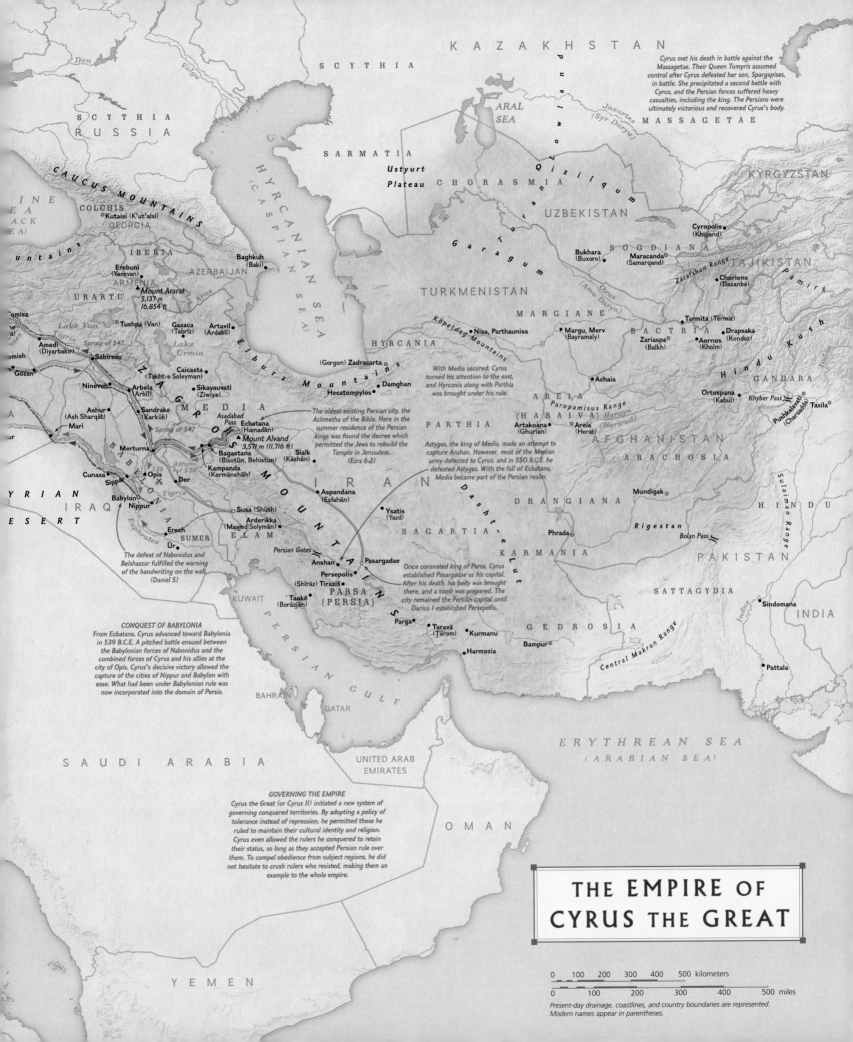

THE EMPIRE OF CYRUS THE GREAT

Cyrus met his death in battle against the Massagetae. Their Queen Tomyris assumed control after Cyrus defeated her son, Spargapises, in battle. She precipitated a second battle with Cyrus, and the Persian forces suffered heavy casualties, including the king. The Persians were ultimately victorious and recovered Cyrus's body.

With Media secured, Cyrus turned his attention to the east, and Hyrcania along with Parthia was brought under his rule.

Astyges, the king of Media, made an attempt to capture Anshan. However, most of the Median army defected to Cyrus, and in 550 B.C.E. he defeated Astyges. With the fall of Ecbatana, Media became part of the Persian realm.

The oldest existing Persian city, the Achmetha of the Bible. Here in the summer residence of the Persian kings was found the decree which permitted the Jews to rebuild the Temple in Jerusalem. (Ezra 6:2)

Once coronated king of Parsa, Cyrus established Pasargadae as his capital. After his death, his body was brought there, and a tomb was prepared. The city remained the Persian capital until Darius I established Persepolis.

The defeat of Nabonidus and Belshazzar fulfilled the warning of the handwriting on the wall. (Daniel 5)

CONQUEST OF BABYLONIA
From Ecbatana, Cyrus advanced toward Babylonia in 539 B.C.E. A pitched battle ensued between the Babylonian forces of Nabonidus and the combined forces of Cyrus and his allies at the city of Opis. Cyrus's decisive victory allowed the capture of the cities of Nippur and Babylon with ease. What had been under Babylonian rule was now incorporated into the domain of Persia.

GOVERNING THE EMPIRE
Cyrus the Great (or Cyrus II) initiated a new system of governing conquered territories. By adopting a policy of tolerance instead of repression, he permitted those he ruled to maintain their cultural identity and religion. Cyrus even allowed the rulers he conquered to retain their status, so long as they accepted Persian rule over them. To compel obedience from subject regions, he did not hesitate to crush rulers who resisted, making them an example to the whole empire.

0 100 200 300 400 500 kilometers
0 100 200 300 400 500 miles

Present-day drainage, coastlines, and country boundaries are represented. Modern names appear in parentheses.

THE PERSIANS

The Persians were the superpower of the sixth and fifth centuries B.C.E. From their heartland in the southwestern part of what is now Iran, they strode boldly onto the world stage to dominate a realm that empires before them had only been able to dream of. Under the rule of the Achaemenid dynasty, they demonstrated their power for all to see by building grand palaces, at Persepolis, Pasargadae, and Susa. These royal residences have yielded a treasure trove of archaeological riches, from life-size bas-relief sculptures, like those at right in Persepolis, to elaborately decorated bowls, goblets, and jewelry.

Dating from the fifth and fourth centuries B.C.E., many of the artifacts on the following pages come from the Oxus treasure, a collection of 170 gold and silver objects so called because they were unearthed near the Oxus River, known today as the Amu Darya. The story of their recovery is somewhat less orthodox than that of most museum artifacts. In 1880, a group of merchants who had acquired the pieces were robbed of them by bandits in Afghanistan. As this was happening, a passing British army officer intervened and helped the merchants recover their treasures. As a mark of their thanks, the merchants allowed the officer to buy one of the pieces, the gold bracelet with griffins (see p. 223), before continuing on their way to Rawalpindi, where they sold the rest of them to the highest bidder. It was thus in the bazaars of British India that the Oxus treasure eventually emerged, and from there found its way to the British Museum in London.

The era of the Achaemenids was brief but glorious, barely 200 years in all. In that time they exerted a huge impact on the peoples of the Near East, particularly the people of Judah. What follows on this and the next pages is a sampling of the physical legacy they left behind.

In solemn procession, envoys from Media ascend the stairs to pay tribute—such as that shown on pages 222-23—to the Persian king, in this relief from the palace at Persepolis. The neighboring Medes were the first people conquered by the rising power of Persia.

A gold plaque depicts a priest in Median costume. The ceremonial staff he carries is much less elaborate than the one at left, which is made of gold and lapis lazuli and adorned with the head of a snarling lion, the latter the hallmark of Achaemenid rule.

The animal motif is repeated in the handle of the gold jug above, right, while the terminals of this gold bracelet are in the form of rising griffins.

Decorative golden archers, in gold inlay, march around the outside of this silver bowl.

CYRUS'S CONQUEST OF BABYLON

"I SETTLED IN THEIR HABITATIONS, IN PLEASING ABODES, THE GODS OF SUMER AND AKKAD, WHOM NABONIDUS, TO THE ANGER OF THE LORD OF THE GODS, HAD BROUGHT INTO BABYLON."

CYRUS CYLINDER

Moving from the religious realm to the geopolitical and back again, the Book of Isaiah expresses great hope about the growing strength of the Persian Empire. Cyrus the Great had been driving all before him in the Near East, and in him the writer of Isaiah sees God's instrument to free the Judean exiles from their Babylonian captivity.

Cyrus was the founder of the mighty Achaemenid dynasty, a ruling family that claimed descent from a legendary ancestor named Achaemenes. Soon after becoming king in 559 B.C.E., Cyrus defeated Astyages, King of Media, and seized control of his empire. Next, he conquered the ruler of Lydia, the fabulously wealthy King Croesus, and extended his reach across Asia Minor. Taking heart at the unfolding events, the writer of Isaiah believed that the

conqueror of the Jews, Babylon, would soon be conquered itself. In chapter 45 he writes:

Thus says the Lord to his anointed, to Cyrus, whose right hand I have grasped, to subdue nations before him and ungird the loins of kings, to open doors before him that gates may not be closed: "I will go before you and level the mountains, I will break in pieces the doors of bronze and cut asunder the bars of iron, I will give you the treasures of darkness and the hoards in secret places, that you may know that it is I, the Lord, the God of Israel, who call you by your name. For the sake of my servant Jacob, and Israel my chosen, I call you by your name, I surname you, though you do not know me. . . . I have aroused him in righteousness, and I will make

straight all his ways; he shall build my city and set my exiles free, not for price or reward," says the Lord of hosts.

The words of Isaiah proved prophetic. In 539 B.C.E., the Persians toppled the Babylonian Empire, which was then ruled by King Nabonidus, an event memorialized in the famous Cyrus Cylinder (below, left).

Discovered in Babylon in 1879, the barrel-shaped clay cylinder was most likely unearthed amid the ruins of the city's temple of Marduk. It was already damaged when it was discovered, and although the clay cylinder contained 36 lines of text it was clear that additional lines were missing. Nearly a hundred years later, a clay fragment from another museum collection containing nine of the missing lines was added. The cylinder is still incomplete, however, and the remaining lines of text have never been found. Even so, the Cyrus Cylinder tells us much about the Persian conquest of Babylon and the events that followed.

The text starts with an unflattering description of Nabonidus himself—"an incompetent person" who "continually did evil against his city," imposing forced labor on the people and "ruining them all." Then the Cyrus Cylinder goes on to describe what the Persian king did after conquering Babylon. In a rare move by a ruler of antiquity, Cyrus decided not only to liberate the local people from forced labor but also to allow all foreigners who lived as captives in Babylon to return home.

And so it was that in 538 B.C.E. the Jews made the journey from Babylon back to Judah, with Cyrus's blessing and his permission to rebuild their Temple in Jerusalem. Before they left, Cyrus restored to them the gold and silver vessels that Nebuchadnezzar had plundered from the Temple. The first chapter of the Book of Ezra records these events, echoing the sentiments on the Cyrus Cylinder:

"The great gods delivered all the lands into my hands," Cyrus the Great declares on the clay brick at left, which was found in Ur and dates from the sixth century B.C.E. The Cyrus Cylinder (below, left) documents the Persian king's conquest of the Babylonian empire.

In the first year of Cyrus king of Persia, that the word of the Lord by the mouth of Jeremiah might be accomplished, the Lord stirred up the spirit of Cyrus king of Persia so that he made a proclamation throughout all his kingdom . . . "The Lord, the God of heaven, has given me all the kingdoms of the earth, and he has charged me to build him a house at Jerusalem, which is in Judah. Whoever is among you of all his people, may his God be with him, and let him go up to Jerusalem, which is in Judah, and rebuild the house of the Lord, the God of Israel—he is the God who is in Jerusalem; and let each survivor, in whatever place he sojourns, be assisted by the men of his place with silver and gold, with goods and with beasts, besides freewill offerings for the house of God which is in Jerusalem."

The city the departing Jews left behind, Nebuchadnezzar's once great capital, would also be restored. Cyrus himself set about reconstructing the city's walls. The Persian king was now master of a huge realm, the first "world empire." He administered his various territories with remarkable enlightenment and justice. By adopting a policy of tolerance instead of repression, he permitted those he ruled to maintain their cultural identity and religion. Cyrus even allowed the rulers he conquered to retain their status, as long as they agreed to accept Persian rule over them. The latter was no small consideration: To compel obedience from subject regions and rulers, Cyrus did not hesitate to crush local leaders who resisted Persian power, making of them examples and as a warning to the other peoples of his sprawling empire.

REBUILDING JERUSALEM

Satraps

The governors of the various provinces of the Persian Empire were known as satraps. They undertook the administration of the province and ruled in the king's name. Today the term satrap is sometimes applied to a leader who acts as the surrogate of a more influential and powerful regime.

The exiled Jews returned from Babylon with great joy and great expectation, ready to rebuild Jerusalem and restore its temple. But when the Prophet Nehemiah arrived, the city and its occupants were in a sad state.

In Babylon, Nehemiah had been the cupbearer to King Artaxerxes. But in 445 B.C.E., the Persian ruler sent him to Jerusalem to serve as its governor and save it from further decay. Carrying letters of safe-conduct from the king, Nehemiah made his way to the city to see the scale of the problem. He found poor social and economic conditions throughout Jerusalem and the infrastructure in a bad state of repair. During the decades that the Jewish exiles had spent in Babylon, those who remained had taken over other families' homes, and newcomers from Assyria had also moved in. Thus, when the exiles had returned there were more residents than Jerusalem could accommodate. The Book of Nehemiah puts the number of returning Israelites at 42,000 in all. The new arrivals had to cast lots to determine who could settle in the city.

Other challenges loomed for the people of Judah, especially for the poor, who were hit hard by meager harvests. In return for food for their children, many were obliged to give up their land and were reduced to a state of virtual serfdom. Nehemiah introduced debt relief measures to alleviate their plight, calling on the rich to return debtors' fields, vineyards, and olive groves to their original owners.

Nehemiah also carried out religious reforms, instituting observation of the Sabbath and raising revenue for the temple. But he is, perhaps, remembered most for supervising the reconstruction of the city's walls. The raising of the walls was a defensive measure, made especially necessary after threatening moves made by hostile neighbors such as the Samarians and the Ammonites, who had occupied the territory around Jerusalem in the intervening years. Despite their opposition, Nehemiah set about his task.

According to the Bible, Nehemiah's builders worked with great speed and determination. And because of the resistance to their undertaking, they worked as

The Prophet Nehemiah looks on the ruins of Jerusalem in the art (above) by James Tissot. A section of the city's wall (opposite) may be Nehemiah's.

discreetly as they could, and under the cover of darkness. Organized by families and clans, they labored on specific sections of the wall or on individual gates. Remarkably, the entire wall around the city was raised and restored in just 52 days, and Nehemiah himself continued to work in the city for the next 12 years, before returning to the Persian court.

The results of his efforts may have been discovered in 2008. Archaeologists from the Shalem Center in Jerusalem tentatively identified part of the 2,500-year-old "Nehemiah wall," located near the Dung Gate and facing the Mount of Olives. They found the remains of a hundred-foot section of the wall and a nearby tower, which scholars had previously believed was constructed during the time of the Hasmonean kingdom. However, through pottery found at the site, as well as other artifacts such as arrowheads and seals, some archaeologists suspect that the wall may have been built centuries earlier than the time of Nehemiah's governorship of Jerusalem.

THE GREEKS

The advance of Alexander the Great across the Near East and through the lands of the former Persian Empire brought to the region not just a new ruler. It also brought with it a new dominant cultural force—that of Hellenism.

In the wake of the Macedonian armies, the enduring influence of Hellenism was felt by many newly subject people during the fourth century B.C.E.—Egyptians, Parthians, Armenians, Assyrians, Jews, and others. Throughout this realm Alexander founded new cities, many of which were settled by Greeks. The new arrivals brought with them Greek philosophy, religion, art, education, and politics. Greek buildings rose in the cities. Greek was spoken in the streets and the marketplaces, and Greek coins, carrying their leaders' distinctive realistic portraits, were exchanged.

Alexander's generals divided the empire after his death, perpetuating Hellenism through four great ruling dynasties: the Ptolemies, the Seleucids, the Antigonids, and the Attalids. Eventually, these dynasties were overthrown by the Roman Republic. But the new imperial masters adopted many of the cultural manifestations of the Greeks. Thus, in some ways the Romans continued to perpetuate Hellenism in the lands of the Near East.

The most famous of Greek temples, the Parthenon, sits atop the Acropolis in Athens.

This statue portrays the Greek philosopher Socrates, who lived from around 469 to 399 B.C.E. Socrates famously declared, "I know that I know nothing" and was one of the founders of Western philosophy.

This Greek krater, a vase used to mix wine and water, shows Dionysos watching a Maenad dancing. Dionysos was the Greek god of wine, whose Roman counterpart was Bacchus.

At right is a fragment of the 2,100-year-old Antikythera mechanism, a bronze system of cogs and wheels that may be the earliest surviving mechanical computing device, found in 1900 in a Greek wreck.

This famous mosaic from ancient Pompeii shows a
mounted Alexander the Great at the Battle of Issus in
southern Anatolia, where he defeated the Persians in
a famous victory. With the fall of the Persian Empire
to Alexander and his generals, territories like Judah
came under Greek influence.

" . . . BEHOLD, A HE-GOAT CAME FROM THE WEST ACROSS THE FACE OF THE WHOLE EARTH, WITHOUT TOUCHING THE GROUND."

DANIEL 8:5

ALEXANDER'S EMPIRE

In 334 B.C.E. Macedonia's Alexander the Great—believed by some commentators to be the warlike goat of the Book of Daniel—crossed the Hellespont from Europe into Asia to take on the might of Achaemenid Persia. He had unified mainland Greece under his rule and had grown accustomed to carrying all before him. After defeating Persian troops at the Granicus River near ancient Troy, Alexander forged his way across Asia Minor. South of the village of Issus, on the Mediterranean coast, his Greek and Macedonian soldiers encountered a vastly superior enemy force, commanded by the Persian emperor Darius III. During the battle, Alexander mounted his horse, Bucephalos (opposite), and made straight for "the Great King," who had placed himself in the center of the Persian line, flanked by his best warriors. Unaccountably Darius fled. When his soldiers saw this, they abandoned the battlefield. Alexander's cavalry pursued them, slaughtering many and almost snatching the emperor, before darkness brought the battle to an end. Issus was a great victory for Alexander. As was his custom, he founded a city nearby to commemorate the event, which he called Alexandrette and is the present-day Turkish city of Iskenderun.

The Battle of Issus marked the beginning of the end for the Persian Empire—and the beginning of the Hellenization of the Near East. Alexander followed victory with victory, as his armies made a virtual tour of the Persian realm. Leaving Asia Minor, he pushed on down the Mediterranean coast toward Israel and Egypt.

ALEXANDER BESIEGES TYRE

One of Alexander's targets as he drove south was the strategically important port city of Tyre. The Phoenician citizens vainly hoped they would be able to stand aside in the conflict between the Macedonians and the Persians. But Alexander would have none of it. He demanded entry to the city, and when the city leaders refused, he laid siege to it.

Tyre posed particular challenges to the invaders, located as it was on an island about half a mile off the coast, and slowed down the hard-charging Macedonians. The warrior Alexander turned engineer. He decided to build a great causeway from the shore to the port—using cedars from Lebanon as piles and the debris of an abandoned earlier city on the mainland as construction material.

The challenges of the undertaking were considerable, especially as the water got deeper farther out from shore. The Tyrians were accomplished sailors, and their fleet harassed the Macedonians as they labored on the causeway. In response, Alexander scoured the region for ships, traveling to Sidon, Cyprus, and ports in Syria to put together his own navy. Eventually, he assembled a force of some 220 warships, which descended on Tyre and the defenders' smaller fleet.

After seven months, the causeway had reached Tyre, whose 200-foot-high walls shielded the city's landward-facing side. Alexander brought up two huge siege engines, their wooden towers almost as tall as the walls themselves. From these, great catapults targeted defenders on the city walls while ballista below pounded the walls themselves.

The name Alexander was revered in Egypt, one of the lands that made up his vast empire and whose ancient port city is still known as Alexandria. The hieroglyphs on the Egyptian cartouche below spell out the name of the great conqueror.

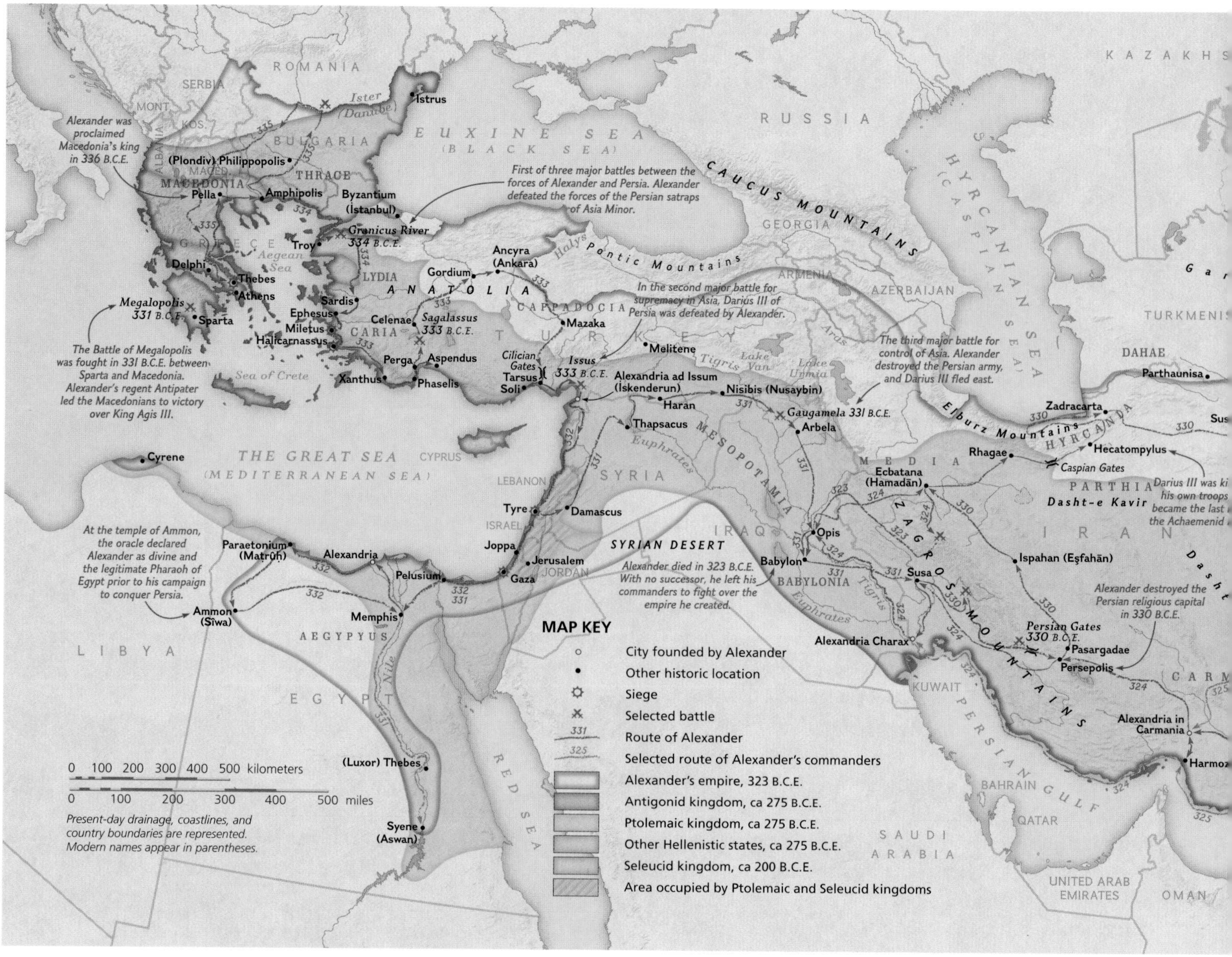

KAZAKHS
ROMANIA
SERBIA
MONT.
KOS.
ALBANIA
Alexander was proclaimed Macedonia's king in 336 B.C.E.
Ister (Danube)
Istrus
BULGARIA
EUXINE SEA
(BLACK SEA)
RUSSIA
(Plondiv) Philippopolis
MACEDONIA
THRACE
Pella
Amphipolis
Byzantium (Istanbul)
First of three major battles between the forces of Alexander and Persia. Alexander defeated the forces of the Persian satraps of Asia Minor.
CAUCUS MOUNTAINS
HYRCANIAN SEA (CASPIAN SEA)
GEORGIA
Granicus River 334 B.C.E.
Troy
GREECE
Aegean Sea
Delphi
Thebes
Athens
Megalopolis 331 B.C.E.
Sparta
LYDIA
ANATOLIA
Gordium
Ancyra (Ankara)
Halys
Pontic Mountains
ARMENIA
AZERBAIJAN
Sardis
Ephesus
Miletus
Halicarnassus
CARIA
Celenae
Sagalassus 333 B.C.E.
CAPPADOCIA
Mazaka
In the second major battle for supremacy in Asia, Darius III of Persia was defeated by Alexander.
TURKMENIS
The Battle of Megalopolis was fought in 331 B.C.E. between Sparta and Macedonia. Alexander's regent Antipater led the Macedonians to victory over King Agis III.
Sea of Crete
Xanthus
Perga
Aspendus
Phaselis
Cilician Gates
Tarsus
Soli
Issus 333 B.C.E.
Melitene
Tigris
Lake Van
Lake Urmia
Aras
The third major battle for control of Asia. Alexander destroyed the Persian army, and Darius III fled east.
DAHAE
Parthaunisa
Alexandria ad Issum (Iskenderun)
Nisibis (Nusaybin)
Haran
Gaugamela 331 B.C.E.
Arbela
Elburz Mountains
Zadracarta
HYRCANIA
Sus
Thapsacus
MESOPOTAMIA
Euphrates
Hecatompylus
Rhagae
Caspian Gates
Cyrene
THE GREAT SEA
(MEDITERRANEAN SEA)
CYPRUS
LEBANON
SYRIA
MEDIA
Ecbatana (Hamadān)
PARTHIA
Darius III was ki his own troops became the last the Achaemenid
Dasht-e Kavir
Tyre
Damascus
ISRAEL
IRAQ
ZAGROS MOUNTAINS
IRAN
At the temple of Ammon, the oracle declared Alexander as divine and the legitimate Pharaoh of Egypt prior to his campaign to conquer Persia.
Paraetonium (Matrūh)
Alexandria
Joppa
Jerusalem
JORDAN
Gaza
SYRIAN DESERT
Opis
Alexander died in 323 B.C.E. With no successor, he left his commanders to fight over the empire he created.
Babylon
BABYLONIA
Susa
Ispahan (Eşfahān)
Pelusium
Alexander destroyed the Persian religious capital in 330 B.C.E.
Ammon (Sīwa)
Memphis
AEGYPYUS
MAP KEY
City founded by Alexander
Other historic location
Siege
Selected battle
Route of Alexander
Selected route of Alexander's commanders
Alexander's empire, 323 B.C.E.
Antigonid kingdom, ca 275 B.C.E.
Ptolemaic kingdom, ca 275 B.C.E.
Other Hellenistic states, ca 275 B.C.E.
Seleucid kingdom, ca 200 B.C.E.
Area occupied by Ptolemaic and Seleucid kingdoms
Alexandria Charax
Persian Gates 330 B.C.E.
Pasargadae
Persepolis
LIBYA
EGYPT
Nile
KUWAIT
PERSIAN GULF
CARM
Alexandria in Carmania
Harmoz
0 100 200 300 400 500 kilometers
0 100 200 300 400 500 miles
(Luxor) Thebes
RED SEA
BAHRAIN
QATAR
Present-day drainage, coastlines, and country boundaries are represented. Modern names appear in parentheses.
Syene (Aswan)
SAUDI ARABIA
UNITED ARAB EMIRATES
OMAN

The map above shows the extent of the empire of Alexander the Great and his successors—from Greece in the west all the way to the Indus Valley in the east.

At last, the wall was breached, and Alexander's men poured up the causeway and inside the port. Frustrated at the resistance of the defenders, they destroyed half the city, leaving it in much the same condition as its mainland counterpart. Alexander lost just around 400 men in the fighting while inflicting some 8,000 casualties on the defenders. Thousands more were seized and sold into slavery. Leaving behind him the ruined city and the great causeway (the remains of which can still be seen today), Alexander pushed on down the coast, ever eager for more conquests.

Gaza Resists the Invaders

And the conquests came. Town after town submitted to the Macedonian invaders as they drove toward Egypt. But before he reached the prize on the Nile, another city would choose to resist the invaders and stall Alexander's plans. A hundred and fifty miles south of Tyre, the people of Gaza refused entry to the Macedonians, and Alexander was forced to lay siege again.

Gaza had once been a port on the Mediterranean coast, like the earlier-inhabited settlement of Tyre. But while Tyre eventually moved half a mile out to sea (to the island redoubt), Gaza had "moved" some two miles inland: Its harbor had silted up over the centuries, leaving the port stranded and landlocked. Alexander would thus not encounter the difficulties he had faced in besieging Tyre. However, while the silting up of its harbor had cut Gaza off from the sea, it had also left the city on a mound more than 60 feet high (around which the Gazans had erected massive fortifications). This posed other problems for Alexander, who could not simply

EMPIRE OF ALEXANDER THE GREAT AND THE SUCCESSOR KINGDOMS

UZBEKISTAN

CHINA

Bukhara

TIAN SHAN

Alexandria Eschate (Khujand)

329

Maracanda (Samarqand)

SOGDIANA TAJIKISTAN

329

Chorienes

Sogdiana Rock

327

Alexandria Oxiana

Alexandria Margiana (Bayramaly)

BACTRIA

Bactra (Balkh)

329

Drapsaca (Kondoz)

Khawak Pass

(Bagram) Alexandria in Caucaso

Shibar Pass

Kabul

327

GANDARA

Aornus 326 B.C.E.

Indus

Taxila

ARIA

Artacana

AFGHANISTAN

Alexandria (Ghazni)

Bucephala

Nicaea

Hydaspes 326 B.C.E.

andria Areion Ierat)

DRANGIANA

Sangala

Alexandria Arachoton (Kandahar)

329

PUNJAB

ARACHOSIA

325

PAKISTAN

Alexandria Prophthasia

325

Bolan Pass

Alexandria in India

In the last major battle fought by Alexander, he defeated the Indian army. Although victorious, Alexander's exhausted army refused to go any farther.

GEDROSIA

Pura (Īrānshahr)

Alexandria Oreiton

325

Pattala

INDIA

Gwadar

325

ERYTHREAN SEA
(ARABIAN SEA)

move his siege engines up to the city and attack it in the usual manner.

Once again, the engineer came to the fore. Alexander built another huge mound adjacent to elevated Gaza. Then he moved the same engines he had used at Tyre to the top of the mound, and from there began to pound the city's walls. Two months after laying siege to Gaza, the Macedonians broke through the walls. According to ancient sources, some 10,000 of the inhabitants were put to the sword and the rest enslaved.

Flush with yet another victory, Alexander's army appeared invincible, an irresistible force bludgeoning its way through all in its path. The way to Egypt lay open. And it was there that the all-conquering Macedonian founded the most famous Alexandria of them all, the great port city on the Mediterranean.

Following well-trodden Fertile Crescent paths, he next swept up to Assyria before turning down the great river valley to Babylon. From here, he struck out to the east, capturing the Achaemenid capitals of Susa and Persepolis. Alexander made it all the way to the Punjab in India before turning back west, and died in the Babylonian palace of Nebuchadnezzar, the previous conqueror of Judah and Jerusalem.

A VISITOR TO JERUSALEM?

The Jewish historian Flavius Josephus later writes a somewhat fanciful account of Alexander's supposed arrival in Jerusalem after his conquest of Gaza. In it, the Macedonian advances on the city, only to be met and welcomed on the way by priests dressed in fine white linen and led by the high priest himself, ceremonially clad in purple and scarlet. According to Josephus, Alexander greeted them warmly: "And when he had . . . given the high-priest his right hand, the priests ran along by him, and he came into the city. And when he went up into the Temple, he offered sacrifice to God, according to the high-priest's direction, and magnificently treated both the high-priest and the priests. And when the Book of Daniel was showed him wherein Daniel declared that one of the Greeks should destroy the empire of the Persians, he supposed that himself was the person intended." Although the story by Josephus is most likely apocryphal, the Greeks had indeed come to Judah, and the process of Hellenization had begun.

Flavius Josephus
A member of the Pharisees, Josephus (ca 37 to 100 C.E.) lived during some of the most momentous decades in human history. As military commander he fought during the Great Jewish Revolt against Rome. Defeated, he changed sides to embrace Rome. After Vespasian was proclaimed emperor, Josephus joined his court and authored *The Jewish War* and *The Jewish Antiquities.*

This limestone relief of Greek soldiers adorned a fourth-century B.C.E. tomb of a prince of Lycia. Alexander and his armies conquered this region of Asia Minor around the year 334.

This bronze bust portrays Seleucus I Nicator—one of Alexander the Great's generals and the founder of the Seleucid dynasty that eventually extended its control over Judea.

"FORCES FROM HIM SHALL APPEAR AND
PROFANE THE TEMPLE AND FORTRESS . . .
BUT THE PEOPLE WHO KNOW THEIR GOD SHALL
STAND FIRM AND TAKE ACTION."

DANIEL 11:30-32

PTOLEMIES AND SELEUCIDS

Just ten years after the Battle of Issus, Alexander the Great died of a fever, in circumstances that have never been fully explained. With his death at the age of 33, his empire split apart. Rival generals struggled for supremacy. Eventually, Cassander emerged as the ruler of Greece and Macedonia, while Antigonus seized control of Asia Minor. Ptolemy established himself in Egypt, where he moved the capital from Memphis to Alexandria. And Seleucus I Nicator (312-280 B.C.E.) took over in Mesopotamia and Syria.

Judea was a battleground for these rival generals. Initially, the region fell under the rule of Ptolemy, who made it a province of Egypt. Jewish communities had long existed in Egypt: Papyrus records show that after the destruction of Jerusalem in 586 B.C.E., Jewish exiles had settled as far south as Aswan. Now, Jewish merchants and scholars also moved to the flourishing new capital of Alexandria and to other cities.

Meanwhile, Hellenistic influence in philosophy, literature, and theater was spreading throughout Judea itself. As it did, the Greek language began to replace Hebrew and Aramaic as the lingua franca in the arts, politics, and international trade. The latter was further enhanced by the use of a common currency, with the Greek drachma—featuring the owl, symbol of the goddess Athena—the coin of choice. Eventually, the Ptolemies lost possession of Judea to the rival dynasty established by

Seleucus. In 200 B.C.E., the Seleucids won a crushing victory over King Ptolemy V, at the Battle of Paneion, near the Golan Heights. As a consequence, little Judea fell under the rule of another outside power. But despite the goodwill of the region's first Seleucid ruler (see sidebar), the process of Hellenization continued, complete with the building of Greek-style cities based on the grid pattern and boasting theaters, libraries, temples, and gymnasia. Some Jews sought accommodation with the new Greek culture. Others, to greater or lesser degrees, opposed it. The once homogenous society of the Jews began to split apart.

The ruins of the Grand Colonnade in Apamea, Syria, testify to the glory of the Seleucid dynasty.

Antiochus the Great

The Seleucid victor at the Battle of Paneion was Antiochus III (223-187 B.C.E.), and by his decree Judea became part of the Seleucid realm. Antiochus treated the Jews of Judea with tolerance and liberality. He granted them funds for the Temple and exempted the people of Jerusalem from tribute payments, allowing them to live in accordance with the "laws of their fathers."

But if one action by Antiochus had brought the Jews respite, another brought them disaster. After numerous victories in the East, the man who styled himself "the Great King" (after the Persian Achaemenids) overreached. He seized a number of Greek city-states in Asia Minor and, in 196 B.C.E., crossed the Hellespont into mainland Greece and territory over which the new and rising power of Rome claimed dominion.

Routed by the Romans in Europe, Antiochus fled to Asia Minor. The Romans followed (an early foray

into a region where they would later play a major role) and defeated the Seleucid king again. They imposed a punitive treaty on Antiochus, which included the surrender of hostages, territories in Asia Minor, and the fleet that had carried his army to Europe. It also included the payment of crippling reparations, which Antiochus had to levy from the ordinary people of Judea, Syria, and elsewhere in his realm. In 187 B.C.E. the king was murdered in a temple of Baal. The once mighty Seleucid empire was, by this time, virtually bankrupt.

"AND THE KING SENT LETTERS BY MESSENGERS TO
... THE CITIES OF JUDAH; HE DIRECTED THEM TO
FOLLOW CUSTOMS STRANGE TO THE LAND."

I MACCABEES 1:44

ANTIOCHUS IV EPIPHANES

After the reign of Antiochus III, the Seleucid empire may have been in a weakened state, but it was still the imperial power in Judea. When Antiochus's son came to the throne, however, things for the Jews grew worse. Upon becoming king, Antiochus IV (175-164 B.C.E.) adopted a surname that best captured his elevated aspirations: The name Epiphanes is short for "god manifest." Perhaps not surprisingly, then, Antiochus IV—whose likeness is depicted on the gold coin at right—exhibited none of the respect for the Jewish religion that his father had shown. He not only traveled to Jerusalem and removed all the gold and silver objects from the Temple, he also rededicated the sanctuary to Olympian Zeus. Then he proceeded to ban Jewish observance of the Sabbath, forbade circumcision, and tore up copies of the Scriptures.

REVOLT OF THE MACCABEES

But Antiochus IV Epiphanes was not yet done in Judea. Those who resisted his dictates faced death or enslavement, and there are numerous stories from this era of Jews who were martyred for their faith. The martyrdom of seven Jewish brothers is a particularly infamous episode. Given the choice of eating pork or being killed, the eldest of the brothers announced that the family would rather die than violate the Jewish laws. This answer infuriated the king; he had the eldest brother's tongue cut out and his hands and feet chopped off, then he was burned alive in a frying pan. Each of the brothers remained steadfast, and one after another they were tortured and killed in this manner in front of their mother, who was later executed as well.

To further advance the process of Hellenization, the king even began to force Jews to make heathen sacrifices. When a priest named Mattathias saw a Jew obeying this instruction, he became enraged and killed the man along with a Seleucid official. Mattathias then called upon all God-fearing people to join him in revolt. After his death, his son Judas Maccabeus took over leadership of the rebels, who became known as the Maccabees. Books of the

The Durable Drachma

The drachma was the coin of the realm in the ancient Greek world. It was the oldest continually used currency in history until 2001, when it was replaced by another currency serving an even greater realm, the euro.

The ruins of Beth-zur (Khirbat Tubay-qah) in Israel was once a fortress of the Maccabees during their revolt against the Seleucids

same name—I and II Maccabees—recount the barbarity of Antiochus IV Epiphanes and the revolt against his rule. These books are part of what is usually known as the Apocrypha or the deuterocanonical writings.

Most scholars identify Antiochus as the "little horn" who comes forth from the "ten horns" (the Hellenistic kings) in the Book of Daniel, chapters 7 and 8. And, echoing the acts of Antiochus, chapter 11 declares:

Forces from him shall appear and profane the temple and fortress, and shall take away the continual burnt offering. And they shall set up the abomination that makes desolate. He shall seduce with flattery those who violate the covenant; but the people who know their God shall stand firm and take action. And those among the people who are wise shall make many understand, though they shall fall by sword. . . .

The widespread use of tetradrachm (four drachmas) coins like this one featuring Antiochus IV Epiphanes symbolized the increasing Hellenization of the Seleucid empire. Jewish law forbade such "graven images" of men and animals.

THE HASMONEAN KINGDOM

Under the leadership of Judas Maccabeus, the Maccabees launched a campaign of guerrilla warfare against their Seleucid overlords. The tactics proved successful beyond all expectation. The Maccabees seized control of Jerusalem and in 164 B.C.E. took possession of the Temple, which they rededicated to the worship of the Hebrew God. The Temple's rededication is commemorated each year by the celebration of Hanukkah.

For Judas Maccabeus and some of his followers this success was not enough. They wanted full political autonomy for Judea. The Books of Maccabees describe their many successful battles, among them a spectacular victory over the Seleucid commander Nicanor in 160 B.C.E. The following year, though, the Seleucids amassed a large force and dispatched it to Judea to put down the revolt. In response, Judas Maccabeus could muster only 3,000 men to meet them, and many of these fled the field when the Seleucids appeared; only 800 fighters remained. As the Battle of Elasa began, near the modern-day town of Ramallah in what is now the West Bank, Judas Maccabeus, the most important of those 800, was killed. In I Maccabees 9:21, the people mourn: "How is the mighty fallen, the savior of Israel!"

But the Maccabeus family was not finished. One of Judas's brothers, Jonathan (160-142 B.C.E.), took over the leadership of the revolt. Under his command, the Maccabees continued to inflict great losses on Seleucid forces. Finally, in 152 B.C.E. the then king, Demetrius I (162-150 B.C.E.), sued for peace. He appointed Jonathan Maccabeus governor of the Seleucid province of Judea, and two years later the former rebel leader was confirmed as high priest.

ON TO INDEPENDENCE

In Jerusalem and Judea there was great rejoicing. But the celebrations were not universal. For many pious Jews, the appointment of Jonathan Maccabeus as high priest was a step too far. According to Jewish law, the holders of this office had to be a member of the Zadokite family, a man who could trace his ancestry all the way back to Zadok, the high priest of King Solomon. And Jonathan was not a Zadokite. As a result, some Jews withdrew their support from the Maccabees.

Undeterred, the Maccabees continued to plan, plot, and struggle for outright Judean independence, taking advantage of power struggles within the Seleucid empire and growing tensions with Ptolemaic Egypt to advance their cause. When Jonathan Maccabeus was killed by a Seleucid assassin, another brother stepped up. Simon Maccabeus (142-134 B.C.E.) won the final concessions

from the Seleucids. They recognized him not only as high priest but as autonomous ruler of the kingdom of Judea.

Some 445 years after Nebuchadnezzar's destruction of Jerusalem, the kingdom of David and Solomon had been restored. A ruling dynasty emerged, the Hasmonean, named after a forebear of the Maccabeus brothers, a certain Asamonaios. The Hasmoneans reigned for a century, both as high priests and as kings of Judea, their exploits recorded in the Books of Maccabees. Eventually, they would be swept away by the invading Romans.

These arrowheads were found in the citadel in Jerusalem and date to the time of the Maccabean Revolt. The Hasmonean kingdom that resulted (palace ruins, opposite) would rule an independent Judea for nearly a hundred years.

"THE ASSEMBLY OF ISRAEL DETERMINED THAT EVERY
YEAR AT THAT SEASON THE DAYS OF DEDICATION
SHOULD BE OBSERVED WITH GLADNESS AND JOY."

I MACCABEES 4:59

REDEDICATION OF THE TEMPLE

Shortly after the Arab-Israeli Six Day War of 1967, Professor Nahman Avigad of Hebrew University began excavations in the Old City of Jerusalem, now known as the Jewish Quarter, just west of the Temple Mount. The work would go on for the next decade and a half, often 24 hours a day, and in the process turned up archaeological treasures from a part of the city whose ancient past had been virtually sealed.

Among Avigad's finds were the ruins of palaces belonging to the Hasmonean kings, the residences of the high priests, and the homes of ancient Jerusalem's wealthiest citizens. In one of the latter, located just a few hundred yards from the Temple site, Avigad found an important and iconic artifact of the nation Israel. Inscribed on a plaster fragment from one of the walls was the oldest representation that has yet been found of the ceremonial candelabra known as the menorah, a millennia-old symbol of Judaism.

The multibranched menorah, which is said to represent the burning bush that Moses encountered at Mount Horeb in Midian, once burned in the Jewish Temple. It was constructed according to specific divine instructions, as recorded in the Book of Exodus, chapter 25:

And you shall make a lampstand of pure gold. The base and the shaft of the lampstand shall be made of hammered work; its cups, its capitals, and its flowers shall be of one piece with it; and there shall be six branches going out of its sides . . . three cups made like almonds, each with capital and flower, on one branch, and three cups made like almonds, each with capital and flower, on the other branch.

However, when Judas Maccabeus and his fellow Maccabees entered the devastated Temple building in 164 B.C.E., they found only enough ritually pure oil to burn the menorah for one more day. Yet the lights miraculously continued to burn for eight days, until a new supply of the oil could be found. The Maccabees went on to rededicate the Temple to God, an event that triggered great celebration among the people of Jerusalem.

Today, the restoration of the Temple is celebrated every year during Hanukkah, also known as the Festival of Lights, with the lighting of the menorah. The original Temple menorah had six branches extending out from the central candlestick, as shown in the artifact at left. However, because the light in the Temple continued to burn for eight days, the traditional Hanukkah menorah has a central candleholder with eight branches. On each day of Hanukkah, one of these eight candles is lit until all are burning. The ninth, higher branch is known as the *shamesh* (helper or servant), and it holds the candle used to light the other eight.

The branches of a menorah are inscribed on plaster and date to the first century B.C.E.

"Period of John Hyrcanus II, the High Priest and the Council of the Jews"

Two clay emblems, one adorned with a menorah, made to commemorate the rededication of the Temple to the God of the Hebrews in 164 B.C.E.

The horror of the story from the Book of Judith is captured in "Judith and Holofernes" by Artemisia Gentileschi.

Judith and Holofernes

In remembrance of the oil that burned in the Temple, many traditional Hanukkah foods are cooked in oil, such as potato pancakes known as latkes. Another custom associated with Hanukkah is the eating of dairy products, especially cheese. This is done in memory of a beautiful Hebrew heroine from the Book of Judith, one of the deuterocanonical books of the Hebrew Bible.

According to the story, when King Nebuchadnezzar called on the Israelites to fight with the Babylonians against the Persians, they rejected his request. In response, he dispatched a general named Holofernes with an army to punish them. When the Babylonians laid siege to the city of Bethulia, one of its residents, a widow named Judith, resorted to desperate means to save her people. Summoning all her courage, she slipped into the enemy camp and told the Babylonian soldiers she met that she was an Israelite defector.

Taken before Holofernes, Judith extolled the greatness of Nebuchadnezzar. The general, smitten by her beauty and intelligence, took her back to his tent, where Judith put her plans into action. She plied him with cheese and wine until he was drunk. And when he fell asleep, she took a sword and cut off his head. Hiding it in a bag, she carried it off with her as she escaped back to Bethulia.

Later, when the headless body of Holofernes was found, one Babylonian official lamented: "One Hebrew woman has brought disgrace upon the house of King Nebuchadnezzar." Judith's plan had worked. The enemy troops fled, and as they did so were chased and slaughtered by the pursuing Israelites.

Archaeologists unearthed these ruins at Qumran, once the site of a Jewish monastic settlement. It is believed that the scribes who penned the Dead Sea Scrolls lived here.

ESSENES, SADDUCEES, PHARISEES, AND SAMARITANS

"FOR THERE ARE THREE PHILOSOPHICAL SCHOOLS AMONG THE JEWS ... THE PHARISEES ... THE SADDUCEES, AND THE THIRD, WHO PRETEND TO A MORE SEVERE DISCIPLINE, ARE CALLED ESSENES."

JOSEPHUS, *THE JEWISH WAR*

Some scholars have claimed that the scribes who lived at Qumran and penned the famous Dead Sea Scrolls (see pp. 244-45) were members of a little-known sect called the Essenes. Historical records mention them from about 130 B.C.E. until the destruction of Qumran by the Romans in 68 C.E., when the Essenes seem to have disappeared. The Essenes are not mentioned by name in the Scriptures, but they are referred to by the Jewish historian Flavius Josephus and by other contemporary writers.

The Essenes were a separatist, ascetic group who rejected what they considered the corrupt worship in the Temple led by the high priest, and had removed themselves to the Judean desert. There they established a monastic community where the faithful led lives of self-denial, celibacy, study of Scripture, and extreme purity—even to the point of withholding one's bodily functions on the Sabbath. Excavations at Qumran indicate Essene belief in an apocalyptic "War between the Children of Light and the Children of Darkness" and the imminent arrival of the Jewish Messiah, or Anointed One.

The other two "philosophical schools" mentioned by Josephus are the Sadducees and the Pharisees, both familiar to readers of the Gospels. The Sadducees were the priestly aristocracy of Judaism, and differed from the Pharisees in that they did not believe in resurrection of the dead. Based at the Temple, the Sadducees comprised most of the members of the council known as the Sanhedrin, which was Judaism's highest authority on religious questions and the body that would oversee the trial of Jesus.

The Pharisees (literally, the "separated ones") were a strict, legalistic group who, although laymen, followed the same purity laws as the priests. Often depicted in the New Testament as self-righteously pious in their rigid application of Jewish law, they also believed that the oral tradition carried the same authority as Scripture. After the destruction of the Second Temple, the Pharisees were the main group remaining to establish Rabbinic Judaism.

GOOD SAMARITANS?

Another group at this time were the Samaritans, although their history had placed them outside mainstream Judaism. In 722 B.C.E., the Assyrians had conquered the northern kingdom of Samaria and deported part of its population. The Assyrians then resettled in Samaria outsiders from Babylonia and elsewhere, who not only worshipped foreign gods but also intermarried with those Israelites who remained. Their mixed Jewish-gentile descendants became known as the Samaritans.

Relations between Samaritans and Jews were sometimes marked by open conflict. After the Jews returned from exile in Babylon, the Samaritans tried to disrupt their rebuilding of the Temple and the walls of Jerusalem. Eventually, they built their own religious sanctuary at Mount Gerizim. Hostility between the two groups continued into Jesus' day, adding poignancy to his parable of the Good Samaritan, which tells of the kindness of a Samaritan to a Jew who had been set upon by thieves.

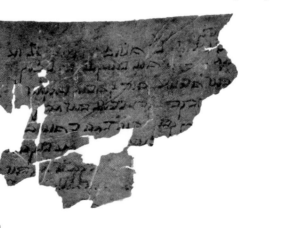

These fragments are from Qumran's Isaiah Scroll, which contains apocalyptic visions that the Essenes—who believed they were living in the "end of days"—may well have applied to themselves.

THE DEAD SEA SCROLLS

"THUS SAYS THE LORD OF HOSTS,
THE GOD OF ISRAEL: TAKE THESE DEEDS . . .
AND PUT THEM IN AN EARTHENWARE VESSEL,
THAT THEY MAY LAST FOR A LONG TIME."

JEREMIAH 32:14

The scrolls were preserved through the ages in cylindrical clay jars like these, found in a cave not far from the Dead Sea. The jars ranged from 18 inches to 25 inches in height.

Sometimes vital artifacts from the biblical past are unearthed by professional archaeologists working in the field, like Hebrew University's Nahman Avigad (see p. 240). At other times they are found by ordinary people going about their daily business, oblivious of the ancient history that surrounds them. Such was the case with the celebrated Dead Sea Scrolls.

The scrolls were first discovered in 1947, by young Bedouin shepherds in one of the many caves near the shores of the Dead Sea, from which the scrolls get their name. While in pursuit of a lost sheep (or possibly a goat), one of the boys came upon seven earthen jars at the back of the cave. Hoping for gold or silver, he and his friends were disappointed to find nothing but debris in the jars and, in one, three leather bundles, two of them wrapped in disintegrating linen. Naturally, they had no idea what they had found—or the fact that it was of far greater value than any treasures they may have found in the caves. What the young Bedouin had discovered would astonish the scholarly world. The bundles contained copies of the Scriptures that were nearly a thousand years older than the oldest complete manuscript of the Hebrew Bible known at that time, which dated from the ninth century C.E.

The discovery set off a nearly decade-long search, by Bedouin and archaeological teams alike, that produced thousands of fragments of biblical documents in 11 of the caves. Together, the texts contained several copies of every book of the Old Testament with the exception of the Book of Esther.

THE ISAIAH SCROLL

Among the most significant discoveries was a scroll found in the very first cave, which contains the first Book of Isaiah. Only the Isaiah Scroll, as it is known, carries the entire text and is the oldest manuscript of a complete book of the Bible. Later on, additional scrolls were discovered, including a second Book of Isaiah. Found in a good state of preservation, the scrolls are in the possession of the Shrine of the Book Museum today. On their journey they passed through the hands of shady antiques dealers, high church officials, bankers, and academics, before they came to rest in the museum built specifically to house them and the other Dead Sea Scrolls.

It is believed that the scrolls had been penned by scribes from the nearby settlement of Qumran. When not in use, the scrolls would be kept in large clay jars, and at some point the jars had been secreted in the caves for safekeeping. However, their caretakers did not return to retrieve them, leaving it to the shepherd boy to stumble upon them generations later. These artifacts have been proclaimed the most important archaeological discovery of the 20th century.

The scrolls showed that, for the better part of a millennium, the biblical text had remained amazingly intact. Scholars have detected only small variations between the Dead Sea version and later manuscripts.

"And God said to Habakkuk to write the things to come upon the last generation but he did not reveal to him the close of the end time."

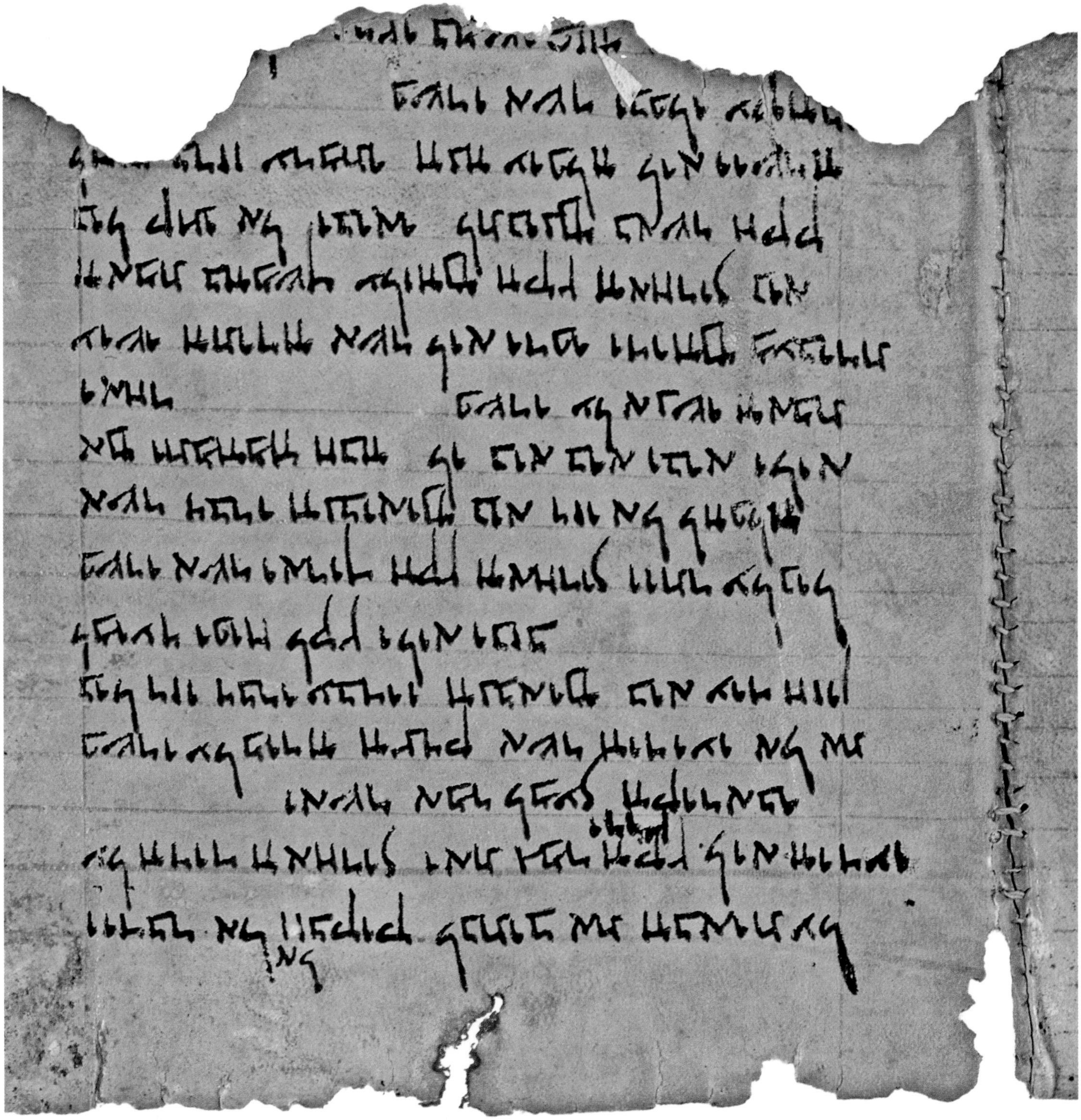

The Dead Sea Scrolls were written in Hebrew, Aramaic, and Greek. In addition to copies of the Scriptures and commentary on the Hebrew Bible such as on the prophet Habakkuk, pictured above, the scrolls also contained sectarian writings of a group of Jewish believers who lived at Qumran.

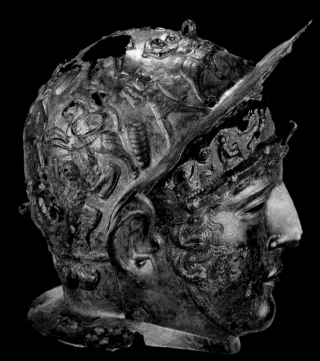

This two-piece visor helmet once belonged to a Roman legionary.

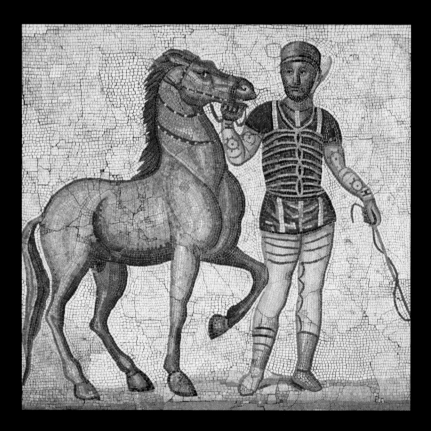

Above, a Roman mosaic depicts a horse and one of the charioteers who raced in the amphitheaters of the capital.

A legionnaire's short sword and sheath. Only the handle and parts of the sheath, which would have been made of leather or wood, are missing.

"RENDER THEREFORE TO CAESAR THE THINGS
THAT ARE CAESAR'S, AND TO GOD
THE THINGS THAT ARE GOD'S."

MATTHEW 22:21

THE ROMANS

The Hellenistic dynasties that ruled the former empire of Alexander the Great had spread Greek influence far beyond the homeland of Greece. However, they in turn eventually succumbed to the rising power of Rome. According to legend, Rome was founded along the banks of the Tiber by the twin brothers Romulus and Remus. After a period of rule by kings, Rome became a republic around 509 B.C.E., governed by a constitution that divided power among a number of entities. These included assemblies of the people, a senate composed of patricians, and elected magistrates. The two most important magistrates of ancient Rome where the consuls, who wielded executive and military power.

The Roman republic began by extending its rule over the Italian peninsula, which it completed by around the year 280 B.C.E. Next, it acquired Sicily and Spain. And an imperial Rome had begun its ascent. With its conquest of Greece, coastal North Africa, and, later, the Macedonian and Seleucid empires, Rome became the premier power in the Mediterranean. The Romans brought many things to the lands that they occupied—their laws, religion, literature, art, architecture, and technology. Wherever Rome went, so did its mighty legions. Well-trained and disciplined, the legionaries enforced Roman rule throughout a vast realm, which at its height stretched from northern Britain to the deserts of Judea.

The ruins of the Roman Forum, with the last remaining columns of the Temple of Saturn in the foreground

THE BUILDING FRENZY OF HEROD THE GREAT

Proclaimed king of Judea by the Roman Senate, Herod I (40-4 B.C.E.) was a man determined to make his mark on the world around him. He presided over a time of peace and prosperity, and mainly earned his sobriquet, "the Great," from his many building projects. These included two forts he had constructed to protect his kingdom, the ruins of which can still be seen today. One is Masada, which overlooks the Dead Sea and would play an iconic role in the history of the Jewish people. Another is the massive palace-fortress of Herodium that continues to dominate the surrounding landscape as it did in Herod's day (opposite).

Herodium rises up in the Judean desert, eight miles south of Jerusalem. Here, Herod's engineers reshaped a cone-shaped hill into a formidable fortress 300 feet high and topped it with a cylindrical outer wall some 200 feet in diameter. They built four great towers to watch, sentrylike, over the four cardinal directions. And below, they amassed tons of earth and rock to create a virtually impregnable redoubt.

But for all its daunting fortifications, Herodium was not a place without luxury or comfort. Atop the height Herod built spacious royal residences. And for good measure, at the base of the mountain he constructed another palace, which boasted formal gardens, a swimming pool almost the size of a soccer field, and a 1,100-foot-long terrace that may have been used to race horses.

According to Flavius Josephus, Herodium is also the site of Herod's final resting place. However, the historian did not record where Herod was buried. Only in 2007 did archaeologists discover halfway up the slopes a mausoleum believed to have contained the king's sarcophagus.

Herod's other great construction (or renovation) project was the building most revered by Jews throughout the ages—the Temple. Eager to win his subjects' favor, impress his Roman masters, and bring glory to himself, Herod determined to bring Solomon's Temple back to its former glory. By all accounts, he more than succeeded. The huge complex known as Herod's Temple was one of the wonders of the ancient world. Religious law dictated that the actual sanctuary had to be the same size as the original shrine. But those laws said nothing about the surrounding area, and here Herod's building ambitions had free reign. Outside the temple he added a large courtyard known as the Court of the Women. At the northern end of the complex he built a bastion called the Antonia Fortress, and at the other a huge columned pavilion called the Royal Stoa.

Only priests were permitted to carry out the construction work on the sanctuary, so one thousand were trained as carpenters and stone masons. The priests finished their task in less than two years. But more than 80 years would pass before the rest of the complex was completed. Only seven years after that, in 70 C.E., the Roman legionaries of Titus conquered Jerusalem and utterly destroyed Herod's great complex, reducing it to rubble.

Visiting the finished temple before its destruction, Josephus describes how it was built with "finely hewn white stones, twenty-five cubits long," while the vast arcade was "four columns deep, their capitals fashioned in the Corinthian order, which amazed visitors with their grandeur." The complex sat on a platform supported by hundred-foot-high retaining walls and covered one-sixth of the area of the city. Only the Western Wall of this platform, also known as the Wailing Wall, remains today.

Mass Murderer
For Christians, the name of Herod the Great will always be associated with the slaughter of the innocents—Herod's systematic murder of boys age two and under as a way of eliminating the infant that the Magi said had been "born king of the Jews" (Matthew 2:2).

This limestone sundial is the only archaeological find that is directly related to Herod's Temple. Priests may have used sundials for the timing of temple services.

CAESAREA MARITIMA

Archaeologists working on the remains of Herod's greatest feat of engineering, Caesarea Maritima, face a challenge: They must exchange their brushes and trowels for diving gear and plunge into the waters of the Mediterranean around the artificial port city.

The city was born out of necessity. King Herod realized that to take advantage of trade between Rome and the rest of its empire, Judea would need a bigger seaport than modest Joppa. However, the coastline offered no natural deepwater harbor. Herod decided to build one—a state-of-the-art facility on the site of an abandoned Phoenician trading post, about 30 miles north of modern Tel Aviv. Ever mindful of his imperial masters, Herod named it Caesarea in honor of the Roman emperor Caesar Augustus.

> "ALONG THE COAST HEROD DISCOVERED A CITY THAT WAS IN DECAY. . . ."
>
> JOSEPHUS,
> THE JEWISH WAR 1.408-410

In 22 B.C.E., Herod's builders set to work. The main feature of Caesarea's revolutionary design was a pair of huge breakwaters. Constructed with a special marine concrete invented by the Romans, the breakwaters were half a mile long and were, according to Josephus, "laid out as a compass toward the land . . . so that the great ships might lie in safety." Stonemasons fitted the breakwaters with docks, an oil-burning lighthouse, and warehouses to store grain, wine, and other imported goods.

Back from the harbor, Herod built a city on the Roman grid pattern, at one time home to 100,000 inhabitants, 3,500 of whom could be accommodated in the city's theater. The city also had temples, a palace, a hippodrome, paved streets, and an elaborate sewer system. A grand temple dedicated to Augustus and Roma towered over the city. All was enclosed by a protective wall, through which passed an aqueduct that brought fresh water from five-mile-distant Mount Carmel to supply the city's many fountains and baths.

St. Paul would be tried in Caesarea, and from here he would be taken in shackles to Rome. The remains of the once thriving port are still visible today.

A bird's-eye view of Caesarea Maritima shows the outlines of Herod's port city. The restored theater in the foreground once staged Greek and Roman plays and today hosts summer concerts by the Israeli Philharmonic Orchestra.

GABRIEL'S REVELATION

In 2008 a polished stone, inscribed with ink like the Dead Sea Scrolls and dating to the late first century B.C.E. or early first century C.E., set off a storm of debate in the scholarly world. A collection of short prophecies in Hebrew proclaiming the "word of YHWH," the stone raises questions about the early Jewish and Christian understanding of a Messiah. And it helps make the case that Jesus and Christianity can best be understood through a better appreciation of contemporary Jewish history and beliefs.

"The Last Judgment" by Rogier van der Weyden shows the archangel Michael weighing souls at judgment day.

Known as Gabriel's Revelation after its apparent author, the artifact has received widespread coverage in the academic and popular press, and scholars are still examining the stone, questioning its authenticity. Its provenance is unknown, although experts believe that it probably was found near the Dead Sea in Jordan. It was purchased from a Jordanian antiques dealer in the late 1990s by a Swiss collector, who kept it in his home in Zurich. Later, it was examined by an Israeli scholar, who, intrigued, eventually published a paper about it, triggering much attention and interest.

Written in the first person, Gabriel's Revelation is presented in two neat columns, much like those in the Torah. The stone, however, is now broken, and some of its text is faded, making it hard to read and leaving interpretations open to debate. The text does include a number of biblical phrases. Many of its prophetic declarations begin with "Thus said the Lord of Hosts," and other lines use terms like "the God of Israel" and "My servant David." The expression God shows "steadfast love to thousands" is found in Exodus, chapter 20, and elsewhere in the Old Testament, and the quotation "I will shake the heavens and the earth" is from the Book of Haggai. The text also has strong apocalyptic overtones. It makes reference to the archangel Michael, for instance, who is mentioned in the Old and New Testaments, as well as in several extrabiblical sources, often in conjunction with the archangel Gabriel and the end times.

Significantly, the author of Gabriel's Revelation seems to make reference to two different concepts of the returning Messiah. According to one, that event is associated with a "day of battle," after which the triumphal Messiah will make his enemies his "footstool." According to the other, it involves a suffering Messiah, in the manner of Jesus, dying and rising from the grave. The author of Gabriel's Revelation leaves his readers, down through the ages, in no doubt about his preference. Rather than the servant savior in the mode of Jesus, the writer makes it clear his vision of the Messiah is the victorious, all-conquering one.

"Here is the Glory of YHWH the Lord of Hosts, the Lord of Israel."

Three feet tall, "Gabriel's Revelation" comprises 87 lines of text in two columns. Unlike the text on other stone artifacts, the inscriptions are not engraved but written in ink.

A decree, written in three different scripts, served as the key to deciphering hieroglyphs.

The Rosetta Stone

It has been called the most famous piece of rock in the world, and over the years has drawn millions of visitors to Room 4 of the British Museum in London. Why? Because the 45-inch-tall Rosetta Stone has provided a key to unlocking the mysteries of the ancient world through an understanding of Egyptian hieroglyphics.

The stone was discovered near Rosetta (Rashid) by French scholars during Napoleon's invasion of Egypt, and two years later it was captured from them by the British. A year after that the Rosetta Stone was on display in the British Museum.

The stone records a decree issued in 196 B.C.E. by the priests of Memphis honoring an Egyptian ruler. Of more importance, however, is the fact that the ancient decree was written in the three languages that were in use in Egypt at the time. One was Greek, the "official" language of the Ptolemaic rulers. The second was demotic, the cursive script used by literate Egyptians. And the third, and most important, was hieroglyphic, the picture-symbol system of writing that was used exclusively by the priestly class.

Eighteenth-century scholars understood ancient Greek. So when the tri-language stone was discovered, they had a means to solve the riddle of hieroglyphs, which had up until then successfully hidden its meaning from the modern world. It took a team of scholars more than 20 years, but at last they deciphered a writing system that the Egyptians had used for more than 3,000 years and was the key to unlocking other ancient histories.

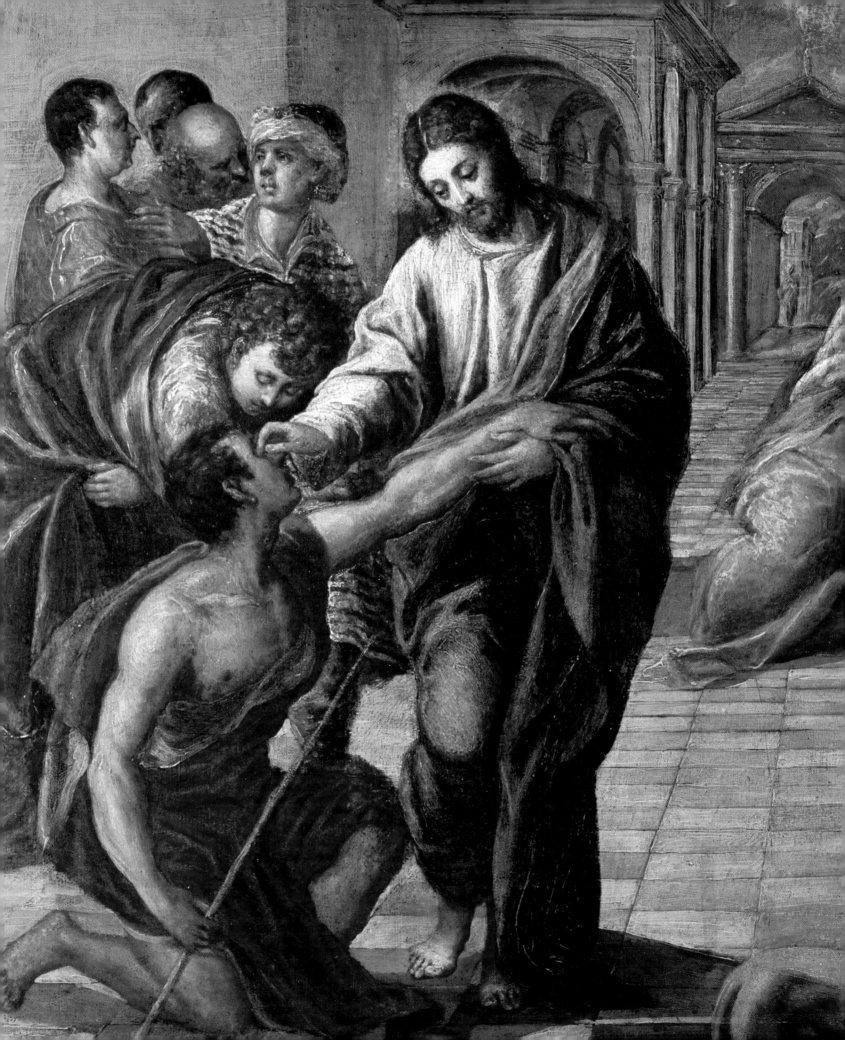

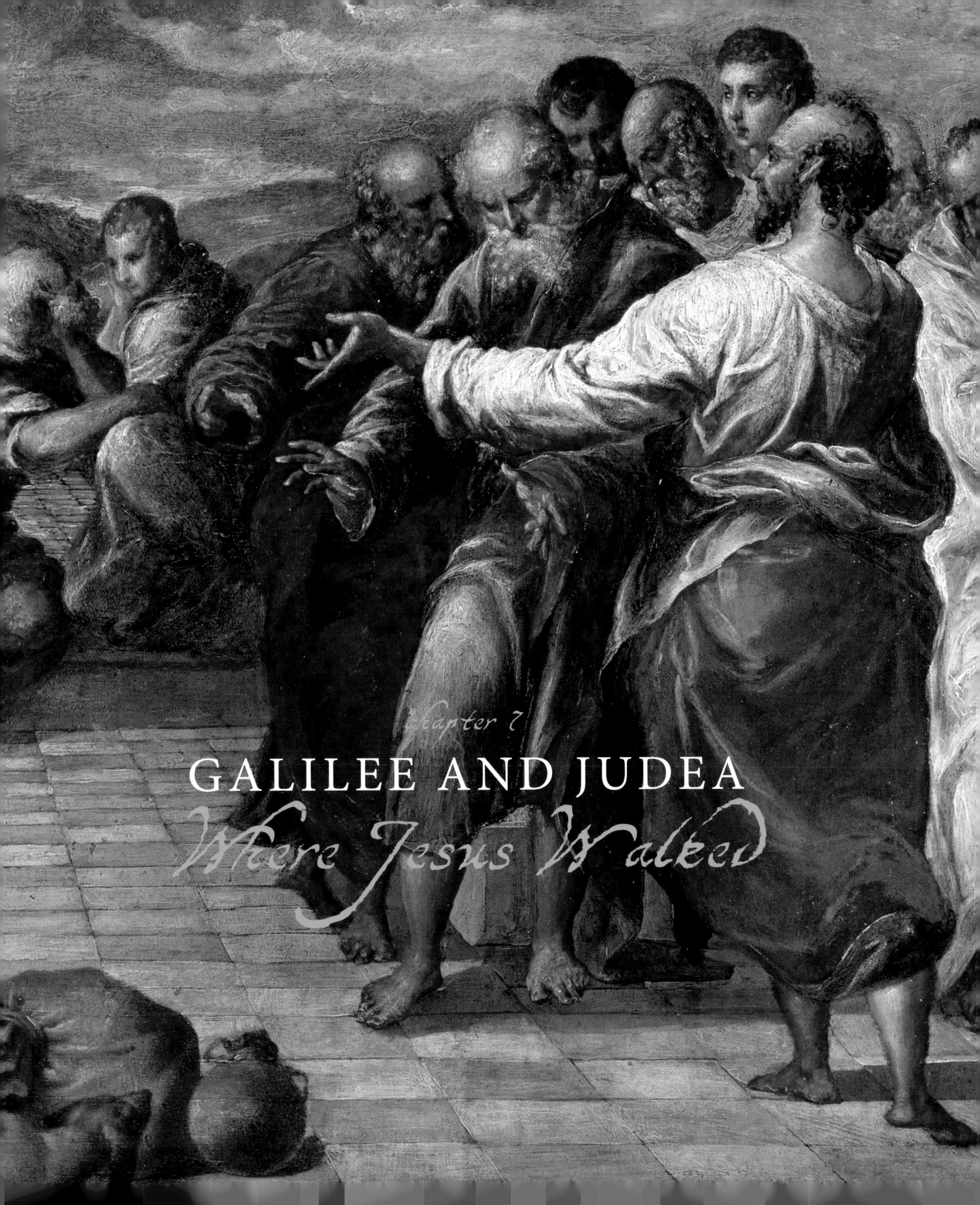

chapter 7

GALILEE AND JUDEA

Where Jesus Walked

GALILEE AND JUDEA

Roman rule in the province of Judea was marked by periodic rebellion and repression. In the year 6 C.E., a small group of resistors, known as the Zealots, staged yet another revolt, promising deliverance for the Jewish people. It ended when two Roman legions crushed the uprising, crucifying 2,000 of the rebels and deporting 6,000 others. Less than a quarter century later, the Romans would find themselves confronted by another man claiming to be Israel's Messiah, a young carpenter who began with just a dozen followers. He, too, would die on a Roman cross, but his ideas would be harder to stop.

According to the gospels, Yeshua bar Yosef (Jesus, son of Joseph) was born to a young mother named Mary in Bethlehem in Judea. He was raised in Nazareth, a village in northern Galilee, where he likely learned his carpentry working alongside his father, whose lineage traced back to "the house of David." The canonical gospels say little about the childhood of Jesus. He had four brothers and several sisters. The Gospel of Luke records one of Jesus' first public acts when, as a boy, he went to the synagogue in Nazareth and read from the Book of Isaiah. A Muslim cemetery occupies the area where scholars suspect the synagogue once stood. Four granite columns found there are thought to be the remains of an earlier Byzantine church. Greek Orthodox belief holds that this marks the site of the synagogue that Jesus visited.

When he was about 30, in the 15th year of the reign of the Emperor Tiberius, Jesus heard his cousin, John the Baptist, preaching in the wilderness about a coming Messiah who would deliver Israel. John called on his followers to repent of their sins and baptized them, in a symbolic cleansing, in the Jordan River. According to Scripture, Jesus asked John to baptize him, and when he rose from the waters he was ready to begin bringing God's message to the world. Today, clergy from the nearby Monastery of St. John still conduct baptisms in the Jordan where John is said to have baptized Jesus. It is at a spot not far from where the prophet Elijah had taken refuge after fleeing from Queen Jezebel.

But Jesus also learned from John the dangers of speaking truth to power. The power in question was the tetrarch Herod Antipas, son of King Herod the Great, who, the Bible says, had tried to thwart the rise of a rival king of the Jews by slaughtering all the male children around the time of Jesus' birth. Antipas had scandalously married Herodias, the wife of his half brother, and suffered denouncement by John the Baptist as a result. Stung by the holy man's words, Herodias sought a way to hit back. It came when, at a royal banquet, Herodias's daughter Salome had danced so well that Antipas offered her whatever she asked of him. Her mother seized the chance and had Salome ask for the head of John the Baptist. Antipas had no choice but to comply. He ordered a guard to chop off John's head, which he then brought on a platter to Salome.

Soon after, Jesus began his own ministry, beginning in the town of Capernaum. Centrally located on the north shore of the Sea of Galilee, Capernaum had prospered through trade in basalt, olive oil, and wine. It was also a thriving fishing port and the hometown of the fisherman Simon Peter. Like his brother Andrew and the brothers James and John, Peter left his nets to

> "HE STIRS UP THE PEOPLE, TEACHING THROUGHOUT JUDEA, FROM GALILEE EVEN TO THIS PLACE."
>
> LUKE 23:5

Previous pages: "The Healing of the Blind" by Spanish Renaissance painter El Greco
Opposite: Wildflowers bloom in the hill country of Galilee, where Jesus carried out much of his ministry.

follow Jesus and become a "fisher of men." With 12 disciples in all, Jesus walked from Galilean village to Galilean village, teaching in parables, healing the sick, and spreading the "good news" of the gospel.

JESUS IN JERUSALEM

Eventually, Jesus would make his way to Jerusalem, the City of David. By the time he did, the Jewish religious leaders were watching him closely. Jesus gave them much to watch. After he reached the city, he made his way to the Temple and there confronted the money changers who were profiting from the faithful who had come to make offerings. This was a different Jesus from what anyone had seen. Wielding a knotted rope as a whip, he drove the traders out of the Temple and overturned their tables. "My house shall be a house of prayer," he declared. "But you have made it a den of robbers."

The high priests and the Pharisees were paying attention now. Here was a direct challenge to their authority—and from one who was nothing more than the son of a carpenter. What's more, this rabble-rouser was getting the people stirred up. Something would have to be done about the upstart Galilean. The religious leaders began to hatch a plot against him. By the time Jesus and his disciples gathered to celebrate Passover, his enemies were poised to make their move.

During the traditional Passover feast, his "last supper," Jesus broke bread and blessed the wine, symbolically foretelling his friends what was about to come. After the meal, he went to the nearby Garden of Gethsemane to pray. Near dawn, armed soldiers arrived to arrest him, led to Jesus by one of his own disciples, Judas Iscariot, who betrayed him with a kiss. They hauled him before the Roman governor, Pontius Pilate, and the religious leaders, Sadducees and Pharisees, began to make their case against him. They said that Jesus was a dangerous agitator, guilty of stirring up the people against Rome and claiming to be the new king of Judea. "Crucify him! Crucify him!" the mob screamed. Pilate, reluctantly at first, handed Jesus over to be put to death.

Death at the hands of the Roman authorities was a gruesome affair. Soldiers mocked Jesus, beat him, and spat on him.

A fourth-century fresco shows Christ's encounter with the Samaritan woman at the well, a story that appears only in John's gospel (John 4:4-42). The fresco was preserved in the catacomb of the Via Latina in Rome.

Then they took him to a hill called Golgotha and nailed him to a cross. Even in death, according to the gospel accounts, he appealed for mercy for those around him, for those who put him to death. "Father, forgive them," he pleaded from the cross before he died, "for they know not what they do." He was buried in a tomb cut in a rock. Terrified that they would be next, Jesus' disciples fled.

However, the gospels go on to record that when some of his followers visited the tomb two days later, they found that his body was gone. The resurrected Jesus appeared to them soon after, comforting them and instructing them to continue his work and take his message to the world. Some of their fellow Jews began to believe, accepting that Jesus was what he had claimed to be—Christ (from *christos*, Greek for "Messiah"), the Son of God—and that he had risen from the dead on the third day. The number of Christians began to increase.

THE CHURCH IS BORN

As the number of these *Christians* grew, they faced mounting opposition from the Jewish leaders. Among the latter was a young Pharisee from Tarsus named Saul. Saul was present in Jerusalem when an angry mob stoned to death a follower of Jesus named Stephen, the first Christian martyr. He determined to help crush the new faith, which was already spreading beyond Judea. Saul headed north to Syria to arrest the Christians there. But on the road to Damascus, the New Testament records, he encountered the risen Christ. Blinded by a great light, he fell to the ground and heard the words "Saul, Saul, why do you persecute me?"

Saul was converted. To signal the change, he changed his name to Paul. From a persecutor of Christianity, he became its greatest missionary. As an Apostle, or "sent out one," Paul devoted the rest of his life to spreading the gospel message. Over the course of the next 20 years, he traveled throughout the eastern Mediterranean, establishing new Christian communities everywhere in his wake and writing letters that would make up much of the New Testament. The once-Jewish church became increasingly more gentile, taking root in the Greek city-states of Asia Minor, across to Europe, and eventually all the way to Rome itself.

The map at right shows the footsteps of Jesus during his two-year ministry in Galilee.

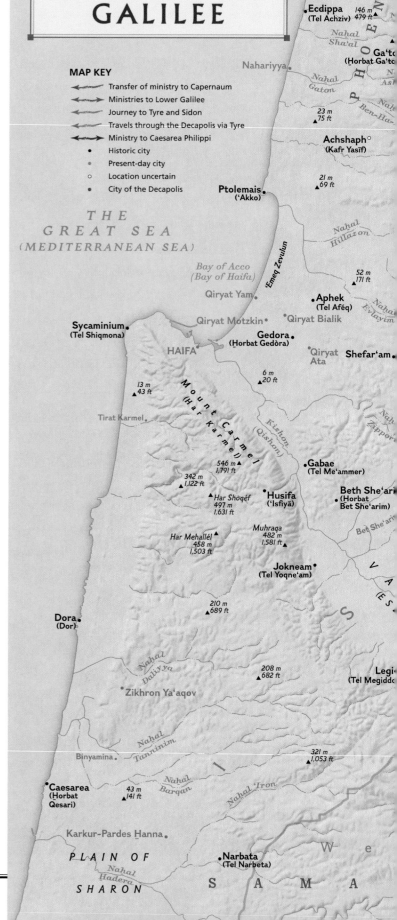

THE MINISTRY OF JESUS IN GALILEE

MAP KEY
← Transfer of ministry to Capernaum
← Ministries to Lower Galilee
← Journey to Tyre and Sidon
← Travels through the Decapolis via Tyre
← Ministry to Caesarea Philippi
• Historic city
• Present-day city
○ Location uncertain
• City of the Decapolis

THE GREAT SEA
(MEDITERRANEAN SEA)

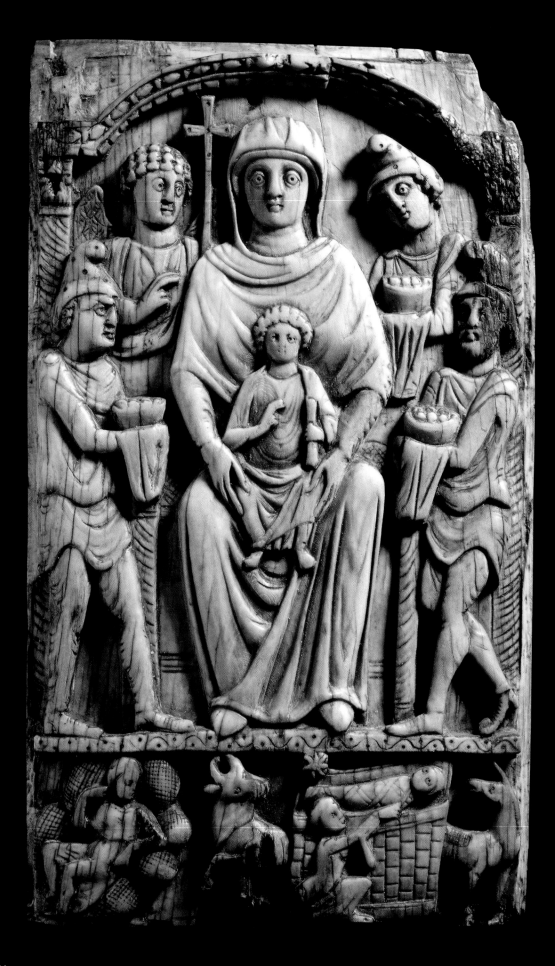

This ivory plaque of the Adoration of the Magi is dominated by the Virgin Mary, who holds the Christ child, making a gesture of blessing, in her lap. The early Byzantine plaque dates to the sixth century C.E.

"BUT STANDING BY THE CROSS OF JESUS
WERE HIS MOTHER, AND HIS MOTHER'S
SISTER, MARY THE WIFE OF CLOPAS,
AND MARY MAGDALENE."

JOHN 19:25

THE EARLY CHRISTIANS

The Jewish prohibition against graven images would have been well known by the early Christians, most of them Jews themselves. Yet as they looked back on the life of Jesus, they began to create images and symbols depicting his birth, death, and resurrection. Skilled craftsmen began to preserve the stories of Jesus in stone, marble, and ivory. And in their work they began increasingly to concentrate on depictions of the cross.

The earliest Christians may have eschewed representations of the cross, the method of crucifixion of their Lord, and it is rare in their iconography. But eventually the cross became the most identifiable symbol of Christianity and of the church. Even in the ivory plaque opposite—of the adoration of the Christ child by the magi—it is present, in the form of a cross-staff held by the angel standing behind the Virgin Mary. Thus, this depiction of the birth of Christ still has within it a reference to the brutal means by which he would die.

For the Eastern Orthodox Church, iconic representations of Jesus, Mary, and the saints became a particularly important aspect of the faith. Icons (from the Greek for "image") would develop into sacred objects in themselves, to be venerated in the same way that the person being depicted is venerated. Thus, for an Orthodox believer the act of kissing an icon of Christ is to show love for Christ himself.

In the 11th-century Church of the Nativity in Bethlehem, a silver star marks the spot believed to be the birthplace of Jesus.

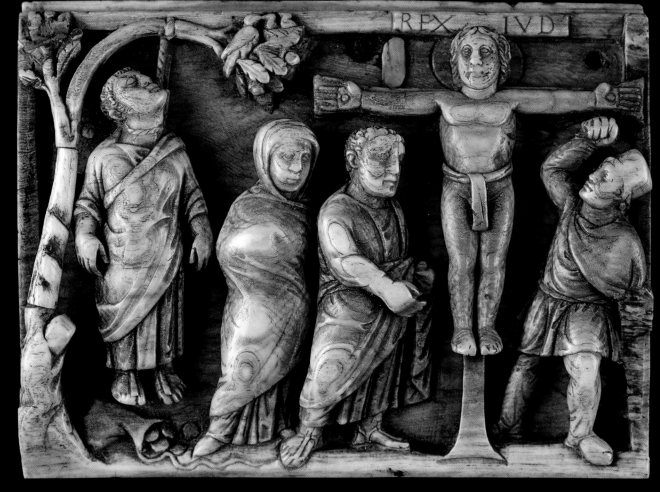

At right, a fifth-century ivory panel juxtaposes Judas's suicide by hanging with Christ's sacrificial death for all. Below, a cross topped with the Chi-Rho monogram and other scenes from the Passion adorn a marble sarcophagus dating from around the year 340.

REX IVD

Despite his youthful look, Tiberius—Rome's second emperor—would have been in his early 40s when this marble bust was commissioned.

A New Emperor

Around the year 4 B.C.E., Emperor Augustus—adopted son of Julius Caesar—adopted Tiberius Claudius Nero to succeed him. When Augustus died, the Roman Senate conferred full imperial powers on him. He thus ruled as emperor (14-37 C.E.) during the years of the ministry of Jesus and at the time of his crucifixion.

There is one reference in the New Testament to Tiberius by name. Luke 3 begins: "In the fifteenth year of the reign of Tiberius Caesar, Pontius Pilate being governor of Judea, and Herod being tetrarch of Galilee . . . in the high-priesthood of Annas and Caiaphas, the word of God came to John [the Baptist] the son of Zechariah in the wilderness."

The "Caesar" mentioned in Matthew 22, Mark 12, and John 19 are all references to Tiberius. His image would have been familiar to Jesus as the face on some of the coins in everyday use in Judea. When the Pharisees sought to trap Jesus by asking whether it was lawful to pay taxes to Caesar, the prop he used to illustrate his answer to them was a silver denarius that carried the image of Tiberius. According to the account in Matthew, Jesus answered them, "Show me the money for the tax." When they did so, he asked them, "Whose likeness and inscription is this?" When they answered, "Caesar's," Jesus then instructed them, "Render therefore to Caesar the things that are Caesar's, and to God the things that are God's." When his enemies heard this, Matthew records, "they marveled; and they left him and went away."

Roman Emperor Octavian, known as Caesar Augustus, ruled from 27 B.C.E. to 14 C.E., during the time of Jesus' birth and childhood.

"'FOR THIS MAN PERFORMS MANY SIGNS. IF WE LET HIM GO ON THUS, EVERY ONE WILL BELIEVE IN HIM, AND THE ROMANS WILL COME AND DESTROY BOTH OUR HOLY PLACE AND OUR NATION.'"

JOHN 11:47-48

THE ROMAN OVERLORDS

When Jesus was born, the Romans were the ruling power in the Near East, at a time when their republic had just given way to the Roman Empire. The emperor at the time of the birth of Jesus—Rome's first—was Caesar Augustus, the man after whom Herod the Great took care to name his new port of Caesarea.

Augustus was born Gaius Octavius ("Octavian"), the son of a Roman senator and, more significant, the great-nephew of Julius Caesar, who adopted him as his own son upon the death of the boy's father. The assassination of Caesar in 44 B.C.E. had brought the republic that had ruled Rome to an end. A power struggle then ensued, eventually pitting against each other Mark Anthony, the soldier and orator who ruled the Roman east, and Octavian, Caesar's heir who ruled the west. The struggle ended when Octavian defeated Mark Anthony's fleet off the coast of Greece at the Battle of Actium about 31 B.C.E.

The calculating King Herod, who had been a longtime friend of Mark Anthony, quickly made his way to Octavian's field headquarters on the island of Rhodes. There he pledged his allegiance to the victor of Actium and laid his crown at the young man's feet. Octavian was impressed. He confirmed Herod as king of Judea, then proceeded to pursue Mark Anthony across the Mediterranean to Alexandria. Defeated again, Mark Anthony and his lover, the Ptolemaic Queen Cleopatra, committed suicide, and Egypt was reduced to the status of a province of Rome.

Three years later, Octavian became the first Roman emperor, and changed his name to Augustus, "the exalted one." His rule would last for 40 years, longer than that of any subsequent Roman emperor. And it ushered in a new period of prosperity and tranquillity across the Mediterranean world—the "peace of Augustus" that would merge into the celebrated 200-year Pax Romana.

By the time of the birth of Jesus, the "Caesar Augustus" referred to in the Gospel of Luke calling for a census (see pp. 270-71) would have been about 58 years old and would rule for nearly 20 years more. As the reference in Luke indicates, the emperor's word was law in Judea and across the Roman realm.

For Jews, the other representation of Roman power in Judea was, of course, King Herod. And the man whom Christians, down through the centuries, have held guilty of the slaughter of the innocents was himself dying, suf-

OTTAVIO   LIVIA

fering a slow and painful death. When he passed away in 4 B.C.E., Herod was succeeded by his three sons, one of whom took over the lion's share of the kingdom: Archelaus, the eldest, became ethnarch (ruler of the people) of Judea, Idumea to the south, and Samaria to the north. One of his early acts was to send in Roman troops to crush a tax protest by Jewish dissidents outside the Temple, convinced a major revolt was under way. About 3,000 Jews died in the incident, most of them innocent bystanders.

Archelaus would exercise a decade of misrule before the Romans intervened. Around 6 C.E., Emperor Augustus removed him as ethnarch, and Judea became a Roman province, led by a governor known as a prefect. The most notorious of these prefects was the one who held the office in the early 30s C.E., Pontius Pilate.

"The Banquet of Octavian and Livia" by late Renaissance painter Domenico Passignano

"IN THIS CITY THERE WERE GATHERED TOGETHER AGAINST THY HOLY SERVANT JESUS, WHOM THOU DIDST ANOINT, . . . PONTIUS PILATE, WITH THE GENTILES AND THE PEOPLES OF ISRAEL."

ACTS 4:27

PONTIUS PILATE, GOVERNOR OF JUDEA

The Governor
In the gospel accounts, Pilate comes across as a rather pathetic figure, forced somewhat against his will into condemning Jesus. Other contemporary Jewish writers are less charitable, portraying him as excessively cruel. Eastern Orthodox tradition holds that Pilate committed suicide in despair at having sentenced Jesus to death.

D uring excavations at Herod's port city of Caesarea in 1961, a team of Italian archaeologists came across a limestone slab bearing the name of Pontius Pilate, the man who replaced Herod's son as Rome's administrator of Judea. They found the stone while working on the city's ancient theater. It is believed that the stone, which was only partially intact, may originally have been a dedicatory plaque inserted in the wall of a newly constructed building. Another word in the three-line inscription, "Tiberieum," suggests that the tablet may have once been part of a temple that Pilate had dedicated to the emperor Tiberius.

However, by the time it was discovered, the stone had been used for another, less lofty purpose. It had apparently been repurposed years later by workmen who scavenged it from its original site, split it in two, and used it in the repair of a flight of steps at the theater. This secondary use, possibly during a renovation of the theater during the fourth century C.E., is perhaps a fitting end for so infamous a name.

That name appears in numerous contemporary written accounts of the time. In addition to the gospel writers, Josephus, Philo of Alexandria, and the Roman historian Tacitus all mention Pontius Pilate. The Caesarea stone, however, was the first inscriptional record of the name ever found.

PREFECT OF JUDEA

Scholars believe that Pilate served as prefect of Judea from 26 to 36 C.E. Philo characterizes his governorship as one of "violence, robberies, ill treatment of the people, grievances, continuous executions without even the form of a trial, endless and intolerable cruelties."

This notwithstanding, Pilate's decade in power was longer than that of most of his predecessors. As prefect, his official residence was in Caesarea, on the shores of the Mediterranean (see pp. 250-51), where the stone bearing his name was found. However, during times of unrest among the Jews, such as at Passover—which was always a time of potential trouble—Pilate would relocate to

A 16th-century painting of Pontius Pilate (above, right), who is the only historical figure, except for Jesus and Mary, to be mentioned in the Christian creed

Jerusalem, some 55 miles to the southeast. There he would take up residence either in the royal palace or in the Antonia Fortress, the bastion at the northern end of the temple complex built by Herod the Great. If any trouble broke out, Pilate would be well placed to deal with it.

And according to Josephus, trouble is exactly what Pilate got when he appropriated monies from the Jerusalem treasury for construction of an aqueduct for the city. Despite the need for such an undertaking, the Jews in Jerusalem protested and a threatening mob managed to surround the Roman prefect. But Pilate had been forewarned of what was brewing and had placed a number of his soldiers, in civilian garb and armed with clubs, among the crowd. At Pilate's order, they quickly pulled out their weapons and beat several of the unarmed protestors to death. Eventually, Pilate was recalled to Rome in disgrace after the slaughter of a group of Samaritans at Mount Gerizim.

[ ]s Tiberieum
[Pon]tius Pilate
[Pref]ect of
Jud[ea]

Approximately 32 inches high and 27 inches wide, this inscribed limestone slab carries three lines of partially legible Latin text that includes the name of Pontius Pilate. It was found in Caesarea Maritima and dates from 26-36 C.E.

"IN THOSE DAYS A DECREE WENT OUT
FROM CAESAR AUGUSTUS THAT ALL
THE WORLD SHOULD BE ENROLLED."

LUKE 2:1-3

CENSUS ORDER

In his *Antiquities of the Jews*, Flavius Josephus recounts how, after the dismissal of Herod Archelaus, Emperor Augustus appointed new officials to carry out a census of Syria and Judea:

Now Cyrenius, a Roman senator . . . came at this time into Syria, with a few others, being sent by Caesar to be a judge of that nation, and to take an account of their substance. Coponius also, a man of the equestrian order, was sent together with him, to have the supreme power over the Jews. Moreover, Cyrenius came himself into Judea, which was now added to the province of Syria, to take an account of their substance, and to dispose of Archelaus's money.

Coponius was the first prefect of Judea, who served under the authority of Cyrenius, Roman governor of Syria. The purpose of their census was taxation. The Jews resented the imposition of Roman taxes. And according to Josephus, "they took the report of a taxation heinously." Indeed, one of their number, a certain Judas of Galilee, "became zealous to draw them to a revolt, who both said that this taxation was no better than an introduction to slavery, and exhorted the nation to assert their liberty."

This, Josephus claims, marked the beginning of the Zealot movement. Despite its failures in this instance,

the Zealots would go on to mount stiffer challenges to Roman rule in Judea. The census decreed by Augustus is also mentioned in the Gospel of Luke. In chapter 2, Luke writes: "This was the first enrollment when Quirinius [Cyrenius] was governor of Syria. And all went to be enrolled, each in his own city."

The papyrus opposite, which dates from 160/161 C.E., records a census statement from a certain "Paesis" in response a census decree similar to the one that Joseph had to obey. This one was issued by Gaius Vibius Maximus, the Roman prefect in the province of Egypt, and commanded all in his province to return to their homes in order to give account of their wealth. The papyrus fragment records the following from Paesis:

From Paesis son of Nebteichis . . . I declare for the house-by-house census of year 23 of our lord Antoninus Caesar: myself, Paesis, son of Nebteichis, over-age 72 years; Horus, my son whose mother is Athenais alias Kinna daughter of Besis, under-age in Year 23, 8 years; Women: Athenais alias Kinna, my wife 57 years; Tereus, my daughter, whose mother is the same; Athenais 40 years. And there are in the possession of my wife Athenais daughter of Besis son of Harpechis shares in landed property in Alabanthis, and in other places other shares inherited from her father in other

In this ca 100 B.C.E. relief, Roman officials conduct a census of citizens. Such registrations were carried out for purposes of raising taxes throughout the empire.

landed property and appurtenances. And I swear by the Fortuna of Imperator Caesar Titus Aurelius Hadrianus Antoninus Augustus Pius . . .

Likewise, in response to Augustus's decree, Joseph had to travel from his home in Galilee to register in Bethlehem in Judea. The journey was necessary, since Joseph was a descendant of the House of David, which was based in Bethlehem and was therefore the city in which he had to register. And so he set out from Nazareth.

In verse 5 of chapter 2, Luke adds more startling detail about Joseph's journey: "He went there to be enrolled with Mary, his betrothed, who was with child." By now, this may have been "old news" to Joseph. But when he first learned about Mary's condition, Joseph had planned to "divorce her quietly." Elsewhere in the gospels, though, an angel is said to have appeared to Joseph and told him that Mary's conception was through the Holy Spirit. Thus, they traveled together from Galilee to Bethlehem. Luke 2:6 then announces the next dramatic development in the story, "While they were there, the time came for her to be delivered."

A papyrus dating to ca 160 C.E. with part of the census return from "Paesis, son of Nebteichis," a Roman citizen of the province of Egypt.

The Byzantine relief above dates from the sixth century and is one of the earliest depictions of the Nativity of Jesus as recounted in the Gospel of Luke.

"AND SHE GAVE BIRTH TO HER FIRST-BORN SON
AND WRAPPED HIM IN SWADDLING CLOTHS,
AND LAID HIM IN A MANGER, BECAUSE THERE
WAS NO PLACE FOR THEM IN THE INN."

LUKE 2:7

BIRTH OF JESUS

The Gospel of Luke provides the most detail about the birth of Jesus, describing how he was brought into the world in a Bethlehem stable. The first to come visit the child were the shepherds, who had themselves been visited by the angel of the Lord, declaring: "Be not afraid; for behold, I bring you good news of a great joy which will come to all the people; for to you is born this day in the city of David a Savior, who is Christ the Lord. And this will be a sign for you: you will find a babe wrapped in swaddling cloths and lying in a manger."

After the angels' departure, the shepherds left their flocks and pasture, by tradition the Field of the Shepherds a mile to the east of Bethlehem, near the present-day Arab village of Beir Sahur. They hastened to Bethlehem and found Joseph and Mary, and the baby lying in a manger. When they had seen him, they praised God, and told the people all they had experienced.

But where did these events take place exactly? And when? According to later tradition, the place of Jesus' birth was a cave (over which the original Church of the Nativity was built). And indeed, from ancient times caves in this part of the world have been used as stables for livestock. Justin Martyr (100-165 C.E.) wrote in his *Dialogue with the Jew Trypho:* "But when the Child was born in Bethlehem, since Joseph could not find lodging in the village, he took up his quarters in a certain cave near the village; and while they were there Mary brought forth the Christ and placed him in a manger, and here the Magi who came from Arabia found him."

VISIT OF THE MAGI
The story of the visit of wise men, or magi, from the East to pay homage to "the King of the Jews" is told only in the Gospel of Matthew. Despite Justin Martyr's assertion, they were probably astrologers from Babylon and followed a star all the way to Jerusalem.

When the magi found Jesus in Bethlehem, they presented him with gold, frankincense, and myrrh. Another notable was searching for Jesus at this time, one who considered himself the true king of the Jews.

Herod took the most draconian of measures to protect his position: He had all children age two years and younger murdered.

The New Testament does not mention a date for the birth of Jesus. Christians celebrate the incarnation of God in Jesus at Christmas. The first recorded celebration of Christmas on December 25 stems from the year 336 C.E. and was originally connected to the winter solstice. As for the year of his birth, scholars offer dates ranging from 7 B.C.E. to 2 B.C.E. The Gospel of Matthew merely places it at the time of Herod's reign, which came to an end in 4 B.C.E.

"Adoration of the Shepherds" by 17th-century C.E. Danish artist Henrich Dittmers

"AND LEAVING THE CROWD, THEY TOOK HIM
WITH THEM IN THE BOAT, JUST AS HE WAS.
AND OTHER BOATS WERE WITH HIM."

MARK 4:36

GALILEE BOAT

Galilee
In Roman times, ancient Israel was divided into Judea, Samaria, and Galilee, with the latter the largest of the three. Galilee was ruled by the tetrarch Herod Antipas, son of Herod the Great. Unlike the Samaritans, the Galileans recognized the authority of the Temple in Jerusalem.

When in 1986 the waters of the Sea of Galilee dropped to record-low levels, they revealed the distinctive outline of a boat buried in the mud along the shoreline. Excavation yielded the remains of what looked like an ancient wooden fishing boat some 30 feet long and 8 feet wide. No vessels of antiquity had ever been discovered in the lake. This one had been found just five miles from Capernaum, the hub of Jesus' ministry in Galilee.

A scholar dispatched from the Israeli Department of Antiquities immediately knew that this was a significant find. A quick examination showed that the boat exhibited a construction technique used up until Roman times, in which the planks of the hull were edge-joined with mortise and tenon joints held together by wooden pegs. But just how old was it? Seventeen pottery fragments found in and around the boat, as well as a complete cooking pot and an oil lamp, provided the answer. Based on these artifacts, scholars date the boat to between the latter part of the first century B.C.E. and the mid-first century C.E., a finding also confirmed by carbon dating. Newspaper headlines were soon proclaiming the discovery of the "Jesus boat."

Such vessels were once a common sight on the Sea of Galilee. As many as 2,000 of them may have been afloat during the life span of the boat's use. Evidence suggests that the latter could either have been rowed or sailed with a mast. Either way, it had the capacity to carry Jesus and the 12 men who made up his inner circle across the waters of the lake. Today, the preserved remains have a more landbound location, in a custom-built exhibit hall at a nearby kibbutz.

Discovered along the shores of the Sea of Galilee (right), the ancient boat opposite dates back to the time of Jesus' ministry in this part of Israel.

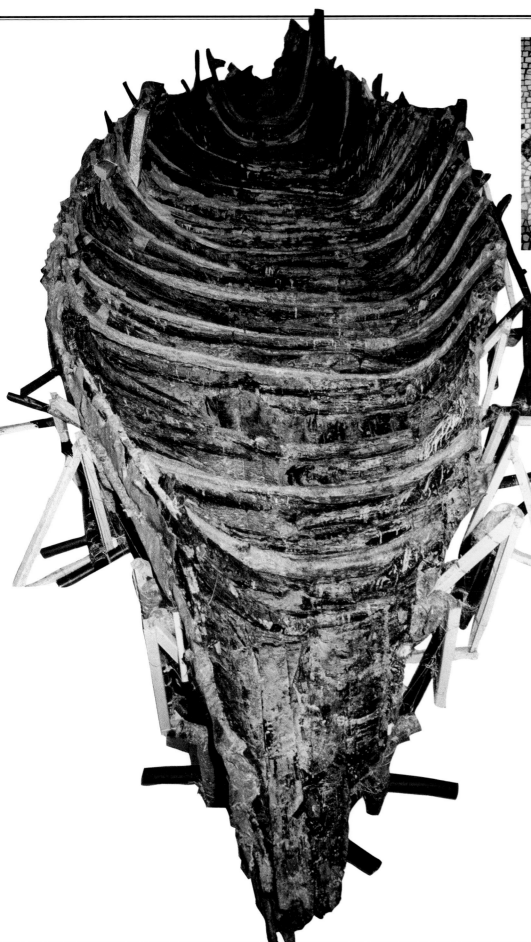

A Byzantine mosaic commemorates Jesus' multiplication of the loaves and the fishes.

Loaves and Fishes

The story of Jesus feeding the 5,000 with five loaves and two fishes is among the best known of Jesus' miracles and the only one recounted in all four of the gospels. According to the gospel writers, it happened after large crowds had followed Jesus to a deserted place along the shores of the Sea of Galilee, eager to hear his words and his teachings. As the day draws to a close, his disciples suggest he send the people back to their homes so they can eat. But Jesus tells the disciples to feed the multitude.

The disciples have no food themselves and scramble to find what they can come up with. Andrew, the brother of Simon Peter, reports to Jesus: "Here is a boy who has five barley loaves and two fish; but what are they among so many?" (John 6:9). Jesus blesses the loaves and fish, then he divides them into baskets that the disciples carry to go back and forth to distribute the food, until everyone has eaten their fill. And still there are 12 basketfuls left over.

The fifth-century mosaic above celebrates the miracle of the loaves and the fishes. The art is preserved under a modern church, at Tabgha, two miles west of Capernaum, but it once was part of an earlier Byzantine sanctuary on the same site. The craftsman who created the mosaic was, it seems, unfamiliar with the fish in the nearby Sea of Galilee, none of which have a pair of dorsal fins.

Despite their importance in the region surrounding the lake, fish were likely not an important source of food in ancient Israel. Not one single species is mentioned in the Bible.

The ruins of a dwelling found underneath a Byzantine church in Capernaum are traditionally regarded as the home of the Apostle Peter. In the background are ruins of a fourth-century c.e. synagogue.

"AS [JESUS] WALKED BY THE SEA OF GALILEE, HE SAW TWO
BROTHERS . . . CASTING A NET INTO THE SEA;
FOR THEY WERE FISHERMEN. AND HE SAID TO THEM,
'FOLLOW ME, AND I WILL MAKE YOU FISHERS OF MEN.'"

MATTHEW 4:18-19

FISHERS OF MEN

According to the gospel accounts, after Jesus left Nazareth he began his public ministry in Capernaum, an ancient fishing village on the western shore of the Sea of Galilee. The second chapter of Mark's gospel records Jesus' visit to the village and how "when the Sabbath came, Jesus went into the synagogue and began to teach." It was here that Jesus was also confronted by a "man with an unclean spirit" and healed the servant of the Roman centurion.

Many synagogues were destroyed by the Roman general Vespasian after the Jewish revolt in 70 C.E. The Jerusalem Talmud, for example, claims some 480 of the buildings were destroyed in Jerusalem alone—an exaggeration, perhaps, but an indication of the likely scale of the damage done to these Jewish centers of teaching and worship throughout Palestine. Excavations at Capernaum begun in 1905 led to hopes that the synagogue Jesus had visited had been found, though scholars continue to disagree on the matter. The ruins of basalt walls were found underneath the foundations of a later synagogue, built at the end of the third or fourth century C.E.

The Capernaum of Jesus' day probably had a population of around a thousand inhabitants, their livelihoods dependent on the nearby body of water. Among them was the fisherman Simon Peter, one of the first Jesus called to be an apostle, or messenger, of the good news of the gospel. More evocative for a man of Peter's background, perhaps, was Jesus' promise to make those who followed him "fishers of men."

While in Capernaum, Jesus stayed at Peter's home, where he taught and healed the sick. The site traditionally known as the House of Peter (opposite) was found in 1968 beneath the remains of several churches built there. Archaeologists dug down until they reached the oldest layer of construction, which dates to the first century B.C.E. On the plastered wall of one house, they found a number of inscriptions mentioning both Simon Peter and Christ.

Peter's life was transformed by his encounter with Jesus. In the Scriptures, he appears courageous and loyal but also impulsive and inconsistent. When Jesus asks the disciples who they thought he was, it is Peter who unhesitatingly responds: "You are the Christ, the son of the living God." Jesus then replies, "Blessed are you, Simon Bar-Jona! For flesh and blood has not revealed this to you, but my Father who is in heaven. And I tell you, you are Peter, and on this rock I will build my church, and the powers of death shall not prevail against it" (Matthew 16:13-20). Yet it was also Peter whom Jesus at another time addresses with the words "Get behind me, Satan!"

In Matthew, chapter 14, after the disciples are caught in a storm on the Sea of Galilee and Jesus comes walking across the water to them, it is Peter who climbs out of the boat and tries to reach him. When he starts sinking, Jesus reaches out a hand and saves him. So, too, it is Peter who reaches for a sword when the Romans come to arrest Jesus in the Garden of Gethsemane and slices off the right ear of one of Caiaphas's guards.

When Jesus is taken off for trial, Peter continues to exhibit the same inconstancy. Soon after expressing his undying loyalty to Jesus, he denies knowing him three times. When a cock crows after the third denial, just as Jesus had predicted, the fisherman weeps tears of shame. Yet it was this same man who was the first male witness to the resurrected Christ on Easter morning.

Peter would later lead the first Christian community in Jerusalem. The Book of the Acts of the Apostles reports how he and the other apostles went on to preach in the city, drawing many believers to the early Christian community in the manner of true "fishers of men."

Ichthys

The plaster-covered walls of the House of Peter carried references to *ichthys*, the Greek word for "fish" that has taken on a double meaning. It relates to the Apostles' being called "fishers of men." It is also an acronym in Greek of the phrase "Jesus Christ Son of God Savior."

Small fishhooks like the ones at left, from Capernaum and dating to between the first and third centuries C.E., were found on the floor of the House of Peter.

"NOW THERE IS IN JERUSALEM BY THE SHEEP GATE
A POOL, IN HEBREW CALLED BETH-ZATHA, WHICH
HAS FIVE PORTICOES. IN THESE LAY A MULTITUDE
OF INVALIDS, BLIND, LAME, PARALYZED."

JOHN 5:2-3

POOLS OF BETHESDA

Bethesda, meaning "house of mercy," was one of the purification pools used for ritual bathing by the many pilgrims who flocked to Jerusalem to take part in religious festivals. The spring-fed pool may have been designed by Herod the Great. The Gospel of John describes the site as having five porches, or covered colonnades. A clay urn, adorned with snakes reminiscent of a caduceus, found on the site suggests that the pools may have been a shrine to Asclepius and a place for healing even before Herod's time.

According to the account in John, a belief had taken hold that at certain times an angel would visit Bethesda to stir the waters and infuse them with healing powers. As a result, the blind, lame, and paralyzed would wait at the side of the pool, in expectation and in hope, ready to enter the disturbed waters. John records an encounter there between Jesus and a paralyzed man one Sabbath day. John tells how Jesus heals the man, who had been lame for 38 years, and instructs him, "Rise, take up your pallet and walk."

After the New Testament, the oldest description of the pool of Bethesda is found in the writings of Eusebius (ca 262-ca 339 C.E.), bishop of Caesarea and a chronicler of the history of the early church. In his *Onomasticon,* an alphabetical listing of biblical place names, the bishop describes Bethesda thus: "A pool in Jerusalem . . . which formerly had five porticoes. And now it is shown in the twin pools which are there, each of which is filled by the yearly rains."

The ancient writings give no indication of the location of Bethesda in Jerusalem. But tradition had long held that the site of the pool was in the east of the city, near what had been the Antonia Fortress, though the historicity of the site had been in question. However, excavations carried out there in 1956 confirmed the New Testament's, and Eusebius's, description of the site. Digs were undertaken near the church of St. Anne. They revealed a rectangular pool (opposite) with a portico on each side and a fifth one dividing the pool into two separate compartments. To facilitate access, flights of steps

with intermittent landings led down to where the waters would have been. The pool was some 350 feet long and 200 feet wide, and the waters 25 feet deep.

The story in the Gospel of John continues after the healing of the paralyzed man with a famous encounter between Jesus and some of the legal-minded religious leaders of the day, who found fault in his healing on the Sabbath. Later, Jesus performs a miracle in connection with another of Jerusalem's purification pools, the Pool of Siloam. He meets a man who had been blind from birth. Spitting on the ground, Jesus makes some mud and puts it on the man's eyes. Then he instructs him to wash in the pool, and when the man does, he receives his sight.

Once more, though, the actions of Jesus offend the religious authorities. Again, because of the day on which he performed the healing, some of the Pharisees concluded, "This man is not from God, for he does not keep the sabbath."

"Christ Healing the Lame Man at the Pool of Bethesda" by Sebastiano Ricci

II KINGS 18:17 | JOHN 5:2-3 | JOHN 9:16

"AND HE ENTERED THE TEMPLE AND BEGAN
TO DRIVE OUT THOSE WHO SOLD AND THOSE
WHO BOUGHT IN THE TEMPLE . . ."

MARK 11:15

TEMPLE TAXES

Jesus had come to Jerusalem with his disciples to celebrate the great Jewish festival of Passover. He had arrived in the city from the Mount of Olives, riding on a donkey and was received by the people like a king. His triumphal entry recalled the words of the Prophet Zechariah: "O daughter of Zion! . . . Lo, your king comes to you; triumphant and victorious is he, humble and riding on an ass" (Zechariah 9:9).

In Jerusalem, Jesus spent time in the vicinity of the Temple, teaching and praying. The Gospel of Mark records that it was almost Passover, a time when every Jewish male was expected to travel to the Temple with a lamb for sacrifice (the poor could opt for a dove instead). The requirements for the animal were exacting; it had to be older than eight days but no older than a year, and free of any blemishes. These standards were rigorously enforced, and as a result many families waited until they got to Jerusalem to buy a Paschal lamb; those on sale in the pens set up in the Temple forecourt were guaranteed to pass priestly inspection.

Steps lead up to the Temple Mount in Jerusalem, where the Second Temple once stood.

In order to purchase the lambs, however, the pilgrims first had to exchange their everyday, Greek currency into Temple shekels; the latter, in keeping with Jewish law, were free of any kind of graven image. To accommodate this exchange, the area outside the Temple had been turned into a place of business, where the new arrivals could trade in their Greek coins for Temple shekels and then move on to pick out a Paschal lamb.

The gospels tell of Jesus' shock at this commerce. According to Matthew, "Jesus entered the temple of God and drove out all who sold and bought in the temple, and he overturned the tables of the money-changers and the seats of those who sold pigeons. With righteous fury, he drove the terrified merchants before him, admonishing them: 'It is written, "My house shall be called a house of prayer"; but you make it a den of robbers'" (Matthew 21:12-13).

SHEKELS AND DRACHMAS

In addition to the annual Temple sacrifice, Jewish families also had to pay annual Temple taxes. In ancient Israel, when Solomon's Temple still stood on the Temple Mount, every adult male had to pay a half shekel into the treasury every year for the upkeep and maintenance of the sacred building. By Jesus' day, the shekel had mostly given way to Greek coinage, which had been in use since the Seleucids, and as a consequence the Temple tax had been set at two drachmas.

Matthew 17 tells how, during his earlier ministry in Galilee, Jesus gets a visit from the tax collectors. While he and his disciples were in Capernaum, collectors come to Peter and ask him about Jesus' payment of the two-drachma tax. Jesus then instructs Peter, "'Go to the sea and cast a hook, and take the first fish that comes up, and when you open its mouth you will find a shekel; take that and give it to them for me and for yourself'" (Matthew 17:27).

Another form of taxation since ancient times in Israel was forced labor. Often the practice of compelling people to work was regarded as oppressive. Earlier in Matthew, however, Jesus' exhortation to "go two miles" recommends compliance with such forced labor.

One side of this silver tetradrachma coin carries the image of Caesar Augustus (above); the other, the city goddess of Antioch, seated in front of the river god Orontes. Such coins had been in circulation since 5 B.C.E. and were in common use in Judea.

"The Parable of the Pharisee and Tax Collector"
by Julius Schnorr von Carolsfeld

Pharisee and Tax Collector

In the days of Jesus, tax collectors were considered to be the lowest of the low. But for Jesus, these despised members of society—shunned as collaborators with the Roman rulers—were less guilty than some of the religious rulers of the day. While tax collectors were often all too aware of their faults, members of Judaism's religious elites took pride in their holier-than-thou behavior and a law-observing life that they thought made them superior to others.

While Jesus had kind and comforting words for most people he encountered, he reserved special condemnation for the Pharisees. In Luke, chapter 18, he tells a parable to a group of listeners who are described by the gospel writer as individuals "who trusted in themselves that they were righteous and despised others." The parable is a short one, about two men who went up to the Temple to pray, the first a Pharisee, the other a tax collector. The Pharisee, Jesus says, prayed thus: "God, I thank thee that I am not like other men, extortioners, unjust, adulterers, or even like this tax collector. I fast twice a week, I give tithes of all that I get."

Then Jesus addresses the tax collector, who stood some way off from the Pharisee and would not even raise his eyes to heaven. "God, be merciful to me a sinner," he cries, in recognition of both his sins and his need for forgiveness. "I tell you," Jesus concludes for his listeners, "this man went down to his house justified rather than the other; for every one who exalts himself will be humbled, but he who humbles himself will be exalted."

This elaborate ossuary contained the bones of Joseph Caiaphas (Yehoseph bar Qypa), possibly the same high priest named in the gospels.

"THEN THOSE WHO HAD SEIZED JESUS
LED HIM TO CAIAPHAS, THE HIGH
PRIEST, WHERE THE SCRIBES AND
THE ELDERS HAD GATHERED."

MATTHEW 26:57

THE BURIAL OF JESUS

Jewish custom required that the dead be buried within 24 hours of dying. Once the corpse was cleaned and covered with linen, it was laid to rest. Just how this was handled depended on the wealth and status of the deceased. The bodies of the poor were usually interred in the ground, while the wealthy placed their dead in family tombs hewn out of rock. The latter often underwent a "secondary burial": After the body was laid out for about a year to decompose, the bones were gathered up and preserved in an ossuary. The sides of these ossuaries were often decorated, with the names of the interred etched on the sides.

In 1990, a tomb was uncovered that held an ossuary bearing a name right off the pages of the New Testament and lifted straight from the final days of Jesus (opposite). The tomb was found during the construction of a water park two miles south of the Old City of Jerusalem, when a bulldozer operator broke through the roof of the ancient burial site. The tomb had four fingerlike shafts extending out from a central chamber that contained a collection of ossuaries that date from the first century C.E.

Six of the boxes were strewn across the tomb floor, the way they had been left by grave robbers centuries ago. Six others were still stowed away in wall recesses. The most elaborate of these, beautifully decorated with rosettes and covered with a faded orange wash, con-tained the bones of a 60-some-year-old man. Etched on the end of the ossuary, possibly with one of the two nails found nearby, was the Aramaic inscription Yehoseph bar Qypa—Joseph Caiaphas. Some scholars believe that this ossuary may have contained the bones of the high priest who presided over the trial of Jesus.

In the Passion account of the trial in the Gospel of Matthew, Caiaphas interrogates Jesus, demanding to know if he really claims to be "Christ, the Son of God." Jesus' answer, "You have said so," sends Caiaphas into a fury. "He has uttered blasphemy," rages the high priest, tearing his robes. The punishment for blasphemy was death.

How Caiaphas himself died is not known. But it is clear from the burial site that many in the high priest's family met untimely deaths. Archaeologists from the Israel Antiquities Authority identified 63 other skeletons buried in the tomb. Of these, 40 percent had died by the age of five, stark testimony to the fragility of life and prevalence of infant mortality in the days of Jesus, even for members of wealthy families like the family of Caiaphas the high priest.

The window on the past that was suddenly opened with the discovery of the tomb of Caiaphas was just as soon closed. The authorities resealed the burial site and the Ministry of Religious Affairs took charge of its human remains for reburial on the Mount of Olives.

"Christ before Caiaphas" by Palma Giovane

THE TOMB

After the crucifixion of Jesus, the gospels tell how a wealthy man named Joseph of Arimathea laid the body in a new tomb in a garden. He was helped by another of Jesus' followers, Nicodemus, and by Mary Magdalene and Mary, the mother of James. Once the burial rites had been completed, the entrance to the tomb was sealed by a heavy stone, called a *golal*.

The day after the Sabbath, at dawn, the two Marys set out to visit the tomb again, wondering how they will roll away the stone. But when they get there, they find it already rolled aside. Entering the tomb, they see a young man in a long white garment sitting to one side. "Do not be amazed," he tells them; "you seek Jesus of Nazareth, who was crucified. He has risen; he is not here." He instructs them to tell the disciples that they will find Jesus in Galilee. The women, terrified, flee from the scene.

Today, the Church of the Holy Sepulchre is said to mark the site where these dramas played out. The original church was built in the fourth century C.E., after Emperor Constantine's mother, Helena, made a pilgrimage to Jerusalem and selected a site. However, the church lies within Jerusalem's crowded old city, in apparent contradiction of New Testament details about Jesus' crucifixion being outside the city walls (also where all Jewish burials would have taken place). The discrepancy can be explained by dint of an expanding city; a new wall, built in 44 C.E., incorporated within the city limits places that in Jesus' day would have been outside. Moreover, archaeological evidence shows that the area of the church was once a garden, in accordance with the gospel accounts.

Other sites in present-day Jerusalem have been suggested for the tomb of Jesus. For believers, the power of the gospel message lies not in the location of the tomb, but in the words the women heard that first Easter Sunday morning: "He has risen; he is not here."

> "THIS MAN WENT TO PILATE AND ASKED FOR THE BODY OF JESUS. THEN HE TOOK IT DOWN AND WRAPPED IT IN A LINEN SHROUD, AND LAID HIM IN A HEWN TOMB."
> LUKE 23:52-53

The tomb at left is at Bet Guvrin, near Mareshah and dates from Roman times. It was sealed by a huge, round stone that was rolled across the entrance.

"AND SUDDENLY A LIGHT FROM HEAVEN FLASHED ABOUT HIM.
AND HE FELL TO THE GROUND AND HEARD A VOICE SAYING
TO HIM, 'SAUL, SAUL, WHY DO YOU PERSECUTE ME?'"

ACTS OF THE APOSTLES 9:3-5

THE STORY OF PAUL

Unlike Peter, Paul was not one of the original 12 disciples. Yet he became the most important Apostle of the Christian church and is referred to as "the second founder of Christianity." A Roman citizen from the city of Tarsus in modern-day Turkey, Paul was a Pharisee and an early persecutor of the followers of Jesus. Indeed, Acts of the Apostles tells how Saul, as he was known then, was on his way from Jerusalem to track down Christians in Damascus when he encountered the risen Christ and spent the rest of his life telling people about him, his crucifixion, and resurrection.

That missionary work began in Damascus itself, where Paul (the new name of the new convert) preached in the synagogues that Jesus was the Messiah, the Son of God. But the Jews in the city tried to arrest him, and Paul had to flee back to Jerusalem. The Christian community there was suspicious of him, however, because of his past persecution of them. Barnabas, an important member of that community, was the first to welcome him. The other believer whose name is most associated with Paul's is Timothy, who often accompanied him on his missionary journeys throughout the eastern Mediterranean.

Paul's travels took him to Asia Minor, especially to Ephesus (opposite). Paul spent more than two years in the city, which—with a population estimated at up to 250,000—was the third or fourth largest in the Roman Empire. One Ephesian maker of statues of the goddess Artemis complained, "This Paul has persuaded and turned away a considerable company of people, saying that gods made with hands are not gods." (Acts of the Apostles 19:26).

From Asia Minor, Paul crossed over into Europe, to the city-states of Greece, and eventually traveled all the way to Rome. His visit to Rome was not one of Paul's planned missionary journeys; after he had been arrested by the authorities in Jerusalem and imprisoned in Caesarea, Paul decided to appeal his arrest before Caesar in person, the right of every Roman citizen. But despite the purpose of his travel to the imperial capital, he continued to spread the gospel; Acts of the Apostles closes with him being held in a low-security prison that still allowed him to preach the message of the risen Christ. While legend holds that Paul met his end in Rome sometime after 60 C.E., executed by the sword, history shows that the power of Paul's writings testifies to the primacy of the pen.

Through the work of the Apostle Paul, Ephesus became a major center of the early church. The ruins of the Gate of Herakles (opposite) symbolize the triumph of Christianity over Greco-Roman paganism in the city. In the 14th-century manuscript illumination below, the seated apostle Paul is at work on an epistle with his traveling companion, Titus.

Paul's Epistles

Everywhere he traveled, the Apostle Paul set up local churches of believers—in Ephesus, Corinth, Thessalonica, Philippi, Colossae, Athens, Rome, and elsewhere. He stayed in contact with these churches through long letters, or epistles. These show that Paul was not just the mighty evangelist of the early church who spread the news of Jesus as the Christ to the corners of the Roman Empire, but that he was also the first great Christian theologian. More forcefully than any other Apostle, he insisted that the goods news of Jesus as the Messiah—*Christos* in Greek—was for all people, Jew and gentile alike. It was through the writings of the Greek-speaking Paul that Jesus of Nazareth first became known as Jesus Christ.

The writing and preaching of Paul turned what might have remained a small Jewish sect into a faith that transformed the world. In his epistles to infant churches, he encouraged the new believers, instructed them in doctrine, settled disputes, and exhorted them to steadfastness. Incorporated into the New Testament, the words have done the same for Christians down through the ages—to persecuted early believers, to the leaders of the Protestant Reformation, and to powerful church leaders and humble missionaries around the world.

chapter 8

JERUSALEM
A Land Besieged

JERUSALEM

In the decades after the crucifixion of Jesus, belief in his resurrection as the Christ began to spread. Communities of Christians, as they came to be known, took root in cities across the Roman world, linked with each other by excellent Roman roads. In many instances, the communities must have been small and isolated, but in the major cities they were sizable and well-known. Indeed, the number of Christians in Rome must have been substantial. For when a terrible fire destroyed half the imperial capital in 64 C.E., the fiddling emperor Nero (54-68 C.E.) felt able to blame the disaster on this section of the population.

Some of Nero's fellow citizens had their own suspicions about what had happened to their city, believing that their increasingly erratic emperor had set the fire himself as a way of clearing space for his new urban building plan. The fire raged unchecked for a week. The historian Tacitus (56-117 C.E.) concluded that Nero *was* the culprit and had then decided to shift blame for the disaster by making Rome's Christians the scapegoats.

Christians had aroused opposition before—in Jerusalem, Damascus, Ephesus, and elsewhere—and the Apostle Paul had often been forced to flee for his life. Many had already perished for their belief in a risen Christ. But it was in Nero's Rome that the first organized and "sanctioned" persecution began. Tacitus records how Christians were arrested in "large numbers" and condemned to death, many of them crucified.

THE ROMANS IN JUDEA

While the Romans targeted Christian believers in the imperial capital, the Jews of Jerusalem were finally completing the vast new Temple precinct begun during the reign of Herod the Great. But the achievement of this historic undertaking came at a time of increasing Roman misrule in Judea. Conflict with the imperial overlords had been brewing for years. Eventually it would erupt in war between Romans and Jews.

For the people of Judea, matters had begun to take a turn for the worse following the death of Emperor Tiberius in 37 C.E. In his place arose a new Roman leader—Emperor Gaius Caesar, better known by his nickname, "Caligula." But being the supreme ruler of a mighty empire wasn't enough for Caligula.

Shortly after becoming emperor, he declared himself a god. Now, what most pagans did or believed may have had little impact on the Jews. But not in the case of this particular pagan. Caligula soon commanded that sacrifices be made in his honor in temples and sanctuaries throughout the empire. This included Judea and, specifically, the Temple in Jerusalem. The Jews refused to commit such sacrilege in their holy sanctuary. Only the death of Caligula—assassinated in a plot involving Rome's senators and his own Praetorian Guard just four years into his reign—averted open conflict with the imperial power. Still Jewish resentment continued to simmer.

In Rome, Caligula was succeeded by his uncle, Claudius, himself a nephew of the emperor Tiberius. The new ruler appointed a Roman procurator to govern the province that the Romans now called Palestina, or "the land of the Philistines," rather than Judea, "the land of the Jews" (see map, p. 295).

Most of the appointees who held the post were incompetent at best, and one, Gessius Florus, was in the words of the contemporary chronicler Josephus "an executioner rather than

> "FOR I DESIRE STEADFAST LOVE AND NOT SACRIFICE, THE KNOWLEDGE OF GOD, RATHER THAN BURNT OFFERINGS."
>
> HOSEA 6:6

Previous pages: Emperor Titus destroys the Temple in Jerusalem, in a 17th-century painting by Nicolas Poussin.
Opposite: Two third-century C.E. frescoes from the Synagogue of Dura Europos in Syria depict scenes from the life of the prophet Ezekiel and the high priest Aaron.

a governor." Once again, Jewish resentment began to heat up, especially among groups like the Pharisees and the Essenes. But the biggest threat to Roman rule arose from a new group of dissidents known as the Zealots. The Zealots not only resented the foreigners but were prepared to take up arms against them.

THE JEWS REVOLT AGAINST ROME

The Zealot movement had first come to the fore in its opposition to paying Roman taxes. But now they were a more lethal group, with a cadre of dedicated *sicarii,* or "dagger men," ready to take on the Romans. In 66 C.E., the Zealots launched a second revolt against their imperial masters. By this time, Nero was emperor and his capital in turmoil, so the Romans were at first slow in responding to the revolt (further hampered by the fact that the increasingly paranoid emperor had just executed several of his leading generals). Eventually, Rome dispatched one of its most accomplished commanders, Vespasian, to deal with the revolt.

In the spring of 67 C.E., Vespasian arrived in the Mediterranean port of Ptolemais, and with the Tenth Legion and the Fifth Legion he marched into Galilee. There he crushed a Zealot force under the command of none other than Josephus, the historian. Then he moved on south and proceeded to lay siege to Jerusalem. With Nero's Rome still in political upheaval, Vespasian's troops proclaimed the general as emperor, and so he set off for the capital. Left to conduct the war against the rebels was Vespasian's son, Titus.

The new commander began to tighten the noose around Jerusalem, which had been weakened by internal dissent and rivalry among various rebel groups. Roman troops encircled the city walls with a trench and breastworks. Any citizens who tried to escape were seized and executed—crucified in full view of those who remained inside the city. After enduring two years of siege, Jerusalem's starving defenders could mount little more resistance. The legionaries of Titus managed to fight their way inside the city. Then they relentlessly closed in on what, inevitably, would be the last holdout of the Zealots: the Temple.

In the final days of August in the year 70, Roman troops reached the spot that had been Judaism's sacred sanctuary,

Left: Among the most significant of the Dead Sea Scrolls finds, 122 biblical scrolls or fragments were found in Cave 4, the center outcrop, at Qumran.

the center of the nation's spiritual life since the reign of King David—and burned it to the ground.

Thousands perished in the fires that raged throughout the city and at the swords of the vengeful legionaries. As many as 100,000 may have died, with as many more carried off as slaves. Some of the rebels fled to Masada, Herod's fortress-palace on the shores of the Dead Sea. There they made a final stand against the Romans, again holding out bravely before succumbing to inevitable defeat. But in reality, the end had come with the fall of Jerusalem. Henceforth, a Roman legate would administer Judea, and he would report directly to Rome. Jews were banned not only from rebuilding but even from returning to Jerusalem.

JUDAISM ENTERS A NEW ERA

With the destruction of the Temple of Herod and the Jews' exclusion from the City of David, the practice of Judaism was about to change fundamentally. No longer able to perform sacrifices on the Temple Mount, Jews turned to their Scriptures and to the rabbis, or teachers, who studied and interpreted the ancient writings. With this turn of events, the era of rabbinic Judaism had begun.

By the first century C.E., the canon of the Hebrew Bible—what Christians call the Old Testament—had come together. It consisted of three major sections. The first was the Torah, the five books of Moses: Genesis, Exodus, Leviticus, Numbers, and Deuteronomy. The second was the books of the Prophets: Isaiah, Jeremiah, Ezekiel, and the 12 Minor Prophets. And the third was a section called the Writings, an assorted collection that included such books as Esther (unique in not being found among the scrolls at Qumran) and the Song of Songs (a seemingly secular book interpreted as a sacred love song between God and Israel).

The canonization of the Hebrew Scriptures had come at a time that the Jews considered a "postclassical age." They believed that they now entered a period when God no longer spoke to them through prophets, as he had to their ancestors. But that did not mean they were not able to know the will of God. This, they believed, could be learned through the Scriptures, which captured God's revelation to their ancestors down through the ages. Through these, they maintained, they could still hear the voice of God.

But the voice of God in the Scriptures could sometimes be inaccessible and hard to understand, communicated through the prophets in different times and circumstances. And although it contained eternal truths, those truths would often have to be explained and made relevant to believers. Thus, while there may have been an "original intent" to a particular passage of Scripture, there also needed to be an "application" for the circumstances of today. These interpretations and applications were carried out by the rabbis.

And so Judaism began to enter a new era. The destruction of the Temple, which had been central to the faith's sacral practices, had seemed a fatal blow. But it had spurred its movement toward the increased study of the Scriptures.

In diaspora communities throughout the Near East and the Mediterranean, Jews met in synagogues to pray and read the Scriptures. And in Palestine, they set up a school for rabbis, at Tiberias, on the shores of the Sea of Galilee. There, rabbis were trained in their new roles and in the scholarship that would lead to three new types of work on the Scriptures: biblical translation, biblical paraphrase, and biblical commentary. The rabbis were guided by a belief that in addition to the Torah, Jewish oral law and tradition were an integral part of the faith, too. Eventually, rabbinic discussion and debate about the Torah and legal arguments surrounding it were recorded in a series of books collectively known as the Talmud.

New Christian Scriptures were also coming together at this time. Most of the books that would make up the New Testament were written between around 70 C.E. and 120 C.E. After Paul's Epistles—his letters of encouragement and instruction to young churches—the four gospels appeared, telling "good news" of the life, death, and resurrection of Christ. These, together with the Hebrew Bible, were read during Christian services.

The Judeo-Christian Scriptures that took final form during the first century C.E. have since transformed the world. Throughout, they tell a story firmly rooted in ancient Israel and in the people who lived there and left their mark on the land. The destruction of the Temple in Jerusalem in 70 C.E. was thus not an end of that story. Rather, it was a point along a journey that continues today—one that began when the biblical patriarch Abraham left his home in Ur of the Chaldees and traveled with his family to the land that God had promised him.

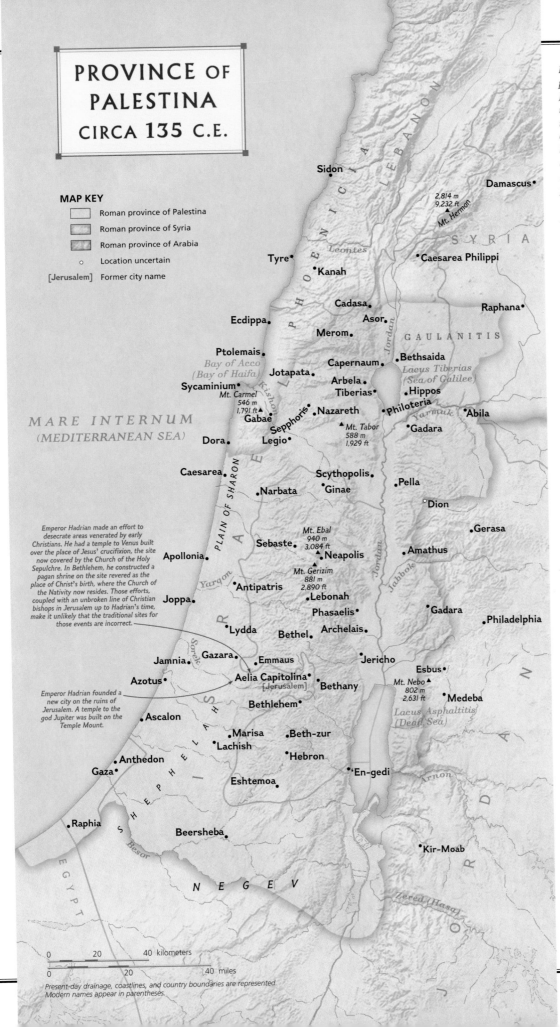

PROVINCE OF PALESTINA
CIRCA 135 C.E.

MAP KEY

- Roman province of Palestina
- Roman province of Syria
- Roman province of Arabia
- ○ Location uncertain
- [Jerusalem] Former city name

MARE INTERNUM
(MEDITERRANEAN SEA)

Sidon

Damascus

2,814 m
9,232 ft
Mt. Hermon

S Y R I A

Tyre
Kanah

Caesarea Philippi

Cadasa
Asor

Raphana

Ecdippa
Merom

G A U L A N I T I S

Ptolemais
*Bay of Acco
(Bay of Haifa)*
Jotapata
Capernaum
Bethsaida
*Lacus Tiberias
(Sea of Galilee)*

Sycaminium
*Mt. Carmel
546 m
1,791 ft*
Gabae
Sepphoris
Nazareth
Arbela
Tiberias
Hippos
Philoteria
Abila

Dora
Legio
*Mt. Tabor
588 m
1,929 ft*
Gadara

Caesarea

Scythopolis
Pella

Narbata
Ginae
Dion

Gerasa

*Emperor Hadrian made an effort to
desecrate areas venerated by early
Christians. He had a temple to Venus built
over the place of Jesus' crucifixion, the site
now covered by the Church of the Holy
Sepulchre. In Bethlehem, he constructed a
pagan shrine on the site revered as the
place of Christ's birth, where the Church of
the Nativity now resides. Those efforts,
coupled with an unbroken line of Christian
bishops in Jerusalem up to Hadrian's time,
make it unlikely that the traditional sites for
those events are incorrect.*

Sebaste
*Mt. Ebal
940 m
3,084 ft*
Neapolis
Amathus

*Mt. Gerizim
881 m
2,890 ft*

Apollonia

P L A I N   O F   S H A R O N

Antipatris
Lebonah

Joppa
Phasaelis
Gadara
Philadelphia

Lydda
Bethel
Archelais

Jamnia
Gazara
Emmaus
Jericho
Esbus

Azotus
Aelia Capitolina
[Jerusalem]
Bethany
*Mt. Nebo
802 m
2,631 ft*
Medeba

*Emperor Hadrian founded a
new city on the ruins of
Jerusalem. A temple to the
god Jupiter was built on the
Temple Mount.*

Bethlehem

*Lacus Asphaltitis
(Dead Sea)*

Ascalon

Marisa
Beth-zur
Lachish
Hebron

Anthedon
Eshtemoa
En-gedi

Gaza

Raphia
Beersheba

Kir-Moab

N E G E V

E G Y P T

Zered (Hasa)

0   20   40 kilometers
0   20   40 miles

*Present-day drainage, coastlines, and country boundaries are represented.
Modern names appear in parentheses.*

Rome administered this land as a
provincial backwater, content to leave
Judea to the governance of local puppet
monarchs. But when anti-Roman senti-
ment exploded in the Jewish Revolt of
66 C.E., the Roman Empire came down
hard: Roman legions crushed the rebels,
and some Jews were dispersed. After the
Bar Kochba revolt in 132 C.E., Rome deported the remaining Jews and renamed
the region Palestina, for the Philistine
people who predated them.

Three tools of the Jewish scribe—a menorah-adorned oil lamp in the shape of a bird (left), a paper weight (above), and a quill (below)

At left, another oil lamp, and at right an inkwell found at Qumran and dating to between the third century B.C.E. and the first century C.E.

JEWISH SCRIBES

With the birth of rabbinic Judaism came a renewed focus on the application of the Law—and on the role of scribes, the professional interpreters of that Law, both oral and written. The Hebrew Law regulated every aspect of daily life for pious Jews. Such regulations were many and difficult to meet, and for help with the practical application of the Law the faithful increasingly turned to the scribes.

Scribes were not a new class that began with rabbinic Judaism. The profession originated during the period after the Babylonian Exile, when piety became more formal and legalistic. While the priesthood occupied itself with the ritual and sacrifice of temple worship, the scribes were called upon for their expertise in studying the sacred writings and, as copyists and editors, in safeguarding the purity of the original texts.

At various times, Hellenistic influences in Judea had threatened to undermine the practice of Judaism. The priesthood lost much popular support among the people as a result of its backing of Hellenism. But the scribes, through their fidelity to the Law, grew in stature and respect. By the time of the New Testament, they had become leaders of the Pharisee party. With their growing power, many of the scribes neglected their essential spiritual function, of interpreting the will of God as expressed in Scripture and the oral law. Instead, they became narrow jurists, emphasizing the letter of the law over its spirit.

A first-century B.C.E. papyrus scroll of commentary on the Book of Habbakuk

EARLY CHRISTIAN ART

The earliest Christians, as members of an outcast and often persecuted group, would have had little time or resources to express their new faith in elaborate works of art. The fish symbol *ichthys* that the first believers scratched on the walls of the catacombs in Rome was a quick, easy, and covert way to signify their new faith. Only later, as Christianity grew in acceptance throughout the empire, would more elaborate works of Christian art emerge.

Christian artists used the same media as those carrying out secular works, such as mosaics, frescoes, and sculpture. The earliest artworks date from the times of persecution, when members of the church sought refuge underground, in the catacombs of Rome. There, on the walls of Christian tombs, they created frescoes that depicted scenes from the life of Jesus and of Old Testament stories and figures like Jonah and Daniel, as well as Christian symbols like the fish and the dove.

At the other end of the spectrum in sophistication were mosaics—the creation of images with small pieces of stone or colored glass. And instead of the catacomb walls of the persecuted church, they adorned the walls and ceilings of the first Christian basilicas. Mosaics became particularly central for the Byzantines, who adorned the interiors of their churches with the most spectacular examples of this art form.

Since the earliest days of the persecuted church, Christian artwork has been about more than simple aesthetics. For believers unable to read the Scriptures, mosaics and frescoes, sculptures, and carvings brought alive the message of the gospel of Christ.

A stela with a Coptic cross from the fifth or sixth century is shown at right, and above it a terra-cotta portrait of Christ from a century or more earlier.

Christ appears as a warrior, with snake and lion under his feet, on a fifth-century Roman mosaic.

A third-century fresco from the catacomb of Callixtus in Rome depicts seven disciples at a meal around a table, celebrating the Lord's Supper.

Underground Church

Because public Christian burials were impossible in Rome, during the first century C.E. the faithful began to use underground chambers located on the outskirts of the city. This network of narrow subterranean passageways was known as the catacombs. Here, Christians would hollow out grooves in the soft rock to bury the bodies of their dead. In times of severe persecution, believers would also take refuge in the catacombs. They would gather underground to pray, to celebrate the Eucharist, and to honor the dead who were present all around them.

Archaeologists have uncovered some 40 catacombs in Rome, like the one pictured below. Many were adorned with inscriptions and early Christian symbols that give an insight into the lives, hopes, and fears of these early believers; frequent symbols included a dove with an olive branch (for peace or salvation), an anchor (hope), and most common of all the fish (*ichthys,* Christ).

Over time, artists added wall frescoes of Jesus delivering his Sermon on the Mount or seated with the Apostles at the Last Supper. Paintings also showed other characters and stories from the Scriptures, often depicting heroes of faith in particularly trying and perilous times: Noah and the Flood, Moses in the wilderness, David going up against Goliath, Daniel in the lions' den. The Christians of the Roman catacombs looked to God to similarly deliver them in their hour of need.

An underground portico in the Catacomb of Priscilla, Rome

Roman emperor Nero is immortalized in this large bronze statue that was cast shortly after his death in 68 C.E.

"WHO SHALL SEPARATE US FROM THE
LOVE OF CHRIST? SHALL TRIBULATION, OR
DISTRESS, OR PERSECUTION, OR FAMINE,
OR NAKEDNESS, OR PERIL, OR SWORD?"

ROMANS 8:35

THE ROMAN RULERS

By the time the 14-inch bust of Nero opposite was commissioned—part of a bronze equestrian statue—the emperor was approaching the end of a tumultuous 14-year reign. Few such depictions of this most unpopular of Roman rulers survive. After his death, the senators of Rome ordered that all traces of him be obliterated, and indeed this artifact was found far from the halls of the Senate, in Cilicia in distant Asia Minor.

It was during Nero's oppressive rule that the Jews revolted in Jerusalem and the persecution of Christians began in Rome. The martyrdom of the church's two great leaders, the Apostles Peter and Paul, is said to have happened in the imperial capital at this time—the former crucified upside down, the latter beheaded, in the manner of execution reserved for citizens of Rome. Nero would meet his own gruesome end, in a parody of Roman execution: As troops sent to arrest him drew near, he stabbed himself in the neck and dying exclaimed, "What an artist the world is losing in me!"

A self-styled musician and poet, Nero is said to have strummed a lyre and sung of the destruction of ancient Troy as he watched the great fire of Rome in 64 C.E. Some of his fellow citizens were quick to pin blame for the blaze on him. Suspicions intensified after Nero, who initially provided relief to those who lost their homes, later constructed a grandiose palace called the Golden House on the former residential site. However, Nero identified the city's Christian community as the guilty party, and before the embers had burned themselves out was making his ruthless plans.

Cruelty had long been a hallmark of Nero's life. Early in his reign he had poisoned his brother, whom he saw as a rival. And when his mother, Agrippina, overstepped the mark, behaving as if she were the power behind the throne, he showed no greater leniency toward her. As Nero's tutor, the philosopher Seneca, observed, "the over-watchful, over-critical eye that Agrippina kept on whatever Nero said or did proved more than he could stand." The emperor first banished his mother from the court, then, when she continued to try to exert her influence over him, tried to poison her—three times, it seems, before succeeding. He also killed two wives and various other family members, and would have felt little compunction about sending to their deaths unknown members of this new religious sect in Rome.

Contemporary sources document Nero's pogroms against Rome's Christian community (significantly, now seen as a sect distinct from Judaism) in the aftermath of the city's great fire. The historian Tacitus records their

barbaric treatment at the hands of the emperor. At Nero's orders, some were dressed in animal skins and turned loose into the arena, where they were ripped apart by wild dogs. Others were crucified, as the Jesus that they proclaimed had been, their bodies then set on fire, human torches to illuminate the sides of the emperor's highways.

However, Tacitus also notes that far from thrilling in the spectacle, the spectators were moved to sympathy for the victims. For the next 200 years, the Christians of Rome would experience times of tolerance interspersed with periods of persecution. The persecutions seemed only to strengthen their determination and make their numbers grow.

A 17th-century tapestry from Flanders depicts the conquest of Jerusalem by Vespasian and his son Titus in 70 C.E.

EARLY SYNAGOGUE

The term "synagogue" (from the Greek for "assembly") was traditionally applied not only to the building in which Jews congregated for prayer and worship but also to the people who gathered there themselves. In much the same way, "church" can likewise be understood in both ways. Synagogues would have been a common sight in Jerusalem in the years before the Roman destruction of the city in 70 C.E. (see pp. 304-305). And since times of antiquity, these houses of worship had existed across the Mediterranean world and the Near East, wherever communities of the Jewish Diaspora were found. Indeed, during his missionary journeys, the Apostle Paul is said to have visited the synagogue whenever he arrived in a new city, a place where he knew he would meet fellow Jews.

Synagogues likely originated during the time of the Babylonian Exile to meet the need for non-temple worship and gathering. Many Jews chose to remain in exile after Persia's King Cyrus gave them permission to return to Judea, suggesting that their needs for non-temple gatherings were being met.

By the time of the New Testament era, the synagogue had become a dominant institution in Jewish religious life. Jerusalem alone, it has been estimated, had hundreds of such gathering places. But despite numerous mentions of synagogues in the gospels, the Acts of the Apostles, and in the writings of the Jewish historian Josephus, archaeologists and scholars had been unable to find physical evidence of such buildings in Jerusalem before 70 C.E. None had been unearthed until 1913, when a French team discovered the "Theodotus plaque" at right, in an area south of the Temple Mount.

The limestone tablet was inscribed with ten lines of Greek text that describe a synagogue built by a priest named Theodotus. Most likely a building block for a synagogue, its inscription documents the purposes of such a structure—"the reading of the Law and for the teaching of the commandments, and . . . as an inn for those in need from foreign parts." Synagogues thus became models for the growing number of churches in the lands of the Roman Empire.

The development of the synagogue was one of the premier accomplishments of Judaism. Synagogues survived the destruction of Jerusalem by the Romans and the further dispersion of Jews from Judea and, in the absence of a central Temple, became enduring focal points for Jewish scholarship, worship, and community in the many lands of the Jewish Diaspora.

This mosaic floor adorns a sixth-century synagogue in the Bet Shean Valley in Israel. The signs of the zodiac encircle a depiction of the Greek sun god Helios.

"AND PAUL WENT IN, AS WAS HIS CUSTOM, AND FOR THREE WEEKS HE ARGUED WITH THEM FROM THE SCRIPTURES, EXPLAINING AND PROVING THAT IT WAS NECESSARY FOR THE CHRIST TO SUFFER AND TO RISE FROM THE DEAD, AND SAYING, 'THIS JESUS, WHOM I PROCLAIM TO YOU, IS THE CHRIST.'"

ACTS 17:2-3

"Theodotus, [son] of Vettenus, priest and archisynagogos [ruler of the synagogue], son of an archisynagogos, grandson of an archisynagogos, built the synagogue for the reading of the law and the teaching of the commandments."

The Theodotus inscription was found among a heap of building fragments at the bottom of an ancient cistern in southeastern Jerusalem. Dating to the time of Herod the Great, it measures 30 inches by 16 inches and is inscribed with ten lines of Greek text.

Located in the Upper City section of Jerusalem, these are the remains of a home put to the torch by the Romans in 70 C.E. Now a museum known as the Burnt House, it contained the bones of a young woman who perished when her home collapsed.

"AS FOR THESE THINGS WHICH YOU SEE, THE DAYS WILL COME WHEN THERE SHALL NOT BE LEFT HERE ONE STONE UPON ANOTHER THAT WILL NOT BE THROWN DOWN."

LUKE 21:6

THE SACKING OF JERUSALEM

For most Jews, Roman rule remained a foreign and hated imposition on Judea—and resistance grew to the idea of paying tribute to Caesar. Jews were offended at the notion of a divine emperor, whose face on their coins further offended against the Torah's prohibition on graven images. And according to Josephus, Rome's governors not only imposed punitive taxes but also extorted bribes from the people. The governor in charge between 64 and 66 C.E., the historian claimed, "virtually announced to the entire country that everyone might be a bandit if he chose, so long as he himself received a rake-off."

Even so, some counseled against open resistance to Roman rule. Their troops might mistreat the local people, and the Roman eagle might be paraded around the streets of Jerusalem like a heathen idol. But more could be gained by cooperating with the Romans than by rebelling against them. Josephus himself was of this opinion. But such collaborative voices were being drowned out. When, in the year 66, the already unpopular governor decided to appropriate money from the Temple's treasury "on the pretext that Caesar required it," in the words of Josephus, a riot broke out. Roman troops crushed it, at a bloody price, and the cause of the more militant Jewish leaders gained widespread sympathy. The crushed riot led to an open revolt, and the rebels seized control of Jerusalem.

The task of reconquering the city and ending the Great Jewish Revolt fell to the future emperor Titus. He marched four legions up to a well-protected city huddled behind several layers of walls bristling with towers and battlements. The Romans laid siege to the city, but the inhabitants held out with great determination. The siege dragged on, reducing the defenders to starvation, until the city's walls were finally breached in 70 C.E. and Roman troops poured through.

While they sometimes spared the citizenry of hostile regions if they surrendered, the Romans were ruthless with those who resisted. They took out a terrible revenge on Jerusalem, destroying the city and reducing the Temple to rubble. They slaughtered thousands of Jerusalem's inhabitants and carried those who survived off into slavery.

Excavated by Israeli archaeologists following the Six Day War, the remains of the burned house, opposite, bear testimony to the destructiveness of the Romans, who systematically looted and torched their way through Jerusalem. In his *Jewish War,* Josephus records: "They massacred indiscriminately all whom they met, and burnt the houses with all who had taken refuge within. Often in the course of their raids, on entering the house for loot, they would find whole families dead and the rooms filled with the victims of the famine, and then, shuddering at the sight, retire empty-handed."

Shekel of Israel

During their revolt against Roman rule, the Jews of Judea minted their own coins. The coins, which were actually over-struck Roman pieces, carried a variety of images, such as a lyre, a cluster of grapes, and a wreath with a palm branch in the center. The coins also bore various Hebrew inscriptions that were designed to uplift the Jewish people. These include such phrases as "Jerusalem the Holy," "To the deliverance of Jerusalem," and "First year of the redemption of Israel."

The coin at right carries the inscription "Shekel of Israel" and a depiction of the Omer cup of the Temple. The Omer was a golden vessel that, on the second day of Passover, was used to hold an offering of barley as the fruit of the fields. During the ceremony it was waved in all directions.

The other side of the coin carries the image of a pomegranate, said to have the same number of seeds as the number of commandments in the Torah.

A silver shekel adorned with an Omer cup from Judea, minted in the fourth year of the Jewish Revolt against Rome

FALL
OF MASADA

The final act of Jewish resistance to Roman rule was played out at the stronghold of Masada. Built by Herod the Great, the fortress sat atop a plateau overlooking the Dead Sea. Here, the Zealots held out for three years after the fall of Jerusalem, succumbing only after the Romans constructed a huge assault rampart of earth and stones against Masada's western side. But there would be no surrender. Faced with inevitable defeat, the defenders chose suicide over continued Roman rule.

> "FOR JERUSALEM HAS STUMBLED, AND JUDAH HAS FALLEN; BECAUSE THEIR SPEECH AND THEIR DEEDS ARE AGAINST THE LORD, DEFYING HIS GLORIOUS PRESENCE."
>
> ISAIAH 3:8

At Masada, nearly a thousand Jews determined to end their own lives. Under the leadership of a man named Eleazar ben Yair, each Zealot warrior slew the members of his own family. When this was done, the remaining warriors then cast lots to select ten men among them who would kill the others. This accomplished, the men who were left cast lots once more, to choose one of their number to kill the others. He then would take his own life.

The famous Israeli archaeologist Yigael Yadin, who worked at Solomon's city of Hazor and the fortress of Megiddo, also carried out excavations at this other great iconic site for the Jewish people. In the 1960s he discovered the luxurious palaces of Herod, complete with their storerooms and casemate walls, large bathhouse, ritual bathing pool, and huge reservoirs. A copy of the Book of Ecclesiastes was found as well as other ancient manuscripts. He also unearthed what he considered the most significant find of all—11 potsherds, or ostraca, each inscribed with a Hebrew name.

Yadin speculated about just what he had unearthed: "Had we indeed found the very ostraca which had been used in the casting of lots? We shall never know for certain. But the probability is strengthened by the fact that among these eleven inscribed pieces of pottery was one bearing the name, 'ben Yair,'" who had resolved "never to be a servant to the Romans."

The hilltop fortress of Masada sits more than 1,300 feet above the surrounding Judean desert. The remains of its three-tiered palace can still be seen, as can the Dead Sea in the background.

An ancient papyrus manuscript containing an order from the rebel leader Bar Kokhba to one of his followers

"We want to apprise you that the cow which Yehosef, son of Yaaqov, son of Yehudah, whose house is in Beth-Mashko, belongs to him. And if the foreigners were not so close upon us, I would have gone up and declared you free of obligations of this account."

BAR KOKHBA REBELLION

At a lecture in Jerusalem in 1960, the celebrated Israeli archaeologist Yigael Yadin addressed a hushed, distinguished audience that included both the president and prime minister of Israel. "Your Excellency," he declared to the current head of the Jewish state, President Ben-Zvi, "I am honored to be able to tell you that we have discovered 15 dispatches written or dictated by the last president of Israel 1,800 years ago." The silence in the lecture hall was shattered as the audience erupted in celebration.

What Yadin was referring to was one ancient document in particular. He had recently found it in a cave in the Judean desert, at Wadi al Murabbaah near the Dead Sea. The document had been written by Shimeon bar Kokhba, "President over Israel." Subsequent searches were carried out by teams of volunteers, in and around nearby caves in the sheer walls of the wadi. They revealed more finds of scrolls and other objects that had been secreted there by Jewish refugees during the Second Revolt against Rome in 132-135 C.E.

Sixty years after their first revolt had ended at Masada, the Jews launched a second attempt to overturn Roman rule, this under the direction of a leader of almost mythical repute known as Bar Kokhba, or "son of a star." In 132 C.E., he led an army that seized Jerusalem, then proceeded to liberate all of Judea. The emperor at this time was Hadrian, whose imperial realm was the greatest that Rome had ever seen. He was unwilling to let any of it slip away, and dispatched his legions to crush the rebellion, otherwise known as the War of Bar Kokhba.

As the conflict in Judea raged, more than half a million Jews perished. Bar Kokhba's troops, defeated in battle outside Jerusalem, fled to the Judean desert, where they and their families took refuge in remote caves. The Romans pursued them, and set up a siege camp nearby to prevent the fugitives from slipping away. Many of those holed up in the caves starved to death rather than surrender to the enemy.

It was to this remote spot that Yigael Yadin came in search of this piece of Israel's storied past. He found the site of the Roman camp, perched strategically above the caves in which the resisters sheltered. And in those caves he discovered many of the mundane items of the people who hid out there, such as drinking vessels, coins, and jewelry. He also found evidence of the horrific end of some of those who died in the caves—baskets filled with skulls of some of the resisters, most likely gathered by relatives after the lifting of the Roman siege. One cave, dubbed the "Cave of Horrors," contained some 40 skeletons of adults and children.

Hidden in a niche deep inside one cave, he also found a small bundle of writings by Bar Kokhba himself. The crumbling papyri contained a set of commands to his officers from the legendary leader. "I did not dare touch the papyri themselves," Yadin later recalled, "but I managed carefully to pull out of the bundle two [of them]. I copied the letters on to a piece of paper, one by one. My hand copied automatically without my mind registering the words. When I finally looked at what I had scribbled, I could not believe my eyes. It read: 'Shimeon bar Kosiba, President over Israel.'" Yadin's find has contributed greatly to our understanding of second-century Judaism.

Entranceway to the Cave of Letters at Wadi al Murabbaah, where Yigael Yadin found the Bar Kokhba manuscripts

GOSPEL OF JOHN

"IN THE BEGINNING WAS THE WORD, AND THE WORD WAS WITH GOD, AND THE WORD WAS GOD. HE WAS IN THE BEGINNING WITH GOD; ALL THINGS WERE MADE THROUGH HIM. . . ."

JOHN 1:1-3

The papyrus fragment opposite, shown on both sides, is the oldest existing copy of any part of the New Testament Scriptures. It contains verses from the Gospel of John, which is generally accepted to be the last of the four gospels to be written. And unlike most artifacts from biblical times, this one had to be discovered twice.

The fragment is actually a tiny leaf from the upper corner of a page in a bound bible (as opposed to a

"The Evangelists" by 17th-century Dutch painter Abraham Bloemaert

scroll). It was one among many thousands of such papyrus fragments obtained on the Egyptian market by the University of Manchester, England, in 1920. The provenance of the fragment is not known for sure, but it may have come from the famous site of Oxyrhynchus, the ruined city in Upper Egypt. And for 14 years its meaning and significance lay undiscovered, just one of a collection of papyrus fragments waiting to be translated.

A university student eventually took the task on, thrilled when he discovered that portions of the seven lines of Greek text were from John's gospel. The translator dated the fragment to the first half of the second century, a date generally accepted by most scholars now. This makes it the earliest New Testament text ever found.

Such a date has also revised scholarly thinking about when this gospel was written. Previously scholars believed that it was penned around 160 C.E. But this fragment came from a copy that was in circulation some time before that date. Furthermore, it was in use not in the great port city of Alexandria but in a provincial Egyptian town, far from the city of Ephesus, where many authorities believe the Gospel of John to have been written. This showed that Christianity had quickly spread far from the land of its origin. Based on this tiny papyrus fragment—three and a half inches high and less than three inches wide—the date of authorship of the original Gospel of John is now generally accepted to be the latter part of the first century C.E.

The St. John fragment (opposite), as it is known, has text written on its front and its back. Both scriptures are from chapter 18—part of verses 31-33 on one side and verses 37-38 on the other. They are believed to have made up a codex (handwritten leaves bound like a book) some 150 pages long that contained a full account of John's gospel. The text is written in dark ink on light-colored papyrus of good quality. Experts can tell that the writer was a practiced but not a professional scribe.

Most authorities believe that the original author of the Gospel of John, John the Evangelist, was the Galilean fisherman (and brother of James) that Christ called as one of his original 12 disciples. John was the only one of the 12 to live on into old age, in exile on the island of Patmos. The author of the last of the gospels, he also wrote the last book of the New Testament and the Christian Bible, the Book of Revelation, penned on Patmos.

This fragment of the Gospel of John dates to the second half of the first century of the current era and is the oldest existing copy of any book in the New Testament.

"The **Jews** said to him, 'It is not lawful **for us** to put **any man** to death.' This was to fulfill **the word** which Jesus **had spoken to show** by what death he was **to die. Pilate entered** the praetorium again and called Jesus, **and said** to him, 'Are you the King of the **Jews?**' "

JOHN 18:31-33

" '. . . I am a king. **For this I was born,** and for this I have come into the **world, to bear witness** to the truth. Every one who is **of the truth** hears my voice.' Pilate **said to him,** 'What is truth?' After he had said this, he went out to **the Jews** again, and told them, 'I find **no** crime in him.' "

JOHN 18:37-38

"THE SENATE AND PEOPLE OF ROME [DEDICATE THIS] TO THE DIVINE TITUS VESPASIANUS AUGUSTUS, SON OF THE DIVINE VESPASIAN."

INSCRIPTION, ARCH OF TITUS

THE CONQUERORS

After the Romans sacked Jerusalem in 70 C.E., they shipped thousands of those enslaved to Rome. They were paraded through the streets as part of a spectacular triumph that the all-conquering Titus celebrated with his emperor father, Vespasian.

Father and son, adorned in laurel leaf crowns and crimson robes, watched the triumph from a raised platform, both seated in ivory chairs. The citizens of Rome thronged the streets, eager to see the spectacle as the triumphal procession began. According to the historian Josephus, they were treated to the sight of great traveling stages that rolled through the streets and depicted scenes from the recent war in Judea. "Here was to be seen a smiling countryside laid waste," Josephus wrote, "there whole formations of the enemy put to the sword; men in flight and men led off to captivity; walls of enormous size thrown down by engines, great strongholds stormed."

The parading Roman soldiers acclaimed the general and the emperor as they marched in formation past them. Some carried the trophies of their recent victory, the most prized of which was the golden seven-branched menorah (opposite). They also carried through the streets other spoils from the Temple in Jerusalem, including a scroll of "the Jewish law" (probably the Torah with its books of the Mosaic law) and silver trumpet-shaped offering containers.

The scene, indeed the whole Roman conquest of Jerusalem, is commemorated in the Arch of Titus, a marble triumphal arch that still sits on the Via Sacra amid the ruins of the Forum in Rome. Some 50 feet high, 44 feet wide, and nearly 16 feet deep, the arch was erected shortly after the death of Titus and is adorned with a relief that shows the parading of the menorah and trumpets during the triumph. The famous—infamous—relief provides the only contemporary depiction of these sacred articles plundered from Herod's Temple.

The main inscription on the Arch of Titus reads: "The Senate and people of Rome [dedicate this] to the divine Titus Vespasianus Augustus, son of the divine Vespasian." (The Roman square capitals of the inscription were originally ornamented with precious metals, silver or perhaps even gold.) Titus became emperor himself nine years after the conquest of Jerusalem, upon the death of "the divine Vespasian."

Upon his deathbed, Vespasian is supposed to have famously uttered, "Oh no! I think I am becoming a god." The Roman Senate subsequently confirmed Vespasian's inclination by deifying him. When in 81 C.E. Titus's brief reign came to an end, when he died suddenly of a fever at the age of just 40, the Roman Senate bestowed the same honor on him. Doubtless, it would all have come as little surprise to devout Jews and to those who had seen fit to rise up in rebellion against the imperial—and blasphemous—power of Rome.

The Arch of Titus, which still stands in the ancient Roman Forum (detail opposite), celebrates the general's victory in Jerusalem in 70 C.E.

A bronze torso and
head of the emperor
Hadrian dating from
around 135 C.E.

HADRIAN'S ROMAN CITY

Many Roman leaders, be they local governors or emperors in Rome, were held in low regard by the people of Judea. But as the quotation above indicates, few were as hated as the man whose actions provoked the Bar Kokhba Rebellion in 132 C.E. —the emperor Hadrian (117-138 C.E.).

After the conquest of Jerusalem by Titus, the Jewish people were forbidden from returning to their ruined capital to rebuild it. Eventually, it was an outsider who took on the task of restoring the city, none other than Hadrian himself, after the emperor paid a visit to what was left of Jerusalem in 130 C.E.

Hadrian planned out a "new Jerusalem," naming it: Aelia Capitolina. "Aelia" comes from Hadrian's family name of Aelius, and "Capitolina" indicated that the city would be dedicated to the god Jupiter Capitolinus. This was to be a city most distinctly Roman and (from the perspective of the Jews) most distinctly pagan.

Hadrian's new city delivered on its name. It was a typical Roman settlement, based on the traditional grid pattern with the main thoroughfares crisscrossing lengthwise and widthwise. It was also pagan. The emperor raised temples to Roman deities throughout Aelia Capitolina. Indeed, the temple to Jupiter he placed on the site of the now-demolished temple of Herod. Furthermore, Jews were prohibited from living in the city, or even visiting it, except for one day a year, a day of fasting and prayer when they came to commemorate the destruction of the Temple.

Hadrian enacted other punitive measures on the Jews, such as outlawing circumcision, which the Romans— recent killers of so many men, women, and children in

Judea—regarded as barbaric. Jewish anger erupted in the 132 C.E. rebellion. In the aftermath of the failed revolt, the Romans continued to enforce their strict exclusion of Jews from the city. A garrison of legionaries was tasked with preventing them from moving back into the (wallless) city. And the Talmud records how Hadrian also targeted Judaism in general by banning the use of the Hebrew calendar and the Torah, and by the persecution of Jewish scholars.

As with other emperors, Hadrian's image adorned the coins of the realm. The Jews were less keen on depictions of this particular emperor. In an act of defiance, they would over-strike images of Hadrian on their coins with their own patriotic symbols.

The gold coin at left dates from around the time of Hadrian's construction of Aelia Capitolina, which came near the end of his reign, although both sides of the coin show a distinctly youthful emperor. In the view at top, he is depicted as a bareheaded young man. On the reverse of the coin, a spear-wielding Hadrian stands between army standards and is wearing military dress, in a scene typical of the induction of a Roman nobleman into the Roman army.

The emperor would be dead a few years after these coins were minted. As he neared death, he is said to have composed the following poem:

Little soul, roamer and charmer
Body's guest and companion
Who soon will depart to places
Darkish, chilly and misty
An end to all your jokes . . .

The Talmud's final words on Emperor Hadrian, less poetic, are certainly more succinct.

Hadrian the Builder
Hadrian's most famous building project is the great, defensive wall that was constructed in Britain in 122 C.E. and bears his name. Hadrian's Wall, close to the present-day border between Scotland and England, marked the northern limits of an empire that stretched all the way south and east to Palestine.

Two sides of the same coin show the same side to Hadrian— a man keen to be depicted as young and vigorous, even during the last years of his reign.

BIRTH OF RABBINIC JUDAISM

The year 70 C.E. marks the end of what is known as Second Temple Judaism and the beginning of Rabbinic Judaism. With the destruction of the Temple that year by Titus, and the later prohibition by Hadrian on Jews returning to Jerusalem, Judaism seemed cut off from its very foundations. During this period, study of the Torah came to replace the sacrificial cult as the essence of Judaism. Thus the focus of Jewish worship changed from the Temple to the synagogue and from the high priest to the rabbi.

> "LET YOUR HOUSE BE A GATHERING PLACE FOR SAGES . . . DRINK THEIR WORDS WITH GUSTO. LET YOUR HOUSE BE OPEN WIDE, AND SEAT THE POOR AT YOUR TABLE."
>
> YOSÉ BEN YOZER AND YOSÉ BEN YOHAN, MISHNAH, TRACATE AVOT I

The synagogue became the place for faithful Jews to conduct their religious services with instruction from the Torah, or Pentateuch, the first five books of the Hebrew Bible. A shrine of the Torah was at the heart of each synagogue.

Despite the blows it had suffered at the hands of the Romans in the new millennium, Judaism would survive. The new rabbinic movement was led by the Pharisees, the "separated ones" (now literally separated from their sacred Temple). Rabbinic teachings were captured in what would become known at the Talmud (from the Hebrew for "teachings"), which was after the Bible the most important text in Judaism.

After the fall of Jerusalem, Rabbi Johanan ben Zakki established a center for rabbinic Judaism at Jamnia, near the Mediterranean coast. After the failure of the second Jewish revolt against Rome, the center moved to Tiberias (right), on the Sea of Galilee, the very region where another rabbi had spent most of his ministry and whose teachings would touch millions of lives.

Tiberias was the center of Rabbinic Judaism after the destruction of the Temple in Jerusalem. The ruins of the Galilean settlement are shown at right.

"Donated by Akaptos lover of God who contributed the table to the god Jesus Christos as a memorial."

This ancient Greek inscription was found on the mosaic floor of the Megiddo church in northern Israel. A translation of the inscription is shown at top.

THE EARLIEST CHRISTIAN CHURCH

"SO THE CHURCH THROUGHOUT ALL JUDEA AND GALILEE AND SAMARIA HAD PEACE AND WAS BUILT UP; AND WALKING IN THE FEAR OF THE LORD AND IN THE COMFORT OF THE HOLY SPIRIT IT WAS MULTIPLIED."

ACTS OF THE APOSTLES 9:31

During construction work at Megiddo prison in northern Israel in the late 1990s, one of the prisoners clearing away rubble struck a distinctly hard surface with his shovel. Using a sponge and buckets of water, he uncovered part of a mosaic floor. Construction was halted, and archaeologists from the Israel Antiquities Authority were called in to investigate the find.

What the worker had discovered was part of an ancient church. Using potsherds and coins found at the site, scholars have dated it to as early as the first half of the third century C.E., and identified it as a place of worship used both by local believers and by those from a nearby Roman camp, where two legions were garrisoned. This was at a time long before Constantine the Great legalized Christianity in the empire in the early fourth century, making the church the oldest discovered in Israel and among the oldest anywhere in the world.

The beautifully preserved mosaic was the floor of a room where the faithful celebrated the Eucharist, the commemorative reenactment of the Last Supper at which bread and wine are symbolically turned into the body and blood of Christ. The mosaic held three inscriptions in rectangular panels. One showed the names of four individuals, presumably members of the congregation and, significantly, all women: Primilla, Cyriaca, Dorothea, and Chreste. The second one commemorated two other members: "Gaianus, also called Porphyrius, centurion, our brother, has made the pavement at his own expense as an act of liberality. Brutius carried out the work." The third inscription, shown opposite, refers to another woman, Akaptos, and makes clear the room's use as a place to celebrate the Eucharist. It may be the oldest inscription that includes the words "Jesus Christ."

The center of the the mosaic depicted two fish facing in opposite directions. At this stage in the development of Christianity, the cross used to crucify Christ had not yet become the common symbol of the faith. For early believers, the universal symbol was the fish, adopted because the initial letters of the Greek word for fish, *ichthys,* stand for "Jesus Christ, Son of God, Savior."

The Megiddo church was in use at a time when congregations first began to meet in dedicated houses of worship and prayer, led by ordained members of the clergy, and is thus among the earliest examples of this kind of church building. Prior to that time, the faithful met in the homes of members of their community, in house churches, or *domus ecclesia,* much as believers do today in countries where they face persecution.

The Megiddo church seems to have been abandoned at some stage during the fourth century. The archaeological evidence does not suggest that it came to an abrupt end, through some form of destruction. Rather, the congregation appears to have left deliberately, taking care to cover the mosaic floor with a protective layer of plaster that accounts for its excellent condition today. It has been suggested that the church fell into disuse as a result of the departure of the local Roman garrison.

Armies return to this corner of Israel in the last book of the Christian Bible. The prophetic Book of Revelation speaks of Megiddo—Armageddon—as the great battleground where the forces of good will eventually triumph over the forces of evil.

A pair of fish, an early symbol of Christ, adorn the mosaic floor at Megiddo.

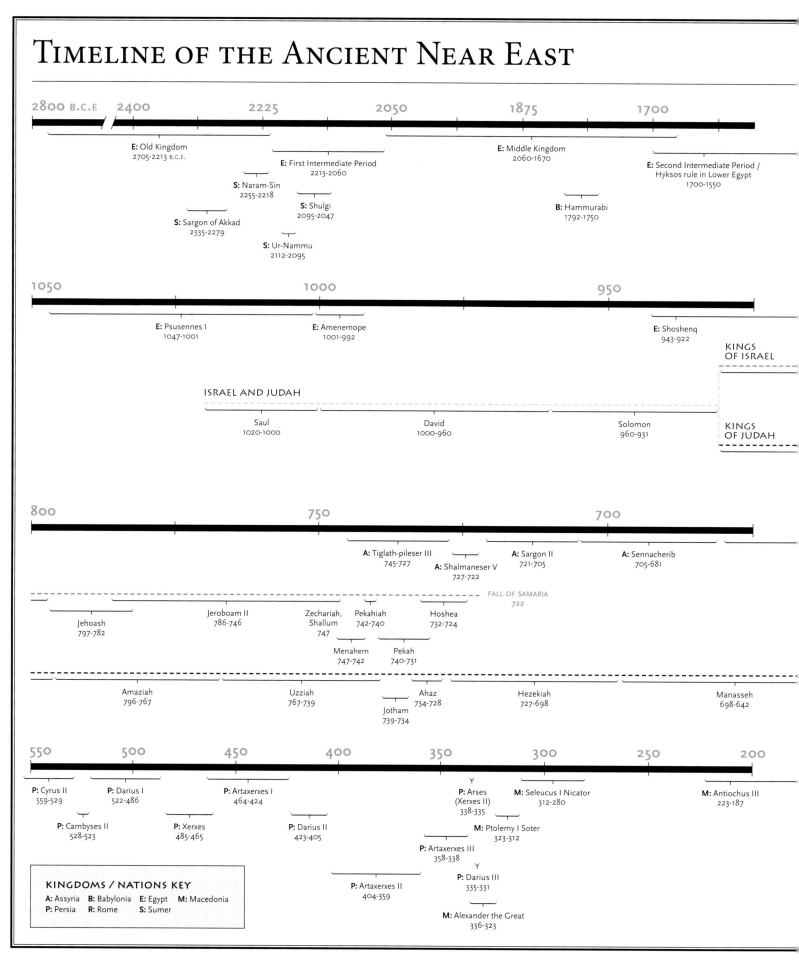

TIMELINE OF THE ANCIENT NEAR EAST

2800 B.C.E 2400 2225 2050 1875 1700

E: Old Kingdom
2705-2213 B.C.E.

E: First Intermediate Period
2213-2060

E: Middle Kingdom
2060-1670

E: Second Intermediate Period /
Hyksos rule in Lower Egypt
1700-1550

S: Naram-Sin
2255-2218

S: Shulgi
2095-2047

B: Hammurabi
1792-1750

S: Sargon of Akkad
2335-2279

S: Ur-Nammu
2112-2095

1050 1000 950

E: Psusennes I
1047-1001

E: Amenemope
1001-992

E: Shoshenq
943-922

KINGS
OF ISRAEL

ISRAEL AND JUDAH

Saul
1020-1000

David
1000-960

Solomon
960-931

KINGS
OF JUDAH

800 750 700

A: Tiglath-pileser III
745-727

A: Sargon II
721-705

A: Sennacherib
705-681

A: Shalmaneser V
727-722

FALL OF SAMARIA
722

Jeroboam II
786-746

Zechariah,
Shallum
747

Pekahiah
742-740

Hoshea
732-724

Jehoash
797-782

Menahem
747-742

Pekah
740-731

Amaziah
796-767

Uzziah
767-739

Ahaz
734-728

Hezekiah
727-698

Manasseh
698-642

Jotham
739-734

550 500 450 400 350 300 250 200

P: Cyrus II
559-529

P: Darius I
522-486

P: Artaxerxes I
464-424

P: Arses
(Xerxes II)
338-335

M: Seleucus I Nicator
312-280

M: Antiochus III
223-187

P: Cambyses II
528-523

P: Xerxes
485-465

P: Darius II
423-405

M: Ptolemy I Soter
323-312

P: Artaxerxes III
358-338

P: Artaxerxes II
404-359

P: Darius III
335-331

M: Alexander the Great
336-323

KINGDOMS / NATIONS KEY
A: Assyria **B:** Babylonia **E:** Egypt **M:** Macedonia
P: Persia **R:** Rome **S:** Sumer

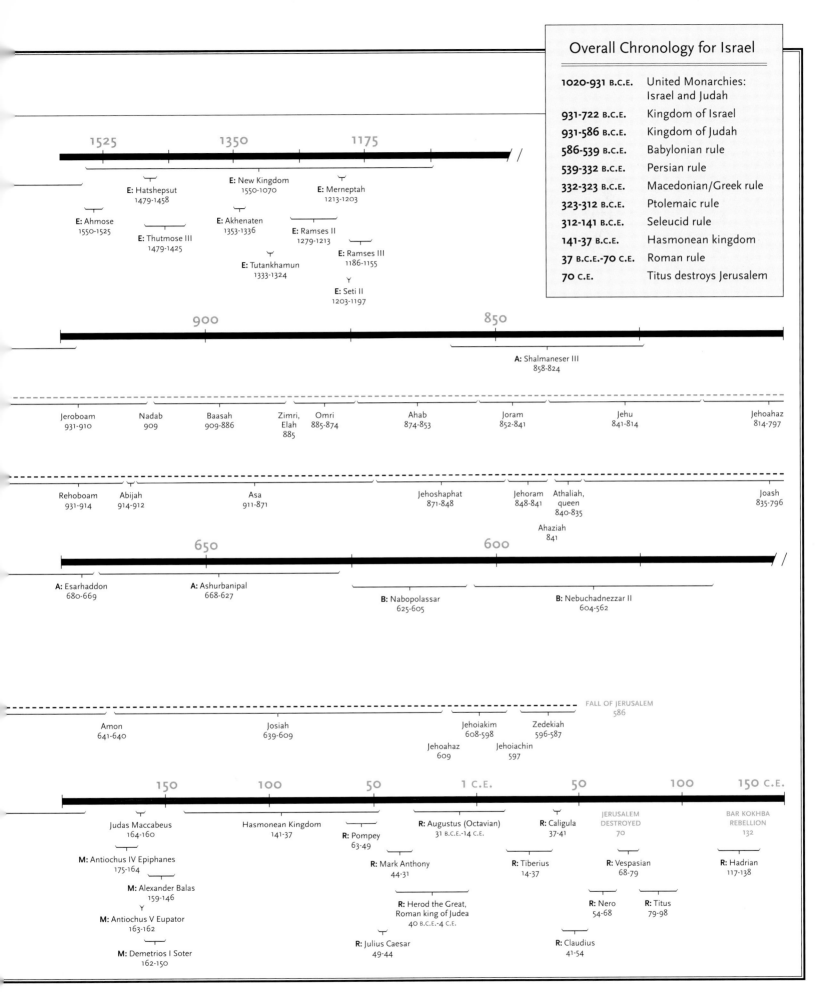

Overall Chronology for Israel

1020-931 B.C.E.	United Monarchies: Israel and Judah
931-722 B.C.E.	Kingdom of Israel
931-586 B.C.E.	Kingdom of Judah
586-539 B.C.E.	Babylonian rule
539-332 B.C.E.	Persian rule
332-323 B.C.E.	Macedonian/Greek rule
323-312 B.C.E.	Ptolemaic rule
312-141 B.C.E.	Seleucid rule
141-37 B.C.E.	Hasmonean kingdom
37 B.C.E.**-70** C.E.	Roman rule
70 C.E.	Titus destroys Jerusalem

1525 · 1350 · 1175

E: Ahmose 1550-1525
E: Hatshepsut 1479-1458
E: Thutmose III 1479-1425
E: Akhenaten 1353-1336
E: Tutankhamun 1333-1324
E: New Kingdom 1550-1070
E: Ramses II 1279-1213
E: Merneptah 1213-1203
E: Ramses III 1186-1155
E: Seti II 1203-1197

900 · 850

A: Shalmaneser III 858-824

Jeroboam 931-910
Nadab 909
Baasah 909-886
Zimri, Elah 885
Omri 885-874
Ahab 874-853
Joram 852-841
Jehu 841-814
Jehoahaz 814-797

Rehoboam 931-914
Abijah 914-912
Asa 911-871
Jehoshaphat 871-848
Jehoram 848-841
Athaliah, queen 840-835
Ahaziah 841
Joash 835-796

650 · 600

A: Esarhaddon 680-669
A: Ashurbanipal 668-627
B: Nabopolassar 625-605
B: Nebuchadnezzar II 604-562

FALL OF JERUSALEM 586

Amon 641-640
Josiah 639-609
Jehoahaz 609
Jehoiakim 608-598
Jehoiachin 597
Zedekiah 596-587

150 · 100 · 50 · 1 C.E. · 50 · 100 · 150 C.E.

M: Antiochus IV Epiphanes 175-164
Judas Maccabeus 164-160
M: Alexander Balas 159-146
M: Antiochus V Eupator 163-162
M: Demetrios I Soter 162-150
Hasmonean Kingdom 141-37
R: Pompey 63-49
R: Mark Anthony 44-31
R: Julius Caesar 49-44
R: Herod the Great, Roman king of Judea 40 B.C.E.-4 C.E.
R: Augustus (Octavian) 31 B.C.E.-14 C.E.
R: Tiberius 14-37
R: Caligula 37-41
R: Claudius 41-54
R: Nero 54-68
JERUSALEM DESTROYED 70
R: Vespasian 68-79
R: Titus 79-98
BAR KOKHBA REBELLION 132
R: Hadrian 117-138

Ben-Tor, Amnon, editor. *The Archaeology of Ancient Israel.* New Haven: Yale University Press, 1992.

Biran, Avraham. *Biblical Dan.* New York: Hebrew Union College, 1994.

Borowski, Oded. *Daily Life in Biblical Times.* Atlanta: Society of Biblical Literature, 2003.

Bowker, John. *Aerial Atlas of the Holy Land: Discover the Great Sites of History from the Air.* Ontario, Canada: Firefly Books, 2008.

Brown, Michelle P. *In the Beginning: Bibles Before the Year 1000.* Washington, D.C.: Arthur M. Sackler Gallery/ Smithsonian Institution, 2006.

Charlesworth, James H., editor. *Jesus and Archaeology.* Grand Rapids, Mich.: Eerdmans Publishing Company, 2006.

Cline, Eric H. *Biblical Archaeology: A Very Short Introduction.* New York: Oxford University Press, 2009.

——. *From Eden to Exile: Unraveling Mysteries of the Bible.* Washington, D.C.: National Geographic, 2007.

——. *Jerusalem Besieged: From Ancient Canaan to Modern Israel.* Ann Arbor: University of Michigan Press, 2004.

Cohen, Shaye J. D. *From the Maccabees to the Mishnah,* 2nd edition. Louisville, Ky.: Westminster John Knox Press, 2006.

Crossan, John Dominic, and Jonathan L. Reed. *Excavating Jesus: Beneath the Stones, Behind the Texts,* revised edition. San Francisco: HarperSanFrancisco, 2001.

Davies, Philip R., George J. Brooke, and Phillip R. Callaway. *The Complete World of the Dead Sea Scrolls.* London: Thames and Hudson, 2002.

Davis, Miriam C. *Dame Kathleen Kenyon: Digging Up the Holy Land.* London: UCL Institute of Archaeology, 2008.

De Hamel, Christopher. *The Book: A History of the Bible.* New York: Phaidon Press, 2001.

Dever, William G. *What Did the Biblical Writers Know and When Did They Know It?: What Archaeology Can Tell Us about the Reality of Ancient Israel.* Grand Rapids, Mich.: Eerdmans Publishing Company, 2001.

——. *Who Were the Early Israelites and Where Did They Come From?* Grand Rapids, Mich.: Eerdmans Publishing Company, 2003.

Fant, Clyde E., and Mitchell G. Reddish. *Lost Treasures of the Bible: Understanding the Bible through Archaeological Artifacts in World Museums.* Grand Rapids, Mich.: Eerdmans Publishing Company, 2008.

Finegan, Jack. *The Archaeology of the New Testament: The Life of Jesus and the Beginning of the Early Church,* revised edition. Princeton, N.J.: Princeton University Press, 1992.

——. *Handbook of Biblical Chronology: Principles of Time Reckoning in the Ancient World and Problems of Chronology in the Bible,* revised edition. Peabody, Mass.: Hendrickson Publishers, 1998.

Finkelstein, Israel, and Neil A. Silberman. *The Bible Unearthed: Archaeology's New Vision of Ancient Israel and the Origin of Its Sacred Texts.* New York: Free Press, 2001.

Freedman, David Noel, editor. *The Anchor Bible Dictionary,* 6 volumes. New York: Doubleday, 1992.

Friedman, Richard Elliott. *Who Wrote the Bible?* San Francisco: HarperOne, 1997.

Gibson, Shimon. *Flights into Biblical Archaeology.* Herzlia, Israel: Albatross, 2007.

Hoffmeier, James K. *Israel in Egypt: The Evidence for the Authenticity of the Exodus Tradition.* New York: Oxford University Press, 1997.

Hurtado, Larry W. *The Earliest Christian Artifacts: Manuscripts and Christian Origins.* Grand Rapids, Mich.: Eerdmans Publishing Company, 2006.

Isbouts, Jean-Pierre. *The Biblical World: An Illustrated Atlas.* Washington, D.C.: National Geographic, 2007.

Isserlin, B. S. J. *The Israelites.* London: Thames and Hudson, 1998.

King, Philip J., and Lawrence E. Stager. *Life in Biblical Israel.* Louisville, Ky.: Westminster John Knox Press, 2001.

Kitchen, Kenneth. *On the Reliability of the Old Testament.* Grand Rapids, Mich.: Eerdmans Publishing Company, 2003.

Laughlin, John C. H. *Archaeology and the Bible.* London: Routledge, 2000.

Levy, Thomas E. *Journey to the Copper Age: Archaeology in the Holy Land.* San Diego, Calif.: Museum of Man, 2007.

Magness, Jodi. *The Archaeology of Qumran and the Dead Sea Scrolls.* Grand Rapids, Mich.: Eerdmans Publishing Company, 2002.

Marcus, Amy D. *The View from Nebo: How Archaeology Is Rewriting the Bible and Reshaping the Middle East.* Boston: Little, Brown and Company, 2000.

Maxwell, Miller J., and John H. Hayes. *A History of Ancient Israel and Judah,* 2nd edition. Louisville, Ky.: Westminster John Knox Press, 2006.

Mazar, Amihai. *Archaeology of the Land of the Bible, Volume I: 10,000-586 B.C.E.* New York: Doubleday, 1990.

McRay, John. *Archaeology and the New Testament.* Grand Rapids, Mich.: Baker Book House, 1991.

Metzger, Bruce M., and Michael D. Coogan, editors. *The Oxford Companion to the Bible.* New York: Oxford University Press, 1993.

Mitchell, T. C. *The Bible in the British Museum: Interpreting the Evidence.* New York: Paulist Press, 1988.

Pritchard, James B., editor. *Ancient Near Eastern Texts Relating to the Old Testament.* Princeton, New Jersey: Princeton University Press, 1969.

Provan, Iain, V. Philips Long, and Tremper Longman III. *A Biblical History of Israel.* Louisville, Ky.: Westminster John Knox Press, 2003.

Reed, Jonathan L. *The HarperCollins Visual Guide to the New Testament: What Archaeology Reveals About the First Christians.* San Francisco: HarperOne, 2007.

Shanks, Hershel, editor. *Ancient Israel: From Abraham to the Roman Destruction of the Temple,* 2nd edition (revised). New York: Prentice Hall, 1999.

Stern, Ephraim. *Archaeology of the Land of the Bible, Volume II: The Assyrian, Babylonian, and Persian Periods (732-332 B.C.E.).* New York: Doubleday, 2001.

VanderKam, James, and Peter Flint. *The Meaning of the Dead Sea Scrolls: Their Significance For Understanding the Bible, Judaism, Jesus, and Christianity.* San Francisco: HarperOne, 2002.

Vermes, Geza, translator. *The Complete Dead Sea Scrolls in English,* revised edition. New York: Penguin Classics, 2004.

ABOUT THE WRITERS

ROBIN CURRIE is an editor and writer, whose books include Time-Life's *What Life Was Like in the Land of Druids and High Kings* and *Lost Civilizations: Anatolia.* He was an author of National Geographic's *Concise History of the World* and has edited *National Geographic Traveler* guides on New York, Hawaii, South Africa, and Greece. His writing has been published by the Smithsonian Institution, McGraw-Hill, the National Endowment for the Humanities, and America Online, where he was senior editor of the AOL home page.

STEPHEN G. HYSLOP is the author of several books on American and world history, including *Eyewitness to the Civil War* and *National Geographic Almanac of World History* (with Patricia S. Daniels). Formerly at Time-Life Books, he served as editor for the historical series Time Frame and the books *What Life Was Like on the Banks of the Nile* and *What Life Was Like When Rome Ruled the World.* His articles have appeared in *American History* and the *History Channel Magazine.*

ABOUT THE CONSULTANTS

ERIC H. CLINE is the author of eight books, including *From Eden to Exile: Unraveling Mysteries of the Bible.* He currently serves as associate professor and chair of the Department of Classical and Semitic Languages and Literatures at the George Washington University. Cline is also associate director (USA) of the ongoing excavations at Megiddo in Israel.

RANDALL W. YOUNKER is professor of Old Testament and biblical archaeology and director of the Institute of Archaeology at Andrews University. He has been a field archaeologist for the past 29 years in Israel and Jordan and currently directs the ongoing excavations at Tall al Jalul in Jordan.

ACKNOWLEDGMENT

The authors and the editor would like to thank researcher and virtual archaeologist Karin Kinney, who in preparing the outline for this book located sites, dug up artifacts, and retrieved inscriptions. She guided us in our own research and helped keep this project on the correct course from start from finish.

ILLUSTRATION CREDITS

INDEX

INDEX

4/03